Independent Traveller's Guides
CENTRAL ITALY

Independent Traveller's Guides
CENTRAL ITALY

Florence, Tuscany, Umbria, Marche, Northern Lazio

Fiona Duncan and Peter Greene

Duncan Petersen

First published 1996
Second edition published 1999 by
Duncan Petersen Publishing Ltd
31, Ceylon Road,
London, W14 OPY

Sales representation and distribution in the U.K. and Ireland by
Portfolio Books Ltd
Unit IC, West Ealing Business Centre, Alexandria Road, London W13 0NJ
Tel: 0181 579 7748

© Text Fiona Duncan and Peter Greene 1996, 1999
© Maps and other material Duncan Petersen Publishing Ltd, 1996, 1999

Conceived, edited, designed and produced by
Duncan Petersen Publishing Ltd from a concept by Emma Stanford

Originated by Reprocolour International, Milan

Typeset by Duncan Petersen Publishing Ltd,
text film output by MHA, London

Printed by Delo-Tiskarna, Slovenia

A CIP catalogue record for this book is available from the British Library

ISBN 1 872576 88 5

Every reasonable care has been taken to ensure that the information in this guide is accurate, but the publisher and copyright holders can accept no responsibility for the consequences of errors in the text or in the maps, particularly those arising from changes taking place after the text was finalized. The publisher is always pleased to hear from readers who wish to suggest corrections and improvements.

Editorial director Andrew Duncan
Revisions editor Nicola Davies
Assistant editor Leonie Glass
Art director Mel Petersen
Design assistants Beverley Stewart, Chris Foley
Maps by Chris Foley and Beverley Stewart
Illustrations by Beverley Stewart

Many thanks also to Rita Cecchini, Alba Donati, Claudia Galli, Nicky Swallow, Lucinda Cookson, Peter Kennealy, Amanda and Alastair Parker and Helen and Marco Vidotto.

Photographic credits
All photographs by **Mel Petersen**
except **The Bridgeman Art Library** p43, 62, 66; **John Freeman** p2, 70, 139, 146; **Neil Setchfield** 47, 50, 55, 59, 75, 207.

Peter Greene, one-time press officer for London's Royal Festival Hall, lives and works in Italy's northern Marche. In 1988, he left London to start a new life in a small farming community in the Appennines, where he ekes out a living as a freelance writer amidst the distractions of making wine and killing pigs. He has written articles for many magazines and newspapers, including *The Independent.* Together with his partner, Richard Dixon, he has written two other Duncan Petersen guides, *Italy on Backroads* and *3-D City Guides: Rome.*

Florence, Seeing the Region: 1 and Local Explorations: 1, 2 and 4 are the work of **Fiona Duncan,** who has been a regular and enthusiastic visitor to the region for 25 years. A freelance writer, she devised the *American Express Pocket Travel Guides* while working at Mitchell Beazley Publishers, and has written guide books on London, Paris, Manhattan, Amsterdam and France.

The authors are much indebted to **Richard Dixon** for his background research, a major contribution to the guide.

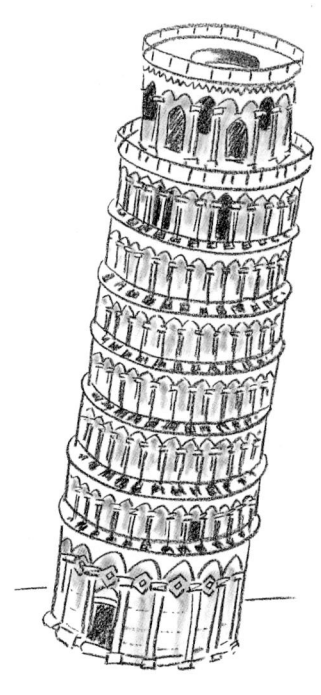

Master contents list

This contents list is for when you need to use the guide in the conventional way: to find out about where you are going, or where you happen to be. The index, pages 238-240, may be just as helpful.

Conventions used in this guide	12
Something for everyone	13
Central Italy: an introduction	14
Before you go	15
Getting there / Getting around	17
Essential practical information	18
A brief history of Central Italy	21
Key dates	22
Some key cultural themes and places	26
How the Renaissance came about – an instant guide	27
An A to Z of artists and architects	29
Art, architectural and general Italian terms	32
Food	35
The region's wines	37
Florence	**39, 81**
Tuscany	**82, 98, 110, 130, 150, 160, 170, 186, 204, 232**
Umbria	**118, 160, 176, 210**
Marche	**98, 118, 210, 220**
Northern Lazio	**110, 196**
Index	238

HOWEVER
There is much more to this guide than the region by region approach suggested by the contents list on this page. Turn to page 8 and also pages 10-11.

Contents

Central Italy: seeing the region
– *master map*

Central Italy: Seeing the Region, pages 82-129, is a traveller's network for taking in the whole country, or large parts of it.

Each 'leg' of the network has a number (i.e., Central Italy: Seeing the Region: 1); you will also find it described as a National Route, plus the number.

The term National Route does *not* simply mean a line on a map. Each route 'leg' features a whole region, and describes many places both on and off the marked route. Think of the routes not only as physical trails, but as imaginative ways of connecting all the focal points of Central Italy and of describing and making travel sense of the region as a whole.

They are designed to be used in these different ways:

1 *Ignore the marked route entirely:* simply use the alphabetically arranged Gazetteer of Sights & Places of Interest, and the map at the start of each route, as a guide to what to see and do in the region, not forgetting the hotel and restaurant recommendations.

2 Follow the marked route by public transport (see the transport box), ferry, or by car. You can do sections of the route, or all of it; you can follow it in any direction. Link the routes to travel throughout Central Italy.

1 Between Livorno and Florence Pisa, Lucca and Pistoia: the western approach to Florence	82
2 Between Florence and Pesaro Arezzo, Urbino, the Marches and the Adriatic	98
3 Between Florence and Viterbo The Via Cassia	110
4 Between Pesaro and Spoleto Umbria and Upland Marches – the Via Flaminia	118

CENTRAL ITALY OVERALL – *master map*

Some practical hints on how to travel red, blue and green are given in the introductory pages and the simplified maps, including key roads and their numbers. Generally, though, there are no absolute rules for going red, blue or green and you are meant to link the places, using a detailed road map, in whatever way suits you best.

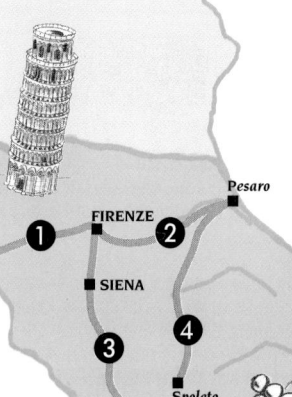

The routes are broken down into manageable 'legs'. Each leg has a section to itself, beginning with an introduction and a simplified map. The page number for each such section is shown on this master map.

Always use the simplified maps in conjunction with detailed maps (suggestions are given on the introductory pages).

On the simplified maps:

RED *marks key sights and centres, not to be missed.*

BLUE *marks important places, certainly worth a visit.*

GREEN *places are for those who aren't in a hurry and want to experience the region in some depth.*

Florence has a section of its own, pages 39–81

The *Central Italy: Seeing the Region* section is ideal for:

- Planning, and undertaking, tours of the whole, or parts of it.

- Making the journey to or from your eventual destination as interesting and as rewarding as possible.

- Linking the in-depth explorations of localities provided by the Local Explorations section, pages 130-237.

Contents

The Local Explorations
- *master map*

The Local Explorations – strategies for exploring all the interesting localities of Central Italy – complement the regional routes, pages 8-9. **They are designed to be used in these different ways**:

1 *Ignore the marked route entirely*: simply use the alphabetically arranged Gazetteer of Sights & Places of Interest, and the map at the start of each Local Exploration, as a guide to what to see and do in the area, not forgetting the hotel and restaurant recommendations.

2 Use the marked route to make a tour by public transport (see the transport box), ferry, or by car. You can do sections of the route, or all of it. (In the introduction it tells you how long you might take to cover everything the quickest way, by car.)

If you are driving, you can generally follow the tour in any direction; usually, the route as marked is an attractive and convenient way to link the places of interest; you may well find other ways to drive it. Always use our map in conjunction with a detailed road map (suggestions are given on each introductory page).

1	**Siena, San Gimignano and Volterra**	130
2	**Chianti**	150
3	**Cortona, Montepulciano and Lake Trasimeno**	160
4	**Montalcino, Val d'Orcia and Monte Amiata**	170
5	**Perugia, Orvieto and Todi**	176
6	**Monte Argentario, Isola del Giglio and the Lower Maremma**	186
7	**Southern Etruria – the Etruscan Trail**	196
8	**The Upper Maremma and Metal Hills**	204
9	**Gubbio and its Mountains**	210
10	**Inland from Ancona – Hill Towns of the Central Marche**	220
11	**The Garfagnana, Lunigiana and Versilia Coast**	232

THE LOCAL EXPLORATIONS – *master map*

The Local Explorations, pages 130-237, generally follow each other in a north-south/west-east sequence.

Florence has a section of its own, pages 39-81

The *Local Explorations* are ideal for:

■ **Planning single-centre holidays**: each Local Exploration encapsulates an area which would make a great holiday. The introductory page to each section is designed to tell you whether the area will suit you: what you can expect; and something of its history, geography, people, customs and food.

■ **Entertaining yourself while you are there**: each section is packed with ideas for things to see and do. The tour, followed in full, can fill several days, and will always make a memorable journey, but most of the sights and places of interest make fascinating day or part-day trips in their own right, not to mention the detours.

■ **Planning multi-centre holidays**: the map on this page shows you at a glance all the interesting parts of Central Italy. Combine them at will to experience the different faces of the state; or link them, by means of the regional route network.

11

Conventions used in this guide

> A single *lira* sign – **L** – or several *lire* signs, such as **LLL**, in a hotel or restaurant entry, denote a price band. Its object is to give an indication of what you can expect to pay. Accommodation offered at any one place may well span two price bands.

Hotels
Double room with shower:
L	Up to L120,000
LL	L120,000-L220,000
LLL	More than L220,000

Italian hotels are given an official star rating by the tourist authorities. Four or five stars will usually be in our LLL price bracket; three stars in LL; one or two stars in L.

Restaurants
Full meal for one, including modest quantity of local wine:
L	Up to L50,000
LL	L50,000-L80,000
LLL	L00,000 L120,000
LLLL	More than L120,000

Hotels and restaurants in this guide are a selection of personal recommendations – not exhaustive lists. They have been chosen to represent interest and quality, more often than not with an eye to value for money.

Opening times – hotels and restaurants
Where hotel and restaurant opening times are not specifically mentioned in this guide, assume they follow these general rules.

Larger city hotels are open all year and staffed day and night. In deeply rural areas and purely tourist locations, such as the Tuscan islands, hotels sometimes close between October and Easter. Smaller establishments in both town and country frequently close for a month in the depth of winter, and sometimes for a fortnight in August.

Restaurants normally open for lunch and dinner, though country *trattorie* occasionally serve only lunch – remember that the mid-day meal is still the most important in Italy. *Pizzerie*, though open for pasta and main courses at lunchtime, usually only light their pizza ovens in the evening. In the grander city restaurants, dinner is generally available up to 10 or 11 pm. However, in humbler places, particularly in country areas, don't expect much of a choice after 9 pm. *Pizzerie*, however, often keep late hours.

By law every restaurant must close for one day a week; often all the restaurants in smaller towns close on the same day. We have indicated the weekly closure in the restaurant entries. All bars open early in the morning to provide the inimitable Italian breakfast – a shot of caffeine-laden *espresso* coffee, or a lip-smacking, frothy *cappuccino*, and a sticky pastry. Many then stay open until late at night or the early hours of the morning, while others close around 8 pm.

Opening times – museums, galleries, churches and tourist attractions
This guide only gives opening times for places described if they depart from the norm, *except* in Florence, where the number of variations makes it essential to give comprehensive opening times.

Otherwise, the following general rules should enable you to time your visit. If in doubt, enquire at the local tourist office.

Museums and art galleries open from 9 am to 2 pm on weekdays and 9 am to 1 pm on Sunday. Most close on Monday. Moves to extend the opening hours of major museums and galleries are underway and Florence's Uffizi Gallery is already open from 9 am to 7 pm on weekdays. Important outdoor archaeological sites and gardens also close on Monday, but are usually open from 9 am through to 7 pm in summer with earlier

> ⌂ after a heading in **Sights & Places of Interest** means that there is an accommodation suggestion for that place in **Recommended Hotels**.
>
> ✕ after a heading in **Sights & Places of Interest** means that there is a suggestion for that place in **Recommended Restaurants**.
>
> ↗ after a place on a map means that the sight or place of interest is covered in detail in another part of the book. To find out exactly where, look up the place in the **Sights & Places of Interest** gazetteer which follows the map: a cross reference is given in every case

closing in winter. Many churches, particularly in country towns, are only open in the morning. More important churches, however, re-open between around 4 and 6 or 7 pm. In some out-of-the-way corners, church doors may be kept locked – an enquiry at the nearest bar will often get the doors opened for you.

Remember that works of art in churches are covered up during the week before Easter.

Mileages for routes and tours are approximate and represent the shortest possible distance you could expect to cover, excluding detours.

Something for everyone

Getting the most from your guide
Here is a small selection of ideas for enjoying Central Italy. The list is just a start: the guide offers many, many more ideas for what really matters – suiting yourself.

City sights
Florence city section plus Pisa in Seeing the Region: 1; Siena in Local Explorations: 1; Perugia in Local Explorations: 5 and Ancona in Local Explorations: 10.

Rugged uplands for walkers
Seeing the Region: 4 and Local Explorations: 9.

Masterpieces of art and architecture
Florence city section plus Arezzo and Urbino in Seeing the Region: 2; Pisa and Lucca in Seeing the Region: 1; Pienza in Seeing the Region: 3; Siena in Local Explorations: 1; Montepulciano in Local Explorations: 3 and Perugia in Local Explorations: 5.

Quintessential Tuscany
Seeing the Region: 3 and Local Explorations: 2.

Medieval Umbria
Seeing the Region: 4; Local Explorations: 5 and Gubbio in Local Explorations: 9.

Sun and sand
Seeing the Region: 2 and 4; Local Explorations: 6, 8 and 10.

Lakeside idylls
Lake Bolsena in Seeing the Region: 3 and Local Explorations: 6; Lake Trasimeno in Local Explorations: 3.

Before the Romans – on the Etruscan trail
Local Explorations: 6 and 7; museums at Florence (pages 42-63), also at Volterra, Chiusi and Cortona in Local Explorations: 1 and 3.

Wine tours
Local Explorations: 2 for Chianti Classico; Local Explorations: 3 for Vino Nobile di Montepulciano; Local Explorations: 4 for Brunello di Montalcino and Local Explorations: 10 for Verdicchio.

Voyages of discovery – hidden Central Italy
Local Explorations 2, 7, 9 and 10.

Interesting towns, often overlooked
Lucca and Pistoia in Seeing the Region: 1 and Arezzo in Seeing the Region: 2.

CENTRAL ITALY:
an introduction

Stendhal was so overwrought with emotion on his first visit to Tuscany that he wrote 'I was seized with a fierce palpitation of the heart; I walked in constant fear of falling to the ground.' While modern tourists are more likely to be legless for reasons other than overwhelming beauty, for most of us the region still embodies a certain type of perfect idyll – the greatest art and architecture of the Italian Renaissance set against a sun-soaked rural backdrop of olive, vine and cypress.

'Tuscany' in the popular imagination usually means just the great cities of Florence and Siena and the quintessential Tuscan countryside that lies between them. But there is much more to Tuscany than these – and indeed much more to Central Italy – than the modern tourist imagines. This guide is the most convenient and stimulating key available to discovering these many facets.

In Tuscany, for instance, there are the windswept moors of the coastal Maremma, haunted by the shadowy Etruscans; the art treasures of Arezzo; the mineral-rich, arched Metal Hills around Volterra; the Appennine fastness of the Garfagnana. Each of these areas, and many others, have their own particular character, each as 'Tuscan' as 'Chiantishire', and, for the time being, unblighted by the coach parties that are turning mainstream tourist Tuscany into a Renaissance Disney World.

Umbria, Tuscany's land-locked neighbour, may not boast quite such a staggering abundance of great Renaissance art and buildings (some may secretly see this as a virtue) but in Gubbio, Orvieto, Perugia and Todi, it has some of Italy's finest medieval towns. The countryside, so much greener, so less assertive than the Tuscan landscape, has a benign aspect fitting the birthplace of St Francis of Assisi and as the evening calm descends it rarely fails to cast its spell. But Umbria, like Tuscany, is fashionable. Tourism is growing fast. The area around Lake Trasimeno now seems to have more resident foreigners than Umbrians.

Fashion, however, has yet to catch up with Central Italy's third region, Le Marche. Even Italians often have difficulty describing where it is. True, the Adriatic coast has for decades been a Mecca for 'sun 'n sand'. But few venture far from the crowded beaches. Inland, perhaps more so than anywhere else in Central Italy, you will find mountain villages where, in the usually inept guidebook cliché, time really has stood still. In the Marche, culture comes in easily digestible proportions – which is not to say that the quality (witness Urbino) is not of the very best. But perhaps the greatest attraction of the Marche is discovering delightful small towns, just as attractive as their celebrated neighbours in Tuscany and Umbria, that haven't yet been done to death by the purple prose of a thousand guidebook writers.

Buon viaggio

Peter Greene
Cagli, 1995

BEFORE YOU GO

When to go
If possible avoid mid-July to mid-August, when Central Italy swelters under *il solleone*, the sun in the constellation of Leo. Inland cities become crowded heat-traps and many museums, shops and restaurants close.

May and September are the ideal months to tour Central Italy. The landscape is clothed in fresh spring green or the first tints of autumn, any rain tends towards brief showers rather than endless drizzle, you can take lunch *all'aperto* (NB *al fresco* is Italian slang for 'in prison', not 'outdoors') and it is usually possible to find a bed without booking.

The wettest seasons are mid-February to mid-April and mid-October to mid-December, when days of grey mist and rain can set in. It can also be devilishly cold, particularly when the bitter northerly Bora or Tramontana winds blow. If your main interest, however, is to see city sights, you will often have museums and galleries to yourself and be able to knock down the price of a hotel room. A visit in late autumn will also allow you to indulge in Central Italy's gastronomic treasure, the white truffle. If frequently sub-zero temperatures don't worry you, you will often find gloriously bright days in January, but rather too many restaurants and *alberghi* will be closed for annual holidays. Remember that while the climate is generally temperate down by the coast and in the lowlands, up in the mountains snow can lie until the spring.

Finally, over the Easter weekend many hotels are full up, and be warned that April is the month when museums and galleries reverberate with the din of parties of Italian school children.

Clothing
Travel light, even in your own car. Formal clothes are unnecessary unless you stay in the grand hotels. A smarter outfit, however, for the evening stroll and dinner will help you feel less like a tourist. Many visitors who would never dream of visiting their own churches back home in shorts and halter top get huffy when frowned upon for doing it in Italy: respect convention and cover up bare flesh when visiting religious places.

While lightweight clothing is essential in high summer, you'll need a sweater or jersey and raincoat in the spring and autumn. In winter, expect the worst.

Documentation
Citizens of the EU, the U.S.A., and numerous other countries only require a valid passport for visits not exceeding three months. Citizens of Shengen Agreement countries need carry only a valid identity document. If in doubt, consult your travel agent or the Italian Embassy. Drivers need a current licence: if it is not the pink EC type it should be accompanied by a translation in Italian, available from the Italian State Tourist Office (ENIT) in your own country or the frontier offices of the Italian Automobile Club (A.C.I). Travelling in your own car you need the vehicle registration book – if it is not in your own name you must have the owner's written permission to drive the car. You will also need your insurance certificate, preferably with a policy extension (in the U.K. a green card) to make the cover comprehensive while motoring abroad – without it your insurance is only the legal minimum. The international green card comes with a standard accident report form which must be filled in at the time of an accident. Motorists must have all their documents with them while driving and police spot-checks are common.

Medical and travel insurance
EU residents should carry the E111 form entitling them to reciprocal health care in other EU states. In practice, the bureaucratic fuss involved in using the E111 (make for the local U.S.L. – Unità Sanitaria Locale – office if you need to use it) makes it only worthwhile if you need costly treatment. For minor aches and pains make straight for the *farmacia*, the pharmacist.

Other nationals are strongly advised to purchase (or to arrange on an existing policy) medical and travel insurance before departure.

If you buy insurance against loss or theft of personal belongings, the policy will nearly always require you to produce a certificate from the police to show that you have reported any loss or theft.

Money
The standard unit is the Italian *lira* (L), plural *lire*. Notes are in thousands (*mille*, plural *mila*), 1, 2, 5, 10, 50 and 100. Although lower denominations still exist, coins in common use are 50, 100, 200, 500 and 1000 *lire* (the last two, in nickel and bronze, are the prettiest).

Travellers cheques in major foreign

Before you go

currencies are widely acceptable; the once notoriously poor service in Italian banks has improved in the last few years but you still have to penetrate the metal-detecting, airlock-type door.

Read the instructions that come with the cheques in the event of loss or theft. With Eurocheques, you can cash L300,000 per day. The major international credit cards, such as Visa, can be used to get cash in the automatic cash dispensers that are now the norm outside banks across Central Italy – don't forget your PIN code.

Credit cards in place of cash transactions are not yet as widespread in Italy as in Northern Europe and the States, but they are catching on fast. All but the humbler guest-houses and simpler restaurants in Central Italy now accept them, but petrol stations, except motorway service areas, rarely do. The most common card sign in Central Italy is Carta Si, which means that Visa, Mastercard and Eurocard are accepted.

Florence apart, Central Italy is still an *isola felice*, a 'happy island', relatively free from the street crime that plagues the peninsula's big cities. Sensible precautions, however, are still wise – carry cash, cards and passport in a zipped inside pocket, carry bags on the side away from the kerb and keep them on your lap in bars and restaurants. In Florence beware the crafty bands of street urchins and consider using a money belt.

Import duty

The regulations follow general EU rules for the import and export of such goods as wines, spirits and tobacco for personal use across EU borders where duty has already been paid in a member state. Customs officers still maintain their vigilance against prohibited goods such as drugs, weapons and antiquities without export certificates. Get advice before travelling with pets or citizens' band radio – complicated subjects.

Tourist information outside Italy

The Italian State Tourist Board (ENIT) has branches in most capital cities offering a wealth of free tourist literature – most useful is the annual *Traveller's Handbook*.

ENIT Amsterdam Stadhouderskade 6, 1054 ES Amsterdam.
ENIT Frankfurt Kaiserstrasse 65, 6000 Frankfurt/Main 1 (*also in Düsseldorf and München*).
ENIT London 1 Princes Street, London W1R 8AY.
ENIT Madrid Calle de Alcalà 63, Madrid 28014 (*also in Barcelona*).
ENIT New York Suite 1565, 630 Fifth Avenue, New York NY 10111 (*also in Chicago, Montreal and San Francisco*).
ENIT Paris 23 rue de la Paix, 75002 Paris.

You will find the ENIT Website at www.enit.it

Local customs: what to expect, how to behave

Italians in this central region of the peninsula combine the best of North and South. You will rarely meet extravagant displays of Neapolitan emotion, nor the cool indifference of Milan. Try speaking a few words of Italian and your welcome will be that much warmer. If you can only master one line, at least try asking *in Italian* if people speak your language – *Lei parla inglese?* Remember that outside the tourist spots, you will not necessarily find people who speak English. French is a common second language and German is catching on.

The key to Italian social behaviour is often to be found in the idea of *bella figura*, or cutting a fine figure. This is not just a matter of dressing smartly, though that is part of it. *Bella figura* embraces correct formal address; staying relaxed while waiting; not getting aggressively drunk and even the knack of negotiating fly curtains without appearing to be locked in mortal combat with an octopus. Dirt in all its forms cuts a decidedly *brutta figura*.

Fundamentalist non-smokers had best be warned that the rules of *bella figura* don't yet cover smoking in restaurants and bars; despite recent anti-smoking laws that bring Italy into line with other EU countries, smokers still often outnumber non-smokers in public places.

The Italian working day begins early and if you are arriving by car you will often find it hard to park between 9 am and 1 pm. Lunch is the main meal of the day, followed in summer by a short siesta. Between 2 and 4 pm town centres are deserted – except for heat-befuddled foreign tourists. Things get going again in the late afternoon, climaxing in the early evening with the *passeggiata*, or promenade, up and down the main street or square. It fulfills many purposes: gossip, matchmaking, showing off new clothes.

Not until 8 do the restaurants start filling up. Theatres and cinemas begin around 9 and go on until midnight.

Despite the lowest birthrate in Europe, Italy is still a country that dotes on children, and parents will find their offspring fussed over in even the smartest restaurants and hotels.

GETTING THERE

By air
If you are heading for northern and central Tuscany, Pisa is the nearest airport served by direct scheduled flights from Europe's principal capitals. For southern Tuscany and Umbria, Rome is a better alternative. For the Marches, Bologna makes the handiest touchdown.

Alitalia offers the most comprehensive scheduled service to all three destinations. Prices vary dramatically according to season and type of ticket – shop around for the best deal. Year-round charter flights at knock-down prices are also available to all three airports; in the summer they also serve Rimini and Ancona – beware frequent delays and occasional re-routing. Florence's own small Peretola airport is gearing up to handle international traffic, but as yet takes few flights from abroad.

By rail
Unless you loathe flying, competitive air fares make the train journey really only worthwhile when combined with a cut-price rail pass allowing further travel within Italy. The Eurail Pass in North America and the Inter-Rail pass (for the latter you have to have been resident in Europe for at least six months) provide economic and unlimited travel throughout Italy and the rest of Europe. If you are under 26, or a senior citizen, there are further tempting discounts: enquire at a main railway station for details.

By coach
The cheapest, by a hair's breadth, and most uncomfortable option: it takes around 30 hours to get from northern Europe to Florence. If you are this desperate to save money, hitch a lift with a long-distance lorry driver.

By car
If you want to take home crates of Chianti or litres of olive oil and enjoy long-distance driving, take your own car. Otherwise you may find a fly-drive package with Alitalia or one of the other airlines a cheaper way of having your own wheels while in Italy. Motorway tolls, petrol, meals, overnight accommodation, and, for drivers from Britain, ferry or tunnel fares soon mount up. At the time of writing, a one-way ticket through the Mont Blanc or Fréjus Tunnels costs start at L46,000 and are worked out on vehicle length.

GETTING AROUND

By rail
The *Ferrovie dello Stato* (FS), the Italian State Railways, together with a couple of privately-run local services, link up most of the larger towns in Central Italy. Smaller places in more rural areas, however, are poorly served. Details of stations and lines are given by this guide in the individual Sights & Places of Interest entries. If you intend to do much travel by train, buy a copy of the yellow *orario* for Central Italy, a comprehensive timetable for all FS services in the area – cheap and easy to find in most station news kiosks. Note that between the end of September and the end of May a limited winter timetable operates.

As well as being efficient, the FS is remarkable value for money, with fares based on a sliding scale: the further you travel, the better the deal. The low fares make travelling first class on crowded trains a worthwhile option. For the fastest services – *super-rapido* and *Intercity* – you will have to pay a supplement of around 30 per cent on the normal ticket price: ask for a *supplemento rapido* when you buy your ticket or face a substantial extra charge on board.

For short journeys in Central Italy you will mostly rely on the semi-stopping *diretto* and, if you are unlucky, the interminably slow-stopping *locale* services.

Return tickets, *andata e ritorno*, simply cost double the one-way fare, and have a limited validity – better to buy a single, *solo andato*. Remember that before making your journey you must validate your ticket by stamping it in one of the yellow machines at the platform entrance. Failure to do so makes you liable to a substantial fine.

Always check your platform, or *binario*, number on the monitor screens as they sometimes differ from the printed

Getting around

timetables and avoid travelling on Friday and Sunday evenings and in August when overcrowding is the norm.

By car

Unless you intend to stay put in one of the larger towns, a car is of course ideal for discovering Central Italy. The main toll motorways (*autostrade*) are: the A1 through the heart of Tuscany and a short stretch of Southern Umbria, with spurs off to Siena and Perugia; the A11 from Florence to Lucca and Pisa linking up with the west coast A12; and the A14 along the Marches' Adriatic coast. A number of the main SS (*strada statale*) routes are toll free, fast dual-carriageways, or *superstrade*. Travelling east-west you are going against the grain of Central Italy and will have to put up with slower roads over the Appennines.

But the real point of a car is to leave the crowded highways to meander along the deserted country roads armed with your *Versatile Guide* and a Touring Club Italiano (TCI) 1:200,000 map. Many of the region's smallest roads are un metalled gravel 'white roads': although these roads are usually well enough kept, beware of potholes.

The region's antique towns were never built for cars and you will find that many historic centres are now closed to unauthorized traffic. Downtown Florence and Siena are no-go areas for motorists. Parking, particularly in the morning and early evening, is often a headache. If signs indicate a time limit you must set a *disco orario* to your time of arrival. You can buy the disc from most newsagents and garages.

Off the motorways, petrol stations close for up to three hours at lunchtime and all day Sunday. Carry a few uncrumpled L10,000 banknotes for use in the 24-hour, self-service petrol dispensers now common in garage forecourts. Lead-free petrol (*senza piombo*) is widely available now.

Traffic rules follow European norms and signs follow international conventions. If in doubt over precedence at a junction, give way to traffic coming from the right. Seat belts are compulsory and you must carry a reflective warning triangle to be placed at least 50 m behind your car when broken down. Speed limits are 50 kph in built-up areas, 90 or 110 kph on country roads and 130 kph on motorways. Police speed checks are frequent and on-the-spot fines are severe. Contrary to received opinion, the standard of driving in this part of Italy is generally good and, avoiding city centres, you shouldn't return home prematurely aged.

Away from the big cities, your car is unlikely to be stolen, particularly if it is right-hand drive. Car radios, however, seem irresistible to petty crooks across Italy – if you can't take them with you, make sure windows are closed and doors locked. Stories of thefts from moving cars are needlessly alarmist.

Magic of Italy, the London-based travel company (tel. 0181 748 7575) offers some of the most imaginative available flight-car-accommodation deals to Florence, Tuscany and Umbria. Their approach is especially sympathetic to the traveller who wants freedom of movement combined with economical charter flights, car rental and hotel bookings.

Taxis

Metered taxis are widely available in most towns – usually in ranks by the station or off the main square. Fares, which are always displayed, vary according to location. For long journeys in country areas agree the price beforehand. If you summon a taxi by telephone, it is usual to be charged for the journey to the pick-up point as well as for the journey itself.

By bus

While larger centres are well served by trains, much of rural Central Italy relies on a network of private bus services. Comfortable modern coaches are the norm, but fares are often more expensive than train fares. Timetables and routes, usually tailored to the needs of school children rather than tourists, are available from tourist information offices. Sunday services are infrequent. Florence's two largest long-distance operators are:

Lazzi, *Via Mercadante* 2.
SITA, *Viale dei Cadorna* 105.

Phoning Italy from abroad This guide gives telephone numbers starting with the code used within Italy. When calling from abroad, the zero at the beginning of the number **must also be included**.

ESSENTIAL PRACTICAL INFORMATION

Accommodation
Tuscany and Umbria now boast a greater concentration of attractive hotels than any other part of Italy. The choice in the Marches is, however, still limited. In the large towns and smart seaside resort the bill for four-star luxury can be outrageously high and in July and August prices are universally jacked-up.

Italy's hotels and guest houses, *alberghi* and *pensioni*, are graded by stars. One and two stars mean basic but cheap. Three stars – the majority of our recommendations are in this category – means a pleasant, all-round hotel without expensive frills and a wide price range depending on location and season. Four-star hotels offer every comfort you would expect at this high price. Five stars denote world-class establishments. Displayed on the door of every room in every hotel is the official tarif. If you are charged more, demand an explanation. Guest houses in seaside resorts in high season sometimes only offer half-pension terms, otherwise you are not expected to eat in the hotel restaurant, indeed many hotels do not have one.

Central Italy, particularly Tuscany, is in the forefront of *agriturismo*, the scheme whereby farmers offer accommodation and meals. The ENIT tourist office in your country can give you lists of such accommodation for Tuscany, Umbria and the Marches. Often it will be self-catering apartments or cottages available for a minimum of three nights.

Banks and currency exchange
Banks open Monday-Friday 8.30 am-1.30 pm and one hour in the afternoon sometime between 2.30 and 4.00.

Currency exchanges (*cambii*) keep longer hours, but they are thin on the ground outside the main centres – you will find them at larger railway stations as well as airports, ferry terminals and city centres.

Breakdowns
Motorways have SOS telephones with two buttons: one for medical assistance and one for breakdowns. On other roads, dial ACI (Italian Automobile Club) on 116 for foreign-language assistance.

Electricity
As in most of Europe, Italy is 220V, 50 AC. Take an adaptor for foreign electrical appliances.

Embassies and consulates
Some countries maintain consulates in Florence; otherwise you need the consular section in your country's Rome embassy. In southern Umbria, the Rome embassies will in any case be nearest.

Australia Rome: Via Alessandria 215; tel. 06 832721.
Austria Rome: Via Pergolesi 3; tel. 06 868241. Florence: Via dei Servi 9; tel. 055 215352.
Canada Rome: Via GB de Rossi 27; tel. 06 8415341.
France Rome: Piazza Farnese 87; tel. 06 686011. Florence: Piazza S. Trinità 1; tel. 055 213509.
Germany Rome: Via Po 25; tel. 06 8441812.
Great Britain Rome: Via XX Settembre; tel. 06 4825651. Florence: Lungarno Corsini 2; tel. 055 284133.
Ireland Rome: Largo del Nazareno 3; tel. 06 6782541.
Netherlands Rome: Via Mercati 8; tel. 06 3221141. Florence: Via Cavour 81; tel. 055 475249.
New Zealand Rome: Via Zara 28; tel. 06 4402928.
Spain Rome: Largo Fontanella Borghese 19; tel. 06 6878264. Florence: Piazza di Salterelli 1; tel. 055 212173.
U.S.A. Rome: Via Vittorio Veneto 119; tel. 06 46741. Florence: Lungarno Amerigo Vespucci 38; tel. 055 298276.

Emergencies
For the public emergency service telephone 113 (manned by multi-lingual operators). Police immediate action service (crime and road accidents), telephone 112. Use the above numbers only in real emergencies.

Measurements
Italy operates on the metric system:
One litre, *un litro*, = 1.7 pints
(1 imperial gallon = 4.5 litres);
1 U.S. gallon = 3.7 litres.
One kilo, *un chilo*, = 2.2 lbs.

Foodstuffs are commonly sold in units of an *etto* (plural *etti*) which is 100 grams or 3.5 ozs.

One kilometre, *un chilometro*, = 0.62 miles. To convert kilometres to miles multiply by five and divide by eight, and vice-versa.

Medical matters
The Italian Health Service operates through local health units – see under

Essential Practical Information

Unità Sanitaria Locale in the telephone directory. EC nationals should show their reciprocal health care form (see Medical and travel insurance, page 15).

In the event of serious illness or injury, head for the 24-hour first aid, *pronto soccorso*, at any hospital, airport or large railway station. Pharmacies (*farmacista*) keep normal shop hours and can be spotted by a green cross outside; they operate an emergency 24-hour service on a rotating basis, details are displayed in the window.

Bring any proprietary medicines you may need with you as their equivalent in Italy are usually expensive. Dental treatment is of a high standard, but costly.

National holidays

January 1 and 6; Easter Monday; April 25; May 1; August 15; November 1; December 8, 25 and 26. Towns also close down on the feast day of their local saint – for example Florence on June 24 (St John the Baptist).

Shopping hours

Italians either shop early or late and shops remain firmly closed for around four hours in the middle of the day. In country areas, shops are open from around 8 am to 12.30 pm and from 4 to 7.30. In the city, they tend to open and close later in the afternoon. Everything closes on Sunday and one (variable) afternoon per week. In tourist haunts, many shops drop afternoon closing in high season. In Florence a few large shops are beginning to operate all-day opening, as are the out-of-town hypermarkets that are taking Italy by storm.

Post and telephone

Post offices are open weekdays and Saturday from 8 am to 1.30 pm. Central offices in principal towns stay open until 7 and also have a Sunday and holiday telegraph service from 8 to 1. If you just want stamps, get them from a tobacconist where you see the 'T' sign. Post offices will hold letters addressed to individuals on the move until collected in person. The envelope should carry the name of the recipient, the words *Fermo posta* and the name and post code of the locality. The recipient pays a fee and must show identification to collect the letter.

Standard payphones, found both on main streets and in many bars, take 100, 200 and 500 lire coins as well as *gettoni*, the 200 lire telephone tokens. Many also now take phonecards – ask for a *carta telefonica*, available in units of L5,000 or L10,000 from post offices, tobacconists and many bars. Break off the top left-hand corner before use.

In principal towns Telecom Italia (alas no longer called SIP) has offices where you can take a cabin and pay for your call afterwards. Some bars also operate this service, *a scatti*.

Calls from your hotel will cost more than from standard payphones.

To make international direct-dial calls use 00 + your country code. To get help from the operator for calls within Italy, dial 10. For information on international calls, dial 176 for Europe and Mediterranean countries, 1790 for other countries. To make operator-assisted international calls, dial 15 for the former and 170 for the latter.

Rush hour

Between 7.30 and 9.30 am, around 12.30 pm, and in the evening between 5.30 and 7.30, roads in and out of towns are at their busiest.

Time

Italy is one hour ahead of Greenwich Mean Time in winter and two hours ahead in summer. From the United States, Italy is six hours ahead of Eastern Standard Time. Summer Time applies from the last weekend in March to the last weekend in September.

Tipping

Tipping in Italy is nowhere near as common as it once was. Most restaurants now include a service charge and you should only leave a few notes if service was outstanding. In cities, customers often leave their loose change in smarter bars, particularly for table service. In the country, tipping in bars and restaurants is the exception rather than the norm. Attendants in some public WCs expect a few hundred lire and sacristans who open normally closed parts of churches expect an *offerta* – a L1,000 note or two. Hotel porters, taxi drivers and ushers in theatres and cinemas should be tipped.

Tourist information

Italy is a country hooked on acronyms and there are plenty to choose from when it comes to tourist information offices – ignore the plethora of initials and look for the 'i' information symbol.

A BRIEF HISTORY OF CENTRAL ITALY

Few regions in the world are infused with such a strong sense of historical continuity as Central Italy. From the myths that surround the birth of the Etruscan civilization to the foundation of United Italy in the 19thC, past and present are wound together in a seamless web that stretches back over three millenia. This short account provides a thread to guide you through the labyrinth of the complex story; to fill in the details, see the entries for the most important towns under Sights & Places of Interest within the guide itself.

Before the Romans Our knowledge of the early peoples of Central Italy is hazy and often draws on the unreliable writings of later Roman historians. The Umbri tribes who dwelt in the area between the Tiber and the Appennines (more or less the eastern half of modern Umbria) have left us few relics of their passage, while the Piceni, who peopled the eastern seaboard of what is now the Marches or Marche, remain firmly in the shadows.

Only with the **Etruscans** do we find early inhabitants who left their mark on history. Their culture took root in the region between the rivers Arno and Tiber and the Tyrrhenian Sea somewhere around the 8thC BC. They built their prosperity on the mineral wealth of the area, particularly the iron ore of Elba, and by the 6thC BC their influence was felt from the River Po to the Bay of Naples. Their major centres organized themselves into the Dodecapolis, a loose confederation of 12 city states. There is much debate as to exactly which cities formed this grouping, but likely candidates include Tarquinia, Vetulonia, Populonia, Roselle, Chiusi, Cortona, Perugia, Arezzo and Volterra. The most significant relics they have left us are great necropoli. Understanding the nature of their civilization has been plagued by contrasting interpretations that often say more about the writers than the Etruscans themselves.

For the Ancient Greeks, with whom they had close cultural and trading links, they shared a common origin from Asia Minor; Imperial Roman historians, keen to show their own superiority, put them down as primitive aborigines. In our own century, the novelist D.H. Lawrence cast them as the antithesis of the cold military machine of Rome and saw the vitality of the modern Italian as the triumph of Etruscan over Roman values. Others point out that many aspects of Ancient Rome were inherited from Etruria. As all schoolchildren who studied Latin will remember, Rome in its infancy was ruled by the Tarquin dynasty of Etruscan kings.

Roman Central Italy
With the expulsion in 509 BC of **Tarquinius Superbus**, the last of the Etruscan monarchs, the new **Republic** of Rome gradually began to make its presence felt. Already weakened by attacks from the Greek colonists in southern Italy and by Celtic inroads from the north, the Etruscans soon came under the sway of Rome. The beginning of the end was marked by the Roman conquest of the Etruscan city of Veio in 396 BC. Over the next hundred years both warfare and cultural absorption sealed the fate of Etruria. The founding of Roman colonies such as Sena Julia (Siena) and Florentia (Florence), and the construction of highways such as the Via Aurelia and Via Flaminia consolidated Roman dominion. Under the first Roman Emperor, Augustus, Central Italy was divided into Tuscia, covering much the same area as modern Tuscany; Umbria, comprising present-day Umbria east of the Tiber and the northern Marches; and Picenum, now the southern Marches.

Arrival of the Barbarians
In AD 476, Rome, already weakened by the split between the Western and Eastern Empires and the first forays by Goths and Vandals from the north, finally fell to the barbarian warrior Odoacer. His reign as the first King of Italy was shortlived, however, with the arrival in 489 of **Theodoric, King of the Ostrogoths**, who established a 33-year rule of relative tranquility in Italy. On his death, the Eastern Emperor **Justinian** in Constantinople tried to revive imperial power in Italy through his celebrated generals Belisarius and Narses. Although they finally managed to topple the Gothic King Totila in 552, Central Italy was in no fit state to resist yet another invasion from the north, this time from the Lombards in 568. For 200 years these warriors from the

A brief history of Central Italy

Danube valley held loose control over much of Central Italy, ruling from Lucca and Spoleto. Only in the northern Marches and part of Umbria did the Byzantine powers manage to keep a toe-hold under the protection of the Exarchate of Ravenna.

The Holy Roman Empire
Although converted to Christianity by Pope Gregory the Great, the Lombards were regarded as unwelcome guests by later popes. It was Pope Stephen II who first hit on the idea of calling in foreign help to oust the Lombards and in 754 Pepin the Short entered Italy at the head of his Frankish army. The expulsion of the Lombards proved difficult and it was only under Pepin's son, the great Charlemagne, that the work was completed. As a reward to his Frankish champion, Pope Leo III crowned Charlemagne as the first Holy Roman Emperor. Although at the time it was little more than an honorary title, the Holy Roman Empire thus founded was to last on and off for a thousand years and to become the focus of continual strife between the rival claims of successive popes and emperors. Although Charle-

KEY DATES

Prehistory
Earliest human settlements in Central Italy date back more than 100,000 years	Early Stone Age
Earliest Indo-European settlement in Italy possibly on Monte Cetona in Tuscany	Early Bronze Age

Etruscans & Romans
Etruscans established in Central Italy	8thC BC
Legendary founding of Rome	753 BC
Roman Republic founded	509 BC
Etruscan dominance from Naples to the River Po	6th-5thC BC
Southern Etruria under Roman dominance	350 BC
Via Flaminia completed	222 BC
Hannibal routs Roman army at Battle of Lake Trasimeno	217 BC
Julius Caesar founds Florentia	159 BC
Western Roman Empire falls to Odoacer, King of the Goths	AD 476

The Dark Ages
St Benedict born in Umbria	480
Central Italy invaded by Totila	552
Lombards invade Central Italy and rule from Lucca and Spoleto	570
Charlemagne's Frankish Empire dominates Central Italy	774

The Middle Ages
Death of Matilda, last Germanic ruler of Florence, ushers in age of independent city states	1115
Florence sacks Fiesole and begins its long ascent to power	1125
St Francis of Assisi born	1181/2
Coronation of Frederick II as Holy Roman Emperor lays the foundations of the Guelf-Ghibelline rivalry that splits Central Italy for centuries	1220
Dante born	1265
Giotto born	1267
Black Death	1348

The Renaissance
Masaccio begins frescoes for Brancacci Chapel, Florence	c. 1425

A brief history of Central Italy

magne's empire flourished, it depended too heavily on his guiding hand; when he died in 814, things rapidly fell apart. Italy was again plunged into anarchy with imperial officials setting themselves up as local despots.

Increased security only returned with the revival of the power of the Holy Roman Empire under the Saxon King, Otto I. Trade and industry began to flourish and, while Emperor and Pope argued over who should rule, many of the cities of Central Italy had their first taste of independence. Although they paid lip service to one side or the other, in truth they found themselves able to decide their own future. Bereft of effective central government, these early

• *Roman Temple of* Minerva, *Assisi.*

Cosimo becomes first de' Medici to control Florence	1434
Brunelleschi's dome for Florentine Duomo raised	1436
Donatello's bronze *David* cast	c. 1440
Duke Federico succeedes to the Duchy of Montefeltro and Urbino's golden age begins	1444
Lorenzo the Magnificent rules Florence	1469
Michelangelo born	1476
Charles VIII of France invades Italy and Savonarola holds sway in Florence	1494

The Aftermath

Siena sold to Florence	1557
Florentine control over all Tuscany, Lucca apart, sealed as a de' Medici becomes Cosimo 1, Grand Duke of Tuscany	1570
Montefeltro lands handed over to Pope Urban VIII – the final stage in the consolidation of Papal power over Umbria and the Marches	1624
Tuscan Grand Duchy passes to House of Lorraine	1737
Napoleon conquers Italy	1797
Tuscany votes to join United Italy and the Papal States fall to Garibaldi's troops	1860
Florence capital of Italy	1865-71
Allied forces break German Gothic Line with heavy fighting across Central Italy	1944

A brief history of Central Italy

city states bred fierce local patriotism and ceaseless rivalry with their neighbours. The greatest of them, Florence, earned its freedom in 1115 when the city was bequeathed to its citizens by its last Imperial ruler, the Countess Matilda. With the Florentine sack of Fiesole ten years later, the city began its slow climb to the total domination of Tuscany.

Guelfs and Ghibellines

The rivalry between the Papacy and the Holy Roman Empire came to a head under the rule of the brilliant medieval German Hohenstaufen Emperor, Frederick II, the man who earned the title Stupor Mundi for his dazzling talents. Although he almost succeeded in creating a united Italy under his banner, his death in 1250 marked the eclipse of German imperial power in the peninsula. Central Italy was deeply bound up in this conflict, with loyalties tied either to the Guelf or Ghibelline parties. The supporters of the papacy took their name from Frederick's rival for the empire, the Welf Otto, while the imperialists became known as Ghibellines from the Italianized Hohenstaufen battle-cry *Hie Weibling*. Behind the simple struggle between the two powers lay a deeper political battle between the new middle class of merchants and artisans, who allied themselves with the Guelfs, and the old feudal aristocracy who saw that the tide of democracy could best be held in check by the Emperor's Ghibelline faction. Into this fundamental struggle all the warring factions of Central Italy poured their energies. The Guelf cause can be said to have triumphed with the arrival of the French under Charles of Anjou in the middle of the 13thC at the invitation of Pope Urban IV; from now on France rather than Germany was to be the dominant foreign power in Italy. The Guelf and Ghibelline labels, however, lingered on for centuries. Long after they had lost their original significance, they remained as a cover for just about any difference of opinion, even as an excuse to settle old scores.

Despots and republics

The absence of the papacy in Avignon from 1305 to 1377, the subsequent Great Schism which saw up to three candidates claiming the Throne of St Peter, and the arrival of the Black Death in 1348 all provided fertile soil for the flowering of local despotism across Central Italy, particularly in Umbria and the Marches. The careers of these petty tyrants were briefly interrupted by the arrival of the ruthless Cardinal Albornoz, sent by the Avignon popes to reimpose their rule over the Papal States, and finally went into decline with the restoration of the papacy in Rome in 1421 under the determined Pope Martin V.

Florence and the Early Renaissance

While the Papal States in Umbria and the Marches fell to despots, the course of the 13thC witnessed a different story in Florence. With the close of the Middle Ages, Florentine merchants had made their city one of the richest in Europe, mostly through the wool trade. This new-found wealth in turn encouraged the rise of banking; even in 1342 when Edward III of England reneged on enormous debts with two Florentine banks, it only proved to be a temporary setback. Prosperity, and the political stability that went with it, provided the ideal conditions for the great flowering of art and architecture of the Italian Renaissance. The keystone of this cultural explosion was patronage. Public displays of magnanimity – a fine altarpiece, say, or the facing of a church – brought prestige and power.

In the early days, patronage was in the hands of the great merchant guilds or *arti*. The most important of them, the Arte della Lana, the guild of wool merchants, for example, was responsible for the building and decoration of Florence's cathedral – from Giotto's tower to Brunelleschi's dome. The power of the guilds ensured that Florence managed to resist the rise of despots. It remained, however, firmly under the rule of an oligarchy of the city's wealthiest families, despite the popular uprising of the Ciompi, the poorest wool workers, in 1378.

By 1434, with Cosimo de' Medici, the Medici dynasty, had become the leading family in Florence. For more than another 100 years, Florence carried on with the semblance of a republic but with the Medici effectively ruling through their control of the Signoria. It was only in 1570, when Cosimo I was given the title of Grand Duke of Tuscany, that Medici rule set into total autocracy.

Peace before the storm

The apogee of the Renaissance in the middle of the 15thC was marked by a period of relative stability across Central Italy. This was in no small part thanks to the Italian League, a defensive treaty between the major powers in Italy that held in check both the lesser Italian states and foreign invaders. It is against this background that not only Florence but also smaller centres of art and learning flourished; perhaps none better illustrates the splendour of these lesser courts than that founded by Duke Federico da Montefeltro at Urbino.

Foreign domination and the Papal States

But the days of this prototype of a united Italy were numbered. The individual interests of the leading states soon took priority over the common good, and the arrival of Charles VIII from France in 1494, at the invitation of Milan in their quarrel with Naples, marked the dissolution of the League and the opening gambit in the Wars of Italy. Although the French invasion convulsed Florence and led to the brief rise to power of the reforming Dominican Friar, Girolamo Savonarola, two years later Charles was back in France with his Italian conquests lost. But the French intervention had turned the thoughts of another great European power towards Italian conquests – Spain.

As the 16thC dawned and the Italian Renaissance took root across Europe, Central Italy, along with the rest of the peninsula, became a battleground on which the rival claims to Italian hegemony between Francis I of France and Charles V of Spain were tested. In 1527 a motley army of mercenary soldiers sent by Charles sacked Rome and imprisoned the pope. In the confusion that followed the Sack of Rome, Florentine republicanism staged a last-ditch stand against the emperor, but Charles had already made himself the virtual ruler of Italy by the Treaty of Cambrai in 1529 and the city soon fell to his placeman, Alessandro de' Medici. And with the Treaty of Cateau-Cambrésis in 1559, over a hundred and fifty years of Spanish domination of Italy began.

The Grand Duke Cosimo I ingratiated himself with the Spanish by marrying Eleanor of Toledo, the daughter of one of Charles' most trusted lieutenants and the Spanish Emperor gave him a free hand to rule over the new Duchy of Tuscany. A few important Tuscan ports, known collectively as the Stato dei Presidi, however, stayed under direct Spanish rule as a watchdog over Cosimo's actions.

With the Spanish holding the rest of Italy in check, the Papacy was free to consolidate its rule over Umbria and the Marches; while the centre of Italian culture moved to Counter-Reformation Rome, the Papal States were left to languish under the dead hand of ecclesiastical bureaucrats.

Napoleon and The Risorgimento

The shock waves of the French Revolution of 1789 were felt in Italy and helped to fan the first flames of libertarianism that were to culminate in 1860 with the birth of United Italy. But first it had to submit to the Napoleonic invasion of 1796. Across Italy, Bonaparte first set up client republics – with the Duchy of Tuscany transformed into the Etruscan Republic and the Papal States into the Roman Republic – then the more draconian Kingdom of Italy. The collapse of the regime with the fall of Napoleon was as rapid as its arrival. But, despite its brevity, Napoleonic rule awoke Central Italy and the rest of the country from its long slumber and fostered the rebirth of nationalism. Under the Piedmont King Victor Emmanuel, his wily prime minister Cavour and the heroic if maverick general, Garibaldi, United Italy became a reality. In 1859 the Italian *tricolore* flew from the Fortezza of Florence and the last Grand Duke, Leopold II, abdicated. A year later Tuscany voted to join the new Kingdom of Piedmont. The Papacy, however, proved more intransigent to the onslaught of the Risorgimento and it was only by force that both Umbria and the Marches managed to break free from the Papal States in the same year. Before the fall of Rome in 1870, Florence was for a brief five years the capital of the new Kingdom of Italy. From now on, the history of Central Italy is but part of the story of modern Italy.

SOME KEY CULTURAL THEMES AND PLACES

Pre-history
Museums at Ancona, Florence (Museo di Preistoria), Perugia, and Pontremoli.

The Etruscans
Tombs at Tarquinia, Chiusi, Cortona, Perugia, Orvieto, Vulci. Walls at Roselle, Todi and Volterra. Museums at Volterra, Chiusi, Cortona, Tarquinia, Orvieto, and Florence.

Ancient Rome
Ruins at Fiesole, Spoleto, Spello, Assisi, Arezzo, Ancona, Gubbio, Fano, Civita Castellana, Ansedonia (*Cosa*), Roselle and Ferento (near Viterbo). Many of these places and a number of other towns in Central Italy have important archaeological museums.

• *Ancient ruins, Fano.*

Early churches and monasteries
Pisa, Pistoia, Siena, Spoleto, Assisi, Arezzo, Florence, Orvieto, Portonovo (Monte Conero), Abbadia San Salvatore, Abbazia di San Galgano, Abbazia di Sant'Antimo and numerous small Romanesque churches across Central Italy.

Medieval civic architecture
San Gimignano, Monteriggioni, Siena, Todi, Gubbio, Spoleto, Orvieto, Perugia.

Renaissance architecture
Florence, Pienza, Urbino, Montepulciano, Siena, Perugia, Arezzo, Jesi, and too many others to list here.

Masterpieces of Renaissance fresco painting
Florence (Masaccio and Fra Angelico), Arezzo and Sansepolcro (Piero della Francesca), Perugia (Perugino), Monte Oliveto Maggiore (Il Sodoma), Orvieto (Signorelli), Spoleto (Filippo Lippi).

Outstanding collections of Renaissance painting and sculpture
Uffizi, Pitti Palace, Bargello, Accademia galleries in Florence, galleries in Cortona, Perugia, Siena, and Urbino.

Modern art
Museum of Modern Art in Florence, Burri collection at Città di Castello, Marino Marini works at Pistoia.

Pilgrimage centres
Assisi (St Francis), Loreto (the Holy House), Tolentino (St Nicholas of Tolentino), Osimo (St Joseph of Copertino), Corinaldo (Santa Maria Goretti).

Opera and music festivals
Maggio Musicale in Florence in May; open-air opera in arena at Macerata in July-August; Rossini Opera Festival at Pesaro in August; the open-air Torre del Lago Puccini, August; Spoleto festival of the Two Worlds, June-July; Perugia Jazz Festival, July.

Most spectacular feste
Florence: *Scoppio del Carro* on Easter Sunday and 16thC football in June; Gubbio: *Festa dei Ceri* on 15th May; Lucca: torchlight illuminations for Holy Cross celebrations on 14th Sept; Siena: *Il Palio* 2 July and 16 August; Viterbo: Procession of the *Macchina di Santa Rosa* on September 3.

• *Assisi statues.*

HOW THE RENAISSANCE CAME ABOUT – AN INSTANT GUIDE

It was of course in Central Italy that the Renaissance first took root. The fine things that you see as you travel the region represent an extraordinary cultural explosion, not merely of a school of painting, a style of sculpture or an architectural fashion, but an entirely new way of seeing the world.

Remember that the Renaissance is a catch-all term covering over 200 years of human endeavour. Don't worry if you find it difficult to follow. Lucy Honeychurch, lost in Santa Croce without a Baedeker, in E.M. Forster's novel *A Room with a View*, was also thoroughly confused until '...the pernicious charm of Italy worked on her, and instead of acquiring information, she began to be happy.' (See Florence, page 58.)

The Middle Ages

In the Dark Ages following the collapse of Rome, between the 5th and 10thC, Central Italy was too busy with `barbarian' invaders from north of the Alps to bother much with the finer points of art or architecture. (The barbarians were so called because to Italian ears their speech sounded like a series of 'ba-ba-ba' noises.) The few churches and monasteries that remain from this period are either in the barbarian **Lombard** or the oriental **Byzantine** styles – or an eclectic mix of both.

Only with the increasing wealth and stability of the late medieval period, in the 11th and 12thC, did building fever catch hold of the people of the region. The **Romanesque** style of these years was both the sum of these new influences and a harking back to distant memories of Roman architecture. However, the Pisan style of Romanesque, with its tiers of delicate ornamental arches, introduced something new. As the Romanesque was reaching its peak in Central Italy, northern Europe was being gripped by the construction of the great **Gothic** cathedrals. The solid walls and dumpy round arches of Romanesque were being swept away by soaring pointed arches and flying buttresses that allowed walls to become simply frames for glittering panes of stained glass. The Gothic label was invented by Renaissance Italians as a term of abuse for a style so barbaric it could well have been created by the Goths. For all that, it was a potent influence in Central Italy and churches such as the **Basilica of San Francesco** at Assisi and the **Cathedral at Orvieto**, and many of the great civic buildings of the 12th and 13thC bear a strong Gothic stamp. Gothic architecture, too, was the stimulus for a revival in the arts of sculpture and painting; while **Giotto's** great frescoes and **Nicola** and **Giovanni Pisano's** sculptures were some of the earliest works to break free from medieval two-dimensional formalism, they were firmly planted in the Gothic tradition. It proved a vigorous style that was to run through the Early Renaissance, particularly in the Sienese school founded by **Duccio**.

Its culmination came in the 14thC with the **International Gothic** school, best seen in the mystical works of two artists, **Andrea Orcagna** and **Gentile da Fabriano**.

The Renaissance

It was **Giorgio Vasari** who first drew together all the strands that ran through the great creative flowering in Central Italy. In his *Lives of the Artists*, a collection of well-informed biographies of the protagonists of the Renaissance published in its final form in 1568, he characterized a period of some 200 years, from Giotto to Michelangelo, as a *rinascita*, or rebirth, of art and architecture. But it was not until the 19thC that the French word *renaissance* was used to describe the whole period, set apart from what had come before. And it was with Jacob Burckhardt's *The Civilization of the Renaissance in Italy*, published in 1860, that this region of Italy was identified as the cradle of a chapter in human history that still conditions much of our perception of the world.

What Burckhardt saw as the key to the Renaissance was the growth of individualism – where medieval man had been content to work in collective anonymity to the greater glory of God, his Renaissance counterpart was much more interested in his own greater glory. Fame or notoriety – it mattered little which became the goal, and competitive talent was all. As if to wipe out the nightmare of the barbarian invasions (see A brief History of Central Italy, pages 21-2), poets and painters, sculptors and scholars looked to Ancient Rome and Greece as the source of all nobility and wisdom, while paganism and Christianity uneasily shared the

How the Renaissance came about – an instant guide

same bed. Humanism released thought from the strait-jacket of medieval superstition while wealthy patronage fostered the cult of personality. With human self-awareness came a new interest in the natural world, and artists turned to anatomy and mathematics with as much gusto as they did to the Ancient World. The organization of society, too, became a work of art, both in theory, as in **Machiavelli's** writings, and in practice, as in the glittering court of Urbino. No longer was it adequate for the ambitious to be competent in one chosen craft, for the new age called for the mastery of many talents, and for men to be all-rounders. The ideal of Universal Man was epitomized by that peerless genius, **Leonardo da Vinci**.

And by some mysterious quirk of history, it was Florence, virtually alone, that was responsible for this revolution. Its two great sons, **Dante** and **Giotto**, were born within a year of each other in the 1260s and with them we hear the opening bars of the overture. But the curtain was not to go up on the Renaissance until a hundred years later with the entry of that great Florentine trio, **Masaccio**, **Donatello**, and **Brunelleschi**, in the first half of the 15thC. Although Masaccio (1401-c. 1428) managed to revolutionize art with the first controlled use of perspective in painting and the introduction of full-blown humanism in the realistic portrayal of human suffering, sculpture, because of the ease with which it could render realistically the three-dimensional human form, was the greatest art of the age. Masaccio's solid figures owe a great debt to the most celebrated of Early Renaissance sculptors, Donatello (1386-1466).

Regarded by Vasari as equal to the sculptors of Classical times, Donatello's incisive and emotive realism and sheer versatility have rarely been matched. Both artists were profoundly influenced by the geometric principles of perspective laid down by Filippo Brunelleschi (1377-1446), the leading architect of his day. He is best remembered for the dome of Florence's Duomo, a revolutionary feat of structural engineering, and his creative rediscovery of the *all'antica* vocabulary of the architecture of Ancient Rome.

During the course of the **Quattrocento**, as Italians refer to the 1400s, numerous artists and architects perfected the achievements of the Early Renaissance: **Fra Angelico** with some of the most moving religious images in Western art; **Paolo Uccello** and **Piero della Francesca** with their pioneering exploration of foreshortening and perspective; **Leon Battista Alberti** with his refinement of the Classical style of architecture. The close of the century saw, too, the rise of another great school of painting in Central Italy, the **Umbrian** painters led by **Perugino** and **Pinturicchio**. But it was the first half of the 16thC that saw the apotheosis of the Renaissance ideal of perfect beauty and harmony with the works of **Leonardo da Vinci**, **Michelangelo** and **Raphael**.

This period of the **High Renaissance** was marked by a shift of artistic excellence from Florence to Rome, and, apart from Michelangelo's great Florentine sculptures, few works by this celebrated trinity remain in Central Italy.

Mannerism and beyond

A term that art historians love to argue over, **Mannerism** loosely refers to Italian art between around 1520 and 1600. Many of its greatest artists were Florentines and it was Michelangelo himself whom many regard as its creator. It is characterized by dramatic use of colour, distorted figures, violent compositions and a move towards the grotesque and outrageous. For some it marks the triumph of style over content, a vacuous virtuosity for its own sake; for others, it is an assertive and intellectual breaking-free from the, by now, suffocating restrictions of Classical Renaissance art. Its leading Central Italian exponents include the painters **Rosso Fiorentino**, **Pontormo** and **Bronzino**, and the sculptors **Cellini** and **Ammannati**. Whether or not you take to this highly subjective style, its liberation from the mathematical precision of Renaissance perspective and the confines of the block of marble paved the way for the great Counter-Reformation artistic movement of the 17thC – the **Baroque**.

But with the Mannerists the Central Italian age of artistic glory came to an end; it is to other places, other nations, and other guide books that you must turn to follow the story of Western art and architecture.

AN A TO Z OF ARTISTS AND ARCHITECTS

Alberti, Leon Battista (1404-72)
Born in Genoa as the illegitimate son of an exiled Florentine family, he became an exemplary Renaissance Universal Man. As an architect, his Palazzo Rucellai in Florence was a pioneer in the Classical revival; as a writer, his treatises on architecture and painting profoundly affected the visual arts.

Ammannati, Bartolomeo (1511-92)
A decidedly Mannerist Tuscan sculptor and architect much influenced but little improved by Michelangelo; history's judgement on his *Fountain of Neptune* in the Piazza della Signoria in Florence is harsh.

Andrea del Castagno (active c. 1442, d. 1457)
A painter with a strong sculptural line, much influenced by Donatello (see separate entry); witness his *Last Supper* in Sant'Apollonia, Florence and his painted monument for Niccolò da Tolentino in Florence's Duomo.

Andrea del Sarto (1486-1531)
The leading painter in Florence in the early days of the High Renaissance, his atmospheric paintings, marked by a subtle use of colour, are in sharp contrast to his contemporary Michelangelo, then reaching fame in Rome. See his *Madonna delle Arpie* in the Uffizi.

Arnolfo di Cambio (c. 1244-1301)
Early Tuscan architect and sculptor who studied under Nicola Pisano; famous as the first architect of Florence's Duomo and, probably, the Palazzo Vecchio and Santa Croce.

Bandinelli, Baccio (1488-1560)
Florentine who, as court sculptor to Cosimo I, tried to outdo Michelangelo. His *Hercules and Cacus* in Piazza della Signoria, Florence, shows how dismally he failed.

Beccafumi, Domenico (c. 1486-1551)
Siena's outstanding contribution to Mannerist painting: his best pictures are in the Pinacoteca in Siena.

Botticelli, Sandro (1445-1510)
One of the greatest painters of the Italian Renaissance, he combined faultless virtuosity with sheer poetry. See two of his finest works, the *Primavera* and the *Birth of Venus* in the Uffizi.

Bronzino, Agnolo (1503-72)
The best of the Florentine Mannerists and a master of elegant sophistication – his portraits of Cosimo de' Medici's family and followers are dazzling.

Brunelleschi, Filippo (1377-1446)
Although trained as a goldsmith, he stands as the key figure in Early Renaissance architecture. As his famous dome for Florence's Duomo shows, he was also a brilliant structural engineer. Virtually all his work, including the Innocenti Hospital, San Lorenzo, and the Pazzi Chapel in Santa Croce, is in Florence.

Buontalenti, Bernardo (1531-1608)
Imaginative Florentine architect who turned his hand to toy making, theatre design, military architecture and civil engineering while in the service of Cosimo I. The Belvedere fortress and the grotto in the Boboli Gardens, Florence, are amongst his works.

Cellini, Benvenuto (1500-71)
Celebrated goldsmith, medal-maker and sculptor, part of whose fame rests on his racey *Autobiography*. Of his few surviving works, the best in Florence is the bronze *Perseus* in the Loggia dei Lanzi.

Cimabue, Giovanni (c. 1240-c. 1302)
Florentine painter who was one of the first to break away from the stiff conventions of the Byzantine style, thus paving the way for the naturalism of his pupil, Giotto (see separate entry).

Crivelli, Carlo (c. 1433-c. 1495)
Venetian painter who spent much of his working life in the Marches producing works of bright colour and compelling detail.

Della Robbia, Luca (1400-82)
The founder of the family workshop famed for its blue-and-white glazed terracotta that has become a Florentine trademark. His nephew **Andrea** (1434-1525) continued the

An A to Z of Artists and Architects

Ducal Palace, Urbino — see Luciano Laurana

craft on an almost industrial scale.

Desiderio da Settignano (1428-64)
Sculptor in marble and stone of great charm and delicacy who was possibly trained by Donatello (see separate entry).

Donatello (1386-1466)
The greatest sculptor of the early Renaissance in Italy, responsible for the first life-size nude bronze since Classical times (*David* in the Bargello). Also see his marble statues of Saints Peter, Mark and George for the exterior of San Michele, Florence.

Duccio di Buoninsegna (c. 1260-c. 1319)
The founder of the Sienese school of painting whose influence remained potent in Siena during the 14thC. His masterpiece was the *Maestà* for Siena's Duomo.

Fra Angelico (c.1387-1455)
Dominican monk responsible for some of the most striking paintings in the history of religious art: his most celebrated works are the frescoes in San Marco, Florence.

Francesco di Giorgio Martini (1439-1502)
Sienese painter, architect and military engineer much patronized by Duke Federico da Montefeltro of Urbino for whom he built over 70 fortresses in the Marches. His treatises profoundly influenced High Renaissance architecture.

Gaddi, Taddeo (active c. 1325, d. 1366)
Torch bearer for Giotto with whom he reputedly worked for many years. Compare his frescoes in the Baroncelli Chapel, Santa Croce, with Giotto's in the nearby Bardi and Peruzzi Chapels. His son, **Agnolo** (d. 1396), continued his father's work in Santa Croce.

Gentile da Fabriano (c. 1370-1427)
Leading painter of the International Gothic style whose greatest work, an *Adoration of the Magi* is in the Uffizi. Compare his late medieval vision with the work of his revolutionary contemporary, Masaccio (see separate entry).

Ghiberti, Lorenzo (1378-1455)
Celebrated Early Renaissance Florentine sculptor in bronze who spent most of his career working on

An A to Z of Artists and Architects

the famous bronze doors for the Baptistry in Florence.

Ghirlandaio, Domenico (1449-94)
Outstanding Florentine fresco painter whose large workshop trained the young Michelangelo. His most famous works are in Santa Trinità and Santa Maria Novella, Florence.

Giotto di Bondone (c. 1267-1337)
Perfecting the new style of his master, Cimabue, he revolutionized religious art in his great fresco cycles and stands as Florence's first true genius in painting. His work remained seminal to the course of the Italian Renaissance. Much controversy surrounds the attribution to Giotto of the celebrated frescoes of the *Life of St Francis* at Assisi, but the major part of the frescoes in the Bardi and Peruzzi Chapels in Santa Croce are certainly by his hand.

Gozzoli, Benozzo (c. 1421-97)
A gracious Florentine fresco painter with a fine sense of narrative, though rarely reaching the sublime spirituality of his master, Fra Angelico (separate entry). See his work in the Palazzo Medici-Ricardi, Florence, and at Montefalco and San Gimignano.

Laurana, Luciano (1420/5-1479)
Dalmatian architect, best known for his work on the Ducal Palace at Urbino.

Leonardo da Vinci (1452-1519)
The archetypal Universal Man and one of the titans of Western art: few subjects seemed beyond his genius. Born the illegitimate son of a Florentine lawyer, he began his career in Florence under the painter Verrocchio. His first independent work is the *Annunciation* in the Uffizi, which also holds the only other surviving work from his early Florentine period, the unfinished *Adoration of the Magi*.

Lippi, Fra Filippo (active c. 1432, d. 1469)
Though little suited to his life as a Florentine monk – he eventually eloped with a nun – Filippo added his personal stamp to the gravity and simplicity of Masaccio (see separate entry).
His son, **Filippino** (1457-1504) also became a leading painter of his time.

Lorenzetti, Ambrogio (active 1319, d. ?1348)
Sienese painter, who with his brother **Pietro** (active 1320, d. ?1348) bridged the gap between Sienese and Florentine painting in the wake of Duccio (see separate entry).

Lotto, Lorenzo (c. 1480-1556)
Wandering painter of Venetian origin who left a serendipity collection of his handsome works in the Marches; best collection in Jesi.

Maitani, Lorenzo (active 1310, d. 1330)
Sienese sculptor and architect only known for his outstanding work for Orvieto Cathedral.

Martini, Simone (active c. 1315, d. 1344)
Sienese master of the Gothic style best known for his frescoes on the *Life of St Martin* in the Basilica of San Francesco, Assisi.

Masaccio (1401-c. 1428)
The innovative Florentine genius who in his short life laid the foundations for Renaissance painting. His fame rests on his fresco paintings in Santa Maria Novella and the Brancacci Chapel in Santa Maria del Carmine.

Masolino da Panicale (active c. 1423, d. 1447)
Florentine painter of talent much influenced by the International Gothic style. His reputation has been up-staged by Masaccio, with whom he worked on the Brancacci Chapel.

Michelangelo Buonarroti (1475-1564)
With Raphael and Leonardo, the creator of the High Renaissance and the prototype of the Romantic idea of the tormented artist. Painter, architect and poet of genius, he above all wished to be known as a sculptor.

Michelozzo di Bartolomeo (1396-1472)
Important Florentine architect and sculptor much favoured by Cosimo de' Medici. In Florence his most important building is the Palazzo Medici.

An A to Z of Artists and Architects

Mino da Fiesole (1429-84)
Notable Florentine sculptor in marble much influenced by Desiderio da Settignano (see separate entry).

Nelli, Ottaviano (c. 1375-?1444)
Umbria's best International Gothic painter. His finest works are in his home town of Gubbio.

Orcagna, Andrea (active c. 1343, d. 1368)
International Gothic painter, sculptor and architect who led the pack in mid-14thC Florence with his brothers **Jacopo** and **Nardo di Cione**.

Perugino (active c. 1472, d. 1523)
The great master of the Umbrian school of painting and herald of the High Renaissance, his star pupil was Raphael. Make for Perugia to see some of his best works.

Piero della Francesca (active 1439, d. 1492)
The master of the application of mathematics to painting and a genius of the Renaissance. As a theorist his writings on perspective were of fundamental importance.

Piero da Cortona (1596-1669)
A founding figure of Baroque art whose best works are in Rome. See his ceilings in Palazzo Pitti for a taste of his style.

Piero di Cosimo (1462-1521)
Florentine painter as famous for his odd pictures – for example the *Discovery of Honey* – as Vasari's claim that he lived on hard-boiled eggs.

Pinturricchio, (1454-1513)
Perugian painter who worked with Perugino (see separate entry). His noted use of lavish colour is best seen

ART, ARCHITECTURAL AND GENERAL ITALIAN TERMS

Apse Semicircular recess, especially over main altar in church.

Badia Abbey.

Baldacchino Ornamental canopy especially over altar.

Biblioteca Library.

Borgo Village or suburb.

Bottega Small shop or artist's workshop.

Campanile Bell tower.

Camposanto Graveyard.

Cartoon Full-size preliminary drawing on paper for fresco, tapestry or mosaic.

Caryatid Female figure used as column.

Cattedrale Cathedral.

Cenacolo Fresco of Last Supper.

Centro storico Historic centre of town.

Chancel Part of church near altar reserved for clergy and choir.

Corso Principal street of town.

Chiesa Church.

Collegiata Church with a group of clerics rather than just one parish priest.

Comune The government – and the area governed – of the medieval city states; in modern times the basic unit of Italian local government.

Cortile Courtyard.

Cosmati School of medieval Roman craftsmen celebrated for inlaid marble work.

Convento Monastery or convent.

Cupola Dome.

Diptych Painting on two hinged panels.

Duomo Most important church in town, usually a cathedral.

Eremo Hermitage.

Fresco, affresco Durable wall

in his frescoes for the Piccolomini Library in Siena.

Pisano, Andrea (c. 1290-1348)
Bronze sculptor known chiefly for the south doors of Florence's Baptistry.

Pisano, Nicola (c. 1223-c. 1284)
First great pre-Renaissance sculptor often seen as the father of modern sculpture. With his son, **Giovanni** (c. 1245-c. 1315), he looked to Ancient Rome for his model. The awesome pulpits in Siena, Pisa and Pistoia are their most outstanding works.

Pollaiuolo, Antonio (c. 1432-98)
Florentine of many talents, above all seen as one of the greatest Renaissance draughtsmen. One of the first artists to use anatomical dissection to aid his figure painting.

Pontormo, Il (1494-1556)
Bold distortion and technical mastery mark him out as one of the greatest early Mannerist painters. His acknowledged masterpiece is the *Deposition* in Santa Felicità, Florence.

Quercia, Jacopo della (c. 1374-1438)
Leading Sienese sculptor of the early Renaissance who worked with Donatello and Ghiberti.

Raphael (1483-1520)
Along with Leonardo and Michelangelo, the great name of the High Renaissance and perhaps the best loved of the trio. Born in Urbino, he was much influenced by the city's glittering court. He studied under Perugino.

Rossellino, Bernardo (1409-64)
Sculptor in marble who later became a noted architect, first as assistant to

---

painting where colour is applied directly to wet plaster.

Intarsia Marquetry work.

Loggia Open-sided arcade or gallery.

Maestà Painting of Virgin and Child enthroned and surrounded by angels and saints.

Municipio Town hall.

Nave Main body of church bounded by aisles.

Pala Painting above altar.

Palazzo Palace, mansion, apartment, office-block or large city building.

Palio Banner, given as prize in race, hence the race itself, as at Siena.

Pieve Parish or parish church.

Piano Nobile Grandest floor of palace, almost invariably first floor.

Pinacoteca Picture gallery.

Podestà Ruling official in medieval city.

Porta Town gateway, or door.

Portico Colonnaded covered porch.

Predella Small paintings at base of altar-piece.

Quattrocento Literally '400', but shorthand for the 1400s; alternative expression for the 15thC in Italian art, much used in art history texts. Hence also *Duecento* (13thC), *Trecento* (14thC) and *Cinquecento* (16thC).

Rocca Hill-top fortress.

Sagrestia Sacristy or vestry.

Sgraffito Design scratched in plaster.

Sinopia Preparatory sketch on wall for fresco.

Stemma Coat of arms.

Stucco Decorative lime plaster.

Torre Tower.

Transept Side arms of church.

Triptych Painting on three separate panels.

An A to Z of Artists and Architects

• *Raphael statue, Urbino; below right, Raphael's birthplace.*

Alberti (see separate entry), then as architect to Pope Pius II in the creation of the new town of Pienza.

Rosso Fiorentino (1495-1540)
Central painter in the birth of Florentine Mannerism and, later, a founder of the Fontainbleau School in France.

Sangallo family
Dynasty of architects looked down on by Cellini for their humble origins as carpenters. **Giuliano da Sangallo** (c. 1443-1516) was much favoured by Lorenzo the Magnificent for whom he built the Villa Medici at Poggio a Caiano. His brother, **Antonio the Elder** (c. 1453-1534), brought the Roman High Renaissance to provincial Tuscany with such buildings as the church of San Biagio at Montepulciano. Their nephew, **Antonio the Younger** (1483-1546), is best known for his work in Rome, and, like his uncles, was a noted military architect – the Fortezza da Basso, Florence, and the well of San Patrizio in Orvieto are his work.

Sansovino, Andrea (c. 1460-1529)
High Renaissance Tuscan sculptor noted for his marble work, the most glorious example of which is the cladding for the Holy House of Loreto in the Marches.

Signorelli, Luca (c. 1441/50-1523)
Painter from Cortona noted for his consummate draughtsmanship. His apocalyptic frescoes in Orvieto's cathedral prefigure Michelangelo's *Last Judgement* in the Sistine Chapel.

Sodoma, Il (1477-1549)
Proper name Giovanni Antonio Bazzi. Painter much influenced by Leonardo, who moved to Siena after a training in Lombardy. His masterpiece is a fresco cycle at Monte Oliveto Maggiore.

Uccello, Paolo (1397-1475)
Florentine painter noted for his dramatic use of foreshortening and perspective to produce some of the

most poetic images of 15thC Florence.

Vasari, Giorgio (1511-74)
Though he produced a prodigious quantity of work as both painter and architect, Vasari's reputation rests on his celebrated book, *Lives of the Artists*, the first and still most influential work of modern critical art history. His vision of the *rinascità*, or rebirth, of the arts in Italy between the mid-13thC and the 1560s still colours our outlook.

Verrocchio, Andrea del (1435-88)
Florentine sculptor and painter whose work in bronze is acknowledged as some of the finest of his day.

FOOD

Central Italian cooking is deeply rooted in peasant tradition and remains impervious to the arrival of frozen *bastoncini di pesce* (fish fingers). Here the home cook rather than the professional chef rules and even the smartest restaurants seek to produce food just like *nonna*, or grandmother, used to make.

The use of fresh, top-quality ingredients assembled with the minumum of fuss is common to the food of Tuscany, Umbria and the Marches. But as dishes are strictly based on tradition and local produce, each region has its distinctive *cucina tipica*. As with any rural diet, much use is made of food gathered from the wild; *funghi*, game, nuts, field herbs and – the area's greatest culinary treasure – truffles are an important feature across Central Italy.

Waste is frowned upon, and many of the now most fashionable dishes were first developed to use up such things as stale bread or the less-appealing parts of the pig – the Tuscan *acquacotta* is a good example.

Not surprisingly, the best food is still to be had in private houses rather than in restaurants. The arrival of tourism in smaller towns and villages has often raised the standards in local restaurants and led to the 're-discovery' of long-lost traditional dishes; sometimes, however, particularly in Florence, it has led to indifferent food, catering for the lowest common denominator.

The old labels *ristorante*, *trattoria* and *osteria* have become somewhat interchangeable in recent years; many of the smarter, and most expensive places, call themselves *osterie* and take pride in re-interpreting strictly local dishes with great flair. Generally, though, a *ristorante* will at least have a written menu and a broader choice of wines. In *trattorie*, particularly in country areas, you will often have to cope with a menu rattled off at your table by the proprietor – at your blank looks a son or daughter with a smattering of English or French will often be brought out from the back to assist. Avoid the temptation just to order dishes whose names are familiar to you from back home – you will frequently be missing

the best the house has to offer.

If you are touring in summer or early autumn, look out for posters advertising the local *sagra* – a festival dedicated to a town's particular speciality where you can try the food in question in every guise imaginable. The strangest has to be a *sagra* dedicated to *lardo*, or pig fat, near Carrara.

Region-by-region
Tuscany

A typical Tuscan meal will often start with an *antipasto* of *crostini*, small pieces of toast usually spread with a chicken liver paste, or *fettunta*, toasted bread rubbed with garlic and amply dressed with fine olive oil.

The classic Tuscan *primo* is a hearty soup rather than pasta. The soup could be A*cquacotta*, literally 'cooked water', a simple vegetable soup that varies from place to place but is always served over stale bread; *Ribollita*, a thicker soup which must contain beans and the Tuscan dark cabbage, *cavolo nero*; or a substantial *zuppa di ceci* or *fagioli*, chickpeas or beans. A drizzle of Tuscany's most prized product, the

Food

best olive oil, is often added to the bowl of soup as it is served.

There are two pasta dishes peculiar to Tuscany: *pappardelle con la lepre* and *pici*. The former are wide noodles dressed with a rich hare sauce and the latter are a stubby fat hand-made pasta peculiar to southern Tuscany.

For *secondi*, the celebrated Tuscan dish is *bistecca alla fiorentina*, an enormous steak from Italy's best beef cattle, the Tuscan Chianina breed. It should be cooked fast over charcoal without salt or oil until it is seared on the outside and *al sangue* (rare) within. Never say you don't like tripe until you have tried the rich stew of *trippa alla fiorentina* and don't turn your nose up at *fegatelli*, pieces of pig's liver with bay leaves wrapped in caul fat and sauteed in wine.

In autumn the best game, or *cacciagione*, is often to be had, as well as *cinghiale*, or wild boar.

As you would expect, by the sea the diet turns to fish – if you are near Livorno don't miss a dish of *cacciucco*, the area's famous fish soup-cum-stew. Perhaps the most Tuscan of vegetables are white beans. Try *fagioli all'uccelletto* (with tomato and sage) or, even better, *fagioli cotti al fiasco*, cooked for hours in a chianti flask in ashes.

The best sweets come from Siena but you'll find them across the region: heavy *panforte* packed with candied fruits and the soft almond lozenge-shaped *ricciarelli* are known the world over. Towards Umbria you may find *castagnaccio*, a peasant cake made from chestnut flour, rosemary, pine kernels and raisins.

The local cheese across Tuscany tends to be the sheep milk *pecorino* that crops up all over Central Italy; the best is reputedly from Pienza.

Umbria

In Umbria the best *antipasti* are often the salamis and *prosciutto crudo* (raw cured ham) made from the region's excellent pigs; in summer the *prosciutto* with luscious figs makes a change from the more usual *prosciutto* with melon. Pasta dishes are the common *primo* including Umbria's own thick spaghetti, *umbrici*. Often simple pasta dishes are finished off with a grating of truffle. Minestra di *farro*, an ancient peasant soup made from something similar to buckwheat, is becoming increasingly common on restaurant menus.

Secondi often take the form of simple grilled meat – pork and lamb perhaps the most ubiquitous. Stews of pigeon (*piccione*) and rabbit (*coniglio*) are also frequent. By Lake Trasimeno the best freshwater fish to try are eel, or *anguilla*, and carp, or *carpa*.

On market day make for the *porchetta* van to buy slices of a whole suckling pig stuffed with wild fennel and roasted on a spit.

Some of Italy's best chocolate is made by Perugina at Perugia, including the well-known *baci*, or chocolate 'kisses'.

Le Marche

The *marchigiani* eat more meat than any other Italians and it shows: in many country areas going out to a restaurant is basically an excuse to fuel up on enormous platters of grilled meats. Relief, however, is on hand along the Adriatic coast with the peninsula's most delicious fish.

For an *antipasto*, mountain cured ham and *lonza* (raw salted fillet of pork) reign supreme. The classic *primo* is a generous plate of *tagliatelle* dressed with a *sugo*, or meat sauce, to be avoided by anyone with a high cholesterol level. The region's unique pasta dish is *vincisgrassi*, a baked lasagna without the usual tomatoes. Urbino is also famous for *passatelli*, strands of pasta made from breadcrumbs, parmesan cheese, egg and minced veal cooked in broth. Apart from the ever-present meat grilled *alle brace* (on embers), delicious stuffed pigeons and rabbit cooked with fennel (*in porchetta*) are a Marche speciality. In some areas, stewed snails occasionally creep on to the menu.

By the coast, particularly around Ancona, try *brodetto*, fish stew which must be made with 13 species of fish, no more, no less.

Thin spaghetti dressed with *vongole*, or baby clams, is always tasty in this region.

In the northern Marche look out for *piadina*, a flat, unleavened bread made with lard and often served with cold meats at roadside snack-bars. The sheeps' milk *pecorino* cheese is excellent here and is best eaten in the spring with young raw broad beans.

THE REGION'S WINES

Wine alone could provide an excellent motive for touring in Tuscany. In Umbria and the Marches you can also winkle out some excellent local wines, though rarely up to the class of the better Tuscan estates. Winemaking in Central Italy has been having its own little renaissance over the last 20 years or so, with a move away from quantity towards quality. From producing rough plonk for the masses, Tuscany now boasts some of Italy's finest *vini da meditazione*, wines so good they should be drunk with religious respect. These top-class wines are expensive and cost much the same whether bought in Italy or back home: a bottle of Sassicaia 1991 will cost around L65,000, while the eight remaining bottles of Biondi Santi's Brunello di Montalcino Riserva 1891 are on offer for a staggering 31 million lire – each. But avoiding the fashionable labels, you can drink excellent wines at excellently low prices.

In 1963, the DOC, or *denominazione di origine controllata* laws were introduced. Like the French *appellation* controls, they sought to guarantee the authenticity of wines from a particular region. Unfortunately, however, the DOC label doesn't guarantee that the wine is any good – only that it comes from a certain place and is made in a certain way. Ironically, DOC has given the more creative winemakers in Tuscany something to fight against and some of the region's best wines must carry the undignified label *vino da tavola*. The newer DOCG classification (*denominazione d'origine controllata e garantita*) does include quality benchmarks but as yet only applies to a select group of Italian wines, including three of Tuscany's great reds – Chianti, Brunello di Montalcino and Vino Nobile di Montepulciano.

Joy, however, is not only to be found in the restrained sipping of august bottled vintages, but also in the enthusiastic quaffing of young, local wines. These still-living brews, liable to dramatic alteration at the mere changing of the moon and barely able to withstand the journey from cellar to table, yet alone a long trip north, often delight by their incisive personality and honest price. In wine zones, you will not go far wrong simply sticking to the *vino della casa*.

A region-by-region rundown of wines

Tuscany
Reds: Tuscany means red wine, nearly all of which is made from the Tuscan Sangiovese grape.

Chianti is Italy's best known red wine and comes in two versions, young *normale* and *riserva*, aged for a minimum of three years. Wines vary dramatically from zone to zone and from vineyard to vineyard with the most famous coming from the **Chianti Classico** area between Florence and Siena. Producers to look out for include Badia a Coltibuono, Castello di Uzzano, Fontodi, Poggerino, Rocca delle Macie and Villa Antinori. Only two of the other six Chianti sub-zones produce wines that match the quality of Classico – Frescobaldi's Montesodi Riserva from the small **Chianti Rufina** zone north-east of Florence is amongst the finest Chianti produced, while leading names in the **Chianti Colli Fiorentini** area include Fattoria dell'Ugo, La Querce and Montegufoni. The other four zones – **Colli Senese, Colli Aretini, Colline Pisane** and **Montalbano** tend towards quantity rather than quality with few outstanding producers.

Tuscany's pride amongst red wines is undoubtedly **Brunello di Montalcino**. It is an uncompromisingly old-fashioned full wine made entirely from a Sangiovese clone, aged for at least four years and only produced in a small area around the southern Tuscan town of Montalcino. Names to look out for include Altesino, Biondi Santi, Banfi, Camigliano and San Felice. If your wallet can't stretch to Brunello, settle for the humbler young DOC **Rosso di Montalcino**. Along with Chianti and Brunello, Tuscany's other DOCG red is the chewy and austere **Vino Nobile di Montepulciano**. The top producers include Avignonesi, Contucci, Gracciano and Poliziano. Despite the DOCG label, quality is inconsistent and a bottle of everyday **Rosso di Montepulciano** can sometimes be a better choice. If you are staying to the west of Florence look out for **Carmignano**, a lesser-known but delicious dinner wine with a touch of Bordeaux thanks to the addition of Cabernet Sauvignon grapes to the basic Sangiovese. Other DOC Tuscan

The Region's Wines

• Chianti label – see page 37.

reds include **Montescudaio** and **Morellino di Scansano**.

Whites The region's most properly Tuscan white is the nutty **Vernaccia di San Gimignano**. Top producers include Guicciardini Strozzi, Teruzzi e Puthod and La Torre. Many red wine producers have developed new white wines to use up the white grapes that have gone out of fashion as an additive to Chianti. The most famous of these is the industrially produced **Galestro**, technically faultless but exceedingly boring. In the south, look out for the robust **Bianco di Pitigliano**. Tuscany's greatest white is the ancient **Vin Santo**, made across the region from grapes left to dry in the winery for up to four months. The best Vin Santo, like vinegar, depends on a 'mother' – a small amount of the previous vintage is always left in the barrels when the newly pressed must is added. Traditionalists claim the wine should be sweet, but some producers now make a drier version for modern palates.

Umbria and North Lazio
Whites Umbria is the home of another of Italy's more famous wines, this time white **Orvieto**. But, as with so many of Italy's mass sellers, you have to try it where it's produced to appreciate how it should really taste. Although there are excellent versions of dry Orvieto *secco*, traditionally it is a somewhat sweet *abboccato* wine with the best including a proportion of grapes affected with noble rot as with French *Sauternes*. Top producers include Antinori, Bigi and Barberani. Some of Umbria's best wines are now made by Giorgio Lungarotti at Torgiano and his white **Torre di Giano** is no exception.

In northern Lazio, **Est! Est! Est! di Montefiascone** is of note for its name, certainly not for its quality.

Reds Again Lungarotti at Torgiano produces Umbria's finest reds, **Rubesco** for quaffing, **Monticchio Riserva** for meditation. Near Montefalco, the obscure *Sagrantino* grape is blended with *Sangiovese* to produce the bitter-sweet **Rosso di Montefalco**. *Sagrantino* is also used on its own to produce a delectable dessert *passito* wine. For reliable table wines try **Colli Altotiberini** and **Colli del Trasimeno**.

The Marches
White The Marches' pride is **Verdicchio**, made from the eponymous grape. This green-tinged wine with a distinctive bitter finish goes well with the region's Adriatic fish. Like Orvieto, it is among Italy's best-known dry whites, but has come a long way since the commercially successful but mediocre Verdicchio of Fazi Battaglia in its waisted, 'Gina Lollobrigida' bottle. The two DOC versions are **Verdicchio dei Castelli di Jesi** and **Verdicchio di Matelica**.

A few names worth knowing are Garofoli, Monte Schiavo, Umani Ronchi and Villa Bucci. Other DOC whites include **Bianchello del Metauro** from the north – disappointing after good Verdicchio – and **Colli Maceratesi** from Macerata.

Reds Few notable red wines are made in the region. Around the Conero peninsula, **Rosso Conero**, made from the *Montepulciano* grape, is a rich, perfumed wine that occasionally reaches greatness – leading labels include Garofoli, Umani Ronchi and Le Terrazze. **Rosso Piceno** from the south blends *Montepulciano* and *Sangiovese* grapes and while being pleasant is rarely outstanding. A red sparkling oddity is **Vernaccia di Serrapetrona**, normally a sweet dessert wine but also available in a dry *secco* version. Around Pesaro the undistinguished local tipple is **Sangiovese dei Colli Pesaresi**.

Florence: introduction

There was plenty of domestic strife in medieval Florence but little interference from foreign invaders. The Florentines were therefore able to develop an economy based on silk and wool manufacture and a stable banking system. They flourished while Rome and the cities of Lombardy were tearing themselves apart. They resisted the tyranny of both Pope and Holy Roman Emperor and they enjoyed the nearest thing to a democracy that any city state had known since ancient times. An enlightened business class built itself airy palaces with inner courtyards instead of fortifying their dwellings, setting an example for the graceful urban plan of subsequent ages.

Under its leader Cosimo ('Il Vecchio') de' Medici (1389-1464), a banker and the father of a line of energetic administrators, Florence recovered the Classical virtues and managed to reconcile Christian dogma with pagan wisdom and the natural sciences. Look down on Florence from the surrounding hills and you see, side by side, the two pivots of the citizen's existence: the political centre of Piazza della Signoria and the Palazzo Vecchio; and the religious centre round the green-and-white-marbled Campanile and Baptistry and Brunelleschi's pink-and-grey cathedral dome, the most beautiful in the world, spread like an immense umbrella to protect the spiritual values of the people, as the city walls protected their persons. (The walls of Florence were demolished when she briefly became capital of Italy, 1865-71, but there are a couple of surviving gateways.) Cosimo de' Medici and his grandson Lorenzo ('Il Magnifico') encouraged the phenomenon we call Renaissance Man: the intellectual all-rounder. Florence ushered in the Renaissance, an unprecedented and never-to-be-repeated upsurge of painting, sculpture, architecture, literature and intellectual enquiry.

It was not only art that this city, one-tenth the size of Rome, gave to the world. The financiers of Florence taught Europe banking and invented the florin, the first stable currency. Her physicians turned alchemy into chemistry and biology. (Artists such as Leonardo and Michelangelo profited from their anatomical discoveries.) She was the metropolis of mathematics and astronomy; Amerigo Vespucci, who gave his name to continents, was Florentine; Columbus in 1492 carried a chart drawn up by a Florentine which showed that the Atlantic Ocean was only 2,500 miles wide. She was the cradle of Italian literature: Dante, Petrarch, Boccaccio. Centuries later, the language of Italy is basically the language of Florence.

Even if history leaves you cold, you can hardly fail to discover that this city, spread across a bowl in the Tuscan hills, with its slanting prospects, was designed, as the Italians say, to 'clutch the throat'.

Florence: introduction

USING THIS SECTION
Sights and places of interest in Florence can be found in the A-Z starting on page 42. Four walks are then described, which, if you were to follow them all, would leave you with a thorough knowledge of the city. As with all the itineraries in this guide, the information can just as well be absorbed at a café table; and of course, the hotel and restaurant recommendations, pages 78-81, can also be consulted.

ACCOMMODATION GUIDELINES
Hotel booking services can be found at Santa Maria Novella Station and at exits into the city from the motorways; it is advisable to have booked well in advance – the city is packed from April to October, and particularly during late spring and early autumn, and during the international fashion fair in January and July ('Pitti Uomo'). In central Florence there is a wide range of accommodation. Prices are high, and despite the traffic-restricted 'blue zone', the city is always noisy. Some travellers prefer to stay outside Florence, and commute by frequent fast train to the centre. Pistoia (see Seeing the Region: 1, pages 92-3) makes an attractive base, or, even closer at hand, Fiesole (see Sights Outside Florence, page 77).

ARRIVING
By car Travelling on the *autostrada* from the north or west, exit for Florence at Firenze Nord; from the south and south-east, exit at Firenze Certosa, *not* Firenze Sud. The city has a large *zona a traffico limitato* in which parking is allowed for residents only, and parts of the centre are all-pedestrian. The underground car park at the main railway station is inexpensive – if you can find a space. Further out of town to the north-east, at Fortezza da Basso, is a large car park linked to the city centre by a free bus service. There is also a large, cheaper car park near Piazza Libertà (north side of the city) at the 'Parterre'. Another solution is to book a hotel with garage space.

By train All trains terminate at Santa Maria Novella Station, the city's transport hub.

By coach The main departure point for both long-distance and local services is Santa Maria Novella station. Just about everywhere in Tuscany is served by one of the several bus companies, as well as many long distance routes (run by Lazzi).

By air Peretola Airport is busy, with a large number of flights. Pisa, 85 km away, is linked by a fast train with the Air Terminal at Santa Maria Novella.

Tourist offices (*Ufficio Informazioni Turistiche*) *Via Cavour 1r; tel. 055 290832*; *Borgo Santa Oroce 29r; tel. 055 2340444*; and outside Santa Maria Novella station; *tel. 055 212245*).

PUBLIC TRANSPORT
Bus Maps and route details of the city bus service, ATAF, are available from the tourist office at Santa Maria Novella. Most routes start from there. Tickets must be bought in advance from news stands, tobacconists or street machines, and validated in the stamping machine on the bus. Bus routes are arranged by number. In the text that follows, bus numbers are given for sights best reached by public transport.

Taxi Remember that if you phone for a taxi, the meter starts running the moment the taxi leaves its starting point (Radiotaxi: tel. 055 4798 or 4390). There are taxi ranks at the station, on Piazza San Marco and Piazza Santa Trinità and on Via Pellicceria/Piazza della Repubblica. A 10 per cent tip will be appreciated.

NEIGHBOURHOODS TO AVOID
Florence is a safe city compared with Rome or Naples, but don't relax completely. Wherever tourists are found *en masse*, there too are pickpockets and bag-snatchers – including the Vespa thieves known as *scippatori*. Trouble is most likely to occur at the main railway station, and Piazza Santa Maria Novella, mainly after dark when the pushers and prostitutes are at work. The same goes for Cascine park, and, to a lesser extent, for Piazza Santo Spirito.

FLORENCE: *introduction*

SHOPPING CHECKLIST
Florentines have always been superb shopkeepers, and shopping in Florence is wonderful: beautifully presented stores selling the most elegant and desirable things, all prettily gift wrapped when you have purchased them. Cheap, however, it is not. Here are a few pointers.

Leather goods
Look for the occasional bargain in the **Mercato di San Lorenzo** and **Mercato Nuovo** (just off Via Calimala); also in the Tuesday morning market in **Cascine** park, especially for shoes (and clothes). Many shoe shops are to be found in **Via dei Calzaiuoli**, and cheaper ones at **Borgo San Lorenzo** and around **Via dei Panzani** near San Lorenzo. An interesting, though tiny, shoe shop is **Stefano Bemer**, at Borgo San Frediano 136r. **Gucci** and **Ferragamo** can be found in Via de' Tornabuoni. **Bisonte's** leather goods, in Via Parione, have a natural, easy look. **Madova**, just across Ponte Vecchio in Via Guicciardini, is entirely dedicated to gloves.

Fashion
All the great names in fashion, and others peculiar to Florence, can be found in the streets in and around **Via de' Tornabuoni** and **Via della Vigna Nuova**. Look out for **Luisa** in Via Roma, selling the trendiest designers, plus own-label clothes; also for **Enrico Coveri** and youthful **Emilio Cavallini**, both in Via della Vigna Nuova. The **Coin** department store, Via de' Cerchi, and **Rinascente**, Piazza Repubblica, sell a range of less demanding clothes and accessories.

Marbled papers, stationery
Head for **Il Torchio**, Via de' Bardi, which makes its leather and printed paper combinations to order on the premises. Prices here are generally more reasonable than at the well-known **Il Papiro** shops in Via Cavour and Piazza del Duomo. Also recommended is charming, old-fashioned **Giannini**, found in Piazza de' Pitti.

Ceramics
Sbigoli, in Via Sant'Egidio, a little east of the Duomo, sells traditional hand-made terracotta and ceramics.

Jewellery
There have been jewellers on **Ponte Vecchio** since the late 16thC; or try the grand houses of **Settepassi** and **Buccellati** in Via de' Tornabuoni.

Antiques
Via dei Fossi and **Via Maggio** will keep you busy.

Food
Sant'Ambrogio market is a small-scale, friendly version of the Mercato Centrale; both are superb. Or simply browse with the housewives in the local food stores, particularly around Santo Spirito and Sant'Ambrogio. Gourmet food stores include **Gastronomia** in Borgo Santi Apostoli; **Pegna** in Via della Studio, south of the Duomo; and **Cibreo**, Via de' Macci, near Sant'Ambrogio.

Toiletries
If you want beautifully packaged gifts to take home, try a *farmacia* or *erboristeria*. Best known are the **Farmacia di Santa Maria Novella**, in Via della Scala, and the **Eboristeria Palazzo Vecchio**, tucked away in Via Vacchericcia, near Piazza della Signoria.

Designer objects
The Italian passion for these, from incredible kettles to a little briefcase with a handle which doubles as a portable phone, is displayed at **ViceVersa**, Via Ricasoli 53. **Open House**, behind Ponte Vecchio in Via Barbadori has designer kitchenware.

Florence sights

SIGHTS & PLACES OF INTEREST

ACCADEMIA (GALLERIA DELL')
Via Ricasoli 60; open Apr-Sep, Tue-Sat 8.30 am-10 pm, Sun 8.30 am-8 pm; Oct-Mar, Tue-Sat 8.30 am-6.50 pm, Sun 8.30 am-1.50 pm. My first visit to Florence, in my teens, lasted a couple of hours between bus connections. All we knew was that we had to lay eyes on Michelangelo's **David** before we left, if nothing else. We rushed to the Accademia, queued for ages, saw it and rushed back to the bus station. I would do something quite different now; for a start I would give Michelangelo's original a miss in its inappropriate setting in the Accademia, and view instead the copy which graces the Piazza della Signoria (see page 55). The original stood there until 1873, when it was moved, for protection, to the specially built tribune in the Accademia. Its execution, in 1504, confirmed Michelangelo's reputation, begun with his *Bacchus* (in the Bargello, see page 44) and his St Peter's *Pietà* in Rome, as the greatest sculptor of his day. Its sheer size is awesome, its brand of superhuman beauty and power a metaphor for both Michelangelo and for the Renaissance, but many lovers of Michelangelo will turn with relief to his unfinished and much freer **Quattro Prigioni** (Slaves), begun for the never-realized Tomb of Julius II, a 40 year long saga central to Michelangelo's creative life. As for *David*, made as a symbol of the Florentine republic when the artist was just 26, he is as much of a magnetic crowd-puller as he was when Michelangelo first gave him life. He has had his detractors, however, such as William Hazlitt who wrote in 1821 that he looked 'like an awkward overgrown actor at one of the minor theatres, without his clothes'; or D.H. Lawrence, who found *David* 'shrinking and exposing himself, with his white, slack limbs'.

The **Accademia di Belle Arti** is Europe's oldest art school, founded in 1563 by the leading Florentine artists. The graffitti and the melée of students who are always chatting outside give it a very laid-back appearance these days. Its gallery was founded in 1784, and includes, apart from the Michelangelos, a collection of Florentine painting from the 13th to the 18thC. It contains no real highlights, except perhaps for the painted **Adimari Wedding Chest**.

BADIA FIORENTINA
See Walk Three: East of the Duomo, page 73.

BARGELLO (MUSEO NAZIONALE)
Via del Proconsolo 4; open Wed, Thur, Sat, Sun 8.30 am-1.50 pm, Tue, Sat 8.30 am-5 pm. Closed 1st, 3rd, 5th Sun and 2nd, 4th

---

> **TACKLING FLORENCE'S SIGHTS**
> Florence has such a dauntingly long list of 'must see' sights that it's difficult to know how to cope. Obviously the amount of time you have available is a major factor, but however long you've got, I suggest you adopt this basic strategy.
>
> The Duomo, Piazza della Signoria (with the Palazzo Vecchio) and the Uffizi have great pulling power, and are essential, so see them first. (If you wish, you could do Walk One: South of the Duomo – pages 64-8 – which covers them all.) Then take bus No.13 from the station or Duomo up to San Miniato, one of the city's loveliest places, which is also unmissable. From here there is a glorious view of Florence which will help you to understand the city's layout.
>
> Having had this welcome breather, plunge back into the hard streets, and choose whatever other sights take your fancy to see next, using the A-Z on pages 42-63 as a guide; or follow one of the other walks, visiting whatever places crop up along the way – together they embrace almost all the sights in Florence. Don't neglect Oltrarno (Walk 4, page 74), and try to make time for lesser known delights, such as the Perugino fresco in Santa Maria Maddalena dei Pazzi, the Cenacolo di Sant'Apollonia, the Ghirlandaio frescoes in Santa Trinita, the little church of Santi Apostoli, the Palazzo Davanzati, or the tiny church of San Martino del Vescovo (Walk 3: East of the Duomo). There are many more besides.
>
> Then there's the shopping, the restaurants, the picnic in the Boboli Gardens, the essential escape to Fiesole for a day or just for lunch...

Neptune fountain, Piazza della Signoria.

FESTIVALS IN FLORENCE

Most famous and extraordinary is the **Scoppio del Carro**, held on Easter Sunday at 11 am in Piazza del Duomo. It has its roots in medieval events and involves a firework-filled cart that explodes when ignited by a mechanical dove which zooms down on a wire from the cathedral's high altar.

It's difficult to see much of this in the Piazza because of the crowds, but a tip is to go (around 9-9.30 am) to the street called Il Prato, where, next to the Hotel Villa Medici, the firework-laden cart emerges from two huge doors, pulled by a pair of white oxon, which then proceed to the Duomo. You can watch the beginning of this procession in relative seclusion, then celebrate with a drink at the Bar Curtatone at the junction of Il Prato and Via Curtatone.

Other traditional festivals include the **Festa del Grillo** in the Cascine Park, in which crickets are bought and released from little cages to bring good luck (first Sunday after Ascension Day); and the **Festa delle Rificolone** in which children converge on Piazza della Santissima Annunziata carrying paper lanterns (September 7) – there are floats and stalls selling sweets in the surrounding streets.

Piazza di Santa Croce is the venue for the **Gioco di Calcio Storico**, a very serious football tournament played in 16thC costume between the four medieval quarters of the city. Games are played on June 19, 24 and 28. On June 24, St John's Day (patron saint of Florence), there is a 10-pm **firework display** from Piazzale Michelangelo.

The main cultural festival in Florence is the **Maggio Musicale**, which lasts from early March until early June and covers opera, concerts and ballet. Further information from the tourist office (see page 40); tickets and information also from the Teatro Comunale, Corso Italia 16; tel. 055 211158.

Florence sights

> **MUSEUMS OPEN ON A MONDAY**
> Many museums in Florence, as in the rest of Italy, close on a Monday. If it's Monday, and you are frustrated by this, here is a checklist of ones which are open: Brancacci Chapel; Casa Michelangelo; Galleria dello Spedale Innocenti; Museo Firenze Com'Era; Museo Horne; Museo di Santa Maria Novella; Museo Stibbert; Museo di Storia della Scienza; Palazzo Medici-Riccardi; Palazzo Vecchio. Plus, of course, the churches.

Mon of month. The Bargello's collection of Renaissance sculpture is the equal of the paintings of the same period in the Uffizi (see page 61). The imposing fortress-palace (1255) served first as a seat of the city judiciary (*podestà*) and later of the chief of police (*bargello*). Plenty of rough justice was administered here, with a gallows situated in the lovely courtyard, encrusted with *stemme* (coats-of-arms) of the *podestà*, some by Andrea Castagno. After the executions, post-mortem portraits of victims were gruesomely frescoed on the outside walls; Leonardo sketched a richly robed Pazzi conspirator whose body was left to dangle, as a warning to others, outside a Bargello window (the Pazzi had unwisely tried to overthrow Lorenzo Il Magnifico in 1478).

In the first room, left of the pillars, are a group of sculptures by Michelangelo: tipsy **Bacchus**, done in Rome when he was only 22, his first important work; the **Pitti Tondo**; **Brutus**; and **Apollo (or David)**. Compare the natural grace of the latter to the statue just beyond it: Bandinelli's comically awful *Adam and Eve*, a right pair. Bandinelli, court sculptor to Cosimo 1 (Vasari was his equally vainglorious court painter) was as self-opinionated as he was inept; he thought he could outdo Michelangelo and entered into another bitter rivalry with the waspish goldsmith and sculptor Cellini (see Piazza della Signoria, page 55). The latter's bust of **Cosimo 1** always reminds me of an idealized Pavarotti. Another 16thC contemporary is Giambologna, represented here by his fleet of foot **Mercury**.

Statues in the courtyard require only a glance or two, so proceed upstairs and head for Giambologna's charming **birds** in the Upper Loggia. They originally decorated the grotto at Villa Medicea di Castello (see Sights Outside Florence, page 77). From here a door leads to one of the richest rooms in Florence, filled with the sculptures of Donatello and his contemporaries. The revelation of Donatello's genius (displayed here, in Santa Croce, Palazzo Vecchio and the Museo dell'Opera del Duomo) is a highlight of a visit to Florence, and his bronze **David**, the first free-standing nude of the Renaissance, and a cause of outrage at the time, immediately entrances the eye. Donatello's huge influence on Renaissance artists and sculptors is exemplified by his **St George** (high in a niche at the end of the room), made in 1416 for Orsanmichele (see page 52). Here is a real man, one who knows what he must do, breathing life and vigour. The relief below (sadly eroded) was the first of the Renaissance successfully to create perspective. Other works by Donatello include: the bust of **Niccolò da Uzzano**, a much earlier marble **David**, the dancing **Amor-Atys** and the heraldic lion **Marzocco**.

Two more spine-tinglers are contained in this room: the winning and losing entries, depicting the **Sacrifice of Isaac**, for the great Baptistry doors competition (see Duomo, Baptistry and Campanile, page 49). First inspect Brunelleschi's loser on the left, full of dramatic force, with the angel intervening in the killing. Now look at Ghiberti's winner on the right, far less frenetic, but sweeping the eye towards the beautiful Classical torso of Isaac. The perfect craftsmanship shows his training as a goldsmith. Both panels, done in quatrefoil frames in 1401, point the way out of the Gothic and towards the coming revolution of the early Renaissance. It was a close thing, but Ghiberti was the right choice, not least because it gave Brunelleschi the freedom to pursue his genius for architecture. Later, the two were to clash again: this time when Ghiberti was appointed joint supervisor of the construction of Brunelleschi's great dome. The panels, over on the right wall, are easy to miss unless you are looking for

Florence sights

DONATELLO, BRUNELLESCHI AND MICHELANGELO

Of all the masters who have contributed great works of art to Florence, these three stand out. For a less conventional sightseeing plan, why not follow their trail? Places mentioned in **bold** are described in full in Sights and Places of Interest, pages 42-63.

Donatello (1386-1466)

The **Bargello** contains a marvellous collection of his work, including the early *St George*, which was made for the exterior of **Orsanmichele**, and his much later bronze *David*. Close by, in the **Palazzo Vecchio** is *Judith and Holofernes*. In **San Lorenzo** he decorated Brunelleschi's Old Sacristy. Here too are his last works, a pair of bronze pulpits begun when he was 74 and finished by pupils. In **Santa Croce** is the wooden crucifix which Brunelleschi said he could better. Leave the **Museo dell'Opera del Duomo** until last if you can – here are three later works of great stature: the prophet *Abakuk*, known fondly as *Zuccone* (marrow head); a harrowing, express-ionist Magdalen, *La Maddalena* and the Duomo's original choir loft, decorated with whirling, frenzied urchins. In the Baptistry is the tomb of Antipope John XXIII. Donatello, reserved and modest, was the most astonishing Renaissance artist of all, an innovator to the last.

Filippo Brunelleschi (1377-1446)

First comes his bid to win the famous competition held in 1401 for the commission to create the Baptistry doors. His brilliant entry, along with that of the winner, Ghiberti, is now displayed in the **Bargello**. He then turned to architecture, becoming one of the great progenitors of the Renaissance through buildings which, though based on Classical ideals and building skills, had a monumental authority all their own. His mastery of perspective had a profound influence on contemporary art. A clear example of this influence at work can be seen in Masaccio's pioneering *Trinity* in **Santa Maria Novella**. While there, have a look at Brunelleschi's wooden *Crucifix*, the one which made his friend Donatello drop all his eggs.

Then follow his progress as an architect: the **Spedale degli Innocenti**, begun in 1419 (see Walk Three: East of the Duomo, page 72); **San Lorenzo**; the Pazzi Chapel at **Santa Croce**; **Santo Spirito** and, of course, his crowning achievement, the cupola of the **Duomo**, the construction of which spanned the years 1420-36. Despite its success, he was forced to pitch his design against others for the Duomo's lantern. Begun shortly before his death, the lantern was completed by Michelozzo.

Michelangelo Buonarroti (1475-1564)

His two earliest known works are in the **Casa Buonarroti**, his home for a short time. In the **Bargello**, along with several other sculptures, is *Bacchus*, an important early work. The commission from the Florentine republic for *David* (in the **Accademia**) followed soon afterwards. Here also are the typically unfinished, much freer *Slaves*, meant for the tomb of Pope Julius II.

In **Palazzo Vecchio**, which has a copy of *David* in its original position outside, is *Victory*, also made for the never-realized tomb of Pope Julius. Next door, in the **Uffizi**, is the only painting by Michelangelo in Florence, the sumptuous *Doni Tondo*, depicting the Holy Family.

San Lorenzo sees Michelangelo at his most restless and unsettling, breaking the rules, challenging, always striving for something just beyond his grasp. Here is the Mannerist Laurentian library with its flowing staircase in *pietra serena* sandstone; and the New Sacristy, his answer to Brunelleschi's Old Sacristy opposite. This contains some of his most compelling sculptures, the only ones still in their intended place, the Medici Tombs. The most moving sculpture in Florence is his *Pietà*, now in the **Museo dell'Opera del Duomo**, but intended at one time for his own tomb, which, executed by lesser hands, can be found in **Santa Croce**.

Florence sights

them. Annoyingly, restored panels from Ghiberti's finished doors, the 'Gates of Paradise' as Michelangelo called them, are displayed not here but in the Museo dell'Opera del Duomo (see page 51).

If you haven't squandered all your time in this *salone*, wander through the other rooms: on the first floor, decorative arts, including brilliant Byzantine ivories; on the second, fine collections of Renaissance portrait busts, small bronzes, arms and armour.

BOBOLI, GIARDINO DI (BOBOLI GARDENS)

Main entrance through Palazzo Pitti, Piazza de' Pitti, Via de' Guicciardini; open Nov-Feb 9 am-4.30 pm, Mar, Oct 9 am-5.30 pm, Apr, May, Sept 9 am-6.30 pm, Jun-Aug 9 am-7.30 pm.

This being Florence, the city's main public (though not free) park (there is another one, **Le Cascine**, along the north-western bank of the Arno), is of course a Medici extravaganza, filled with statuary and Mannerist quirks. The gardens were begun for Eleanor of Toledo when she moved to the Palazzo Pitti (see pages 53-4) in 1549 with her husband, Cosimo I. They are shady and well kept and make an excellent place in which to picnic.

The Palazzo Pitti was built with stone quarried from the hillside behind. Facing the *palazzo* is the **amphitheatre**, designed by Ammannati as a garden shaped like a Roman circus in the hollow of the quarry; the theatre was added in the 17thC. From here the gardens spread across the hillside, following the natural contours of the land. The various highlights are well signposted. To the left is the Mannerist folly **Grotta Grande**, in the depths of which Giambologna's *Venus* emerges from her bath. Nearby, at the Bacchus Gate, is the rather horrid **Bacchus Fountain** depicting Cosimo I's naked court dwarf plopped on top of a giant turtle. Three terraces rise above the amphitheatre, leading to the **Museo delle Porcellane** (Porcelain Museum; *open Tue-Sat 9 am-1.30 pm, 2nd, 4th Mon and 1st, 3rd, 5th Sun of month*) and the **Giardino del Cavaliere** which offers superb views. From the first terrace, with its Classical statuary, a path leads left to the pretty rococo **Kaffeehaus**, serving refreshments in summer. To the right of the terrace is the start of the **Viottolone**, a central avenue of cypress trees and Classical statues which sweeps down the slope to **Isolotto**, the lovely Baroque water garden which lies near the Porta Romana exit.

BRANCACCI, CAPPELLA (BRANCACCI CHAPEL)

Santa Maria del Carmine, Piazza del Carmine; open Mon, Wed-Sat 10 am-5 pm, Sun 1-5 pm. It took one man in his early twenties, a man of coarse appearance who died when he was only 27, to light the fuse for the explosion that was Early Renaissance painting. He was Masaccio (a nickname, loosely translated as 'sloppy Tom', which reflected the man's ungainly, dishevelled looks), whose fame rests on his *Trinity* in Santa Maria Novella (see page 59) and his work here in the Brancacci Chapel. What was already underway in sculpture and architecture (spearheaded by Donatello and Brunelleschi respectively) burst forth in an expression of monumental grandeur and realism in the hands of Masaccio, a world away from the courtly and elegant International Gothic style of his contemporary, Gentile da Fabriano (see Uffizi, Rooms 5 and 6, page 62). Suddenly Masaccio was tackling problems of space and volume, and to get help he must have looked back 150 years or so to the paintings of Giotto and the pulpits (see Pisa, Seeing the Region: 1, page 92) of Nicola and Giovanni Pisano, as well as to his contemporary Donatello. His depiction of natural light, is masterly (see how, in *Tribute Money*, it flows from the right, where the real window is, to left). Although the public remained none too impressed, many artists, including Leonardo and Michelangelo, later came to study his work.

The chapel is in the south transept of **Santa Maria del Carmine**, but now disjointedly reached only through the cloister. The frescoes were commissioned in 1423 by Felice Brancacci from Masaccio and an older artist, Masolino. Some scenes are by both artists, some by Masaccio alone, and some by Masolino alone. Others were completed in their style by Filippino Lippi in 1480, 50 years after they had broken off their work and left Florence (the Brancacci were exiled soon after).

An immediate contrast between Masaccio and Masolino can be seen in

Florence sights

their two depictions of *Adam and Eve* on the upper entrance piers. Masolino's is merely decorative, Masaccio's is one of the most harrowing images in western art. Restoration (in the 1980s) removed strategically placed fig leaves, added by more prudish hands.

Other frescoes entirely by Masaccio are *Tribute Money* (left wall, upper level), *St Peter Healing the Sick* (left of altar, lower level), *St Peter Baptizing Converts* and *St Peter Giving Alms* (right of altar, upper and lower level). In all the frescoes concerning St Peter, he is depicted in an orange robe. The famous *Tribute Money* is a 'continuous narration' in which Christ instructs St Peter to catch a fish, in whose mouth he will find the tribute money for the tax collector, depicted on the right.

CASA BUONARROTI (MUSEO MICHELANGELO)

Via Ghibellina 70; open Wed-Mon 9.30 am-1.30 pm. Somewhat disappointing, especially if you go expecting an array of Michelangelo's works or an insight into his personality and lifestyle. Two very early, far-sighted and typically unfinished pieces, however, are worth the trip: **Madonna della Scala** and **Battle of the Centaurs**. Also by Michelangelo on the first floor are a model of the façade of San Lorenzo, never executed, a wooden Crucifix, and a clay and wood model of a River God. The building was only briefly inhabited by Michelangelo, and it was his great nephew who devised the frescoed gallery in homage to his famous forebear. I find it charming, with its nooks

GREAT VIEWS

Perhaps Florence's best sight of all is the city itself, its red-brown buildings huddled under the skirt of the great protective Duomo in a bowl of green, sheltering hills. See it from the **Forte di Belvedere** (a short walk from Ponte Vecchio; see Walk 4: Oltrarno, page 75); from the church of **San Miniato** (see Sights and Places of Interest, pages 57-8) or from **Piazzale Michelangelo**, just below San Miniato. Bus No. 13 reaches both these places from the station.

Within the city, there are of course dizzying views from the top

• *Ponte Vecchio.*

of the Duomo or from its Campanile (see Sights and Places of Interest, page 49). Marvellous river views can be had from **Ponte Vecchio**; or, if you want the best view of Ponte Vecchio and its extraordinary Vasari Corridor, from **Ponte Santa Trinita.**

One of the best things about walking in Florence is the way that Brunelleschi's dome appears and disappears. You turn a corner into some long, narrow street, and there it is, blocking the end. Turn again, and it's lost.

Florence sights

and crannies and panelled study at the end of the gallery.

The drawings on the ground floor are reproductions; a wooden model shows how Michelangelo's *David* was transported from the Piazza della Signoria to the Accademia.

CENACOLO DI SAN SALVI
Via San Salvi 16; open Tue-Sun 8.30 am-1.50 pm (1 pm on Sun). Cenacolo refers to the depiction of The Last Supper, often in fresco, on the refectory walls of monasteries and convents. This one, by Andrea del Sarto, begun in 1520, is off the beaten track, but is well worth seeking out if you have the time (bus No. 6 from the Duomo or Piazza San Marco).

Andrea del Sarto's great gift was as a painter as opposed to draughtsman, and this marvellously preserved fresco is a rich visual treat. Though del Sarto is an important link in the evolution of Florentine painting, he never quite lived up to his promise. The Victorian poet Swinburne put it much more romantically: 'His life was corroded by the poisonous solvent of love, and his soul burnt into ashes.'

CENACOLO DI SANT'APOLLONIA
Via XXVII Aprile 1; open Tue-Sat 8.30 am-1.50 pm, 1st, 3rd, 5th Mon and 2nd, 4th Sun of month. Andrea Castagno's sinister evocation of the Last Supper (1445-50) must have made unsettling company for the gentle nuns of Sant'Apollonia, and in fact they later obscured it with whitewash. (It is not surprising to learn that Castagno was adept at painting *post mortem* portraits on the walls of the Bargello.)

A powerful sense of evil and foreboding hangs over the scene. Judas, satyr-like, is separated from the rest by the long strip of white tablecloth (a traditional device); the walls behind the disciples are panelled in marble, and a jagged vein crackles menacingly over the heads of Judas, Christ and St Peter, like a sign from the heavens. The figures show the influence of Masaccio's scientific realism (see Brancacci Chapel, page 46), but they are frozen, separate, unable to help one another. Above the *Last Supper* are pastoral *Scenes from the Passion* (badly damaged), including a *Resurrection*. The whole story was told, showing that, despite the wickedness displayed in the *Last Supper*, good eventually triumphed. The frescoes' *sinopie* are displayed on another wall.

CORRIDOIO VASARIANO
See Vasari Corridor, page 63.

DUOMO, CAMPANILE AND BATTISTERO (BAPTISTRY)
Piazza del Duomo/Piazza di San Giovanni; Duomo open 10 am-5 pm, Sun 1-5 pm; Campanile open Apr-Oct 9 am-6.50 pm daily, Nov-Mar 9 am-4.20 pm daily; Baptistry open Mon-Sat noon-6.30 pm, Sun 8.30 am -1.30 pm.

The great dome of the **Duomo** (more properly the Cathedral of Santa Maria del Fiore) is the defining feature of Florence, and the greatest engineering feat of the Renaissance. Glimpsed suddenly from a street corner or a bedroom window, it seems to hover in the hazy, smoggy atmosphere like a vast russet-coloured hot air balloon on the point of landing. Having spied it from a distance, one is quickly drawn towards it, unable to imagine what it can be like close up.

By the 13thC, Florence, ever keen to increase its sense of importance, longed for a cathedral that would outdo anything else in existence and in 1296 Arnolfo di Cambio was commissioned to create it. Progress was slow, but by 1418 a vast base for a dome was in place – but how to cover it? Help was solicited from all over Europe, many bizarre theories were propounded, but Florence's own Filippo Brunelleschi, with his clear understanding of Classical architecture, had the answer (see page 49).

The Piazza del Duomo and adjoining Piazza di San Giovanni are disappointments, scrappy spaces besieged by tourists in herds and attendant parasites. The Duomo's main façade is a neo-Gothic shocker, put up in 1875 to match the **campanile**, though it has none of the charm of 'Giotto's Tower' with its candy stick confection of pink, white and green marble. In fact Giotto, who was city architect at the time, died before its completion (1359), which was carried out by Andrea Pisano and then Francesco Talenti; only the first three storeys are exactly to Giotto's design. The originals of their reliefs and sculptures, by Pisano and Donatello, are in the Museo dell'Opera del Duomo (see page 51). You can climb the campanile – take heart, there's a man at the top with oxygen, if needs must. It isn't as tall as the dome, but it feels precarious (tragically, people come from far and wide to jump off it).

Before you enter the cathedral, look up at the dome and notice the ring around its base, an arcaded gallery which suddenly stops. Why was it never completed? Because, the story goes, Michelangelo stood in the square below and said 'What's that, a pigeon loft?' and work ceased then and there.

The interior is a numbingly huge and empty space, and as you look along the length of it, the dome seems to have shrunk. Many of the works of art were removed in the 19thC to the Museo dell'Opera del Duomo (see page 51). Of interest are the *trompe l'oeil* **monuments to Niccolò da Tolentino** and **Sir John Hawkwood** by Castagno and Uccello respectively. Both men were mercenary commanders. The frescoes of the **Last Judgement** beneath the dome, recently revealed after years of restoration, are the work of Vasari and Zuccari. Executed with panache, 150 years later they nonetheless make a gaudy, frenetic lining for Brunelleschi's rational dome. Steps near the south door lead down to the excavated **crypt** of an earlier church called Santa Reparata, and also to the **tomb of Brunelleschi** whose burial here was a rare yet fitting honour.

Brunelleschi's **dome** can be climbed (*open Mon-Fri 8.30 am-6.20 pm, Sat 8.30 am-5 pm*), via the maintanence stairs which inch up between its inner and outer skins. The inner skin supports the outer protective one; the framework consists of eight ribs, bound by chains. The outer skin uses the Roman technique of building up the brickwork in a series of self-supporting rings. Try to make the climb if you can: the view from the lantern of the rusty old city inside its blue girdle of hills is worth the struggle. Imagine, as you ascend, the business of building the dome. At times there were strikes and disagreements, not least between Brunelleschi and the man who, he complained, was foisted on him to help oversee the project, Ghiberti. Brunelleschi was concerned with every detail, watching over the baking of the bricks, and making special tools for the labourers to use. In order to save time, he had canteens specially installed amongst the scaffolding.

The **Baptistry** (Battistero), which cries out for a cleaning (and should be getting one soon) is a mysterious building. Its precise date of construction is unknown (the Romanesque marble cladding was added in the 11thC), but it is surely the oldest building in Florence, and certainly one of the best loved by Florentines. In the days when joyful mass baptisms took place, including Dante's own, the poet called the Baptistry '*il mio bel San Giovanni*'. Not long afterwards, the Guild of Merchants, patrons of the church, decided to grace the building with the most beautiful set of doors that could be summoned.

First orientate yourself. The East Doors face the main façade of the Duomo, with the South Doors to the left of them, the North Doors to the right. The Gothic **South Doors** were designed by Andrea Pisano back in 1330. In 1401 a famous competition was held (see Bargello, page 44) and Lorenzo Ghiberti was chosen to create the remaining two sets. It took him the rest of his life. The **North Doors**, in Gothic quatrefoil frames, were completed in 1424. By the time he started the **East Doors** (1424-52), Ghiberti had taken up the precepts of the Early Renaissance. The panels are now in square, not restrictive quatrefoil frames and the line of perspective is confident. The buildings depicted in the Old Testament scenes are in the new Classical style of Brunelleschi; the scenes are no longer stylized as of old, although the figures still retain a Gothic elegance.

If you are reading this in front of 'The Gates of Paradise' as Michelangelo dubbed them, you may be wondering what all the fuss is about. The ghastly brassy melée which you behold are poor modern copies of the ten panels. An immediate visit to the **Museo dell' Opera del Duomo**, behind the cathedral (see page 51), is essential. Here you can see some of Ghiberti's original, movingly beautiful panels. The rest are still undergoing regilding and cleaning.

The interior of the Baptistry has an intensely spiritual quality. The glittering Byzantine-style **mosaics** date from the 13thC as does the Zodiac **marble floor** around the all-important font. The superb **tomb of Baldassare**

Florence sights

• *The Duomo.*

Coscia, deposed Pope John XXIII, is by Donatello and Michelozzo (1424-7).

MUSEO ARCHEOLOGICO
Via della Colonna 36; open Tue-Sat 9 am-2 pm, Sun 9 am-1 pm. Time is always short, and there is so much glorious Renaissance art to get through in Florence, but all the same try not to miss this superb collection of ancient art: Egyptian, Greek, Etruscan and Roman. It makes a refreshing contrast to the rest of the city's riches, and illustrates Classical influences on the Renaissance. The Etruscan collection (badly damaged during the 1966 flood) will hold you in good stead if you later visit one of the many Etruscan sites in the region (there is another excellent museum of Etruscan art in Volterra; see Local Explorations: 1, pages 147-8. Prize exhibits include the Greek vases, particularly the **François vase**, which was discovered in an Etruscan tomb near Chiusi (it was smashed in the museum in 1900 but restored in the 1970s); the **Egyptian chariot** made of wood and bone found in a tomb at Thebes, and the Etruscan bronze ***Chimera***, found at Arezzo in the 16thC and restored by Cellini.

MUSEO DI FIRENZE COM'ERA
Via dell'Oriuolo 4; open Mon-Wed, Fri, Sat, 9 am-2 pm, Sun 8 am-1 pm. The development of Florence from the 15thC onwards (and its potential destruction in the 19thC), seen through maps, prints and paintings. It is highly illuminating.

MUSEO HORNE

Via de' Benci 6; open Mon, Wed-Sat 9 am-1 pm, Tue 8.30-11pm in summer.
Probably one for a rainy day. Herbert Percy Horne (1864-1916) was an English art historian, a champion of Botticelli who was then little cared for. The *palazzo* in which he lived was built in 1489 for a wealthy cloth merchant (the Santa Croce area was packed with wool traders at the time) in an arrangement which perfectly combined home with work: dyeing vats were stored in the basement, the courtyard was used for drying cloth, and the family lived on the upper floors.

Horne's collection of art and furniture pales into insignificance when compared to the other treasures which Florence has on show. It is, however, notable for having been gathered together by one not very rich man through a love and understanding of Italian art. The Renaissance way of life obviously interested him too: the top floor kitchen contains his collection of cooking pots and utensils.

MUSEO DELL'OPERA DEL DUOMO

Piazza del Duomo 9; open Mon-Sat 9 am-6.50 pm, Sun 9 am-2 pm. The Cathedral Museum houses some lovely things originally made for the Duomo, Campanile and Baptistry, but brought in here for protection. The building, which has been the Cathedral offices since the 15thC, has been improved by new lighting, heating and air conditioning, and plans to expand will allow space for some minor works to be brought out of storage. The famous 'Gates of Paradise' should be restored and on display in all their glory in a new covered courtyard by the beginning of 2000.

The ground floor contains 14thC sculptures made for the Duomo's façade, models and tools for the construction of Brunelleschi's dome, and a facsimile of a 1587 drawing of the unfinished façade.

The intense emotion of Michelangelo's **Pietà**, made towards the end of his life, apparently for his own tomb, stops you in your tracks on the mezzanine. According to Vasari, the head of Nicodemus is a self-portrait, and the damaged parts of the sculpture were caused by the artist himself in a rage. The hopelessly inadequate figure of Mary Magdalene was finished by one of his pupils.

Continue upstairs to see the pair of **choir lofts** by Luca della Robbia and Donatello respectively. This was della Robbia's first major work before he turned to glazed terracotta work, for which he and his family are famous. His frivolous, dancing children have a charming, self-absorbed innocence and humanity: compare them to Donatello's far more dynamic, frenetic interpretation. The power of Donatello's imagination, and his pioneering depiction of expressive realism are well illustrated in his prophet **Abakuk** (1423) (affectionately known as *zuccone* – marrow-head – by locals), and his much later **La Maddalena** (1455).

Also on this floor are Andrea Pisano's original **bas-reliefs** for the base of the Campanile. They depict, with dignified simplicity, man's spiritual redemption through hard work and education. Ruskin wrote of them: 'Read but these inlaid jewels of Giotto's once with patient following,' (they were based on Giotto's designs) 'and your hour's study will give you strength for all your life.'

The restored panels from Ghiberti's **Baptistry Doors** are in the Sala dell' Altare (see under Baptistry in the entry Duomo, Campanile and Baptistry, page 49.

MUSEO STIBBERT

Via Stibbert 26; open Fri-Wed 10 am-1 pm, 3-6 pm in summer; Mon, Wed, Fri 10 am-2 pm, Sat & Sun 10 am-6 pm in winter; bus No. 4 from station. North of the centre, in Montughi, is the weirdest museum in Florence. Like Museo Horne (see above), this is another collection put together in the 19thC by an Englishman – but there the resemblance ends. Horne's collection is measured and Frederick Stibbert's is wild and eclectic.

Stibbert (1838-1906) was in fact half Scottish, half Italian. He inherited a 14thC house, bought the one next to it, and joined them together. He then proceeded to stuff every one of the 64 rooms with – well, things. His collection of armour is said to be one of the best in the world. In the great hall a whole regiment of silent mannequin-knights prepares to do battle.

A little east of here, off the Via Bolognese, lies one of the most beautiful gardens in Tuscany (*visits by special arrangement only*), at **Villa La Pietra**,

Florence sights

former home of the late historian and aesthete, Sir Harold Acton.

MUSEO DI STORIA DELLA SCIENZA

Piazza de' Guidici 1; open Mon-Sat 9.30 am-1 pm and 2-5 pm on Mon, Wed, Fri. The Medici grand dukes (from the 16thC) and their House of Lorraine successors (from 1737) may not have cultivated great art, but they did much to foster knowledge of science. The museum has its foundations in the Accademia del Cimento (Academy of Experiment), founded by Cardinal Leopold de' Medici. He and his brother, the Grand Duke, had studied with Galileo, whose instruments, including the lens with which he discovered the four moons of Jupiter (then called the Medicean planets) are on display. Many of these early scientific instruments are works of art in themselves, like the Arab astrolabes, the Florentine globes, and the huge armillary sphere of 1593. The museum is well-laid out, and foreign language descriptions are lent to you at the start of your visit.

OGNISSANTI

Borgo Ognissanti 42; open 9 am-noon and 3.30-7 pm; Cenacolo del Ghirlandaio open Mon, Tues, Sat 9 am-noon. A Benedictine order of monks established this church (All Saints) in the 13thC. Their skill was wool weaving, which grew to become the basis of Florentine wealth. Later, when the church was handed to the Franciscans, the façade and interior were given an ornate Baroque makeover. The church is worth visiting for its 15thC frescoes which are still in place, unlike an ealier work, Giotto's Maestà altarpiece, now in the Uffizi.

Above the second altar on the right you can see Ghirlandaio's *Madonna della Misericordia*; the onlookers are the donors, the Vespucci family, including the explorer, Amerigo Vespucci, then a boy. On either side of the nave are two frescoes of 1480: *St Augustine* by Botticelli and *St Jerome* by Ghirlandaio. In the **Cenacolo** (refectory) is Ghirlandaio's interpretation of the **Last Supper**, approached through the frescoed **cloister**.

ORSANMICHELE

Via dei Calzaiuoli; open 9 am-noon, 4-6 pm. It doesn't look like a church, and it doesn't sound like one. Its square shape was dictated by its origins: first it was a grain store, then a *loggia* which served as a trading hall for the governing merchant guilds of 14thC Florence. After serious damage during factional fighting, the ground floor loggia was walled in, for use as a church, and the two upper floors, for grain, were added: business and religion under one roof, typically Florentine. Being a guild church, 14 exterior niches were later created, each to be filled with the statue of a guild's patron saint. And being by now the Early Renaissance, some superb sculptures were produced by 'new boys' Donatello (the original of his landmark *St George* is now in the Bargello), Ghiberti and Nanni di Banco. Verrocchio and Giambologna contributed later ones. The empty niches you see today account for statues which have had to be removed. After restoration they should end up in the safety of the Bargello. The strange name, by the way, derives from San Michele in Orto, a religious building which previously stood on this site.

Orsanmichele looks like a mellowed defensive tower from the outside; the interior is a rigid, enclosed space which makes its centrepiece, Orcagna's Gothic **tabernacle**, look all the more extraordinary; some call it grave and majestic, but to me the words 'outlandish and preposterous' can't help but spring to mind. It contains Bernado Daddi's *Virgin and Child* (1347), a painting which replaced an earlier one widely believed to have miraculous powers. The church's pillars are frescoed with the guilds' patron saints.

The superb vaulted upper floors of the church, formerly emergency grain stores, now temporary exhibition space, are entered via an aerial bridge linking the building behind. This was the headquarters of one of the most powerful guilds, the **Palazzo dell'Arte della Lana** (wool merchants).

PALAZZO DAVANZATI

Via Porta Rossa 13; closed for restoration. "My favourite museum in Florence," says my cousin, who lives there. What, better than all the art places? "Well, you rather begin to take all that for granted after a while, and this place shows you what it was like to actually *be* a Florentine nobleman."

The building is mid-14thC, remarkably well preserved. The interior, which constitutes the **Museo dell'Antica Casa Fiorentina**, was sympathetically restored at the turn of the century.

PALAZZO MEDICI-RICCARDI

Via Cavour 1; open Thur-Tues 9 am-1 pm, 3-6 pm (9 am-1 pm on Sun). If the great religious set pieces of Renaissance art are beginning to oppress you, if you crave some secular enchantment, make tracks for the **Cappella dei Magi** in this former Medici palace, now government offices. The frescoes were commissioned by Piero de' Medici to honour the wealthy religious confraternity of the Three Magi, of which he was a member. In the hands of one of the emergent giants of the period (1459) this small, windowless room would have looked very different, but it was Benozzo Gozzoli, pupil of Fra Angelico and jobbing painter whose speciality was charming narratives, who happily got the job. This is without doubt his masterpiece.

Gozzoli's interpretation of the **Procession of the Magi to Bethlehem** is a delightful fairy-tale romp through an enchanting Tuscan landscape, packed with castles, huntsmen, trees, birds and animals of many different types. The splendidly dressed participants are portraits of the Medici family (identifiable by their three-feathers emblem) and other contemporary Florentines; the artist himself can be seen among a crowd of people at the altar end of the right wall, with his name inscribed around his red cap band.

Also on view, in the first-floor gallery, is the **Apotheosis of the Medici**, a ceiling fresco of High Baroque barminess (1683) by Luca Giordano in which the Medici, having had their day in the countryside downstairs, reach spectacularly for the sky. The ceiling fresco was commissioned by the Riccardi family after they bought the *palazzo* from the Medici. Designed by Michelozzo in 1444 for Cosimo II Vecchio, it was the Medici headquarters until Cosimo I moved to Palazzo Vecchio a hundred years later.

PALAZZO NONFINITO

See Walk Three: East of the Duomo, page 73.

PALAZZO RUCELLAI

See Walk One: South of the Duomo, page 67.

PALAZZO PITTI

Piazza de' Pitti; The Palazzo Pitti, built on the principle that big is best, is simply enormous, and the thought of trudging all the way round can be daunting. Visions of a sunny café terrace may swim before your eyes as you contemplate the massive pile of rusticated stone. Persevere: there are rewards.

So much stone was required for the Pitti family to outdo their banking rivals the Medici (who were then completing the Palazzo Medici-Riccardi), that their home had to be quarried from the hillside behind, leaving a great gouge which was later landscaped as part of the Boboli Gardens. Ironically, the cost of the enterprise bankrupted the family and the Medici themselves moved in, less than a hundred years after it was begun in 1550. In the belief that even bigger is even better, Ammannati was commissioned to build the two garden wings, with his stately courtyard in between. More was to come: the north and south wings were added in the 19thC by the Dukes of Lorraine, who ruled after the Medici.

The Palazzo Pitti contains no less than five museums. A ticket to the Palatine Gallery also admits you to the Appartamenti Monumentali; a ticket to the Museo degli Argenti also admits to the Galleria del Costume.

If the Uffizi is an education in great art, the **Palatine Gallery** *(open Mar-Sep Tue-Sat 8.30 am-10 pm, Sun 8.30 am-8 pm; Tue-Sat 8.30 am-6.50 pm, Sun 8.30 am-1.50 pm, in winter)* is playtime. The paintings, many of them masterpieces, are hung not in chronological order, as at the Uffizi, but purely for effect, as in any home. This was, after all, home to the Medici Grand Dukes of the 17th and 18thC, and the pictures hang today much as they did then. So wander through the richly decorated private apartments with their fabulous ceiling frescoes by Pietro da Cortona (1641-7), forget the facts and figures, and just enjoy. By the way, you might notice how muted the colours seem compared to those of the Uffizi, many of whose works of art have undergone recent restoration.

Raphael and Titian are particularly well represented. On the packed walls look out for Raphael's lovely **La Velata**, his tender and dignified **La Gravida**, his brilliantly composed tondo, **Madon-**

na della Seggiola and his **Madonna del Granduca**, so called because Grand Duke Ferdinand III took it wherever he went. One of the greatest masters of the High Renaissance, Raphael (1483-1520), who was born in Urbino and moved in 1508 to Rome, is represented only here and in the Uffizi in Florence. Amongst the works of Titian (Venetian; 1487-1576), the mysterious nobleman in **Ritratto Virile** fixes you with his soulful gaze, while across the doorway **La Maddalena** is a richly sensual depiction of the Virgin. **La Bella** is just that, a ravishingly beautiful young woman, unknown, although she appears in other paintings by Titian.

Amongst other notable pictures are Andrea del Sarto's charming **St John the Baptist**, a **Deposition** by Raphael's master, Perugino, and another by Fra Bartolomeo. Rubens is in full flight in **The Consequence of War**, an allegory on the Thirty Years War (1618-48), which he painted in 1638. Plenty of other big names will catch your eye as you stroll by. Notice too the stiff, naive portraits of Elizabeth I and Catherine de' Medici by 16thC English and French schools.

From the Palatine Gallery, the route continues through the **Appartamenti Monumentali** (Appartamenti Reali, state apartments), a bewildering stroll through endless pompous reception rooms and bedrooms in lavish Neoclassical style. The last is the intricately stuccoed Sala Bianca, where the prestigious Pitti Fashion Shows take place.

From here, stairs lead up to the **Gallery of Modern Art**, which in this case means Italian painting of the late 18th and 19thC. There's plenty of them, and quite honestly, you've got to not want that *cappuccino* a great deal to propel yourself round.

On the ground and mezzanine floors, in the summer apartments of the Grand Dukes, the **Museo degli Argenti** (*open Tue-Sat 8.30 am-1.50 pm; 1st, 3rd, 5th Mon, 2nd, 4th Sun of month*) contains the luxury *objets d'art* collected by the Medici. Not just silverware, but all manner of costly things, from Lorenzo Il Magnifico's priceless antique vases to a stultifying selection of nick-nacks accumulated by later generations. The ground floor rooms are decorated with delightful 17thC frescoes, especially the ebullient Medici allegory in the main hall by Giovanni di San Giovanni. Yet another (Lorraine) extension of the Pitti – Palazzo Meridiana – houses a **Galleria del Costume** which illustrates what the 18th and 19thC rulers would have been wearing about the house. Also on show: 'that dress' worn by Eleanor of Toledo in Bronzino's famous portrait (Uffizi). It was in fact, she, as the wife of Cosimo I, who first purchased Palazzo Pitti, preferring, like so many after her, to live somewhere less built-up than the Palazzo Vecchio for the sake of her health.

PALAZZO STROZZI

See *Walk One: South of the Duomo, page 67.*

PALAZZO VECCHIO

Piazza della Signoria; open Mon-Wed, Fri, Sat 9 am-7 pm, Thu 9 am-2 pm, Sun 8 am-1 pm.

The Gothic Palazzo della Signoria was built as the seat of Florentine government, which was then (around 1300) controlled by the merchant guilds. A great bell rang out from its lofty tower to summon the people to mass meetings in the **Piazza della Signoria** (see page 55), or to warn of danger. In 1540 Cosimo I de' Medici and his wife Eleanor of Toledo moved in to the palace, and when they moved out again a few years later (to Palazzo Pitti), the place became known as Palazzo Vecchio (the Old Palace). Today, it is the city hall, where you might go to pay a fine or to get married; in the fine **courtyard**, graced by Verrocchio's **Putto Fountain**, you might encounter a couple of newlyweds, or long tables laden with local delicacies being laid out for an official reception.

The mostly vapid decoration dates from the time of Cosimo I. Vasari was responsible for much of it, along with many accomplished Mannerist colleagues, but it's pretty bland and sycophantic. However, there are one or two highlights.

In the vast **Salone dei Cinquecento** (first floor), lined with mostly indifferent sculptures, give yourself a quick test. From the doorway, can you spot the Michelangelo amongst the various writhing figures? It is his **Victory**, originally meant for the tomb of Pope Julius II. And it is certainly *not* that one on the right with the beefy guy being hung upside down but still managing to grapple with his equally muscle-bound opponent's private parts. This room, by the way, might have been rather different: Michelangelo and Leonardo each began a great painting at either end of the room; neither was finished and both are now lost.

Off this *salone* is one of the strangest little rooms in Florence – the **Studiolo di Francesco I**, created by Vasari and collaborators as a private sanctum for the equally strange son of Cosimo and Eleanor. The four windowless, richly decorated walls represent Earth, Water, Air and Fire respectively. Whizzing through Vasari's **Quartiere di Leone X**, a staircase with a charmingly decorated ceiling leads to **Eleanor of Toledo's private apartments** (splendid view *en route*). Tucked away there is the **Cappella di Eleanora**, whose bold biblical frescoes by Bronzino, make you sit up and take notice for a change. Continuing onwards, the domestic scale of Eleanor's private quarters is exchanged for elegant grandeur in the **Sala d'Udienza** and **Sala dei Gigli**, with lovely ceilings and a communicating doorway by the da Maiano brothers and frescoes in the latter room by Ghirlandaio. Donatello's ***Judith and Holofernes***, one of the most compelling of his late works, is in the Sala d'Udienza.

The **tower** is usually closed.

PIAZZA DELLA SIGNORIA

Unremarkable 19thC buildings line much of the square. Worse, its ancient paving stones were scandalously replaced by ugly modern slabs during recent archaeological excavations. And yet here, more than anywhere else, you can sense the past in Florence. One can almost see the great crowds of citizens who gathered for public meetings (which often turned into brawls and uprisings). You can stand on the plaque (in front of the fountain) which marks the exact spot where Savonarola held his Bonfire of Vanities, and where, a year later (1498), he was turned into a a bonfire himself; here is Michelangelo pretending to alter *David's* nose to please Soderini, leader of the Florentine Republic, by wielding a chisel and letting marble dust fall from his fingers (Soderini declared it to be much improved). And here are two more

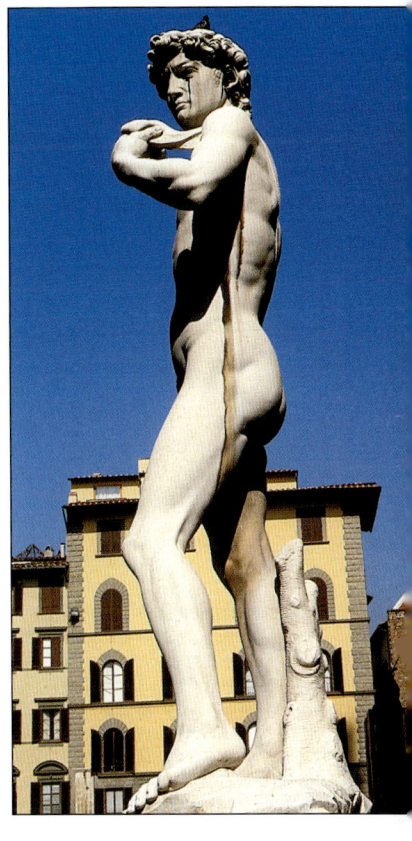

• *David by Michelangelo – the copy.*

sculptors, Cellini and Bandinelli, bickering as usual – "a sackful of melons" remarked Cellini when his rival's **Hercules and Cacus** appeared *in situ*.

But it is the sculpture, much of it Mannerist, which defines the place as uniquely Florentine. The **Loggia dei Lanzi** has been fully restored but some of the statues have been permanently removed. ***Perseus***, is presently being restored and is on display to the public in a room near the Uffizi.

Of course, the copy of Michelangelo's ***David*** dominates the proceedings in front of the Palazzo Vecchio (see Accademia, page 42, where the original now resides). As for Ammannati's **Neptune Fountain**, one glance at the giant fat slob who is supposed to be the God of the Sea (a metaphor in this case for Cosimo I and his naval victories), and I would advise you to look hastily away again.

Florence sights

PONTE VECCHIO
See *Walk Four: Oltrarno, page* 74.

PONTE SANTA TRINITA
See *Walk One: S. of the Duomo, page* 67.

SAN LORENZO AND CAPPELLE MEDICEE (MEDICI CHAPELS)
Piazza Lorenzo di Madonna degli Aldobrandini; church open daily 7 am-noon, 3.30-6 pm. Biblioteca open Mon-Sat 9 am-1 pm; Cappelle Medicee open, Tue-Sat 8.30-5 pm; 8.30 am-1.50 pm on 1st, 3rd, 5th Sun and 2nd, 4th Mon of month; last admission 30 minutes before closing.

The church of the Medici shows only a rough brick façade to the teeming market which surrounds it. Their first family seat was across the piazza – the building now known as the Palazzo Medici-Riccardi (see page 53). It seems odd that none of that showy family ever made it their business to get the church's façade finished. Michelangelo's rejected design can be seen in Casa Buonarroti (page 47).

San Lorenzo was designed by Brunelleschi in 1419. Features of note are: the two **pulpits** by Donatello – his last works, finished by his pupils; Filippo Lippi's *Annunciation*; Bronzino's *Martyrdom of St Lawrence*; and Desiderio da Settignano's superb marble **tabernacle** – look at the angels' faces. A stone slab in front of the high altar marks the grave of Cosimo Il Vecchio.

The left transept leads to the **Sagrestia Vecchia** (Old Sacristy). Notice, to the left of the entrance, Verrocchio's **tomb** of Piero and Giovanni de' Medici, sons of Cosimo. The Old Sacristy is the only one of Brunelleschi's buildings to be completed in his lifetime, a perfect – and perfectly proportioned – expression of his architectural principles. The stucco decorations and bronze doors are by his contemporary Donatello. The tomb of banker Giovanni di Bicci, father of Cosimo Il Vecchio, is positioned in the centre of the room.

The **Biblioteca Medici-Laurenziana** (Laurentian Library) is reached via the lovely **cloister**. It was designed by Michelangelo in the 1520s to house the Medici's extensive collection of manuscripts. Admire it or fear it, Michelangelo's cold, grey torrent of a **staircase** is a sight that remains long in the memory. It connects his equally disturbing **vestibule** with the much simpler and more rational **library**. Michelangelo was above all an innovator: here we can see him happily playing with, and breaking, the strict Classical precepts of 15thC architecture. To see the **Cappelle Medicee** (Medici Chapels) you must walk round to Piazza di Madonna degli Aldobrandini, passing in Piazza di San Lorenzo, the statue of Giovanni delle Bande Nere, father of Cosimo I de' Medici, another awkward effort from the chisel of Baccio Bandinelli.

The Medici chapels were added to San Lorenzo in the 16thC. The **Sagrestia Nuova** (New Sacristy) was Michelangelo's answer to Brunelleschi's Sagrestia Vecchia on the other side, while the dome on the largest of the chapels was the work of Buontalenti. This is the **Cappella dei Principi** (Chapel of the Princes), mausoleum of Cosimo I and his descendants. To modern eyes, it's hard to think of anywhere more oppressive in which to end up, yet it cost the Medici a fortune to create. The crypt below is paved with tombstones of family members.

The New Sacristy is now the only place where Michelangelo's sculptures remain in the setting that he designed for them. Work began in 1520, but his departure for Rome in 1534 meant that the sacristy remained unfinished. Two of the four intended Medici tombs were completed, those of **Giuliano, Duke of Nemours**, flanked by the figures of Day and Night, and, on the left, **Lorenzo, Duke of Urbino**, flanked by Dawn and Dusk. They are among Michelangelo's more extraordinary and compelling works, particularly the brooding, tense, nearly alive quality of the two entirely idealized young dukes. Yet one can hardly bear to look at the splendid reclining figures, so awkwardly placed are they, on the point of slipping off the curved sarcophagus lids, and the dukes look so cramped in their shallow niches...doubtless Michelangelo, had he stayed, would have changed everything around. On the simple tomb of Lorenzo Il Magnifico there is a change of mood with the sculptor's exquisite *Madonna*.

In the siege of 1530, Michelangelo made charcoal drawings on the walls of a nearby corridor. They are on view.

SAN MARCO

Piazza di San Marco; open Tue-Sat 8.30 am-1.50 pm; 2nd, 4th Sun and 1st, 3rd, 5th Mon of month; last admission 30 minutes before closing. It was Cosimo Il Vecchio who, in 1437, commissioned the rebuilding of the run-down Convent of San Marco for a Dominican order. Michelozzo was the architect, and Fra Angelico, one of the monks (born 1400) and already a well-known artist undertook the fresco decorations. He was a devout man who, Vasari tells us, 'lived in purity and holiness' and his paintings are correspondingly direct, sincere and lyrical. While his boldly conceived figures and spatial compositions are legacies of Masaccio, his characters lack the psychological realism of the Early Renaissance, though they convey a calm, convincing spirituality.

The entrance to the former convent, now the **Museo di San Marco** is to the right of the **church**. The core of the building is Michelozzo's tranquil **Sant' Antonino cloister** with its beautiful old cedar of Lebanon. On the right, the **Ospizio dei Pellegrini** (Pilgrims' Hospice) houses a superb collection of Fra Angelico's altarpieces. They include the **Linaiuoli Tabernacle** in its beautiful marble frame by Ghiberti; the moving **Deposition**; and the 35 panels depicting the **Life of Christ** (notice the charming *Flight into Egypt*), which were originally cupboard doors – 'where the silver is kept' wrote Vasari in Santissima Annunziata.

Further round the cloister, the **Sala Capitolare** (Chapter House) is the setting for a marvellous Fra Angelico fresco of the **Crucifixion**. Turning the corner to ascend the stairs, take a peak at the cloister of San Domenico with its palm garden framed by Michelozzo's broad arches. The small refectory on the left of the stairs contains Ghirlandaio's **Last Supper**. Up the stairs, turn a corner...and there it is, Fra Angelico's wonderful **Annunciation** which one knows so well from reproductions and does not disappoint: reverence and modesty personified.

The 44 monks' cells on the first floor were embellished with frescoes by Fra Angelico and his assistants. Lucky the friars who retired to cell numbers **1** (**Noli me Tangere**), **2, 3, 6, 7** and **9**: they have particularly beautiful images. Round the corner, the *Crucifixion* is repeated rather monotonously. Cells **12, 13** and **14** were the religious fanatic Savonarola's quarters when he was Prior: they contain mementos and a portrait of him by *Fra Bartolommeo*. Cells **38** and **39** were kept for Cosimo Il Vecchio when on retreat. Excavations in some of the cells have revealed medieval wall paintings.

On your way out, near the stairs between cells **42** and **43**, take a look into Michelozzo's light and airy **library**.

SAN MINIATO AL MONTE

Via Monte alle Croci; bus No. 13 from station or Duomo (near Via Ricasoli); open daily 8 am-noon, 2-7 pm in summer, 8am-noon, 2.30-6.30 pm in winter. The most perfect church in Florence, perhaps in Tuscany, both inside and out, and the most magnificently sited. I like to save its view until last, arriving by bus or on foot and walking up the long flight of steps without a backward glance. When I have done with the church, I emerge from its shadows, and there, lying in its protective bowl of hills, is Florence, earthy, masculine and secretive, its extraordinary accumulation of treasures hidden from view, waiting to be found and admired.

As one contemplates the **façade**, with its clear and perfectly proportioned patterns of green marble, it is hard to believe that when San Miniato was built, the Classically-inspired Renaissance was not to begin for another 300 years. Indeed, in the 14thC many did believe that, together with the Baptistry (see page 49), San Miniato was a Roman building. In fact, the church was begun in 1018 and the façade added in 1090, a particularly lovely example of the many Tuscan Romanesque churches which stretch inland from Pisa. The mosaic is 13thC, as is the crowning eagle, symbol of the church's then patrons, the Cloth Merchants' Guild (*Arte di Calimala*).

The **interior** lives up to the exterior's promise. Go when it is quietest – early morning or dusk. The choir (or chancel) is raised above the pillared crypt. It contains a marble **pulpit**, with carvings full of playful fantasy. The nave has a beautiful intarsia marble **floor** depicting birds, animals and signs of the Zodiac. At the end of the nave is a tabernacle by Michelozzo, the **Cappella del Crocifisso** (Crucifix Chapel). Renaissance artistic cooperation is on display to the left of the nave in the **Cappella del Cardinale del Portogallo** (Cardinal of Portugal's Chapel). The cardinal died in Florence, aged 25, in 1459, and his memorial was a professional collaboration between Antonio Rossellino (tomb and sculpture), Luca della Robbia (terracotta decoration), Baldovinetti (*Annunciation*), and the two Pollaiuolo brothers (*angels*) on the altar wall).

I recommend a visit to San Miniato as soon as you arrive in Florence; it sets the scene perfectly. You could walk there in the cool of the morning or evening; from Ponte Vecchio, follow Via de' Bardi and Via di San Niccolo where you turn right through Porta San Miniato up Via del Monte alle Croci. The steps up to the church are across Viale Galileo Galilei, to the right.

Below San Miniato is Piazzale Michelangelo, graced by another copy of *David*, a wonderful view of Florence, and dozens of tourist coaches.

SANTA CROCE
Piazza di Santa Croce; church open Mon-Sat 8 am-6.30 pm, Sun 3-6.30 pm in summer, 8 am-12.30 pm, 3-6.30 pm daily in winter; Pazzi Chapel and museum open Thu-Tue 10 am-12.30 pm, 3-5 pm (6.30 pm in summer).

The great Gothic Franciscan church of Santa Croce (about 1294) is not a jolly place. Just as a superbly sited jewel such as San Miniato al Monte can make your spirits soar and your response to Florence hit an all-time high, so Santa Croce can have the opposite effect. The 19thC façade is uninspired; the interior is a huge shadowy barn filled with funerary monuments, and paved with nearly 300 tombstones. In here, the eyes of tour groups glaze over more than usual as they are herded from one lump of marble to the next. So take the advice of Lucy Honeychurch in E.M. Forster's *A Room with a View* who wandered about the church, puzzling things out, until 'the pernicious charm of Italy worked on her and instead of acquiring information, she began to be happy'.

The first **tomb** on the right is that of Michelangelo, who apparently chose the spot. The great man died in Rome in 1564 aged 90 and his body was brought back to Florence a few days later. Vasari designed this plodding memorial to his friend and hero. The *Pietà* Michelangelo intended for his tomb but never finished (now in the Museo dell'Opera del Duomo, see page 51) would have been a much more moving memorial.

Other tombs or monuments of note are those of **Galileo**, who was denied a Christian burial until 1737; of **Dante** (buried in Ravenna); of **Machiavelli**; of **Leonardo Bruni**, a lovely work by Rossellino (1447); of the 18thC poet and dramatist **Vittorio Alfieri** by Canova (1810) (his lover, the Countess of Albany, is buried nearby in the Castellani Chapel). Notice the modest but lovely **pulpit** by Benedetto da Maiano.

If you are interested in tracing the progress of Renaissance painting in Florence, you should start in Santa Croce. To the right of the chancel are two chapels, **Bardi** and **Peruzzi**, frescoed by Giotto. The Bardi shows the **Life of St Francis** (c. 1317) and the Peruzzi the **Life of St John the Divine** (right wall) and **Life of St John the Baptist** (left wall: about 1328). A century passed before another artist (Masaccio, in the Brancacci Chapel) had the stature to draw on Giotto's innovative technique and take it forwards. These monks (Bardi chapel) have a monumental quality quite unknown in contemporary figure painting: their bodies fill their muted brown robes. Standing back from the chapel, look up at the image above the arch: Giotto is able to convey the *feelings* of St Francis as he receives the stigmata. The poor state of repair of Giotto's frescoes are the result of whitewashing in the 18thC, a fate which befell many other frescoes in the church, now lost.

In the right transept, the **Baroncelli Chapel** is frescoed by Giotto's pupil Taddeo Gaddi, including perhaps the earliest night scene in fresco (1338). In the left transept, another Bardi Chapel contains a wooden **Crucifix** by Donatello. Brunelleschi said it looked like a peasant on a cross: he was challenged to do better and his attempt is now in Santa Maria Novella.

Brunelleschi's genius lay in architecture and Santa Croce contains one of his masterpieces. The **Pazzi Chapel** (Cappella de' Pazzi; entrance through the **cloister** to the right of the church) was designed in 1430, a disciplined grey and white Renaissance ideal. Around the cloister is the entrance to

Santa Maria Novella.

the lovely and serene inner **cloister** and to the church's **museum**.

SANTA FELICITA
See Walk Four: Oltrarno, page 75.

SANTA MARIA MADDALENA DEI PAZZI
See Walk Three: E of the Duomo, page 72.

SANTA MARIA NOVELLA
Piazza di Santa Maria Novella; church open 7-11.30 am, 3.30-6 pm (closed Sun am); museum open Sat-Thur 9 am-2 pm (8 am-1 pm on Sun). Santa Croce was the Gothic preaching church of the Franciscans; Santa Maria Novella was the Dominicans', begun 48 years earlier in 1246. The façade is a masterpiece of the Classically inspired Renaissance architect Alberti, who complemented with his rational arrangement of circles and squares the existing (Gothic) lower arcade. The volutes (spiral scrolls) were added to conceal the side chapel roofs. The symbol of a billowing sail, repeated across the centre, shows us that the patron was Giovanni Rucellai, whose family emblem this is.

The interior, mucked about by Vasari in the 16thC (he whitewashed frescoes and shortened windows to make way for side chapels) has an exceptionally long aisle. Or so it seems: it is in fact an illusion created by the Gothic architects who spaced the pillars closer together as they approached the chancel.

Cross to the left side of the nave to see Masaccio's severe and monumental **Trinity**, painted around the same time as his Brancacci Chapel frescoes, about 1425. It is a *tour de force* of perspective and spacial clarity, with a precise architectural background, typical of what Brunelleschi was then creating. It must have seemed very *avant garde* to contemporary eyes. The famous inscription above the skeleton lying on the tomb translates: *What you are, I once was: what I am, you will become.*

Making for the high altar, the chancel behind is frescoed by Ghirlandaio (1485-90). **Scenes from the Life of the Virgin** (left wall) and **Scenes from the Life of St John the Baptist** (right wall) make up in fascinating period detail what they lack in emotional depth. They bear close study.

The chapel to the right of the chancel, the **Filippo Strozzi Chapel**, is frescoed in a rather unappealing frenzy by Filippino Lippi (1487-1502). The scenes are full of references to Antiquity, the result of the artist's stay in Rome. At the same time, Strozzi commissioned Benedetto da Maiano to sculpt the tomb, which is unfortunately hard to see properly. Neither tomb nor frescoes were ready for Strozzi's funeral in 1491. To the left of the chancel, the **Gondi Chapel** is the setting for Brunelleschi's wooden **Crucifix**. He criticized Donatello's effort (in Santa Croce) and was challenged to do better. In Vasari's scenario, Donatello went to Brunelleschi's house with the ingredients for a cosy egg-and-cheese supper held in his apron. When he saw his friend's Crucifix, 'placed in a good light', he dropped the lot in astonishment.

The raised **Strozzi Chapel** holds a fine 14thC altarpiece by Orcagna, and frescoes (faded) by his brother Nardo di Cione on the theme of Dante's *Divine Comedy*.

The cloisters and Spanish chapel form the **Museo di Santa Maria Novella**; entrance to the left of the church entrance. The **Chiostro Verde** (Green Cloister) is so called because of the greenish hue of Uccello's sadly faded frescoes, including the extraordinary *Deluge* (about 1445) which displays the artist's well-known preoccupation with perspective. The **Spanish Chapel** (Cappellone degli Spagnoli) was built and decorated in the mid 14thC but takes its name from Eleanor of Toledo's courtiers, who used it in the 16thC. The fascinating frescoes, by the obscure Andrea Bonaiuti, are an artistic representation of Dominican belief. The dogs depicted on the right wall are a visual pun: *Domini canes* (dogs of God) – Dominicans hounding non-believers. The church in the background is the artist's idea of what the Duomo would look like when it was finished.

If you have a little more time to spare, perhaps before the train departs, cross Piazza di Santa Maria Novella (I wince when I look at those poor about-to-be squashed turtles in Giambologna's two obelisks) and turn right into Via della Scala. At No. 16 is the **Farmacia di Santa Maria Novella**, which has been operated by the convent of Santa Maria Novella since the 17thC. Both the herbal preparations and the interior are little changed.

A left turn away from the piazza brings you to the head of **Via dei Fossi**, full of sumptuous antique shops.

Back at **Santa Maria Novella** station, don't forget to take in the building before you hurry for your train. It was designed by Michelucci in 1935; so well was it designed, however, that it looks much younger.

SANTI APOSTOLI
See *Walk One: South of the Duomo*, pages 65-6.

SANTISSIMA ANNUNZIATA
Piazza della Santissima Annunziata; open 7.30 am-12.30 pm, 4-6.30 pm daily. The **atrium** of Michelozzo's church is notable for its important, though now very faded **frescoes** by leading Mannerist artists of the day. To the right of the entrance into the atrium is Rosso Fiorentino's *Assumption* (1517), painted when the artist was only 17. Looking at this work, you can see how the intensity and spirituality of the High Renaissance, of Raphael and his contemporaries, is no longer a requirement. Here we have characters (to the extreme left and right) who even seem to be laughing at the action taking place. The robes of the onlookers are used to present a wall of colour, as if to obscure the event of the Assumption rather than to celebrate it. To the right of the entrance to the church proper are Andrea del Sarto's *Arrival of the Magi* (1511) and *Birth of the Virgin* (1514). To the left is a much earlier work by Baldovinetti. In his *Nativity* (1460-2), the Arno stretches into the distance, its valley dotted with trees and houses.

Santissima Annunziata is Florence's society church, and its rich ornamentation glitters in the gloom. To the left is the **tempietto** of Michelozzo, commissioned by Piero de' Medici to house an image of the Madonna which, the devout believe, was begun by a monk and finished by an angel. This is perhaps the most revered shrine in Florence. The frescoes in the two chapels nearest to the Tempietto are by Castagno, the **Vision of St Julian** and the **Trinity**, typically compelling and unsettling. The high altar stands in a circular chancel; the chapel at the rear, decorated by the artist, contains the sarcophagus of Giambologna and of his devoted follower Pietro Zacca. To the left is Bronzino's *Resurrection*. Baccio Bandinelli and his wife are buried in a chapel to the right of the steps leading to the chancel; the Nicodemus in his *Pietà* is a self-portrait.

From the left transept, a door leads to the **Chiostro dei Morti**. Above the entrance porch is Andrea del Sarto's

Rest on the Flight into Egypt, known as the **Madonna del Sacco** for the sacks on which Joseph is leaning.

SANTO SPIRITO
Piazza di Santo Spirito; open 8 am-noon, 4-6 pm daily . Santo Spirito is for many the most pleasing of all Brunelleschi's churches. It was his last (1435), and was completed long after his death. The unfinished 17thC façade gives no hint of what lies inside: a serene forest of columns set in a harmonious space. All four arms of the Greek cross are identical, only the nave is larger. All around the perimeter, defining the boundaries of the internal space, march 40 recessed chapels and a colonnaded aisle. Only the entrance wall is excluded, but this is not what Brunelleschi designed; four doors should have opened into the four bays created by the aisle. Can anyone care for the Baroque *baldachino* which blocks the crossing and irritatingly spoils the harmony – again surely not something that Brunelleschi would have tolerated?

Make for the right transept to see Filippino Lippi's lovely **Nerli Altarpiece**, with the donors depicted in the foreground. Left of the nave is a **vestibule** with fine coffered ceiling by Cronaca, and an octagonal **sacristy** by Brunelleschi's follower, Giuliano da Sangallo.

Next door, in the refectory (*cenacolo*), all that remained of the monastery of Santo Spirito after a fire in 1471, is a powerful Gothic fresco of the **Crucifixion**, possibly by Orcagna (*open Tues-Sat 9 am-2 pm; Sun 8 am-1 pm*).

SPEDALE DEGLI INNOCENTI
See Walk Three: East of the Duomo, page 72.

UFFIZI
Pizzale degli Uffizi 6; open Apr-Sep, Tue-Sat 8.30 am-10 pm, Sun 8.30 am-8 pm, Oct-Mar, Tue-Sat 8.30 am-6.50 pm, Sun 8.30 am-1.50 pm (last admission 45 minutes before closing. Advance booking: Tel: 055 2347941). One of the greatest galleries of art in the world, and one of the oldest, inaugurated by Francesco I de' Medici in 1581. The handsome, two-pronged building is the work of Vasari (begun 1560), who designed it as offices (hence the building's title) for Cosimo I. New entrances (one for pre-booked visits, one for groups and one for individuals) have been made nearer the river, and the lofty, vaulted rooms once occupied by the gallery's archive, now contain ticket offices, gift shops, cloakroom and other services.

The Contini Bonacossi collection has been moved here from the Palazzo Pitti. There is a separate entrance on Via Lambertesca, and guided tours (about 45 mins) are by appointment only (*tel.* 055 294883). Tickets are also valid for the Uffizi and vice versa.

The many rooms of the Uffizi in which works of art are hung stretch out along the top floor of the building, starting with Florentine and Tuscan Gothic and Early Renaissance paintings arranged in chronological order. They take up most of the **East Corridor** and include **The Tribune**, the only room in the gallery that isn't reminiscent of an office. There is nowhere better than the first 14 rooms to witness the chain of events in Florentine art.

The short **South Corridor**, parallel to the Arno, connects to the **West Corridor** which is devoted to 16thC Italian painting (High Renaissance and Mannerism) and works by non-Italian artists. The corridors are a delight to walk in, lined by **Classical statues** which, until the turn of the 20thC, were treasured above the paintings.

On the first floor (separate entrance near the river), the museum's library of 50,000 volumes is housed, but general access to the public is not permitted.

Highlights amongst the paintings, many of which have been restored, are:

Room 2: three glowing Gothic altarpieces of the **Maestà** (the Virgin as the Queen of Heaven) from Cimabue (about 1280), Duccio (about 1285) and Giotto (about 1310). Each one makes progressive strides towards naturalism and control of perspective. Giotto, as you can see, makes the greatest leap. You could say that the artistic revolution that took place in Florence over the next 200 years starts here. Room 3: Giotto's genius, and his role as an innovator, was so overwhelming that only followers rather than leaders appeared in his wake in Florence in the 75 years or so after his death. His contemporary Duccio, who was Sienese, had a less stunning effect and in this room you can see how Sienese paintings flowered in the 14thC, especially in Simone Martini's lyrical **Annunciation**. Room 4: 14thC Florentine School – Giotto's suc-

Florence sights

cessors. Rooms 5 and 6: Gentile da Fabriano's **Adoration of the Magi** is the crowning achievement of the International Gothic school. Yet for all the flow and movement, the attention to detail, and the depiction of light (especially in the *Nativity predella*, bottom left), it is remarkable to think that two years after this picture was painted in Florence, in 1423, Masaccio painted his revolutionary *Trinity* in Santa Maria Novella (see page 59), and shortly afterward, the frescoes in the Brancacci Chapel (see pages 46-7). Room 7: Now you step into the Renaissance. Domenico Veneziano, who lived in Florence, left a tiny body of work – only two signed paintings and a few more attributed. His ethereal **Madonna and Saints** (about 1455; an early *Sacra Conversazione* in which the holy participants are seen to communicate or converse) shows Masaccio's influence in the architectural space and solid figures, but breaks new ground with its masterly use of light and harmonious colour. Piero della Francesca was Domenico's gifted pupil: his sense of shape, light and colour and the profound stillness of his paintings are much appreciated by the modern eye. Here is his famous portrait of the **Duke and Duchess of Urbino** (the Duke's weirdly shaped nose was supposedly the result of a sword blow). Piero wrote a treatise on perspective; Uccello was obsessed with the subject: in this panel of the **Battle of San Romano** (the other two are in the Louvre, Paris, and the National Gallery, London) his own battle with it is not won. Room 8: Romantic Madonnas by Filipo Lippi, the lecherous monk/artist who ran away with a nun – the model for his Virgin. Rooms 10-14: One large room devoted to Botticelli and his contemporaries. The mythological paintings executed for the Medici, **Primavera** (c 1480) and **The Birth of Venus** (c 1485), are sensational, full of allegory and considered by many to embody perfectly the Renaissance as well as the Medici ideals of the time. Seen for the first time, these paintings still have the power to overwhelm, despite overexposure in countless reproductions.

In **The Adoration of the Magi,** Lorenzo Il Magnifico, who was himself an accomplished poet, is depicted standing on the left, and the artist is slightly apart on the far right. A few years later Botticelli came under the sway of the religious fanatic Savonarola. The neurotic *Calumny of Apelles* dates from this time. Amongst his earlier religious paintings, the **Madonna of the Magnificent** must be the loveliest. Botticelli belonged to the late *quattrocento*. In his paintings, all but dismissed by the time he died in 1510 and not reappraised until the late 19thC, you see that his interest lies in graceful linear movement, and in figures which have a weightless, ethereal quality rather than in the depiction of space, depth and volume which had preoccupied Masaccio and his followers earlier in the century.

The huge **Portinari Altarpiece** by the Flemish artist Hugo Van der Goes was brought to Florence not long after it was painted in 1476. Its naturalism – notice the weather-beaten shepherds with gnarled hands – had a profound influence on all the Florentine artists represented in this room, and remains one of the masterpieces of 15thC painting and a highlight of the Uffizi.

Room 15: Works attributed to the young Leonardo da Vinci (1452-1519) grace the far wall. The angel in Verrocchio's **Baptism of Christ** is his earliest known oil painting. Vasari says that Verrocchio stuck to sculpture after he saw what his assistant could do. In the unfinished **Adoration of the Magi**, commissioned when he was 29, he first uses the compact yet dynamic pyramidal form for his figures, and light and shadow instead of outline (so different from Botticelli). Leonardo's artistic output was tiny, so busy was he being Universal Man, and although he was Flo-

• Da Fabriano's Adoration of the Magi *alterpiece*, Uffizi.

rentine, this is his only painting to be found in Tuscany. Tribune (Room 18): Built in the 1580s by Buontalenti for Francesco 1's best treasures. It is lined with hard, brilliant portraits of the Medici and their courtiers by Bronzino and other 16thC contemporaries. No one even glances at the statue in the middle: **Venus de' Medici** – how fashion changes. In the 18th and 19thC she was the biggest turn-on in Florence, culture and eroticism neatly combined – although one 19thC writer did have the honesty to remark on her 'pert, petty, insolent and fastidious' face (Leigh Hunt). Rooms 19-24: 15th and 16thC paintings from other parts of Italy, and abroad. Perugino and Signorelli (Room 19); Dürer and Cranach (Room 20); Bellini and Giorgione (Room 21); Holbein, Altdorfer and Memling (Room 22); Mantegna and Correggio (Room 23). Room 24 is decorated with 15th to 19thC miniatures. Room 25: Michelangelo's rich, sculptural **Doni Tondo** (1504) prefigures the Mannerist movement, whose principle exponents were Pontormo and Rosso Fiorentino. Room 26: Raphael and Andrea del Sarto. The former lived in Florence from 1504-1508, and painted the famous **Madonna of the Gold-finch** here. Del Sarto's original **Madonna of the Harpies** takes its name from the figures at the base of the pedestal. Room 27: Pontormo's **Supper at Emaus** is one of his best works. The realistic scene (the diners have dirty feet) is overshadowed by the Masonic symbol over Christ's head. Room 28: The Uffizi's represen-

tation of Florentine art finishes here. Venetian Titian's superbyly voluptuous **Venus of Urbino** stands out among other sensual nudes. Room 29: Parmigiano's elegant, cool mannerist 'Madonna with the Long Neck' (1536). Rooms 30-31: 15th and 16th century Emilian artists (Dosso Dossi, Ludovico Mazzolino). Room 32: Sebastiano del Piombo's melancholy 'Death of Adonis'. Room 34: Paolo Veronese's characteristically glowing 'Holy Family with St Barbara'. Room 35: Tintoretto's : 'Leda and the Swan'. Room 41: Rubens and Van Dyke. Room 42: Sala della Niobe. The latest room to be reopened after bomb damage, housing a collection of sculptures 'Niobe and her sons' (18thC copies of Hellenic works).

Rooms 43-45 are closed for restoration: some Caravaggios are temporarily on show in Room 16.

VASARI CORRIDOR (CORRIDOIO VASARIANO)

(R*estored after* 1992 *bomb damage. Irregular opening hours – check with tourist office*).

By 1565, the Medici and their entourage needed to trot between the Palazzo Vecchio, the adjacent Uffizi, and the Palazzo Pitti across the river. How to do it without mixing with the *hoi polloi*? Simple: Francesco 1 commissioned his court architect Vasari to build an enclosed aerial corridor on rounded arches which clings to the Ponte Vecchio and skirts the church of San Felicità on its way. It is lined with a fascinating collection of artists' self-portraits and offers diverting views.

VIA DE' TORNABUONI

See Walk 1: *South of the Duomo, page* 67.

Florence walks

Orientation Florence is not ideal for a casual stroll. It has neither the enchanting, silent backwaters of Venice, nor the *dolce vita* street life of Rome. Its compact historic centre is infested with merciless cars, buses, taxis and motorbikes roaring down the medieval lanes, parking in the middle of the great squares, blaring and hooting their way along the *lungarni*. Sometimes the pollution levels get so high that the traffic has to be stopped from entering the city. Parking restrictions are very tight.

That said, walking is still the only way to get to know Florence, and to get from treasure to treasure. The good news is that the centre is small, and all but a handful of sights lie within a few minutes walk of the Duomo. The first three walks featured here radiate from the Duomo and have been devised to encompass all the major sights in the city centre. They start on this page, pages 68 and 70.

The Arno river lies to the south of the centre, which is linked by the Ponte Vecchio to one other part of Florence which must be explored: Oltrarno (literally, beyond the Arno). This is better walking terrain: it has its busy streets, yes, but also the Boboli Gardens, shady piazzas and country lanes. A fourth walk, starting on page 74, covers this area.

For those places, such as San Miniato and Fiesole (see page 77) which are further flung, and even for closer sights, should you wish, an excellent bus service exists. If you want a bus, but you don't know its route, head for the terminus at Santa Maria Novella station; most buses stop at either Piazza del Duomo or Piazza di San Marco as well. Bus No. 7 goes from the station to the Duomo to Fiesole; bus No. 10 goes from the station to the Duomo to San Marco to Settignano; bus No. 13 goes from the station to Piazzale Michelangelo and San Miniato.

The four walks vary in length, but if possible, set aside a day for each, especially if you want to include visits to the majority of sights mentioned along the way, and indeed a stop for lunch. I've given passing mentions to good restaurants which lie right on the routes – descriptions of most of them can be found under Recommended Restaurants, pages 78-80.

SOUTH OF THE DUOMO

Walk One – an introductory route – explores the city's most ancient quarter, with echoes of its Roman origins and much evidence of its glory days when guilds, churches, banks, markets and the *palazzi* of powerful families sprang up in the narrow streets.

The walk starts at the Duomo, and ends at one of the cafés of the Piazza della Repubblica. On the way it passes Orsanmichele; the Piazza della Signoria; Uffizi; a network of hardly changed medieval lanes; the fashionable shopping street, Via de' Tornabuoni; a fascinating museum of life in 14thC Florence and the old market place.

Start Piazza di San Giovanni. On the corner of Via dei Calzaiuoli, opposite the South Doors of the Baptistry, stands the **Loggia del Bigallo** where, in the 15thC, abandoned children and babies awaited collection. After three days they were distributed to foster mothers. Later, the charitable body responsible, Misericordia, moved to new premises across the street, where they remain to this day. The ambulances parked outside have taken the places of stretchers, but the lay brothers still wear hooded black capes.

Via dei Calzaiuoli was the main drag in medieval Florence, linking the Duomo with the Piazza della Signoria. The name means 'hosiers' and the wide pedestrian street is still filled with shoe shops. Off to the left is Via dei Tavolini, where **Perchè No?** sells some of the best ice cream in town. There are some interesting food shops here, too, and **Cantinetta Verrazzano** (No. 18/20r; closed Sun), a great place for a quick lunch, always buzzing. The main *raison d'être* here is the 'enoteca' (wine bar) where excellent wines from the Verrazzano estate are served with various snacks. Back in Calzaiuoli, on the right stands **Orsanmichele** (see Sights & Places of Interest, page 52), which you would never guess was a church if you didn't know better. Opposite is little Via dei Cimatori which contains a typical Florentine wine and sandwich booth, and next door, a typical craftsman's *atelier*, unchanged for decades: **Incisore**, brass engraver. (*Cimatori* means shearers – a reminder of the medieval cloth trade.)

Entering **Piazza della Signoria**

Florence walks

SOUTH OF THE DUOMO

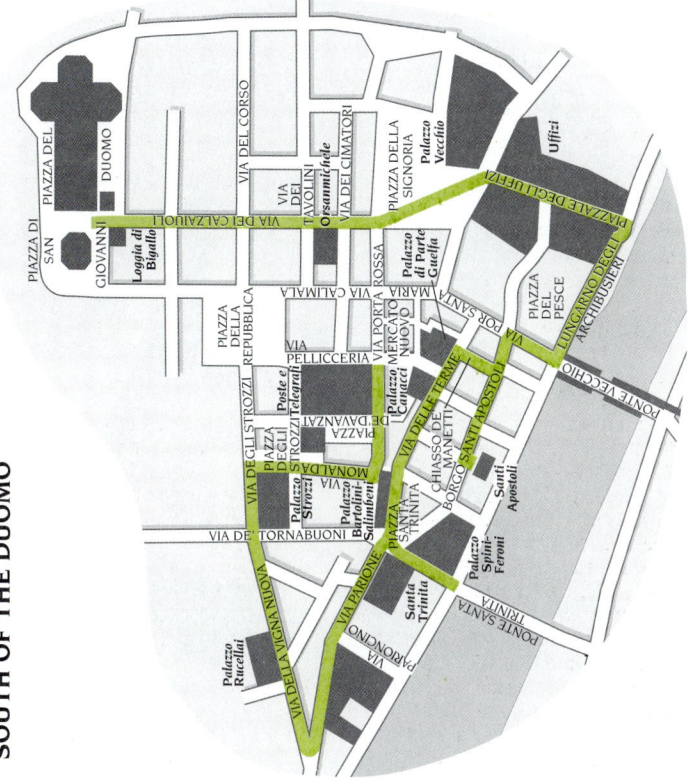

(see Sights & Places of Interest, pages 55-6), notice **Pineider**, for leather-bound stationery and beautifully printed invitations; also the classy café **Rivoire** – expensive but worth it. A rest here gives you time to contemplate the unique collection of buildings and statues now in view. The latter are arranged so that they lead the eye from the **Palazzo Vecchio** towards the **Uffizi** in the corner (see Sights & Places of Interest, pages 54-5 and 61-3).

If now is not the time to visit the Uffizi, you can walk thankfully past the queues along the Piazzale degli Uffizi, lined with mainly 19thC statues of luminary Florentines. On the right, decaying wreaths commemorate the 1992 bombing, which killed five people. Repair work still continues. At the river end there is yet more art – in the form of pavement portrait painters. Turn right here, walking towards **Ponte Vecchio**. Little Piazza del Pesce, site of the medieval fish market, contains a favourite local restaurant, **Buca dell'Orafo** (see Recommended Restaurants, page 78).

Turn left along Via Por Santa Maria, rebuilt since wartime devastation. The speciality here is embroidered linen: the **Taf** shops are a good bet. Turn first left along **Borgo Santi Apostoli**, an old, narrow street lined with crusty *palazzi*. If you look at a city map, you can see that, along with the fashionable shopping street Via de' Tornabuoni, Via de' Cerretani and Via del Proconsolo, Borgo Santi Apostoli forms a ring, marking the line of the first city walls, built in the 11thC. On the right, **Gastronomia** specializes in unusually shaped glass bottles of *grappa*. Further along, on the left, tiny Piazza del Limbo, so named because it stands on a burial ground for unbaptized babies, is easy to miss. **Santi Apostoli** is one of the few surviving Romanesque churches in Florence, and, in its simple way,

• Madonna of the Magnificent, Botticelli

one of the most affecting (sadly, it is often locked).

Having seen it, retrace as far as Chiasso de' Manetti, where turn left. Across Via delle Terme, at the junction of Chiasso delle Misure, a charming group of medieval buildings come into view. Directly opposite is **Palazzo di Parte Guelfa**, its 13thC construction financed by confiscated Ghibelline property. Thirteenth-century Tuscany was riven by bitter and highly complicated factional fighting between the Guelfs and the Ghibellines. In Florence the Guelfs (who themselves divided into Black and White factions) rose to power, and this was their headquarters. The upper storeys were added by Brunelleschi, and there is a staircase by Vasari.

Nearby are the **Palazzo dell'Arte della Seta**, the silkworkers' guild – notice its bas-relief emblem – and the **Palazzo Canacci**, headquarters of the Calcio Storico (annual football tournament in costume) and bedecked with many flags.

Turn left. At the end of Via delle Terme, on the right, is **Palazzo Bartolini-Salimbeni**, once the French Consulate, whose Roman-influenced High Renaissance façade, Vasari tells us, caused a great fuss when it first appeared. Across the road is the fine crenellated **Palazzo Spini-Ferroni** (Via Tornabuoni 2), quite some private house for 1269, and now housing Ferragamo's shop and **museum** (open Mon-Fri 9 am-1 pm, by appointment only, tel. 055 3360456) and a must for shoe fettishists. Apart from displaying some incredible footwear, it documents the personal history and rags-to-riches rise of Ferragamo himself.

Unfortunately, the **Piazza di Santa Trinità** is too much of a busy thoroughfare to allow the buildings to shine. The column in the middle is Roman, from the Baths of Caracalla, a present from Pope Pius IV to Cosimo I. The statue of Justice was plopped on top a few years later.

As you have seen, this patch is thick with the *palazzi* of noble families, and **Santa Trinità**, the local church (*open 8 am-noon, 4-6 pm daily*), was embellished over the years with their private chapels: Strozzi, Doni, Davanzati, Spini, Usimbardi, amongst others. Fourth on the right is the **Bartolini-Salimbeni Chapel**, almost exactly the same as when it was assembled in the 15thC. The frescoes and *Annunciation* were executed by the Sienese Lorenzo Monaco in the early 1420s in International Gothic style – still in vogue even while Masaccio was priming his brushes over the river in the Brancacci Chapel. The real treat here, however, is the **Sassetti Chapel**, second to the right of the chancel, courtesy of Ghirlandaio who once more (see Santa Maria Novella, page 59) gives a fascinating record of contemporary Florentine people and places in his *Scenes from the Life of St Francis*. In the painting you can make out Piazza della Signoria, as well as this church, showing its original Romanesque façade (the present one was put up in 1594). Sassetti, manager of the Medici bank, and his family, mingle with Medicis (Lorenzo Il Magnifico, his sons and tutors) in the top picture.

If you haven't seen **Ponte Santa Trinita** before, you should nip down to the river to appreciate its delicious sweep. It is an exact, painstakingly rebuilt replica of the original which was blown to pieces in 1944. Cosimo I ordered it, Vasari, court architect, oversaw it, Ammannati built it (in 1567)... and Michelangelo suggested its wonderful elliptical curve.

Back in Piazza di Santa Trinita, try to resist the lure of Via de' Tornabuoni for a little longer, and instead head down Via Parione.

Across the road is **Bisonte**, which should be on your list in that hunt for the perfect handbag. Next door is a bookbinder and a perfumery. Nearby in Via Parioncino is **Coco Lezzone** (see Restaurant Recommendations, page 78).

Turn right at low-key but exclusive Via della Vigna Nuova, peppered with fashion designers' stores. There's also the straw shop, **Paoli** (No. 26r). Off to the left, in Via dei Palchetti, is that model of controlled chaos, **Il Latini** (see Restaurant Recommendations, pages 78-9). Next comes the highly influential **Palazzo Rucellai**, which perfectly combines delicacy with rugged strength and was designed by Alberti (1446) for the millionaire intellectual, Giovanni Rucellai, whose charming and cultivated descendants still live there. Just as on the façade of Santa Maria Novella (see page 59) you can see along the frieze the emblems – billowing sail and ring – of the Rucellai and the Medici, united by marriage. **Museo Alinari**, which was once housed on the ground floor, has now moved to Largo Alinari 15 (Piazza Stazione) (*open 9 am-1 pm, 3-7 pm daily*). It is devoted to the history of photography, and the pioneering work of the Alinari brothers, who recorded Florence in the 19thC.

Via de' Tornabuoni, the city's prime shopping – or more probably, window shopping – street stretches to left and right. Amongst all the famous fashion names, look out for **Seeber** at No. 68r, the long-standing foreign language bookshop, and **Giacosa**, at No. 83, an equally venerable café with an elegant clientele. Cross over, turning right into Piazza degli Strozzi. For a private house, **Palazzo Strozzi** is vast, the crazy dream of an enormously rich and egocentric 15thC banker, Filippo Strozzi, who wanted to outdo the Medici. He never lived to see it finished and, of course, the place was the undoing of his successors. Though it was built later than Palazzo Rucellai, the building seems less refined, although it is considered one of the most architecturally important of the Renaissance palaces.

Follow Via Monalda into attractive Via Porta Rossa, opposite the ancient hotel of the same name. Shops selling silks and linens, like **Blue Home** (No. 56r), are clustered in this street; also, on the right, the diverting **Palazzo Davanzati**, currently closed for restoration (see Sights & Places of

Interest, pages 52-3). To the left, in Via Pellicceria, is the vast flank of the main post office.

Continuing along Via Porta Rossa, you reach the **Mercato Nuovo**, still known locally as the Straw Market because of the straw goods which were sold there – though sadly no longer – from the 19thC. Nowadays it's mainly leather: you might well do better here than in San Lorenzo market. In summer the market is open seven days a week; in winter it closes on Sunday and Monday. Even if you don't want to browse, you will be enchanted by the bronze wild boar (the market is also called Porcellino after him), a copy of a copy by Tacca of a Roman statue, now in the Uffizi. Rub his nose to bring you luck and guarantee yourself a return visit to Florence. Around the market are little stalls selling snacks of *trippa* and *lampredotto*. Just off the market square, in Via Val di Lamona, is **Pasquini**, a restaurant which serves reasonably priced food. Notice too, the traditional **Erboristeria** selling herbal remedies, soaps and fragrances in pretty bottles, all beautifully wrapped and perfect as presents.

The Mercato Nuovo has been a market place since the 11thC. The lovely **loggia** was built in the mid-16thC at the behest of Cosimo I for the silk merchants. But this was also the city's banking district, and in the 15thC there were literally dozens of banks around this area.

The medieval food market, Mercato Vecchio, was located where your final goal, **Piazza della Repubblica,** now stands. Before that it was the Roman forum, later it became the Jewish ghetto. In the 19thC its sleazy but picturesque slums were cleared away to create the present piazza, devoid of interest in its slab-like layout and anonymous buildings, but popular for its many pavement cafés. Check out **Gilli**, **Giubbe Rosse** and **Paszkowski** – you deserve them all.

NORTH OF THE DUOMO

This short walk (number two) takes you into the heartland of the Medici and also draws together some of the city's most memorable artistic endevours: the unsurpassed sculpture of Michelangelo in the Accademia and San Lorenzo, the lyrical frescoes of Fra Angelico (San Marco) and of his pupil Benozzo Gozzoli (Palazzo Medici-Riccardi), and the brooding, dangerous vision of Andrea Castagno (Cenacolo di Sant'Apollonia). The route ends at San Lorenzo's famous daily leather and textile market and Europe's largest covered food market. On Saturdays the latter reopens after lunch, making it the best day to make the walk.

Be warned: it's not worth doing this walk unless you intend to visit the various sights *en route*: until you reach Via de' Ginori, the roads in this part of town are long, straight and beseiged by heavy traffic.

Start Piazza del Duomo. Take Via Ricasoli away from the Duomo. On the corner of Via degli Alfani is the **Conservatorio Musicale Luigi Cherubini**. The prestigious music academy has a superb library and collection of musical instruments (closed at time of writing). Almost next door, in Via degli Alfani, is the **Opificio delle Pietre Dure** *(open Mon-Sat 9 am-2 pm – check on times)*. When you get to the Medici Chapels at San Lorenzo you will know *pietre dure*: the walls of the Cappella dei Principi are encrusted with it – intricate patterns of inlaid marble. This workshop for the teaching and making of *pietre dure* was founded in the late 16thC by Ferdinando I de' Medici. A small museum displays tools and examples.

Next comes the **Accademia** (see Sights & Places of Interest, page 42), usually besieged by tourists waiting to see *David* in the flesh. Passing the paint-daubed doors of its parent next door, the **Accademia di Belle Arti**, you emerge into roaring Piazza di San Marco, a useful place to catch a bus, but otherwise unpleasant. Across the piazza stands the church and convent of **San Marco** (see Sights & Places of Interest, page 57), one of the most restful and spiritually uplifting places in the city.

If timing and mood are right, you could make a detour from here. This is the home of the University of Florence, the **Università degli Studi,** and at Via Giorgio La Pira 4 is the entrance to several university museums: **Museo Botanico** *(open Mon, Wed, Fri 9 am-noon and by appointment (tel. 055 2757462); 9.30-12.20 1st Sun of*

Florence walks

NORTH OF THE DUOMO

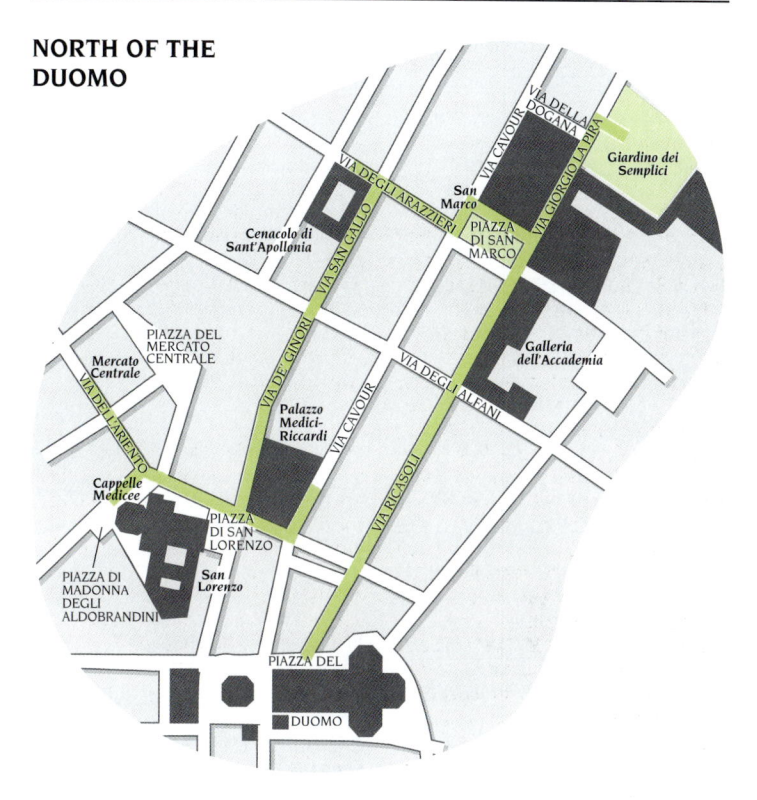

month); **Geology and Palaentogolgy** (*open Mon 2-6 pm, Tue-Sat 9 am-1 pm; 9.30 am-12.30 pm 1st Sun of month*); **Mineralogy and Lithology** (*open Mon-Sat 9 am-1 pm; 9.30 am-12.30 pm 1st Sun of month*). A little further on is the **Giardino dei Semplici**, the botanical garden founded in 1545 by Cosimo 1 (*open Mon, Wed, Fri 9 am-noon*).

Almost opposite the Via La Pira gate into the botanical garden (the main one is at Via Micheli 3), Via della Dogana leads to Via Cavour. Across the street is the Court of Appeal, site of the Medici sculpture gardens where the teenage Michelangelo drew and studied the collection of Classical statuary. Notice, opposite, the original **Farmacia**, one of several remaining in the city. Just to the right, at Via Cavour 69, try ringing the bell of the **Chiostro dello Scalzo** (*supposedly open Mon and Thur 9 am-1 pm, gratuity appreciated*) to gain entry. The cloister is all that remains of the Confraternity of San Giovanni Battista, frescoed in monochrome *grisaille* by Andrea del Sarto. The frescoes depict *Scenes from the Life of St John the Baptist*.

Returning to Piazza di San Marco, take Via degli Arazzieri (meaning tapestry workers' street), walking across Via San Gallo to find the **Cenacolo di Sant'Apollonia** (see Sights & Places of Interest, page 48) on the left. Retrace to Via San Gallo, and turn right. The road becomes **Via de' Ginori**, the most characterful in this part of town, narrow, quiet and lined with high *palazzi*. **Nos 7, 9, 11** and **19** are all fine. Raphael lived in the last-named for a while, and Baccio Bandinelli had his home in this street, next to No. 11. At Piazza di San Lorenzo, turn left and left again for the entrance to **Palazzo Medici-Riccardi** (see Sights & Places of Interest, page 53), where you can hitch your horse to one of the huge iron rings attached to the walls for the purpose, and visit the deliciously decorated Cappella dei Magi.

Piazza di San Lorenzo is the site of Florence's main tourist-Mecca **Mercato di San Lorenzo**, its crowded, bustling stalls spilling over into the side streets. Leather goods predominate, and prices

69

• *Florence, from the top of the Duomo.*

can be fairly reasonable. Across the sea of awnings stands **San Lorenzo** (yes, that humble rough-brick façade – see Sights & Places of Interest, page 56).

Round the back in Piazza di Madonna degli Aldobrandini is the entrance to the church's famous **Medici Chapels**. Leave Piazza di San Lorenzo by Via dell'Ariento, filled with stalls and lined with fabric and clothing shops, emerging at the splendid late 19thC iron and glass **Mercato Centrale**. A wander round this temple of food (*open Mon-Sat 7 am-2 pm, and 4-8 pm on Sat*), with its stalls overflowing with top-quality produce (fruit and vegetables upstairs, everything else downstairs), will make you seriously hungry. In which case, head for one of the many bars or pastry shops in the area, or the lively **Trattoria Zà Zà** in the Piazza del Mercato Centrale; or try a Tuscan take-away from one of the little stalls, such as *trippa* (tripe) or *lampredotto* (pig's intestines) – both are served in a roll or '*panino*'.

EAST OF THE DUOMO
Walk number three is the longest. It takes you out of the clamouring city centre by way of lovely Piazza della Santissima Annunziata, and into the atmospheric working class streets around Sant'Ambrogio and Santa Croce, where few tourists penetrate. Back in the thick of things, the route threads through the medieval lanes of Dante's neighbourhood, before reaching the more familiar shopping streets, packed with boutiques and dedicated shoppers, south of the Duomo.

Start Piazza del Duomo. Take Via dei Servi, the old processional route from the Duomo to Santissima Annunziata. On the left, corner of Via de' Pucci, is the enormous **Palazzo Pucci**, ancestral home of the late designer. While you are here, look too at **No. 21**, directly opposite the church of San Michele Visdomini, its richly coffered ceilings and frescoed walls visible through the first-floor windows. At the junction with Via degli Alfani, you might stop for a glass of wine and a delicious Italian sandwich in the typical panelled wine bar on the corner. At the far end of Via dei Servi, regional government

Florence walks

EAST OF THE DUOMO

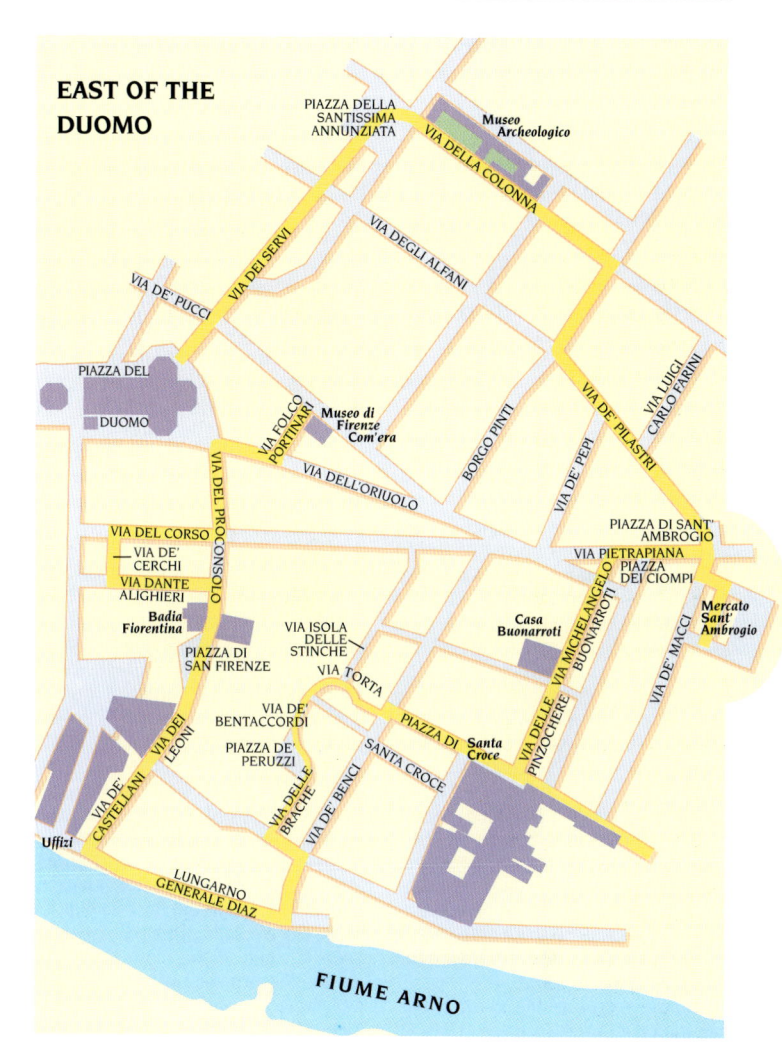

officials toil under fabulous ceilings in Ammannati's rose brick **Palazzo Grifoni**.

Harmonious **Piazza della Santissima Annunziata** (now traffic-free) explodes into life on March 25 each year when a fair is held there to celebrate the Festa dell'Annunziata; there's also a craft fair on the first weekend of September.

Otherwise it has a somewhat scruffy appearance, which does not detract from its appeal. Down-and-outs often doss on the steps near the **Loggiato dei Serviti**, now an atmospheric hotel; next door is a canteen for them run by the church. The *loggia* along this west side of the square, which echoes the Spedale degli Innocenti opposite, was in fact built a century later than the Spedale. The *loggia* which fronts **Santissima Annunziata** (see Sights & Places of Interest, pages 60-1) was added in the early 17thC, unifying the whole square. The statue of *Ferdinando I* is by Giambologna, completed by his pupil Tacca, who was also responsible for the two peculiar fountains.

The *loggia* of Brunelleschi's **Spedale degli Innocenti**, built as an orphanage and still operating, is seminal, the first building (1419-26) to adapt Classical proportion to traditional Tuscan Romanesque architecture. The nine central

Florence

bays (the rest were added much later), adorned with Andrea della Robbia's famous *tondi* of swaddled babies, are very beautiful, as are the two inner **cloisters**. Abandoned babies were handed through a window to the left of the *loggia*. Upstairs, in the **Galleria dello Spedale Innocenti** (*open Thur-Tues 8.30 am-2 pm*) there is a mildly interesting collection of Renaissance paintings on display.

Traffic zooms across the *piazza* in front of Santissima Annunziata. Follow the flow into Via della Colonna, and then, if possible, take refuge in the **Museo Archeologico** (see Sights & Places of Interest, page 50) on the left. Or grit your teeth and keep going until you reach Borgo Pinti, where you turn right.

At No. 58 is the entrance to the church and former convent of **Santa Maria Maddalena dei Pazzi**. The church itself combines Renaissance restraint (architect, Guiliano da Sangallo) with Baroque flourish. Look for a door on the right about half way along the nave which gives on to the sacristy (*open 9 am-noon and 5-7 pm*), whence, having paid, you begin a winding underground journey to the chapter house, and one of the hidden delights of Florence: Perugino's fresco of the **Crucifixion with Saints** (1496). Though Perugino had none of his pupil Raphael's intensity, the quiet behaviour of the drooping, mild-faced participants in the drama and the allure of the softly-lit landscape seem all the more moving for being so hard to find.

Notice, opposite the church, **No. 55**, with a charming garden. Turn left into Via de' Pilastri with its local shops and bars. On the corner of Via Fiesolana is the English-language bookshop, **Paperback Exchange**, strong on guide books, fiction and second-hand books and run by knowledgeable staff. Further on, **Aquacotta**, No. 51r, serving inexpensive Tuscan dishes, is a pleasant choice for lunch. Next door is a tea house, specializing in different varieties of tea. In Via Luigi Carlo Farini, to the left, is the huge synagogue **Tempio Israelitico**. To the right, long, straight Via de' Pepi is permanently bedecked with washing. **Sant'Ambrogio**, with its creamy-apricot 19thC façade, is the local church; the **Cappella del Miracolo**, left of the high altar, contains a marble **tabernacle** by Mino da Fiesole (1482) and his own tomb. Verrocchio is buried here – fourth chapel on the left.

Via de' Macci and then first left will lead you to the neighbourhood **Mercato Sant'Ambrogio**, a scaled-down glass-and-iron version of the city's central market. Close by, **Cibreo** offers diverse eating opportunities: it comprises an up-market restaurant, a cheap *vinaria* serving the same dishes, a café and a gourmet take-out.

From Piazza di Sant'Ambrogio take Via Pietrapiana to Piazza dei Ciompi with its ramshackle little stalls of the daily **Mercato delle Pulci** (flea market), and its charming **Loggia del Pesce**, which was built by Vasari for the fishmongers of the Mercato Vecchio and moved here when that was demolished (in 1890, to make way for the Piazza della Repubblica). Ghiberti lived at **No. 11**.

Take Via Michelangelo Buonarroti out of the piazza (cathedral dome dramatically coming into view) – to **Casa Buonarroti** on the corner of Via Ghibellina (see Sights & Places of Interest, pages 47-8). Now drift towards **Santa Croce** (see Sights & Places of Interest, pages 58-9) as Miss Lavish and Lucy Honeychurch did in E.M. Forster's evocative novel (and film) *A Room with a View* 'through those grey-brown streets, neither commodious nor picturesque, in which the eastern quarter of the city abounds'. This low-lying area, once the hub of the cloth trade and always the province of artisans, was devastated by the 1966 flood. Since then many little workshops have disappeared and the character of the district has become more bland.

Carry on down Via delle Pinzochere into **Piazza di Santa Croce** with its row of overhanging houses supported by stone, formerly wooden, brackets. The piazza has been the site of Medici ceremonies and public executions, and still acts as a pitch for the annual Gioco di Calcio Storico, the period costume football match.

Little Via Torta and its continuations, Via Bentaccordi and Piazza de' Peruzzi, form a curve – they follow the line of the Roman amphitheatre. You can make a pleasant detour right off Via Torta down Via Isola delle Stinche for an ice cream at the famous *gelateria*

Vivoli (*closed Mon*). Proceed through more of E. M. Forster's grey-brown streets, first Via delle Brache, then left into Via de' Neri to emerge opposite the **Museo Horne** (see Sights & Places of Interest, page 51). A quicker route between Santa Croce and Museo Horne, is via **Borgo Santa Croce**, an attractive street lined with *palazzi*, including **No. 8**, which was Vasari's.

You now reach the river, and, walking towards **Ponte Vecchio**, pass the **Museo di Storia della Scienza** (see Sights & Places of Interest, page 52). The peaceful backwaters of Sant'Ambrogio and Santa Croce are forgotten as you plunge back into the centre. Turn right down Via de' Castellani which runs past the **Uffizi** (see Sights & Places of Interest, pages 61-3). Passing the old corn market, the **Loggia del Grano**, continue north, crossing Borgo de' Greci, where, to my mind, one of the most attractive vistas in inner Florence now opens out. On the right, the unexpected sight of splendid 18thC Baroque: the façade of **San Firenze** which unites three earlier buildings and is now partly used as law courts. On the left, Guiliano da Sangallo's late 15thC **Palazzo Gondi**, its arcaded courtyard now a flower shop. Ahead on the right, the medieval bulk of the **Bargello** (see Sights & Places of Interest, pages 42-6); on the left the slim campanile of the **Badia Fiorentina**. It was in this abbey church that the poet Dante (1265-1321) described how he watched his beloved, unattainable Beatrice at mass. And fittingly, it was here, in the 14thC, that Boccaccio gave his lectures on Dante's works. It's worth popping in if only for Filippino Lippi's *Virgin Appearing to St Bernard* and Mino da Fiesole's **tomb of Count Ugo** (about 1470). Count Ugo was the son of Willa, Countess of Tuscany, who founded the abbey in 978.

In Via Dante Alighieri, a little courtyard opens on to **Museo Casa di Dante**, a restored – or, more accurately, mocked-up – 13thC tower that might or might not have been Dante's home (*open Mon, Tue, Thu-Sat 9.30 am-12.30 pm, 3.30-6.30 pm, Sun 9.30 am-12.30 pm*). Back on the street, a wall plaque points out the buildings which existed in Dante's day, including the **Torre della Castagna** on the corner, which was the first seat of city government. Also in this little street: **Da Pennello**, for wonderful *antipasti*.

Opposite the Castagna tower, across the little piazza, is tiny **San Martino del Vescovo**, Dante's parish church, and later, in the 15thC, headquarters of a charity for the poor 'too shy to beg', the Compagnia dei Buonuomini (*open 10 am-noon, 3-5 pm, closed Sun*): it is charmingly decorated with frescoes of the life of St Martin. Typically of Ghirlandaio – an assistant of his carried out the work – they are full of contemporary Renaissance detail. There are also two prized Madonnas, one by Perugino, the other Byzantine. Notice, too, the blocked-up window through which bread was distributed to the shy poor.

Leaving the medieval world of Dante, turn right into Via de' Cerchi. **Coin**, the useful fashion-oriented department store, is on the left. Right again into Via del Corso, lined with boutiques. For a last glimpse at Dante, look down Via del Presto: on the corner is **Santa Margherita de' Cerchi**, where the poet married Gemma Donati in 1295. At the junction with Via del Proconsolo, on the opposite side, are two fine palaces. On the right, **Palazzo Pazzi-Quaratesi** (about 1470). The palace was confiscated after the infamous Pazzi Conspiracy, in which the family and others tried but failed to overthrow their rivals the Medici. The conspirators attacked Lorenzo Il Magnifico and his younger brother Giuliano at mass, slaughtering Giuliano, but were soon caught and lynched. Their palace was confiscated. On the left is **Palazzo Nonfinito**, begun by Buontalenti in the 1590s, but not, as the name suggests, finished, at least until the **Museo Nazionale di Antropologia e Etnologia** moved in (*open Thur-Sat 9 am-1 pm and third Sun of each month*). A left turn down Via del Proconsolo brings you back to the the Piazza del Duomo. If you are feeling strong, a right turn here, followed by a left, leads you to the interesting **Museo di Firenze Com'era** (see Sights & Places of Interest, page 50).

OLTRARNO
Oltrarno refers to the part of Florence which lies 'beyond the Arno'. It was made fashionable in the 16thC when the Medici moved to the Palazzo Pitti,

Florence

OLTRARNO

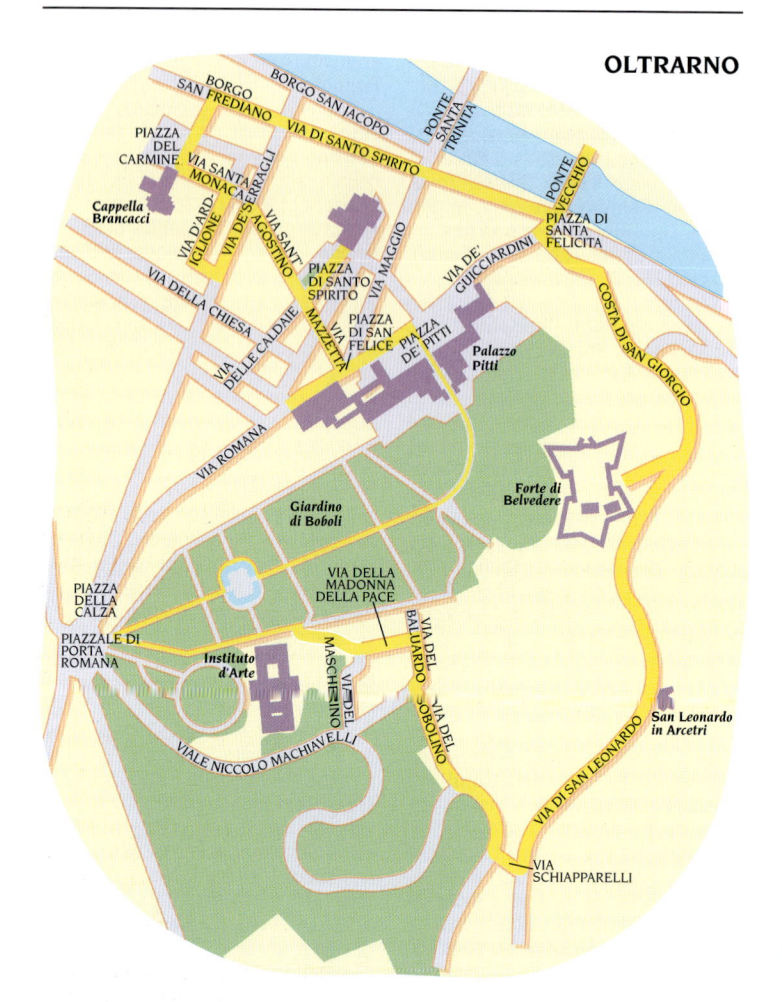

but it has always retained a more tranquil air than the city centre. Apart from the Pitti, two important churches, Santo Spirito and the Carmine (containing the Brancacci Chapel) are to be found here. This walk (number four), with a leisurely stop for lunch or a picnic in the Boboli Gardens, also demonstrates how, in the southern fringes, city and country merge into one.

Start Ponte Vecchio. It must be fun to live in one of the little houses which cling to one side of the famous **Ponte Vecchio**. On the opposite side strides the **Vasari Corridor** (see Sights & Places of Interest, page 63), held on broad arches and pierced by circular windows. Built in 1345, sturdy Ponte Vecchio was the disorderly province of butchers and blacksmiths. Until, that is, the late 16thC when Ferdinando I, even though he was able to cross the bridge in the privacy of the newly built Vasari Corridor, ordered them out, replacing them with the refined goldsmiths and jewellers who are still there. A bust of Cellini, the 16thC Florentine goldsmith, stands in the middle. The Ponte Vecchio has withstood fighting, flooding and bombing; in 1944 it was deliberately spared during Allied bombing raids which all but destroyed the area immediately to the south, which was rebuilt in the 1950s.

In Via de' Guicciardini, notice the wares in the window of **Madova**, the glove factory, then turn left into **Piazza di Santa Felicita**. Notice how Vasari incorporated his corridor into the rebuilt façade of the church. Inside, the **Capponi Chapel** contains two Mannerist masterpieces, not to be missed: the ***Deposition*** and ***Annunciation*** by Pontormo (1525-8).

Now take the right-hand fork out of the piazza, the **Costa di San Giorgio**. As you walk uphill you quickly leave the city behind, and lovely views of it open up here and there to the left. **No. 19** was the home of Galileo. Soon the little houses give way to large villas set in lush gardens. The ancient gateway at the top of the lane is **Porta San Giorgio**, built in 1260.

The **Forte di Belvedere** (to the right through the gate; *open 9 am-7 pm, 6 pm in winter*) was built by Buontalenti in 1590 for the Medici. It commands the most wonderful views from its terraces.

The gate from Belvedere into the Boboli Gardens is now permanently closed, so, back at the road, continue along pretty **Via di San Leonardo**, which in ten minutes or so reaches the church of **San Leonardo in Arcetri**, which boasts a beautiful early 13thC marble pulpit. Push on until you reach a turning on your right, Via Schiapparelli, which makes a short cut to Porta Romana. Emerging on the main Viale Machiavelli, turn right and then take the next right, Via del Bobolino, which leads downhill to a fork, where turn right. Continue down Via del Baluardo to the junction with Via della Madonna della Pace, the centre of the quiet residential area of Bobolino, with pleasant views. Turn left here. At the junction with Via del Mascherino the road broadens into a sort of piazza. Facing you are some iron railings, and set in these, on the right, is an open gate (until 8 pm). A path leads across the park of the

• *Bust of Cellini, Ponte Vecchio.*

Instituto d'Arte (formerly the royal stables) to Porta Romana. A right turn through the city gates brings you into Piazza della Calza from where you can enter the **Giardino di Boboli (Boboli Gardens)** (see Sights & Places of Interest, page 46), emerging at **Palazzo Pitti** (see Sights & Places of Interest, pages 53-4).

At **No. 22** Via de' Guiccardini, opposite the the Pitti, Dostoevsky wrote *The Idiot* struggling the while with his young wife to make ends meet. Close by, in Piazza de' Pitti, **Giannini**, founded in 1856, is famous for its beautiful marbled papers.

Just beyond Piazza di San Felice, in Via Romana, is the entrance to the **Museo La Specola** (*open Thur-Tue 9 am-1 pm*). It is divided into two sections, both riveting, anyway on a rainy day.

Florence

The zoological section displays vast numbers of preserved animals, birds and fish, while the **Cere Anatomiche** is devoted to an extraordinary collection of anatomical wax models, mostly made 1775-1814. In a room of their own, the plague victims made by Gaetano Zumbo for the hypochondriac Cosimo 111 in the late 17thC are truly gruesome. Goes down well with children.

Back in Piazza di San Felice is **Casa Guidi**, home of the poets Robert Browning and Elizabeth Barrett Browning from 1848 until Elizabeth passed away 'as if she had fallen asleep' in 1861. Their apartment, which has been preserved (minus the furniture) is now available for holiday lets through the Landmark Trust in Britain (tel. 01628 825925). From here, dead straight Via Maggio runs towards the river, lined by *palazzi* which sprang up after the Medici moved to the Palazzo Pitti, and filled with impressive antique shops. You, however, should take the Via Mazzetta towards Piazza di Santo Spirito. On the corner of the two, notice **Palazzo Guadagni** (1504), with its trend-setting top-floor open *loggia*, now part of the Pensione Sorelle Bandini.

Piazza Santo Spirito is the hub of one of the last 'local' areas of inner Florence. In the mornings farmers come from the countryside to sell their freshly gathered produce, and housewives come to gossip and haggle. At night the mood changes when, especially in summer, there is often a young late-night crowd, which can be druggy (**Cabiria** is a popular nightlife bar). During the day, the piazza can be the perfect place for an outdoor meal (**Caffè Ricchi, Borgo Antico**). A place where the real locals go is the *latteria* on the corner of Via delle Caldaie and Via della Chiesa. You'll have to rub shoulders and thighs with the workers in the tiny back room as they tuck into delicious home-cooked food at rock bottom prices and then stay to play cards long into the afternoon.

The smooth, yellow, almost Mexican façade of **Santo Spirito** (see Sights & Places of Interest, page 61) dominates the piazza. When you have looked in, turn right along Via Sant'Agostino, the local shopping street dotted with *pasticcerie, pizzicherie, latterie* and grocers spilling over with *primizie* (spring vegetables). Turn left into Via de' Serragli, then first right along Via d'Ardiglione, a quiet backwater with an antique restorers' workshop on the left. There are many similar in the Santo Spirito district, where Florentine craftsmen have quietly pursued their trade for centuries. Further along, at **No. 30**, is the birthplace of Filippo Lippi. In 1421, at the age of 15, Lippi, an orphan, was placed with the monks of **Santa Maria del Carmine** round the corner. He must have watched Masaccio, an early influence on his style, painting the **Brancacci Chapel** there (see Sights & Places of Interest, pages 46-7) during the 1420s; in the 1480s Lippi's son Filippino returned there to complete Masolino's and Masaccio's unfinished frescoes.

A left turn into Via Santa Monaca leads to the Brancacci Chapel. Then head across the somewhat dispiriting Piazza del Carmine (although the **Trattoria del Carmine** may make a lunch break). The landmark dome is that of **San Frediano in Cestello**.

Turn right into Borgo San Frediano, and continue along blackened Via di Santo Spirito, with the traditional *trattoria* **Angiolino** on the left. Notice, next door at No. 14, the splendid frescoed ceiling: Florence is full of these sudden visual treats. Next, on the corner of Via de' Coverelli, comes **Palazzo Coverelli** with its *sgraffito* decoration.

In Piazza de' Frescobaldi, Buontalenti's 15thC corner **fountain** has been a folorn sight: encased for ages in corrugated iron, awaiting restoration; perhaps it is now free again.

The portico of **San Jacopo sopr'Arno**, now a concert venue, is Romanesque, moved in the 16thC from a dismantled church outside the city walls. Across the road, No. 17 is the medieval **Torre di Marsili**, with a charming Della Robbia *Annunciation* over the portal. Further along, another old tower, set back from the road, has been transformed into up-market apartments. And here is the Ponte Vecchio again, to take you back across the river.

SIGHTS OUTSIDE FLORENCE

After a hard day's sightseeing amongst the stone and brick of Florence, you may look longingly at the green hills which encircle it. The countryside around is one of the city's special attractions, and it's wise to plan for a day's excursion sometime during your stay. Here are some of the places you could visit which are not covered in our Local Explorations.

FIESOLE
Just 25 minutes on the frequent bus No. 7 from the station, Duomo or Piazza di San Marco and you are right out in the countryside at charming and sophisticated Fiesole. Many people base themselves here, making day trips into Florence (hotels include the swanky **Villa San Michele, LLL**; tel. 055 59451; fax 055 598734; and the simple pensione **Bencista, LL**; tel./fax 055 59163).

Fiesole's history stretches back further than that of Florence: it was an important Etruscan town and later a Roman one. It was suppressed by Florence in the 12thC. The heart of Fiesole is **Piazza Mino da Fiesole**, site of the Roman forum. Behind the **Duomo** is an excavation site, including the Roman theatre and baths. There are lovely views, particularly from the nearby hamlet of **San Domenico** (reached by Via Vecchia Fiesolana, passing **Villa Medici**). Here is the fine 15thC church of **San Domenico** and, nearby, that of **Badia Fiesolana**, with a pretty Romanesque façade and a truly splendid Renaissance interior.

There are plenty of restaurant/pizzerias in Fiesole. One recommendation is **Da Mario**. It's fun to pop up to Fiesole from Florence just for a meal, although in the summer it can be very crowded.

SETTIGNANO
Bus No. 10 from the station or Piazza di San Marco. A pleasant place to visit for a simple meal or a drink. You might walk there: two hours along lovely roads (Via Ferrucci and Via di Vincigliata) from Fiesole, passing two castles and Bernard Berenson's **Villa I Tatti**, which he left to Harvard University. The village is quieter than Fiesole, and again beautifully situated.

PARCO DEMIDOFF, PRATOLINO
Some 12 km N of Florence; bus No. 25a from the station or Piazza di San Marco; open Apr-Sept Fri-Sun 10 am-8 pm. Another pleasant place to go on a hot summer's weekend. The vast, delightfully shady park was laid out for Francesco I de' Medici. Its villa, along with the famous fountains and grottos designed by Buontalenti, disappeared in the 19thC – only Giambologna's half-stone, half-man fountain **Appennino** (1580) remains.

MEDICI VILLAS
Not suprisingly, the Medici built lavish country retreats in the Florentine hills. North of the city centre there are three which can be visited.

Villa La Petraia (Via della Petraia 40; park open Tues-Sun 9 am-7.30 pm, 4.30 in winter, 5.30 and 6.30 in spring and autumn; (villa closes one hour earlier and is closed 2nd, 4th Mon of month) was remodelled by Buontalenti for Ferdinando de' Medici and has lovely sloping grounds with stunning views over Florence. Close by is **Villa di Castello** (park open Tues-Sun 9 am-7.30 pm, 4.30 in winter, 5.30 in spring and 6.30 in autumn; (closed 2nd, 4th Mon of month). Only the grounds are open, but they are spectacular, with Tribolo's fountain and Vasari's grotto as highlights.

A little to the south-east lies **Villa Careggi** (Viale Pieraccini 17; open only by appointment, tel. 055 4279981). Cosimo Il Vecchio, his son Piero and grandson Lorenzo all died here.

MUGELLO
NE of Florence; access via Pratolino on the SS65. Ideally you need a car to visit this fertile region of gently rolling hills, dotted with the splendid villas of the Florentine élite, but little bothered by tourists.

From Pratolino, head north-east to the **Convento di Monte Senario** from where there are panoramic views. The towns of the Mugello are not particularly interesting (Borgo San Lorenzo, Scarperia, Pontassieve and Rufina, famous for its wine), so stick to the villages: **Bosco ai Frati** and **Sant' Agata**, which both have respectable churches; **San Piero a Sieve**, pleasant for lunch at the hotel **Ebe** or at **La Felicina**; **San Godenza**, over to the east, with its Romanesque abbey; **Vicchio**, the birthplace of Fra Angelico; and tiny **Vespignano**, the birthplace of Giotto. **La Casa del Prosciutto** at **Ponte Vicchio** is great for lunch and for purchasing local goodies.

Florence

RECOMMENDED HOTELS

Casci, L-LL; Via Cavour 13; tel. 055 211686; fax 055 2396461; cards accepted.
Some way north of San Lorenzo, simple and in a relatively busy situation, but welcoming and well run. Rooms are Spartan but clean; those at the rear are peaceful. Once the home of Rossini. Some original frescoes survive in the building.

Excelsior, LLL; Piazza d'Ognissanti 3; tel. 055 264201; fax 055 217400; cards accepted.
The city's grandest old hotel, all marble and polish; now owned by CIGA.

Hermitage, LLL; Vicolo Marzio 1; tel. 055 287216; fax 055 212208; cards accepted.
Everything at the Hermitage is small, like a dolls' house – only upside down, with the neat bedrooms on the lower floors and the pretty sitting room and breakfast room on the fifth floor. A flower-filled terrace offers views across the pantiles to the Duomo; the Ponte Vecchio is right beside the hotel.

J and J, LLL; Via di Mezzo 20; tel. 055 2345005; fax 055 240282; cards accepted.
Bohemian *chic* in a converted monastery peacefully situated between the Duomo and Sant'Ambrogio market. Rooms are all different, mostly spacious, and there are plenty of original features – vaulted ceilings, frescoes, wooden beams. Pretty breakfast area, with a patio garden enlivened by elegant white parasols.

Loggiato dei Serviti, LL-LLL; Piazza della Santissima Annunziata 3; tel. 055 289592; fax 055 289595; cards accepted.
What was once a modest *pensione* has been restored to become one of the city's most atmospheric small hotels. The decoration is a skilful blend of old and new, executed with understated flair. There is a bright breakfast room, and a little bar where you can sip your Campari whilst browsing through glossy magazines. The hotel is in a beautiful square, opposite the Spedale degli Innocenti.

Morandi alla Crocetta, L-LLL; Via Laura 50; tel. 055 234474; fax 055 2480954; cards accepted.
Kathleen Doyle came to Florence as a young woman in the 1920s to be chaperoned by her aunt, a governess whose Italian employers set her up with a *pensione* at Loggiato dei Serviti (see above). Mrs Doyle (as she prefers to be known) settled in Florence, married an Italian and opened her own hotel, which has the feel of a private home, and which she now runs with her son. Like her, it has great character and charm, each room different, and full of eye-catching objects – architectural salvage, fragments of frescoes, old painted tiles, a portrait of Mrs Doyle as a young beauty. Attention to detail in bedrooms and bathrooms is second to none.

Osteria dei Cento Poveri, LLLL; Via Pallazuolo 31r; tel. 055 218846; cards accepted closed Tue, Wed lunch.
Don't be put off by the number of tourists in this tiny restaurant (or go there off-season); it is excellent. It's fun to sit facing the open kitchen and watch dishes being prepared on the spot. Many have a Pugliese influence due to the origins of the owners. Creative and beautifully presented fish and meat dishes (ravioli with seafood, courgette flan with prawn sauce, tagliatelle with baby broad beans and shrimp, pigeon breast filet in a rich wine sauce.

Porta Rossa, LL; Via Porta Rossa 19; tel. 055 287551; fax 055 282179; cards accepted.
There has been a hotel on this site since the 14thC, although the present incarnation dates from the 19thC. The hotel retains its period character, with vast bedrooms, individually decorated, and an air of faded gentility.

Regency, LLL; Piazza Massimo d'Azeglio 3; tel. 055 245247; fax 055 2346735; cards accepted.
Along with the Excelsior, this is the city's best known deluxe hotel, but with one fifth of the number of rooms, it has a much more intimate appeal.

Sorelle Bandini, LL; Piazza di Santo Spirito; tel. 055 215308; cards accepted.

> Many of Florence's restaurants close on Sundays and Mondays. Here is a checklist of recommendable restaurants which are not.
>
> **Open on a Sunday**
> Angiolino (lunch only)
> Aquacotta
> Dino (lunch only)
> Garga (dinner only)
> Latini
> La Maremma
> Omero
> Da Penello (lunch only)
>
> **Open on a Monday**
> Aquacotta
> Borgo Antico
> Cantinetta Antinori
> Carmine
> La Casalinga
> Coco Lezzone
> Enoteca Pinchiorri
> La Maremma
> La Maremmana
> Miro
> Omero
> Sostanza
> Il Teatro

Basic rooms, unstuffy atmosphere, and the bonus of a lovely roof-top *loggia* (the first of its type in the city – built around 1500). Both the *pensione* and its location are best appreciated by the young – or young at heart.

Splendor, LL; *Via San Gallo 30; tel. 055 483427; fax 055 461276; cards accepted.*

A peaceful and still affordable *pensione*, close to San Marco. It has a sunny terrace full of plants and several historic features. The furnishings and some modern additions are not entirely harmonious.

Torre di Bellosguardo, LLL; *Via de'Michelozzi 2; tel. 055 2298145; fax 055 229008; cards accepted.*

In Oltrarno, on hill just south of Porta Romana. Money-no-object, this would be my first choice. The 16thC family home of the owner, Amerigo Franchetti, it has stone walls, tiled floors, Persian rugs, colossal wooden doors and venerable antique furniture; yet, although grand, it is not at all gaunt or dreary. Each room is a separate world, as much sitting-room as bedroom, and the lovely gardens (with secluded swimming pool) are as enticing as the interior. The unassuming gentility of the owners is a refreshing contrast to many a haughty hireling in Florence's central hotels.

RECOMMENDED RESTAURANTS

In Florence it is usually essential to book in advance. The following are my favourites; the restaurants in the additional list are also highly recommended.

Alle Murate, LLL; *Via Ghibellina 52r; tel. 055 240618; cards accepted; closed Mon.*

One of Florence's more elegant restaurants and highly thought-of. The food here is creative and imaginatively served. There are several set menus ('*menu dègustazione*'); fish, 'creative' and Tuscan which all feature some six or seven courses, or choose from the carte. Particularly impressive wine list.

Aquacotta, L; *Via dei Pilastri 51r; tel. 055 242907; cards none; closed Wed.*

A cosy little *trattoria* serving simple Tuscan dishes, including its namesake, the peasant soup *aquacotta* – literally 'cooked water' – but nonetheless delicious when prepared well.

Borgo Antico, L; *Piazza di Santo Spirito 6; tel. 055 210437; cards none; closed Sun, Mon lunch.*

Eating out in this tree-shaded piazza is a delight for lunch or outside on a summer's evening. With its pizzas and fish dishes, some unusual, Borgo Antico, is ideal for a casual meal, though noise levels are high.

Cantinetta Antinori, LLL-LLLL; *Piazza degli Antinori 3r; tel. 055 292234; cards accepted; closed Sat, Sun, Aug.*

Located in one of the most elegant of Florence's 15thC *palazzi*, this is a smart wine bar and restaurant where you can sample wines from the Antinori estates. Food is Tuscan, and

Florence

much of the produce comes from the family farms, including the cheeses. You can have a snack, or a full meal.

Cibreo, LLLL; Via A. Del Verrocchio 8r; tel. 055 2341100; cards accepted; closed Sun, Mon, Aug.

Getting on for 15 years old, and Cibreo has taken over the block: restaurant, trattoria, café and take-out food store. There's a branch in Tokyo too. The restaurant, famous for its superb traditional Tuscan food, and for not serving pasta, is expensive. For half the price you can eat exactly the same fare, minus the flourishes, in the white-tiled trattoria around the corner.

Coco Lezzone, LL; Via Parioncino 26; tel. 055 287178; cards none; closed Sun, Tues dinner, Aug.

The annual bill for olive oil alone is around 20 million lire at Coco Lezzone because, along with the rest of the raw ingredients, only the best is used. The Tuscan food is excellent – you might try trippa alla Fiorentina, the tripe here being particularly tender – but the atmosphere is somewhat po-faced. The self-consciously chic clientele and the clinical white-tiled walls probably don't help. The Prince of Wales has eaten here, amongst other luminaries, which keeps the prices too high.

Garga, LL-LLL; Via del Moro 48r; tel. 055 2398898; cards accepted; closed lunch and Mon.

An intimate spot run by a Florentine chef and his Canadian wife. The Tuscan cuisine has unusual twists, such as pasta served with a sauce of cream, parmesan, lemon rind and cognac, or lamb served with a red pepper sauce. Thanks to the proprietors, Garga has an atmosphere refreshingly different from anywhere else in town. Signor Garga has been known to burst into song.

Latini, LL-LL; Via dei Palchetti 6r; tel. 055 210916; credit cards none; closed Mon, Aug.

A Florentine institution. If you come before 8 pm, be prepared to queue (bring your telefonino and make phone calls to while away the time like everyone else). Once inside you will find a mixture of bemused tourists and well-heeled Florentines, all happy to squeeze up together at communal tables and raise their voices above the racket. Avoid the pasta and stick to the superb prosciutto, salami and bistecca, and dishes such as ribollita or zuppa di farro. Latini has been in the family since the turn of the century when it was a wine shop. Now it is run by one of the original owner's grandson.

La Maremmana, L-LL; Via de' Macci 77r; tel. 055 241226; cards accepted; closed Sun.

A local trattoria which consists of a simple, white-walled room in front, and another entirely encased in bamboo behind. The attraction here is the price: for the full benefit, stick to one of the straightforward fixed-price menus. Service can be surly in the typically Florentine way.

Omero, L-LL; Via Pian dei Guillari 11, Arcetri; tel 055 220053; cards accepted; closed Tues, Aug.

You will feel you have earned your meal if you walk for about half an hour out of the city and into the hills to this beautifully located restaurant (otherwise it's a short taxi ride). When booking, ask for a tavola con panorama to ensure a window seat and a view. Nothing original on the menu, so stick to your favourites – perhaps crostini toscani or salumi misti (excellent) followed by ravioli filled with ricotta and spinach. A small food shop sells cured meats, cheeses and oils.

Over the road is the house where Galileo lived in exile.

Da Penello, L-LL; Via Dante Alighieri 4r; tel. 055 294848; closed Sun dinner, Mon, Aug.

Next door to the Casa di Dante, Da Penello is renowned for its vast selection of antipasti, laid out temptingly on a large central table. Surprisingly few restaurants offer this treat, and you may well want to stick to the delights offered there rather than move on to the traditional pasta and meat dishes on the menu. The trattoria dates back to 1500 when it was patronized by the likes of Cellini and other artists (penello means paintbrush). These day it has a light and airy dining room and a garden for summer.

Da Ruggero, LL-LLL; Via Senese 89r; tel. 055 220542; no cards; closed Tue, Wed, Aug.

A small, traditional but excellent trattoria just south of Porta Romana; booking is essential. Food is traditional, unpretentious Florentine, of the kind that 'Mamma' would make. Thick *ribollita* (bread soup), *pappardelle* with rich, dark hare sauce, mixed boiled meats with pungent '*salsa verde*', home-made puddings. Great value.

Da Stephano LLL; Via Senese 271, Galluzzo; tel. 055 2049105; cards accepted; closed Sun (only open for dinner).

Considered by many to be the best fish restaurant in town, and worth the short taxi ride south to Porto Romana if you don't have a car. Stefano's – bustling and always packed – serves only the freshest of fish and seafood. The set menu is probably the best value and will certainly fill you up, but there is a great variety of dishes à la carte as well. Platters of lightly steamed crustaceans with homemade mayonnaise, steaming pans of tomatoey, garlicky, fishy 'spaghetti allo Stefano', whole fish roasted in the oven on a bed of potatoes and black olives.

Sostanza, L-LL; Via del Porcellana 25; tel. 055 212691; cards none; closed Sat, Sun.

A *trattoria* in the simplest sense since the mid-19thC, Sostanza has retained its communal tables, its excellent no-nonsense food, and its absolutely no-nonsense service. (There's not much room and you're not encouraged to linger.) All that has changed is the clientele – gentrified – and the prices – up. Plenty of well-known faces in search of the 'real' Florence have contemplated a plate of popular *petto di pollo al burro* or *bistecca alla Fiorentina*.

Taverna del Bronzino, LLL; Via della Ruote 25/27r; tel. 055 495220; cards accepted; closed Sun and Aug.

Cool, white-washed, vaulted rooms on an unassuming street north of the central market is the setting for this restaurant which serves Tuscan dishes with a twist. It is an excellent place to try such classics as *Bistecca all Fiorentina* or *ossobuco*, truffle-flavoured *tortelli* or deep-fried brains with artichokes. Often lots of tourists, but they are out-numbered by discerning locals.

ADDITIONAL RECOMMENDATIONS

Alessi (La Pentola d'Oro), L; Via di Mezzo 26r; tel. 055 241821.

Run by food historian Guiseppe Alessi. Pay a small annual membership fee (worth it) to eat in the dining club – excellent value.

Angiolino, L-LL; Via Santo Spirito 57r; tel. 055 2398976; closed Sun dinner, Mon.

Atmospheric traditional *trattoria*, with waiters in long white aprons and a stove in the middle of the room. Surly service.

Carmine, L; Piazza del Carmine 18; tel. 055 218601; closed Sat, Sun, Aug.

Useful place near the Brancacci Chapel, long-established.

La Casalinga, L; Via del Michelozzo 9r; tel. 055 218624; closed Sun, Aug.

Near Santo Spirito. Cheap and cheerful, a haven for hard-up tourists.

Dino, LL; Via Ghibellina 51; tel. 055 241452; closed Sun dinner, Mon, Aug.

Pleasant atmosphere, excellent wine list, interesting food (try the *stracotto del Granduca* or *filetto di maiale al cartoccio*) and wide-ranging cheeseboard.

Enoteca Pinchiorri, LLLL; Via Ghibellina 87; tel. 055 242777; closed Sun, Mon and Wed lunch.

Famous temple of gastronomy, with a world-class wine cellar which makes oenophiles go weak at the knees. The bill may have the same effect. Definitely a money-making operation – smooth and somewhat heartless.

Ricchi, L; Piazza di Santo Spirito.

Popular ice cream bar and café with dining room behind, intriguingly decorated with dozens of outlines of Santo Spirito. Curb your lunchtime hunger with a simple dish such as *bollito misto* followed by ice cream.

Zà Zà, L; Piazza del Mercato Centrale 26r; tel. 055 215411; closed Sun.

Bustling, animated *trattoria* right by the Mercato Centrale.

Seeing the Region: 1

Northern and Western Tuscany
Between Livorno and Florence
Pisa, Lucca and Pistoia: the western approach to Florence

99 km; map Touring Club Italiano Toscana

Each year thousands of people fly to Pisa's International Galileo Galilei Airport, collect a hire car or board a train or a bus and whisk without a backward glance to Florence, a journey of an hour or two. Thousands more alight from their tour buses on the northern fringe of Pisa long enough to see its Leaning Tower before pushing on down the *autostrada*. Exit signs for the cities along the way flash past: Lucca, Pistoia, Prato. The surroundings look unattractive, industrial. They do not know that they are missing some of the loveliest things in Tuscany – churches and sculpture in particular – set in lovely historic centres, full of medieval charm and interest.

Beginning at the important port of Livorno, our route moves north to Pisa and on to enchanting Lucca, and then follows the main road to Florence, taking in the spa resort Montecatini Terme, undervalued Pistoia and finally Prato on an east-west line parallel to the industrialized Arno Valley to the south and shadowed by the gentle foothills of the Alpi Apuane and Garfagnana to the north (see Local Explorations: 12).

If you were to visit each city in turn, you would find that they all have very separate identities and atmospheres, surprising for places so close together, but less so when you consider that Pisa, Lucca, Pistoia and Prato were all independent medieval city-states, battling with varying degrees of success to remain out of Florentine control. Nowadays these are thriving centres of local trade: metalworks, chemicals, horticulture, textiles and so on. Their sprawling suburbs are not pretty, yet their centres have little changed since the glory days. And just a few kilometres from each city you will find unspoilt Tuscan countryside as well as grand villas with splendid gardens: as our suggested detours reveal.

NW TUSCANY / Pisa, Lucca and Pistoia

• Lucca, city wall

TRANSPORT

Air travellers are served by Galileo Galilei airport at Pisa. From the airport, an express train connects with Florence, stopping at Pisa Centrale station where you can take trains to Lucca, then all the towns mentioned *en route* to Florence as well as to Livorno. A coach service runs between Florence and Pisa airport when no train is available. Frequent Lazzi buses also connect the towns: it is quickest to travel by bus from Pisa to Lucca (from Piazza Sant' Antonio, just N of the station). For drivers, the A11 *autostrada* connects Lucca with Florence. A new superstrada connects Pisa/Livorno fo Florence.

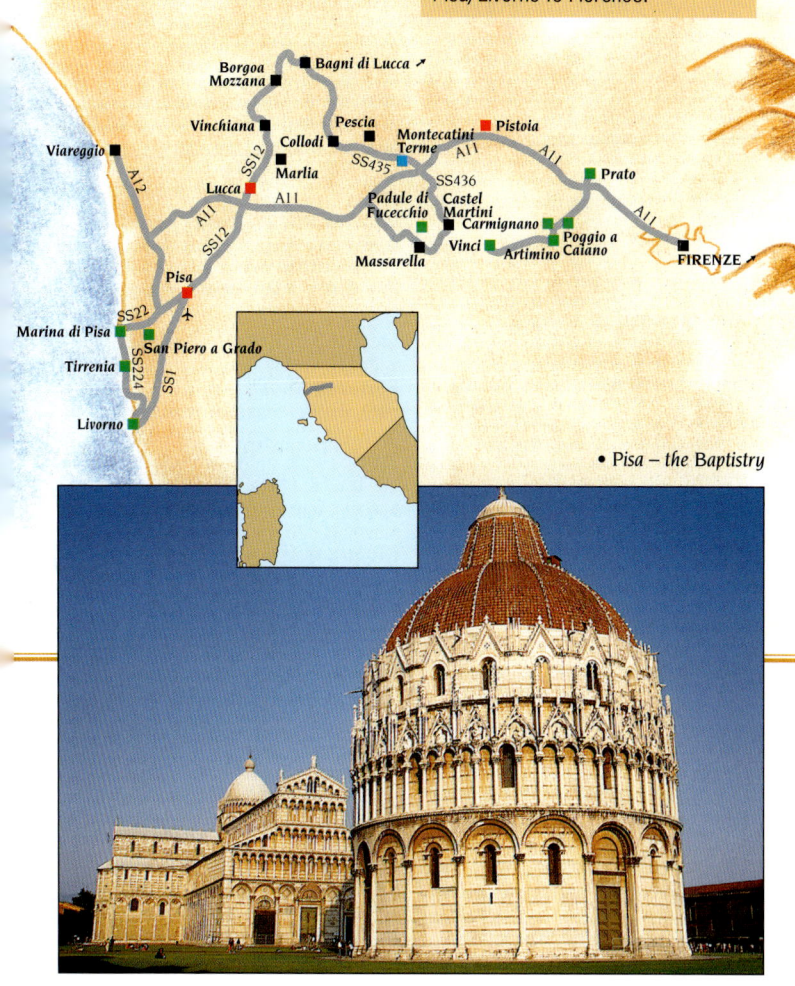

• Pisa – the Baptistry

Seeing the Region: 1

SIGHTS & PLACES OF INTEREST

BAGNI DI LUCCA
See Detour – Between Lucca and Montecatini, page 88.

FLORENCE
See pages 39-81

LIVORNO ×
On the SS1, 22 km SW of Pisa. Tourist information: Piazza Cavour 6, tel 0586 898111; Molo Mediceo (ferry terminal, summer only). Ferries: to Corsica, Sardinia, Sicily and Capraia. Station: Piazza Dante, 2 km E of centre; taxi or No. 1 bus to Piazza Grande. Buses: for Florence, Pisa etc (Lazzi) from just off Piazza Cavour; for southern towns from Piazza Grande. Parking: restricted; best bet is station.

> **DETOUR – CAPRAIA**
> A two-and-a-half hour boat trip from Livorno takes you to this rugged volcanic rock island of the Tuscan Archipelago. There is a tiny harbour and a little town above, connected by the island's only tarmac road, as well as a handful of decent hotels and simple restaurants. You can go diving, bird watching or take a boat trip around the island. The tourist office (Via Assunzione) has details. Best in late spring.

• *Monumento dei Quattro Mori*

Strangely, for it is the second largest city in Tuscany, there is not much to see or to do in Livorno, except to watch the thriving port at work, mingle with the sailors and the African street vendors and then go to a *trattoria* and discover the exceptionally good fish (see Restaurant Recommendations, pages 96-7). This news may well come as a relief – no artistic consience to be pricked here.

You will probably find yourself to begin with in Piazza Grande. The **Duomo** was completely rebuilt in 1959 after the bomb damage which severely affected Livorno. (A U.S. military base, Camp Darby, still operates north of the city, and the **American Market**, famous after the war for its army surplus supplies, continues daily in Piazza XX Settembre, although these days it's an ordinary flea market.) From here, make for the port via Livorno's prettiest corner, **Venezia Nuova**. (From Piazza Grande head north through Largo Municipio.)

The octagonal church of Santa Caterina stands in the middle of this tranquil little 'new Venice' quarter of canals lined with old fisherman's houses and dotted with colourful boats. The moated **Fortezza Nuova** (1590) stands to the east, the **Fortezza Vecchia** (1521) to the west. A bridge at the end of Viale Caprera leads to the harbour, full of fishing boats. Along the quay, in Piazza Micheli, Pietro Tacca's four tense bronze slaves (1626) of the **Monumento dei Quattro Mori** were meant to symbolize naval victories over the North Africans. Instead, they are a powerful reminder of Livorno's once-thriving slave market. They surround an inept earlier statue of Ferdinando I by Bandini.

So where are all the usual medieval buildings and Renaissance altarpieces? The reason they don't exist is that Livorno was not founded until 1571 when Cosimo I de' Medici chose it as the replacement for Pisa's silted-up port. Sir Robert Dudley, son of Queen Elizabeth I of England's favourite, the Earl of Leicester, played a big part in the construction and administration of the port, beginning a long English connection with the city (known to them as Leghorn).

Cosimo's successor, Ferdinando, took the unprecedented step of making Livorno a free port – where both unrestricted trade and religion could be practised. It soon became a refuge for persecuted minorities, who prospered here. Now for the fish.

LUCCA ⚘ ×
On the A11/12 and SS435, 74 km W of Florence. Tourist office: Piazzale Verdi, tel 0583 419689. Station: Piazzale Ricasoli, just S of the walls and the Duomo. Buses (Clap and Lazzi): Piazzale Verdi, just inside the walls. Parking: possible inside the walls in various places including Piazza Napoleone (tariff), but difficult – best to park in one of the free car parks outside such as the one opposite Porta San Donato, near Piazzale Verdi on the city's W side.

Everyone admires Lucca, urbane and aloof within its superb encircling walls, and apparently they always have. The Roman colony was a favourite with Julius

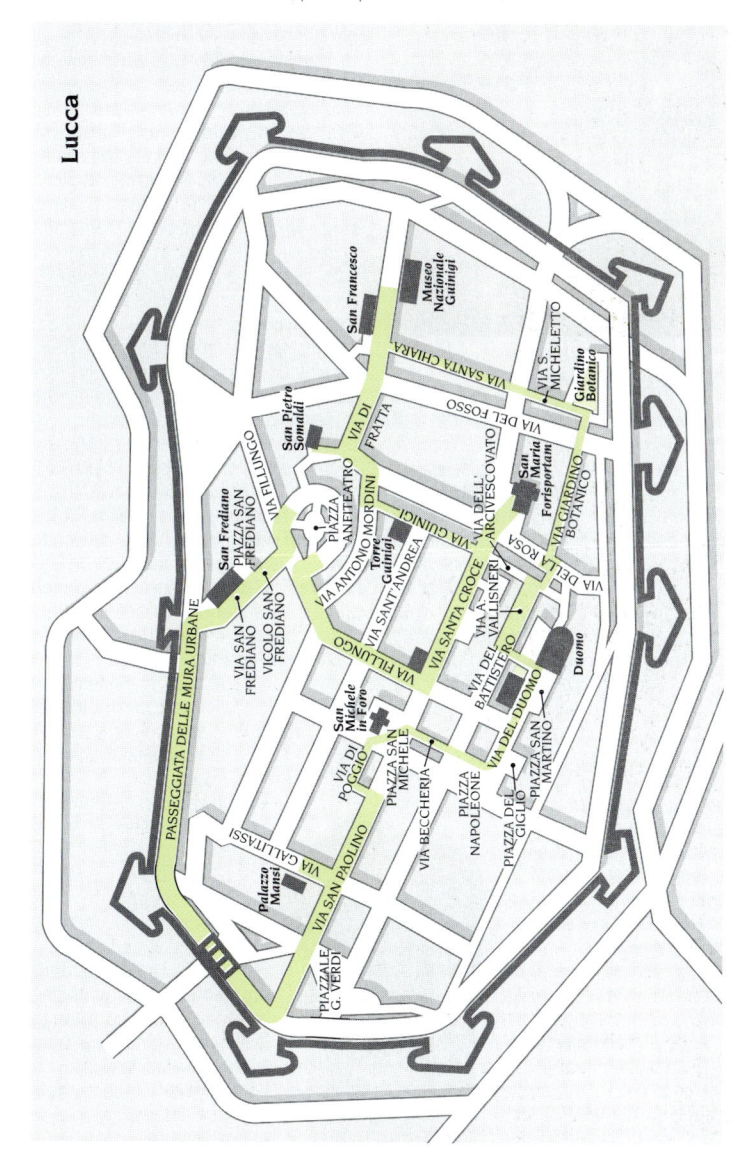

Seeing the Region: 1

• *Lucca, from Guinigi Tower.*

Caesar (it was here that he, Pompey and Crassus met to form the First Triumvirate). By the 14thC, having made its fortune from the production of silk, Lucca was having a hard time keeping the Pisans and Florentines at bay when in 1314, another fan, an exiled nobleman-adventurer called Castruccio Castracani came to rescue his home town from Pisa. He succeeded, and Lucca remained an independent city state, protected and ennobled by its magnificent 16th and 17thC walls, until as late as the 19thC. In 1805 Napoleon gave it as a present to his sister, Elisa Baciocchi; only in 1847 did it became part of Tuscany. Lucca and the Lucchese, now as always: proud, sophisticated, careful, discreet, content.

Walk/bike ride
Lucca has embraced the bicycle: everyone rides one and it is the most amusing – and swiftest – way of seeing the tiny city. Bikes can be hired from 'Barbetti', under the sign Cicli, in Via dell'Anfiteatro 23 (*open 8.30-noon and 2.30-7 pm*) behind the Piazza Anfiteatro. Two very leisurely days, or one brisker day, with a break for lunch, could be spent on the route described below, but to help you see the sights in your own order, they are picked out in bold.

Start Piazza Anfiteatro, an entirely delightful transformation from Roman amphitheatre to medieval marketplace, whose tall, irregular houses trace the ellipse of the Roman walls. Turn left into the fittingly named Via Fillungo, course of the evening *passeggiata*, which threads its way through the city centre and is lined by chic shops (notice **Carli**, selling silver, and **Caffè di Simo**). The charming **San Cristoforo** shelters the names of all Lucca's dead in two world wars. Just past it, a left turn leads towards **Santa Maria Forisportam**, named for having once lain just outside the city walls, with a charming Pisan façade.

From the piazza, follow the sign for **Torre Guinigi** on Via Sant' Andrea, Lucca's famous tower with ilex trees growing on its roof. A stiff climb takes you to the top, with a view over the whole red-roofed city. The Guinigis were for centuries Lucca's leading family, and their *palazzi* lie on either side of Via Guinigi, which you should now follow. A right, then left turn brings you to **San Pietro Somaldi** with a pretty grey and white 13thC façade. Via di Fratta leads to **San Francesco**, a 13thC preaching church with simple façade and barn-like interior. Just beyond, on the right, the **Museo Nazionale Guinigi**, housed in Paolo Guinigi's 1418 villa, contains a respectable mix of sculpture, painting and craftwork. In the painting gallery look out for the intarsia panels, showing views of Lucca.

This is Lucca's dreary eastern quarter, so hurry back to the old core of the city by turning down Via Santa Chiara opposite San Francesco. Continue straight ahead until you reach the **Giardino Botanico**, which is as inviting as it looks behind its high walls, with specimens from all over Tuscany and plenty in flower year round. Now

• *Guinigi Tower.*

Façade of San Michele in Foro, Lucca.

cross the water-filled Via del Fosso (ditch) which marked the outer limits of the Roman city and wiggle your way to the Duomo by turning left into Via della Rosa, immediately right, right again, then first left down the Via Vallisneri.

Piazza San Martino is graced by a palm-filled walled garden belonging to Palazzo Micheletti. The façade of the **Duomo** (San Martino), crushed up on the right to accommodate the campanile, is a Pisan Romanesque masterpiece which captivates the eye with its inlaid marble decorations, its three tiers of columns, each carved differently, and its wealth of sculpture and bas-relief in the portico, well worth inspection.

Local sculptor Matteo Civitali carved the octagonal marble **tempietto** in 1484 to house the revered *Volto Santo* (Holy Face), supposedly a contemporary likeness of Christ by Nicodemus which then made its way by boat and ox cart to Lucca without human help; in fact the cedarwood crucifix dates from the 13thC. In medieval times it was famous throughout Europe; it is carried in a night-time procession every 13th September. In the sacristy, is the lovely **tomb of Ilaria del Carretto** (1405) by Jacopo della Quercia. She was the youthful bride of Paolo Guinigi and many of the Lucchese characteristics seem to be embodied in her still form.

Via del Duomo leads past **San Giovanni** (where excavations dating back to Roman times are on view) to Piazza del Giglio, graced by its famous **Teatro del Giglio** (naturally, hot on Puccini operas), and by the **Hotel Universo** (see Recommended Hotels, page 96) and the

> **DETOUR – THE COAST ROAD**
> If you have time to spare, you could drive between Livorno and Pisa by way of the SS224 coast road. This takes in the seaside resorts of **Tirrenia** and **Marina di Pisa** (featureless, straight coastline, but there's a good fish restaurant in genteel Marina di Pisa: **L'Arsella, LL**; *tel.* 050 36615; *closed Tues eve, Wed*). The road then turns inland to follow the Arno towards Pisa. A right turn leads to the atmospheric Romanesque basilica of **San Piero a Grado**. Frescoes inside tell the *Story of St Peter*, for the church is said to have been built on the spot where he first landed in Italy: excavations show there was indeed a landing stage here.

Seeing the Region: 1

> **DETOUR – PADULE DE FUCECCHIO**
> Leaving Montecatini Terme, travel south on the SS436, turning right for Castel Martini or, 14 km from Montecatini, for Massarella into a most un-Tuscan district – not a vine, olive or cypress in sight. Meandering lanes take you into the *Padule* (swamps). The strange picture of waterways between long curtains of woods is enhanced by poplars and cane-breaks. Punt-like boats of dark wood, occasional disused mills and tiny huts of the L.I.P.U. (a bird-protection society) are the only signs of human life. From Castel Martini you can walk on easy paths (muddy after rain) across the **Paduletta di Ramona**, a more varied marshland with abundant birdlife including bitterns, herons, grebes and snipe.

restaurant **Il Giglio** (see Recommended Restaurants, page 97). This piazza merges into **Piazza Napoleone**, flanked by the unremarkable **Palazzo Ducale**, now government offices. Straight ahead, along Via Beccheria, is the hub of town, Piazza San Michele.

For most onlookers, **San Michele in Foro** (this was the Roman forum) has the pick of all Lucca's fine church fronts, if only for its sheer exuberance and the way that its arcaded Pisan façade goes shooting into the air with nothing behind it as if it were a stage set. (They meant to heighten the church roof to match the height of the façade, but never got round to it.) Again, every candystick column is different, and the theatrical effect is completed by a huge archangel on the very top, flanked by trumpeting cherubs, and by Civitali's golden-rayed *Madonna* on the corner. Admirers of Filippo Lippi should go inside for his painting *Saints Helena, Jerome, Sebastian and Roch*.

Opposite the church, a right turn along Via di Poggio reveals **Casa Museo Puccini**, the composer's birthplace. Cross the little piazza and turn right into Via San Paolino, and then right again into Via Gallitassi where the rococo Palazzo Mansi houses a **Pinacoteca Nazionale** which contains a mixed bag of paintings of the same period. Retrace, cross Piazzale Verdi and mount the **ramparts**, Lucca's most distinctive feature. In the early 19thC a tree-lined promenade was created along the top of the walls which you can now follow; the rest of the world is

> **DETOUR – BETWEEN LUCCA AND MONTECATINI**
> The SS12 follows the River Serchio north towards Bagni di Lucca. After 8 km a road leads east towards three highly recommended 16thC and 17thC Lucchese villas and their gardens which are open to the public. They are: **Villa Reale** at Marlia, with particularly interesting grounds, designed like a series of rooms in thick woodland and including a beautiful open-air theatre, scene of Lucca's Summer Music Festival; **Villa Mansi** at Segromigno; and **Villa Torrigiani** at Camigliano.
>
> Returning to the SS12, continue on to Vinchiana and a turning right to the beautifully sited Romanesque **San Giorgio di Brancoli**, then to the famously curved ancient footbridge, **Ponte della Maddalena** at Borgo a Mozzano.
>
> The church here contains a favourite of mine: a wooden carving of **San Bernardino**, with a movingly pious and gentle expression.
>
> Just beyond **Bagni di Lucca** (see Local Explorations: 11) a turning right off the SS12 leads to **Collodi** where you will find the **Parco di Pinocchio**, a low-key theme park (maze, museum) dedicated to Italy's favourite children's character, whose author used to stay at nearby **Castello Garzoni**. The castle's splendid formal gardens are open to the public. The road to Montecatini passes close to **Pescia**, noted for growing and exporting flowers. Commerce is rather mundane these days, but lavish flower markets are still held in summer. North-west of here stretches the hilly **Valdinievole**, pleasant motoring and excellent walking country dotted with attractive villages.

NW Tuscany / Pisa, Lucca and Pistoia

Tettuccio baths, Montecatini Terme.

kept at bay by a broad swathe of parkland. There are 11 bastions and four gateways.

Just before dropping down from the ramparts at the next exit, notice the rear of **Palazzo Pfanner** with its splendid galleried staircase and (somewhat jaded) formal garden full of classical statuary. Wend your way round to the front of **San Frediano**: you might have spotted the glittering Byzantine-style 13thC mosaic on the façade from Torre Guinigi. Pop into the grand interior where you will immediately see the beautiful 12thC **fonte lustrale**, and behind it, a lunette of the *Annunciation* by Andrea della Robbia. Close by is the chapel of Santa Zita, where lies the ghastly mummified remains of the patron saint of maids: each year on April 26 her uncorrupted body is brought out for people to touch. Also worth lighting up: the second chapel on the left for its recently restored frescoes, including the journey of the *Volto Santo*, by Aspertini (1508).

With San Frediano behind you, head for Via Fillungo and, if you need to give your bike back, into Piazza Anfiteatro once again.

MONTECATINI TERME

On the A11/SS435, 16 km W of Pistoia. Tourist office: Viale Verde 66, tel 0572 772244. Stations: Centrale and Succursale (closest to centre; trains stop at both). Buses: Via Toti, close to Succursale.

With some 250 hotels in all price brackets, a wealth of leisure facilities (swimming, tennis, golf, trotting races, nightclub) and plenty of greenery you could do much worse than to make this genteel, orderly and quietly fashionable spa town, full of well-dressed visitors, your base for summertime exploration of the region (the resort virtually closes down off season). Better still if you want to take the waters or bathe at one of the 11 grandiose thermal *bagni* dotted around the immaculate Parco delle Terme, each specializing in a particular treatment. **Tettuccio** is the most prestigious, while **Excelsior** offers the full range and is open year round (the others from May to Oct). Tickets and information are available from the main office, the Direzione delle Terme, located at Viale Verdi 41.

Ilex-bordered Viale Verdi (the composer was a frequent visitor here) is the

89

Seeing the Region: 1

place for an early evening stroll, a coffee at **Gambrinus** and a wicked whipped cream *cialde*, speciality of the boulevard's *pasticcerie*. Further indulgence is possible in **Montecatini Alto**, reached by funicular (or road). In its friendly little *piazza* the treat is an ice-cream creation called *mangia e bevi*. The idiosyncratic turretted theatre dates from the early 20thC. From the ruined *rocca* there are splendid views of the Valdinievole (Valley of the Mists) and of the neighbouring spa town of **Monsummano**. The surviving turrets of this vast fortress recall desperate battles in the old three-cornered Pisa-Lucca-Florence contest.

PISA ⇌ ✕

On the SS1, 77 km W of Florence. Tourist information: at station, tel. 050 42291, and Campo dei Miracoli, behind the Leaning Tower, tel. 050 560464. Station: Centrale, Piazza Stazione (left luggage office; a 25-minute walk to Campo dei Miracoli; trains for Florence etc. and for Pisa airport). Buses: for town and airport from Centrale Station; for outside Pisa from Piazza Sant' Antonio, adjacent to Piazza Vittorio Emanuele 11, just N of station. Parking: very difficult; try to choose a hotel with a garage.

Pisa was once a great maritime power, at its zenith in the 11th and 12thC. Then the bad times came: its fleet was destroyed by the Genoese, its all-important harbour silted up, and, in 1406, the city, a spent force, fell to Florence. Today its great monuments, including that supreme symbol of tourist Italy, the Leaning Tower, is beseiged by modern hordes, chiefly of the 'Rome-in-a-day-including-the-Pope' brigade. Away from the monuments, the city centre is thronged not by tourists, but by students of the university, which also dates back to the glory days. A sprinkling of sailors on shore leave and of African street vendors add spice. June is a festive time to visit, when the annual **Gioco del Ponte**, a mock battle in Renaissance costume, and the torchlit **Festa di San Ranieri** take place.

Pisa's cathedral complex, the famous **Field of Miracles (Campo dei Miracoli)** is strangely detached from the city, situated in its north-eastern corner. Most tourists, debouching here from their charabangs, never see the rest of the town. It's more interesting, though, to see what else Pisa has to offer and leave the miracles until last: coming across them through a network of small streets helps to put them into context. The following stroll takes in the main sights, but if you wish to see them separately, their names are picked out in **bold** type.

Walk

Start Piazza dei Cavalieri, Pisa's most charming open space, either swarming with students or eerily quiet. On the Palazzo dell'Orologio (the building with the archway and clock above), a plaque recounts that in 1288 Count Ugolino della Gherardesca was walled up and left to die for suspected treachery. His sons and grandsons died with him. The Cavalieri were a so-called order of crusaders begun by Cosimo I de' Medici (statue) in 1561 to combat (and loot) the offending Turks: their palace is the splendid curving building covered in exuberant *sgraffitti* (notice the signs of the zodiac between the ground floor windows) by Vasari. If only Vasari had stuck to this and hadn't been allowed (by his master, Cosimo I) to cover vast tracts of Tuscan churches and palaces with his witless frescoes; but then Cosimo thought he was really good too. The building is now the prestigious University College.

Leave the Piazza by Via San Frediano, passing its little 11thC church, somewhat overshadowed by the adjacent ambulances. Turn right into rectangular Piazza Dante, heart of the university quarter, and at the far end take the left-hand exit, following the street round into broad Piazza Carrara, and here turn right to meet Via Santa Maria. On the right is **San Nicola**, famous for its campanile's splendid spiral staircase, on which Bramante modelled his Belvedere staircase in the Vatican. Ask to see it. In the church, look at the fourth chapel on the right: Pisa being protected from the plague by St Nicholas of Tolentino.

Head for the river, turning right at the **Lungarno** to cross by Ponte Solferino. The Arno here seems moribund, canal-like and strangley devoid of river craft. The two rows of fine orange and lemon *palazzi* on either side are correspondingly subdued, but one can see how literary exiles such as Byron, Shelley and the Brownings were attracted by Pisa's air of faded grandeur.

Santa Maria della Spina resembles a wonderfully decorated cake box plonked on the pavement – literally: it was moved here stone by stone in 1871

NW TUSCANY / *Pisa, Lucca and Pistoia*

from a perilous position closer to the Arno. Spectacular late Gothic flourishes make a surprising contrast to Pisa's earlier religious buildings – High Gothic is rarely seen in Tuscany. There's no cake inside the box: the interior lacks interest.

Continue along the Lungarno past the church to **Ponte di Mezzo**, site of the Romans' bridge and scene of the Gioco del Ponte (see page 89). On the right, the former market place, **Logge di Banchi**, is now functionless, except as a rallying point for student demos. It marks the start of **Corso Italia**, the pedestrianized main shopping street and hub of the evening *passeggiata*. Across the bridge, a right turn takes you along Lungarno Mediceo, past **No. 30**, the *palazzo* rented by Byron (plaque) and on to the **Museo Nazionale di San Matteo**, just before the bridge. You've got to be pretty keen to study Pisan art to make the effort, though, because it's a dreary place. In Room 3 *Madonna del Latte* by Andrea and Nino Pisano is a highlight. You could reward yourself with lunch round the corner at **Kostas** (see Recommended Restaurants, page 97).

Either return to Piazza Garibaldi in front of Ponte di Mezzo (or cut through to Borgo Stretto via pretty Piazza Cairoli and Via Rigattieri); if you decide to skip the detour, carry on along smart, arcaded **Borgo Stretto**, past the charming, typically Pisan façade of San Michele. To the left, in Piazza delle Vettovaglie, is the morning **market**. If it's lunchtime, **Osteria Numero Undici**, offers excellent snacks. A left turn, down Via Dini, returns you to Piazza dei Cavalieri.

The pleasantest way to the Leaning Tower from here (by this time you might have forgotten that Pisa has one) is to leave the Piazza through the archway of the Palazzo dell'Orologio and turn second right down Via della Faggiola. Turn left at the end into Piazza Arcivescovado and (wow!) there it is. As you walk slowly toward the brilliant green sward, the three great buildings, Baptistry, Duomo and its **campanile**, the Leaning Tower, are revealed one by one as the gleaming glories of Pisan Romanesque architecture, monuments to the vivacity, dignity and piety of this once-great Mediterranean power.

Campo dei Miracoli

If you are going to see all the buildings, including the two museums, you should

• *Pisa's leaning tower.*

buy a combined ticket.

The **Leaning Tower** began to tilt when only the third storey had been reached, in 1178, but after a pause of 100 years work continued and was completed in 1350. The cause of the problem was, and is, the sandy subsoil on which it rests and the shallowness of its foundations. It now leans at an amazing (and dangerous) 5.5 degrees. Thanks to the various efforts to keep it upright (including, recently, steel girders being inserted underground, and giant lead ingots being attached as counterweights), the area surrounding it (once a green lawn) has been churned up by bulldozers. It seems unlikely that the public will be able to stand on the ninth gallery and look down vertically to the ground, as Galileo, a native of Pisa, did when he demonstrated the laws governing falling bodies.

The **Duomo** (*open Apr-Oct, Mon-Sat 10 am-7.40 pm, Sun 1pm-7.40 pm; 7.45 am-1 pm, 3-sunset in winter; closed to tourists during certain services*) was the first of the three buildings to go up, begun in 1064 (by Buscheto, whose wall tomb you can see on the left of the façade). If you go to Lucca, Pistoia or Prato you will see many examples of the highly decorated architecture which surfaced in Pisa, but none to surpass the beauty of this richly

Seeing the Region: 1

textured, lace-like **façade**, added in the 12thC by Rainaldo. If you feel an Islamic influence in elements of the Duomo and its sisters, you are right: the Pisans had knowledge of such architecure from their seafaring travels. Before you go in (entrance opposite the Leaning Tower) look at the **doors** by Bonanno Pisano, depicting crude but charming *Scenes from the Life of Christ*. The grand, shadowy interior, much restored after a fire in 1595, holds a masterpiece of Gothic sculpture, Giovanni Pisano's **pulpit**, which was packed away after the fire and only rediscovered in the 20thC. Before inspecting it, however, look at his father Nicola's **pulpit** in the **Baptistry** (*open 8 am-7.45 pm summer; 9 am-4.45 pm winter*). In these, and other pulpits of theirs in Pistoia and Siena, one can trace both their own progress and the emergence of Renaissance sculpture. Nicola was one of the earliest artists to build on the elements he found in Classical sculpture, particularlyRoman sarcophagi. This pulpit, like an exquisite medieval merry-go-round, was his earliest known work, made in 1259. To illustrate the progress, take a close look at the rounded forms in Nicola's panel depicting the *Nativity*. Compare it with the same scene by Giovanni, in the Duomo, carved 43 years later. His figures seem almost freed from the marble; there is light, shadow and space between them and a dramatic unfolding of the scene.

The **Camposanto** or Cemetery (*same opening hours as Baptistry*) lies behind the eery white wall. It overpowers the senses with its paintings, monumental sculptures and collection of Roman tombs. Tragically, most of the famous frescoes which adorned its walls were destroyed by an Allied bomb in 1944: their *sinopie* (sketches on plaster) are preserved in the **Museo delle Sinopie** (opposite the Duomo, between the souvenir stalls). A gallery behind the north wall now houses the grizzly **Triumph of Death** by an unknown 14thC artist. A nobleman pinches his nose at the stench of an open grave; angels and devils wrestle for the souls of the dead; people stand around with their guts hanging out; a green monster from your worst nightmare clutches at a handful of bodies. Liszt was inspired to compose *Totentanz* after seeing these images. An adjoining gallery displays pre-war photos of the lost frescoes, and photos of the war damage and restoration.

The **Museo del Duomo**, beautifully arranged in the old Chapter House, contains works of art from the Duomo and Baptistry. Highlights are (Room 9) Giovanni Pisano's ivory **Madonna and Child** and the 11thC Islamic **griffin** (Room 1) brought back by the Pisans as war booty. Worth a visit, too, for the dramatic view of the Leaning Tower from the museum's pretty cloister.

For most visitors, the contents of the **souvenir stalls** are of as much interest as the contents of the buildings. And who could resist their very own Leaning Tower? Would you prefer it as a lamp or a lollipop, a plate or a pen-set? Kitsch-lovers' heaven.

PISTOIA ⚑ ✕

On the A11/SS435, 33 km NW of Florence. Tourist office: Piazza del Duomo, tel. 0573 21622. Station: Piazza Dante Alighieri, a short walk or taxi ride S of the centre. Buses: Lazzi city buses arrive near the station. Parking: cars with foreign number plates may park in Piazza Spirito Santo (except Wed, Sat am markets) and Via Roma in the centre. All others must use the Ex-Breda car park off Viale Pacinotti, NW of the station.

To my mind, one of the pleasantest towns in all Tuscany in which to while away some time. Pistoia is homely, easy-going and self-reliant with a fine medieval core, a sprinkling of beautiful and unusual treasures, a dirth of tourists and a foul reputation. This last was gained some seven centuries ago when the Pistoiese were famed for their viciousness and intrigue, even in those murderous times. They invented a deadly little dagger, the *pistole*, the better with which to stab one another. Present-day Pistoiese laugh off their murky past, but outsiders seem slower to forget. Today the town still makes its living from metalworks, as well as horticulture, particularly the raising of roses and young trees.

The heart of town is its spacious and quintessentially Tuscan **Piazza del Duomo**, scene of the annual **Giostra dell'Orso** (July 25), a sell-out medieval pageant and jousting competition and part of Pistoia's July festivities, the **Luglio Pistoiese**. The Romanesque **Duomo** and the hexagonal Gothic **Baptistry** are tucked into a corner, the Duomo lurking in the shadow of its huge **campanile**, originally a Lombard watchtower. Inside, the cathedral's treasure

NW Tuscany / Pisa, Lucca and Pistoia

is its silver **altar of San Jacopo** (chapel on the right), worked in incredible detail by a succession of goldsmiths, including Brunelleschi, from 1287 to 1456. Notice too, the lovely **font** (to the left of the main door) designed by Benedetto da Maiano. The rest of the piazza is taken up by civic buildings, notably the **Palazzo Pretorio** and **Palazzo Comunale** in which is housed the **Museo Civico**. Worth a peak for its rather bizarre collection of Pistoian and Tuscan artworks, from Renaissance to contemporary – you can't miss the guinea-a-minute Baroque canvasses on the top floor featuring some seriously hammy acting as in, for example, the *Assassination of Lorenzino de' Medici*.

Pistoia is famous for its beautiful pulpits, showpieces of 13thC Tuscan sculpture. They reside in three charming churches, worth seeking out. From the Piazza, a right turn past the tourist office (where you can pick up a map) and then a left takes you to the first church via Piazza della Sala with its morning fruit market and its pretty **Leoncino Well** (1453). The bustling little streets around the market place, filled with tempting food shops, are pleasant to stroll; on Via degli Orafi, catch sight of the sadly dilapidated Liberty-style Cinema Eden. If it's Wednesday or Saturday morning, take in the shoe market in Piazza Spirito Santo where a bargain may be had. Back on Via Cavour, **San Giovanni Fuorcivitas** (it once lay outside the city walls) presents its dazzling north flank to the street. Of all the stripey Pisan Romanesque churches you may have seen, this has to be the stripiest, made intricate by the row of blind arcades and two rows of blind galleries above. The **pulpit** (1270) is by Fra Guglielmo da Pisa, pupil of Nicola Pisano. His son, Giovanni

• *Frieze detail, Ospedale del Ceppo, Pistoia.*

Pisano, made the **holy water stoup**. Pick out too, a lovely **Visitation** in white glazed terracotta by Luca della Robbia.

San Bartolome stands to the east of Piazza del Duomo, approached down a flight of steps. Its **pulpit** was made in 1250 by Guido da Como. The crouching figure on which one column rests is supposed to be that of the sculptor.

The two most beautiful things in Pistoia are still to come. The first, the painted terracotta **frieze** stretched across the portico of **Ospedale del Ceppo**, is just a few paces to the north-west of San Bartolomeo. When many other images of Tuscan art have faded from your memory, you may find that this one remains clear: especially charming are the freshness of the colours, and the compassion and domestic detail with which the sick and poor, and their carers, are described. It was made by Giovanni della Robbia, last artist member of the famous family, and Santi Buglioni from 1514 to 1525. The last panel was unfinished. The lovely, dignified portico recalls Brunelleschi's Spedale degli Innocenti in Florence. The charity hospital (see Prato, pages 94-5) still operates now, as it has since the 13thC.

A short walk to the west brings you to **Sant'Andrea** with a charming Pisan façade, similar to that of San Bartolomeo. It's a humble setting for Giovanni Pisano's marvellous **pulpit** (1298), modelled on his father Nicola's pulpit in Pisa's Baptistry and a few years earlier than his masterpiece in the Duomo (see Campo dei Miracoli, page 92). Compare his Bible scenes with Guido da Como's charming but static images, and you can again see how Giovanni Pisano took the art of sculpture and ran with it.

Duomo, Prato.

PRATO ⛖ ✕

On the A11, 17 km NW of Florence. Tourist information: Via Cairoli 48, tel. 0574 24112 (behind Carceri church). Station: Piazza della Stazione; buses marked 'Francesco' go to Piazza San Francesco in the centre. Buses: arrive and leave from station, Piazza del Duomo, or Piazza San Francesco (Lazzi). Parking: prohibited in centre; car parks at Piazza del Mercatale (to E, inside walls) and Piazza dei Macelli (to SW, outside walls).

Ask a Florentine what he thinks of the Pratese and you will likely as not be told: 'flashy, *nouveau riche*, uncultured'. Ask a Pratese the same question about Florentines and you might well get: 'Lazy and supercilious'. The fact is that the two cities have never been friends, and they resent one another to this day. Pratese have to live with the fact that everyone zooms past them on their way to visit Florence; Florentines have to live with the fact that Prato is one of the fastest expanding cities in Italy, living healthily on the profits of its textile industry, while they struggle to find a modern economic identity apart from tourism.

Unlike Florence, Prato is a city that doesn't mind getting its hands dirty to earn its living, and it does so very successfully. Its importance as a manufacturer of textiles has not waned since the 13thC; today around 75 per cent of the working population are employed by the trade. Naturally enough it suffers from all the drawbacks of an industrial centre, but it does have a refreshingly earthy and unpretentious quality as well as some beautiful possessions. If you are passing through, it's worth stopping for a few hours, especially if you are travelling by train or bus; fighting your way through the grimy suburbs at the wheel of a car is not so congenial.

Approaching from the station, the first major landmark is the white-walled **Castello dell'Imperatore**, built by Holy Roman Emperor Frederick II on his route from Germany to southern Italy. Opposite, in the *piazza* of the same name, is the church of **Santa Maria delle Carceri**, whose serenly harmonious interior, plainly derived from the works of Brunelleschi and Alberti, is by Giuliano da Sangallo. The lovely terracotta tondi (circular reliefs) are the work of Andrea Della Robbia.

Across the square, the massive flank wall belongs to **San Francesco**, which contains the tomb of Datini, whose frescoed **Palazzo Datini** you will find on the corner of Via Rinaldesca (which leads off Piazza San Francesco) and Via S.L. Mazzei. Francesco di Marco Datini is Prato's most famous son, and the world's most famous accountant. Born in 1330, he became immensely rich through the cloth trade, founded the charity *Ceppo*, which still has its headquarters here, invented the letter of

NW Tuscany / Pisa, Lucca and Pistoia

exchange, and left thousands of business letters and immaculately kept ledgers, each inscribed 'To God and Profit'. His life is described in Iris Origo's superbly detailed book *The Merchant of Prato* (1957). His papers are kept in state archives within the *palazzo*.

Prato's charming **Duomo** wears its loveliest ornament on the outside: the corner **pulpit of the Sacred Girdle**, designed by Michelozzo and sculpted with leaping, laughing cherubs by Donatello (copies of the originals, which are in the cathedral museum). The Virgin's girdle, said to have been handed by her after her Assumption to doubting St Thomas, is displayed there on Easter Sunday, May 1, August 15, September 8 and Christmas Day. It lives in the chapel just left of the entrance, with frescoes by Agnolo Gaddi depicting the story. The *Madonna and Child* is by Giovanni Pisano. One of the highlights (to my mind) of the Early Renaissance is to be seen (as long as you have small change for the electric light, that is) on the walls of the choir: Filippo Lippi's graceful and spontaneous **Lives of Stephen and John the Baptist** (1452-66). Though a monk, Lippi did not, according to Vasari, have monkish habits: the figure of Salome in the superb *Banquet of Herod* is modelled on a beautiful nun, Lucrezia, whom he seduced, horror of horrors, on a day when the Sacred Girdle was displayed from Donatello's pulpit. Her father never smiled again, even though she later married the lusty artist. You can see a work by their son, Filippino Lippi, *St Lucy*, in the **Museo dell'Opera del Duomo** in the *piazza*, as well as Donatello's joyful cherubs.

In the small-scale Piazza del Comune stands the grim Palazzo Pretorio which houses the **Museo Civico,** worth visiting for another Filippo Lippi, this time featuring Datini. In **Madonna del Ceppo**, the five major benefactors of the charity are depicted kneeling before the Madonna and Child: four of the benefactors are pixie-like; Datini, as the largest benefactor, gets to be twice their size.

Also in the Piazza del Comune is Italy's only textile museum, **Museo del Tessuto**, which traces the history of Prato's textile industry from medieval times.

Prato has a famous theatre for plays and concerts, **Teatro Metastasio**, Via Cairoli 59.

VIAREGGIO
See *Local Explorations*: 11, *page* 236.

DETOUR - **SOUTH OF PRATO**
Country villas built by the Medici dot the hills around Florence. Two are located close to one another in the countryside west of Florence and south of Prato. The lovely Classical villa at **Poggio a Caiano** was built for Lorenzo Il Magnifico by Guiliano da Sangallo, although the curved exterior staircase was added later. The great **salone** (*open am only; closed Mon*) is decorated with frescoes by the Mannerists Andrea del Sarto, Franciabigio and Pontormo, whose delicious **Vertumnus and Pomono** surrounds a circular window.
If you admire Pontormo — and who cannot? — you should nip along to Carmignano, 5 km west, to see perhaps his greatest painting, **The Visitation**, in the church of San Michele. The colours are more extraordinary than ever, the figures seem gripped, perhaps by the artist's own troubled, introspective personality.

Five kilometres south of Carmignano is the Medici **Villa Artimino** (*guided tours by appointment, tel.* 055 8718072), designed by Buontalenti in 1594, its roof bristling with ornate chimneys. Artimino, now a quiet village with a fine Romanesque church, was once an important Etruscan settlement and artefacts are displayed in the **Museo Archeologico Etrusco** in the villa's basement (*closed Wed*).

From Artimino head north back towards Carmignano, then turn left to drive 12 km west to **Vinci**, home town of Leonardo. The town's castle is now the **Museo Leonardiano**, (*open daily*) where you can marvel at models of his incredibly precocious inventions, which he designed but never built. Many people walk from Vinci 3 km south-east to his simple birthplace at **Archiano** (*closed Wed*).

RECOMMENDED HOTELS

LUCCA
Universo, LL; *Piazza del Giglio* 1; *tel. 0583 493678; fax 0583 954854; cards accepted.*

Opposite the once-illustrious Teatro del Giglio (Rossini's *William Tell* had its first performance there in 1831), the Universo is another 19thC landmark, a venerable *caravanserai* much frequented by Ruskin and other cultured admirers of Tuscany. Today it has faded in a charming way, full of memories of a gentler age, and if you will forgive its shortcomings, makes a fitting base for visiting the town. Friends speak of a 'heavenly' *spaghetti alla carbonara* in the hotel's restaurant, **Il Giglio**.

Villa La Principessa, LLL; *Massa Pisana, 4 km S of Lucca on SS12r; tel. 0583 370037; fax 0583 379136; cards accepted.*

Luxurious, once a residence of the Dukes of Bourbon and Parma. Formal gardens, swimming-pool, outdoor eating area. The bedrooms and suites have modern furnishings and air-conditioning. Public rooms are more traditional, with marble floors, antiques, family portraits. Excellent food is served in the elegant restaurant. The adjacent building is the **Principessa Elisa**, with ten luxury suites and its own restaurant.

MONTECATINI TERME
The choice is so enormous, at every price level, that it is probably best to consult the town's hotel booking service, Associazione Provinciale Albergatori, 66 Via delle Saline, tel. 0572 70124. Most are closed November-Easter. The best-known hotel is the luxury **Grand Hotel e la Pace, LLL** (*Via della Torretta* 1; *tel. 0572 75801; fax 0572 78451*). Several less expensive options have gardens, including **Torretta, LL** (*Viale Bustichini 63; tel. 0572 70305; fax 0572 70307*) which also has a pool; and **Corallo, LL** (*Via Cavallotti 116; tel. and fax 0572 79642*) which is cheaper still and has a pool too. Also recommended, just off the ring road, close to parkland and the baths, with an indoor pool and a tennis court: **Belvedere, LL** (*Viale Fedeli 10; tel. 0572 70251; fax 0572 70252*).

PISA
Royal Victoria, LL; *Lungarno Pacinotti 12; tel. 050 940111; fax 940180; cards accepted.*

An endearing anachronism, opened in 1842 (Dickens stayed a few years later) and little changed since. The high-ceilinged rooms vary considerably in size and style, but all are fairly basic; some of the *en suite* bathrooms have comfy baths, some splashy showers. A sign in the lift advises you to walk downstairs to see the rest of the hotel, with its lobbies and hallways and patterned marble floors. No restaurant now.

PISTOIA
There are very few hotels in Pistoia, reflecting its surprising lack of tourists. Choose between cosy little **Patria, LL** (*Via Crispi 8; tel. 0573 25187; fax 0573 368168*) opposite our recommended restaurant San Jacopo and **Milano, LL** (*Viale Pacinotti 10; tel. 0573 975700; fax 0573 32657*). The latter was restored and modernized a few years ago.

PRATO
Villa Rucellai, LL; *Via di Cannetto 16, 4 km NE of Prato on SS325; tel. and fax 0574 460392; cards none.*

Industrial Prato creeps almost to the door of this mellow old villa, the country home of the Rucellai, a venerable Florentine family, but this should not deter you from staying in a very special place. Guests have the run of the main part of the house, with its baronial hall and comfortable sitting room filled with pictures and books. Bedrooms are simply furnished and full of character: they reflect the rare attribute of the place – that of a well-run hotel which gives no hint of being anything but a cultivated family home.

RECOMMENDED RESTAURANTS

LIVORNO
Fish dishes come in all shapes and forms in Livorno, but the most famous is the stew *cacciucco*. Freshness and quality is assured, but don't expect prices to be much cheaper than anywhere else. Take your pick from large and lively **La Barcarola, LL** (*Viale Carducci 63; tel. 0586 40 23 67; closed Sun*); up-market, elegant

La Chiave (*Scali delle Cantine 52; tel. 0586 88 86 09; closed Wed*); or a neighbourhood *trattoria* such as **Carlo, L-LL** (*Via Caprera 43*) near Venezia Nuova.

LUCCA
Il Buatino, L; *Borgo Giannotti 508; tel. 0583 343207; cards none; closed Sun.*

In a cobbled street full of agricultural shops leading to one of Lucca's gates, Locanda Buatino began life a century ago as a meeting place for farmers when they came to town. Nowadays the clientele is far more cosmopolitan, but the simplicity of the place can be little changed. The menu – rabbit, chicken, guinea fowl, tripe, cod – is written on rough brown paper, while the decoration is that of a Bohemian '50s café with basic tables and chairs. Monday is jazz night (book ahead).

Buca di Sant'Antonio, LL; *Via della Cervia 3; tel. 0583 55881; cards accepted; closed Sun eve, Mon, July.*

Traditional country cooking from the Garfagnana is the mainstay of this well-known restaurant, which has served food since the 18thC, and also preserves a Michelin star.

Il Giglio, LLL; *Piazza del Giglio 2; tel 0583 494058; cards accepted; closed Tues eve, Wed, first two weeks Feb.*

Traditional restaurant specializing in seafood as well as typical Tuscan *crostini* and *stracotto* (braised beef). Faultless presentation. Outdoor dining in summer months.

Da Giulio in Pelleria, L; *Via delle Conce 45; tel 0583 55948; cards accepted; closed Sun, Mon, Christmas and New Year, first two weeks Aug.*

You usually need to reserve ahead for Lucca's most popular local restaurant (near the tourist office, just north of Piazza San Donato). The food is simple but reliable, and the atmosphere bright and animated.

PISA
Osteria dei Cavalieri, L; *Via San Frediano 16; tel 050 580858; cards accepted; closed Sat lunch, Sun.*

Near Piazza dei Cavalieri, in whitewashed rooms with lofty vaulted ceilings, a very pleasant place for lunch or dinner. Lunch can be a quick, light affair (it is often packed with a rushed business crowd) when single dishes (one meat, one fish, one Pisan) are offered, disigned to reduce eating time (fast food at its best). Dinner is more leisurely with a fuller menu; light courgette soufflé, taglioni with rabbit sauce or with shrimps and canellini beans, *'tagliata'* (steak grilled and sliced) with wild mushrooms, grilled fish and, to finish (remember to order in advance), a superb hot grand marnier soufflé

Taverna Kostas, L-LL; *Via del Borghetto 39; tel. 050 571467; cards accepted; closed Mon.*

Popular spot decorated in Greek Island pinks and blues and featuring an appetizing Greek menu as well as an Italian one – just right if you are temporarily pooped on pasta. The gambas grilled with garlic were delicious.

PISTOIA
San Jacopo, L; *Via Crispi 15; tel. 0573 27786; cards accepted; closed Mon and Tue lunch.*

A delightful, rather chic little restaurant whose best feature is its lovely vaulted brick ceiling. The owner, Signor Bruno, who spent 15 years working in London, orchestrates the polite, efficient service. Fresh fruits and vegetables are displayed on a central table. If *porcini* are in season, ask for them raw, sliced thinly and served with slithers of Parmesan and a little lemon juice – wonderful.

Another local favourite is **Pizzeria Tonnino, L** (*Corso Gramsci 159; closed Mon*), a tiny bar where housewives, businessmen and *carabinieri* from the local station tuck into first-class pizzas.

PRATO
La Fontana, L; *Via di Cannetto 1, 4 km NE of Prato on SS325; tel. 0574 27282; cards accepted; closed Sun dinner, Mon*

Most convenient for anyone lucky enough to be staying just up the road at Villa Rucellai (see Recommended Hotels), this is a simple and often crowded *trattoria* – wobbly tables, café chairs and perfect food – perhaps salad of fennel and Parmesan, *bistecca alla Fiorentina*, grilled vegetables, *biscotti* dipped in Vin Santo.

Seeing the Region: 2

The North-East
Between Florence and Pesaro
Arezzo, Urbino, the Marches and the Adriatic

220 km; map Touring Club Italiano Umbria and Marche

The gentle, olive-clad slopes of eastern Tuscany; the voluptuous curves of the Marches' uplands and, in between, the barren limestone heights of the Appennine mountains: variety of landscape is the outstanding attraction of this region. But it offers much else to charm you, including half a dozen unforgettable small towns in which you can pay homage to one of the greatest Renaissance artists, Piero della Francesca.

The Appennines form a mountainous spine from the top to the toe of Italy. The suggested route crosses the range at one of its narrowest points, but in doing so climbs one of the highest passes in Central Italy, with sweeping views over the Upper Tiber Valley. The road twists, but otherwise makes pleasant driving, with no dizzying drops to frighten the nervous driver.

The mountains created a cultural barrier which is still noticeable. Leaving the Tuscan sophistication of Arezzo, you will feel the difference as you enter Le Marche, the Marches. Here the Appennines have held back the tourist hordes who have invaded Tuscany and Umbria, while the package holiday crowd who throng the Adriatic beaches rarely leave the shade of their umbrellas to venture inland. The few who do, discover Urbino, one of the most beautiful pocket cities in this guide, the perfect embodiment of the Renaissance ideal.

If you like rally driving, you could do the journey in around four hours. Allow at least three days if you want to get the most from it. If you are not following the route, but want to see the sights, be sure to allow a day each for Arezzo and Urbino.

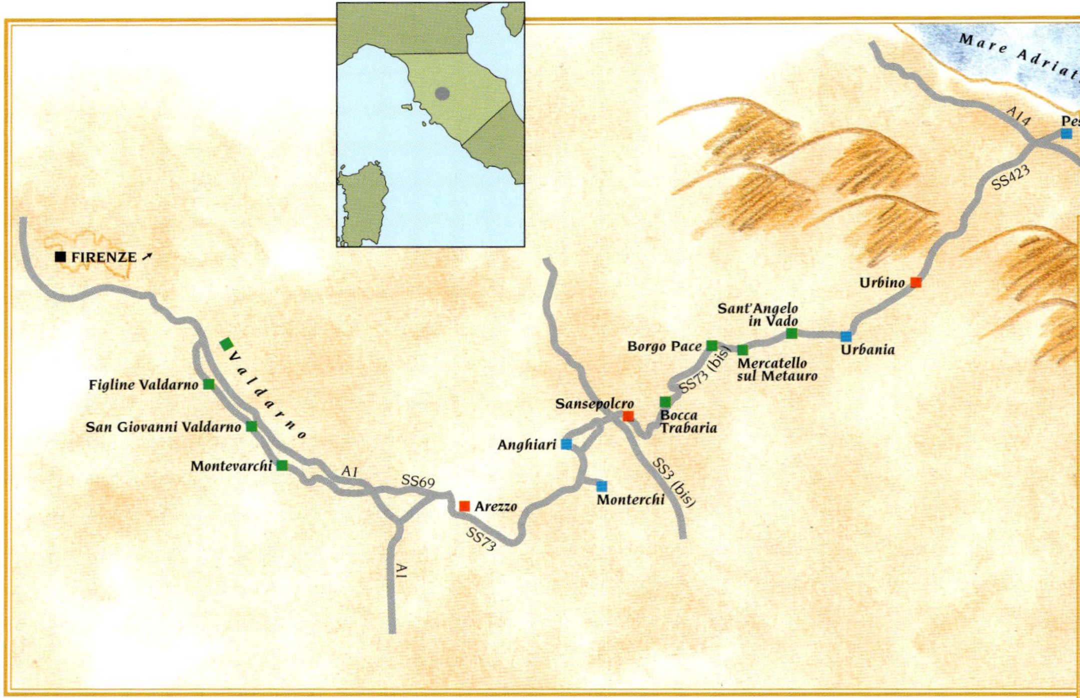

THE NORTH-EAST / Arezzo, Urbino and the Marches

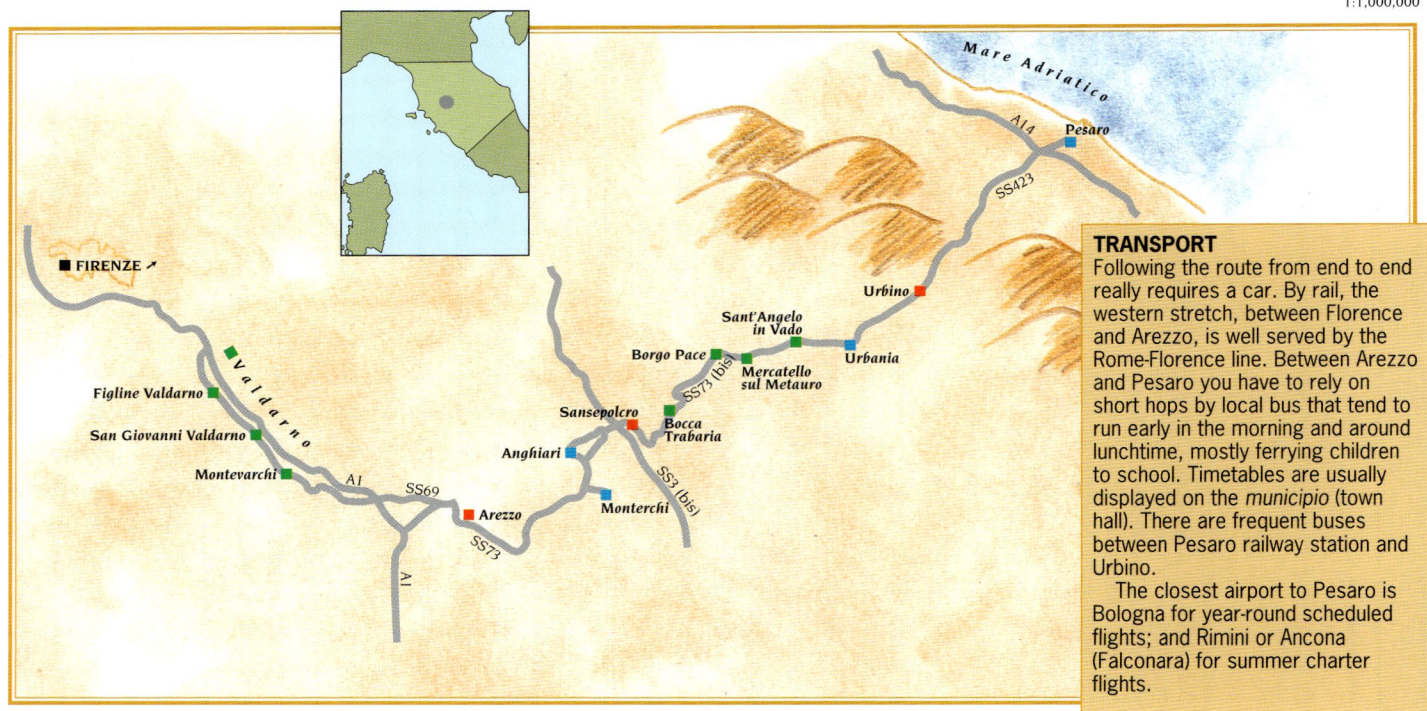

TRANSPORT

Following the route from end to end really requires a car. By rail, the western stretch, between Florence and Arezzo, is well served by the Rome-Florence line. Between Arezzo and Pesaro you have to rely on short hops by local bus that tend to run early in the morning and around lunchtime, mostly ferrying children to school. Timetables are usually displayed on the *municipio* (town hall). There are frequent buses between Pesaro railway station and Urbino.

The closest airport to Pesaro is Bologna for year-round scheduled flights; and Rimini or Ancona (Falconara) for summer charter flights.

Mare Adriatico

Pesaro
A14
SS123
Urbino
Urbania
Sant'Angelo in Vado
Mercatello sul Metauro
SS73 (bis)
Borgo Pace
Bocca Trabaria
SS3 (bis)
Sansepolcro
Monterchi
Anghiari
Arezzo
SS73
SS69
A1
Valdarno
Montevarchi
San Giovanni Valdarno
Figline Valdarno
FIRENZE

SIGHTS & PLACES OF INTEREST

ANGHIARI ⇌ ×
A short detour 8 km SW from Sansepolcro.
An unassuming little Tuscan hill town, remarkable for its architectural *ensemble*. The arresting **Piazza Baldaccio**, a proper old market square, elegantly links the huddle of the walled medieval *borgo* with the more open spaces of the later town. The urbane Renaissance **Palazzo Taglieschi** in Piazza Mameli houses a **museum** of the arts and popular culture from the Upper Tiber Valley – the liturgical objects are the best part of the collection.

At the edge of town on the road for Sansepolcro (pages 103-4) pause to admire the unusual 8thC Byzantine church of **San Stefano,** built in the shape of a Greek cross, with arms of equal length.

The plain below was the scene of the **Battle of Anghiari** in 1440 when the Florentines trounced the powerful Milanese Visconti family, finally putting paid to their designs on Tuscany. Leonardo da Vinci was commissioned to celebrate the victory in a great fresco for Florence's Palazzo Vecchio. He only completed a small section, and this was later covered by Vasari with the insipid frescoes that remain today. Notwithstanding their brief life, the Leonardo fragments were a major influence on the development of Florentine Mannerism (see page 28), and suggest that they might well have been one of the great masterpieces of Western art.

AREZZO ⇌ ×
Off the A1, 77 km SE of Florence. Tourist information: Piazza della Repubblica in front of railway station, trains for Florence and Rome. Centre closed to private traffic; highest concentration of well signposted car parks to SW of city around station.

A proud city with an abundance of first-rate sights, it deserves at least a day of your time. Ignore the ugly urban sprawl that has grown up around the main Rome-Florence railway line and make for the **historic centre** straddling the hill.

Heading up the main street of **Corso Italia** you arrive in front of one of Tuscany's most outstanding Romanesque churches, the 12thC **Pieve di Santa Maria**. The sandstone façade made up of three tiers of ever-diminishing arches owes something to the Pisan style, but the bell-tower with its fretwork of windows is a one-off. Inside is Pietro Lorenzetti's earliest masterpiece, a sternly Gothic polyptych over the high altar of the Madonna and Child with Saints (1320).

Behind the church stands **Piazza Grande**. Some consider it amongst Italy's finest squares – scene-stealing certainly, but losing points, in my opinion, for its lack of animation (except on the first Sunday of each month when it is given over to an antiques fair). Giorgio Vasari, whose *Lives of the Artists* established him as the father of modern art history, designed the striking **Palazzo delle Logge** that flanks the higher side of the sloping square.

Vasari was born here and you will find **Casa Vasari**, the house that he later planned, furnished and decorated himself, in Via XX Settembre.

From the Pieve you can continue up the hill to visit the **Duomo** with its enigmatic **fresco of Mary Magdalene** by Piero della Francesca, and on to **San Domenico** to admire the great austere painted **Crucifixion** by the young Cimabue, that great herald of the Gothic style. If time is short, however, make straight for **San Francesco** (back down Corso Italia a short way and right into Via Cavour). The 14thC Gothic church guards one of the most important creations of the Italian Renaissance, Piero della Francesca's frescoes of **The Legend of the Cross** (currently undergoing restoration). Painted over a period of more than ten years, they recount the miraculous story of the wood of the Cross (see Piero della Francesca, page 103).

For a glimpse of earlier times, stop off at the **Museo Archeologico Mecenate** housed in the ruins of the **Roman Amphitheatre** down near the station. Arretium was one of the most important of the ruling league of 12 Etruscan cities and in Roman times was famed for its ***vasi corallini***, ceramics with an unusual red glaze – the museum has a big collection.

Arezzo is a city with a strong secular tradition. Its famous son, Pietro Aretino, made his mark as one of the greatest writers of his time by penning vitriolic attacks against 16thC worthies both religious and secular. Known as the Scourge of Princes, he is reputed to have made his fortune by accepting bribes not to write about people. One of the city's finest buildings is the 14thC **Palazzo della Fraternità dei Laici** on Piazza Grande, built for a brotherhood of laymen dedicated to good works.

BOCCA TRABARIA PASS

The road from Sansepolcro to Urbino rises sharply through tight hairpins to arrive after 15 km at the highest pass (1,049 m) in this section of the Appennines.

Looking back there are sweeping views over the fertile Upper Tiber valley. This wild country marks the boundary between Umbria and the Marches. Take snow chains if you are crossing in the depth of winter.

BORGO PACE ⇆ ×

On the SS73 bis (Trabaria Pass), 28 km from Sansepolcro. This pocket-handkerchief commune of some 700 souls has high claims for the origin of its name: Roman Burgo Pacis earned its title when a peace treaty between the warring Mark Antony, Lepidus and Octavian (later to become Caesar Augustus) was drawn up here. The treaty was later ratified in 42 BC near Bologna.

It is still a peaceful *borgo*, except when the hunters are out in the autumn stockpiling game for the annual **Sagra del Tordo** (Thrush Feast).

FIGLINE VALDARNO

See Valdarno, page 107.

FLORENCE

See pages 39-81.

MERCATELLO SUL METAURO

On the SS73 bis (Trabaria Pass), 32 km from Sansepolcro. Hemmed in by mountains, the people of this small market town on the river Metauro carry on their traditional industries of lace making, tobacco curing and furniture restoration. A medieval atmosphere still pervades the centre. The worn sandstone church of **San Francesco**, which was started by the Franciscans in 1235, is reckoned to be amongst the Order's oldest buildings.

MONTERCHI

A short detour off the SS73, 16 km SW from Sansepolcro. This crumbling hill village would hardly be worth a mention if it

• *Carnival poster, Arezzo.*

didn't shelter one of Piero della Francesca's great works. Originally frescoed for the tiny chapel of the local cemetery where it remained until its recent restoration, the **Madonna del Parto** (Our Lady of Childbirth) is now housed in the centre of the village. This rare portrayal of a deeply pregnant Madonna, flanked by twin angels, is a universal icon for the travails of childbearing, as moving now as when it was painted.

MONTEVARCHI

See Valdarno, page 107.

PESARO ⇆ ×

At end of the SS423, 34 km E from Urbino. Tourist information: APT on Via Rossini just off main square. Station on Viale Risorgimento serves main Milan-Bari line with frequent trains to Bologna and Ancona. Parking usually easiest towards seafront, except in July and Aug.

This well-heeled provincial capital is a major centre for furniture manufacture – even its renowned basketball team is named after a fitted kitchen company – but in summer it moonlights as an attractive seaside resort. The elegant open streets have worthwhile sights to hold your attention and after a day on the beach a fish dinner by the port is hard to beat.

Sea-horses and tritons decorate the fountain in the centre of the broad

Seeing the Region: 2

Piazza del Popolo fountain, Pesaro.

Piazza del Popolo, at the heart of the city. Flanking it, the **Palazzo Ducale** vies for your attention with the pompous post office building. The clean-limbed Renaissance palace was built in the middle of the 15thC by the ruling Sforza family.

Leaving the square along **Via Rossini**, you find on your right the modest **house** where Gioachino Rossini was born in 1792. His operas, along with those of Verdi, Bellini and Donizetti, brought the Italian art of *bel canto* (literally, beautiful singing) to its apogee in the early decades of the 1800s. The house is now a small shrine to the composer. The annual **Rossini Opera Festival** in August has earned a worldwide reputation for dusting off works from his seemingly endless repertoire of forgotten operas.

The city was once noted for its painted ceramics and in the **Musei Civici** in Piazza Toschi Mosca (just behind the tourist office in Via Rossini) you can enjoy one of Italy's finest collections of Renaissance and Baroque pottery.

If pots leave you cold, the warmth of Giovanni Bellini's masterpiece, the ***Coronation of the Virgin*** in the adjoining **Pinacoteca** shouldn't. The castle in the background of the painting is the Sforza stronghold at **Gradara**: if you're driving north on the motorway you will catch sight of it a few kilometres from Pesaro – it hasn't changed since the day Bellini painted it.

For lost property from Roman **Pisaurum** visit the **Museo Archeologico Oliveriano** in Via Mazza to the west of the main square.

Keep heading straight down Via Rossini and you will eventually find yourself on the seafront and looking at one of the city's most flamboyant buildings, the **Villino Ruggeri**. This heavily stuccoed confection is one of the finest examples of the Italian Liberty style that swept the Adriatic Riviera at the turn of the 20thC.

Like most Italian beaches, the 3-km strand here is laid out with ranks of umbrellas and deck chairs, but it is rarely overcrowded.

THE NORTH-EAST / Arezzo, Urbino and the Marches

• *Detail from Villino Ruggeri, Pesaro.*

SANT'ANGELO IN VADO
On SS73 bis (Trabaria Pass), 27 km W of Urbino. This small agricultural and commercial backwater with an attractive *centro storico* was the unlikely birthplace of several important Baroque artists and architects including the brothers Taddeo and Federico Zuccari.

Nowadays it is known for its contribution to gastronomy: Italy's first nursery to commercially cultivate the much-prized truffle is here. Saplings of selected trees have their roots impregnated with the spores of the underground fungus, then are planted in areas with the very distinctive type of soil which they require in order to thrive. After a wait of some ten years and much luck, the first truffles are ready to be dug up. The technique has proved so successful that large tracts of the Umbro-Marchegiani Appennines are being turned over to truffle reserves.

SAN GIOVANNI VALDARNO
See Valdarno, page 107.

SANSEPOLCRO ×
Off the SS3 bis and on the SS73, 35 km E of Arezzo. Tourist information: Via della Fonte, behind Duomo. Station in Piazza Battisti serves slow local line for Perugia and Terni; LFU bus service for both Arezzo and Florence.

The Florentines bought Borgo San Sepolcro in 1441 from the Pope for 25,000 florins, and the mark of Florence is unmistakable on this com-

---

PIERO DELLA FRANCESCA
Long neglected, Piero della Francesca is now regarded as one of the greatest Renaissance painters – perhaps we needed Cézanne and Cubism to teach us to appreciate his perfect use of form and colour. Born sometime between 1410 and 1420, he remained faithful to his native town of Borgo San Sepolcro (modern Sansepolcro) for the rest of his life, despite travelling far. In 1442 he was made a member of the Priori (town council), a post he retained until his death.

His earliest known painting is the Madonna della Misericordia at Sansepolcro, but like many of his works it took years to complete: it was ordered from him in 1445 for delivery in three years but was finally paid for some 17 years later.

A master of the impersonal, his mathematical clarity and absence of sentimentality produced images whose spiritual depth still confounds us. Always seeking to redraw the boundaries of art, he was also a great theorist and wrote two of the most important treatises of his time on perspective. The last record we have of him painting was in 1478, but he lived on until 1492 – tragically, blindness seems to have blighted his last years.

To follow a pilgrim's trail of his works, visit the Uffizi in Florence to see his famous twin portraits of *Federico da Montefeltro* and *Battista Sforza*. Go to Arezzo for his great fresco cycle of the *Legend of the Cross*. Visit Monterchi for the *Madonna del Parto*; Sansepolcro for his *Resurrection*, and Urbino for the *Flagellation of Christ*.

pact town, built along pure Renaissance lines and boxed in by massive walls. Stroll along central **Via Matteotti** to see the best of its noble palaces and towers.

Piazza Torre di Berta provides a fitting backdrop to the Palio della Balestra, a deadly serious annual crossbow competition on the second Sunday of September. The piazza's name records a medieval tower destroyed by bombing in 1944.

Sansepolcro was the native town of Piero della Francesca and the best reason for coming here is to see his famous fresco of the **Resurrection**. As the grey dawn spreads over hills that are clearly those around Piero's birthplace, a majestic Christ steps from the tomb, fixing us with an unflinching stare. The soldier was said by Vasari to be a self-portrait of the artist. You will find the masterpiece in the **Museo Civico** at the corner of Via Matteotti and Via N. Aggiunti. The collection also includes one of Piero's earliest works, the **Madonna della Misericordia**, the great Mother gathering humanity in the folds of her mantle.

URBANIA ✕

On the SS73 bis, 17 km SW from Urbino. If you arrive from Sant'Angelo in Vado look out for the striking **Renaissance villa** just before the town – it was once a hunting lodge of the Dukes of Urbino.

Formerly known as Castel Durante, this pleasing old town was renamed by Pope Urban VIII in 1636, shortly after the last Duke of Urbino handed over his lands to the Papal States. For such a small place it is surprisingly rich in impressive buildings and works of art. The imposing **Palazzo Ducale** was originally a 13thC feudal stronghold later given airs and graces by Duke Federico of Urbino – his favourite architect, Francesco di Giorgio Martini, was largely responsible for the facelift. Cross the gracious courtyard to see an appealing **museum** of paintings, old maps and globes and Renaissance ceramics (16thC Castel Durante boasted 32 majolica workshops).

Other monuments to note while strolling in the shade of the arcaded streets include the **Bramante Theatre** (Urbania is one of two cities claiming the great Renaissance architect as one of its sons) and the church of **Santa Chiara**. The last Duke of Urbino, Francesco Maria II Della Rovere, is buried in the **Chiesa del Crocifisso**: like many other buildings in Urbania this church was badly damaged by Allied bombing in 1944.

You'll find the town's strangest offering behind the altar of the **Chiesetta dei Morti** in Via Ugolini – the **Cimitero delle Mummie**. Here a dozen leathery mummified corpses hang like washing in a row of glass-fronted cabinets. They were put on display in 1813 after their discovery in the ground below, preserved by a rare type of mould. The custodian takes great delight in opening the cupboards to show you the body with stab wounds and the pregnant woman with a mummified foetus – great fun for children.

URBINO ⇌ ✕

On the SS423, 35 km SW from Pesaro; tourist information office on square at side of Ducal Palace; ill-served by public transport, easiest by bus from Pesaro Station as the pretty railway line to the coast has long since closed; simplest car park to find is by city walls directly below Ducal Palace (partly underground).

For the second half of the 15thC Urbino's windy hill was the setting for one of the most illustrious courts in Europe. Duke Federico da Montefeltro gathered around him the greatest painters, poets and scholars of his day and housed them in one of Italy's most beautiful Renaissance palaces, a palace that still stands as an eloquent memorial to this quintessential Renaissance man.

For the best first impression, approach the town from Arezzo to see the fairy-tale **twin towers** of the palace that give Urbino its unmistakable skyline: already you will see that it was built by a benevolent and secure ruler who had no need to intimidate or to brag.

The hub of the town is the animated triangle of **Piazza della Repubblica** that lies in a dip between the twin humps of a hill. From here follow the signs up to the **Palazzo Ducale**. As you arrive at the entrance you may feel let down – the palace presents an undistinguished face to the town. Once inside, however, you will find one of the most kindly and exhilarating palaces you will encounter in Italy. The **courtyard** sets the tone: a masterpiece of proportion and light carried out with the deftest of touches. Remember that this was the first of its kind; the others you will see across Italy are mere copies. None of the **rooms** of the palace were designed to oppress with grandeur, but were built on a human scale and decorated with glad-hearted sobriety. Nowadays they house the **Galleria Nazionale delle Marche**, a remarkable collection of paintings including one of the world's greatest and most enigmatic images, Piero della Francesca's **Flagellation of Christ**. Other great pictures here are Piero's **Madonna di Senigallia** that could almost be an interior painting by Vermeer; Raphael's **La Muta** (The Silent One), an anonymous portrait of a gentlewoman who we feel might talk to us if she only wished to; and a famous vision of the **Ideal City** by an unknown hand (possibly Piero della Francesca's) and much used by graphic designers to illustrate books on the Renaissance.

The Duke's **Studiolo** is the most remarkable room in the palace. His tiny study was entirely decorated in exquisite *trompe l'oeil* inlaid woodwork panels, a number based on designs by Botticelli.

To understand the complex domestic organization that propped up what W.B. Yeats called 'that mirror-school of courtesies', visit the vast warren of cellars, kitchens, laundry rooms, stables and even an ice store in the **Sotterranei** or basements.

No single architect can be credited as the creative genius behind this blueprint for the unfortified Renaissance dwelling, although Luciano Laurana and Francesco di Giorgio Martini figure large. It has to be seen rather as the sum total of Duke Federico's enlightened patronage.

Few traces remain of earlier Roman Urbinum Metaurense, but you can see some in the exhaustive collection of ancient stone inscriptions in the **Museo Archeologico** on the ground floor of the Ducal Palace. Virtually the entire city within the walls dates from the 15th and 16thC – the ghost of Federico would still not lose his way in the maze of pink-bricked alleys.

FEDERICO DA MONTEFELTRO

Federico da Montefeltro was born in 1422 to a small-time noble family that ruled over an insignificant square of the chess-board that was then Central Italy. Yet within 60 years he had become 'the light of Italy' and the paradigm of Renaissance man, as skilled in letters as in arms. His portrait in Urbino's Ducal Palace, together with that of his young son, Guidobaldo, by the Spanish painter Pedro Berrugue neatly portrays this duality of scholar and warrior – studiously reading a weighty manuscript, he keeps his helmet by his side. As in all portraits of the Duke, including Piero della Francesca's famous painting in the Uffizi, we only see his left profile: a swordblow earlier in his life had cost him his right eye and the bridge of his nose.

He made his money as one of the most successful *condottiere*, or hired generals, of his time. Always fighting on short-term contracts and strictly for cash on the nail, he displayed the timeless Italian ability of never taking sides – he managed once to fight for Florence against the Pope only later to take up the Papal banner against the Florentines. His fortune made, he turned to the arts as enthusiastically as he had to war and settled down to create his shining court. Almost all the great names of the Quattrocento passed through his palace, and his library was reckoned amongst the largest in Europe. On his death in 1482 his sickly son Guidobaldo managed to keep alive the splendour of the court with the help of his emancipated wife Elisabetta Gonzaga. Baldesar Castiglione wrote his famous book, *The Courtier*, the classic account of the Renaissance ideal, as a member of Guidobaldo's retinue.

On Guidobaldo's death in 1508 the dukedom passed to the Della Rovere family and Urbino's decline began. The light was finally extinguished in 1626 when the last duke handed over the duchy to the Papal States – its palace stripped of its treasures, Urbino sank into unbroken torpor.

Seeing the Region: 2

The North-East / Arezzo, Urbino and the Marches

Giovanni Santi was a court painter at Urbino who might have been consigned to the lumber room of art history if he hadn't been the father of the immortal Raphael. Few can doubt that Raphael's childhood at the court helped mould his genius. The **house** where he was born is now a delightful little museum – a simple **fresco** of the Madonna and Child in one of the rooms may have been one of his earliest works. You will find it in Via Raffaello, which runs up from Piazza della Repubblica. Stagger on up to the summit of the steep hill to find a striking **statue** of the painter and grandstand views of the countryside around Urbino.

If you are not yet sated with art, hunt out the **Oratorio di San Giovanni Battista** in Via Barocci in order to see a small church entirely decorated in 1416 with wall-to-ceiling **frescoes** by the Marchegiani painters Jacopo and Lorenzo Salimbeni. Ignore the fact that few outside the Marches have ever heard of the brothers: use your eyes and enjoy the brilliance of their earthy vision of the life of St John the Baptist and a terrifying Crucifixion – or just count the number of playful small dogs you can spot in the lively scenes.

A rarely visited but nevertheless delightful stop is the **Orto Botanico**. This small, walled botanic garden is full of rare plants, the shade is welcome, and there are definitely no paintings. The entrance is in Via Bramante.

As you leave Urbino pause to pay your last respects at the **tombs** of Duke Federico and his son, Guidobaldo, in the fine church of **San Bernardino**. It was built in 1491 by Francesco di Giorgio Martini and stands on the hill above the junction for the Pesaro road: follow the signs.

VALDARNO, THE

Follow the A1 or the SS69 SE from Florence. The twin demons of steam and petrol have shattered the calm of the Valley of the Arno and much of its beauty has been effaced by concrete. If you

• *Urbino.*

• Opposite: *Urbino – statue of Raphael*

are leaving from Florence you might wish to draw a veil over the area and speed straight down the motorway to exit at Arezzo. However, with time on your hands, put up with the traffic lights and lorries on the old SS69 and stop off at one of the towns on the way.

The most interesting is **San Giovanni Valdarno**. Despite being a major industrial centre – large amounts of electricity are generated by burning the locally mined lignite – it has a noteworthy old centre. You can also take pride in being one of the few tourists who bother to stop here. Florence founded the town in the 13thC to curb Arezzo's ambitions and had the versatile Arnolfo di Cambio draw up its defences. Although San Giovanni was the birthplace of Masaccio you won't find any of his work here.

Instead, the town's finest heirloom is the ***Annunciation*** by Fra Angelico to be seen in the **Museo della Basilica** adjacent to the church of Santa Maria della Grazie. The most outstanding building is the **Palazzo Pretoria** on the main square. Its portico is festooned with the coats of arms of great Florentine families.

Some 4 km south of San Giovanni is **Montevarchi**, a major market centre for Valdarno chickens, wine, hats and shoes. In the **fossil museum** you can see the remains of the beasts that stalked the valley long before the arrival of the chickens, wine, hats and shoes. About 8 km north of San Giovanni lies **Figline Valdarno**, twice razed to the ground, first by the Florentines then by the Pisans. Despite a stormy past it managed to foster one of the most important Renaissance scholars, the great humanist Marsilio Ficino (1433-99). He produced the first Latin translations of Plato's complete dialogues, thus making the Greek philosopher's thought directly available to the West for the first time. Seeing Plato as a 'Greek-speaking Moses', he officiated at the uneasy Renaissance marriage between Christianity and Paganism.

107

Seeing the Region: 2

RECOMMENDED HOTELS

ANGHIARI
Locanda al Castello di Sorci, L; Via S Lorenzo 21; tel. and fax 0575 788022; cards accepted.

An old feudal castle and outbuildings lovingly converted to a country guesthouse, 3 km south of the town. The 20 bedrooms in this rambling warren are delightful. If you can't stay here you should at least try the restaurant (see below).

AREZZO
Lovely town, shame about the hotels. These are the best of the bunch:

Continental, LL; Piazza Guido Monaco 7; tel. 0575 20251; fax 0575 350485; cards accepted.

Albergo built in 1946 between station and historic centre. Spacious rooms, well-appointed bathrooms, and views over Arezzo from 6th-floor terrace.

Minerva, LL; Via Fiorentina 4; tel. 0575 370390; fax 0575 302415; cards accepted.

Classic modern Italian hotel with 118 decent rooms. Identical prices to Continental, above. Convenient for motorists as it is near the city gate on the road that leads to the motorway.

BORGO PACE
Oasi di San Benedetto, L; Via Abbazia; tel. 0722 80133; fax 0722 80226; cards accepted.

A bucolic idyll in a former Benedictine monastery high in the hills. Twelve double rooms and five larger family rooms with private services. Mountain fare in the restaurant (see Recommended Restaurants, page 109).

PESARO
Villa Serena, LL; Via San Nicola 6/3; tel. 0721 55211; fax 0721 55927; cards accepted.

Just nine bedrooms in the frayed gentility of a 17thC country villa standing in a fine park some 4 km from the beach. Plenty of character – all the bedrooms are different. Still run by members of the family that built it. Restaurant with interesting dishes cooked by the owner; swimming pool. A lovely place.

Des Bains, L-LL; Viale Trieste 221; tel. 0721 33665; fax 0721 34025; cards accepted.

Handy for beach and old centre, this sound-value hotel is built on Belle Epoque lines. Double glazing and carpets keep the noise down and many rooms have balconies with sea views.

Ambassador, LL; Viale Trieste 291; tel. 0721 34246; fax 0721 34248; cards accepted.

Another attractive choice on the seaside drag of Viale Trieste, this time right on the beach. Many of its 50 spacious rooms look out over the Adriatic.

URBINO
The town hides its few small *alberghi* up blind alleys but there are helpful pedestrian direction signs at every corner. The *alberghi* are popular, so it is advisable to telephone before arriving if you want to be sure of a room.

Bonconte, LL; Via delle Mura 28; tel. 0722 2463; fax 0722 4782; cards accepted.

Urbino's 20-room four-star hotel down by the walls.

Raffaello, LL; Via Santa Margherita 40; tel. 0722 4896; fax 0722 328540; cards none.

Another comfortable small hotel just behind Raphael's House. Lovely views from the upper floors.

Italia (L-LL; Corso Garibaldi 32; tel. 0722 2701; fax none; cards none, and **San Giovanni (L-LL**; Via Barocci 13; tel. 0722 2827; cards none) are both humbler and cheaper establishments than our other recommendations – but with a degree of moth-eaten charm.

Locanda la Brombolona, L-LL; località Sant'Andrea in Primicillio 32, Canavaccio; tel. 0722 53501; fax 0722 53501; cards accepted.

A country guest-house in a 16thC church, 8 km out of Urbino on the Fano road. Beautiful setting in the Marche hills – you may well be tempted to stay for more than one night.

RECOMMENDED RESTAURANTS

ANGHIARI
Locanda al Castello di Sorci, LL; Via S Lorenzo 21 tel. 0575 788022; cards accepted; closed Mon.

An old feudal castle and outbuildings lovingly converted to a country guesthouse 3 km south of town. Studied recreation of simple peasant dishes such as pasta with beans, and polenta. Taste the smoke in the roasts produced in the wood-fired oven. This is also a great place to stay (see Recommended Hotels, page 108).

AREZZO
No shortage of acceptable, fairly-priced Tuscan restaurants here.

Buca di San Francesco, LL; Via S Francesco 1; tel. 0575 23271; cards accepted; closed Mon eve, Tues.

Excellent abundant Tuscan fare under 14thC vaulting, right by the church of San Francesco. Outstanding robust soups.

Antica Osteria l'Agania, L; Via Mazzini 10; tel. 0575 295381; cards none; closed Mon.

Faithfully maintains the tradition of the fast-disappearing simple Tuscan *osteria* – the same family have been running the place for more than 30 years. Hearty rustic food. You may wish to know that *grifi* is stewed calf's muzzle.

BORGO PACE
Oasi di San Benedetto, L-LL; Via Abbazia; tel. 0722 80133; cards accepted.

Idyllic *locanda* in a former Benedictine monastery high in the hills. You might well need to stay the night if you indulge in the rich mountain dishes – *lepre* (hare) or *cinghiale* (wild boar). (See Recommended Hotels, page 108.)

PESARO
Some of Italy's finest fish comes from the Adriatic, so it is no surprise that *la cucina Pesarese* is based on the daily catch. The best way to try the full range is to order the filling *antipasti di pesce* – endless small dishes, both hot and cold, of every type of seafood including clams, winkles, prawns and anchovies – followed by a *risotto di pesce* or spaghetti with a fish sauce. If your appetite and wallet allow, follow with *pesce arrosto* – mixed roast fish. Remember fish is always relatively expensive. Have a seafood pizza if your *lire* are running low.

Da Teresa, LLL; Viale Trieste 180; tel. 0721 30096; cards accepted; closed Sun eve and Mon lunch.

Pesaro's best restaurant, with both fish and meat on the imaginative menu.

La Baita, LL; Strada tra i due Porti; tel. 0721 25672; cards accepted; closed Tues.

Fish only at this popular place down by the yacht-building yards – might be best to take a taxi as it's difficult to find. If you stick to *antipasti* and spaghetti it won't break the bank.

SANSEPOLCRO
Da Ventura; LL; Via Aggiunti 30; tel. 0575 742560; cards accepted; closed Sat.

A notch-above-the-average version of *la cucina di territorio* with the pasta dressed at your table. Near the museum.

URBANIA
Big Ben, LL; Corso Vittorio Emanuele 61; tel. 0722 319795; cards none.

Smart but unfussy Marchegiano restaurant that draws its customers from miles around. Imaginative interpretation of traditional recipes.

Del Cucco, L; Via Betto de' Medici 9; tel. 0722 317412; cards none; closed Sun eve and Mon.

A wonderfully friendly, cramped place with an incongruous mix of bibulous old men at the bar and bemused young foreigners from the local Italian language school. The husband and wife team who run this old *osteria* together do interesting things with vegetables.

URBINO
The *Marchegiani* eat more meat than anyone else in Italy and it shows on the menus of Urbino's full range of restaurants. Meat *alla brace* (charcoal grilled) is a staple along with *coniglio in porchetta* (roast rabbit stuffed with wild fennel), excellent cured pork – *prosciutto*, salami and *lonza* – and *piccione ripieno* (stuffed pigeon).

Tre Pianti, L; Via Voltaccia della Vecchia 1; tel. 0722 4863; cards none; closed Mon.

Off the tourist beat but little signposts will lead you to this unpretentious *trattoria* much favoured by students from Urbino's university. Pleasant verandah overlooking countryside in summer. Also has real pizzas at budget prices.

Vecchia Urbino, LL; Via dei Vasari 3; tel. 0722 4447; cards accepted; closed Tues.

Urbino's most refined restaurant offering classic regional cooking at classic prices.

Seeing the Region: 3

The Centre

Between Florence and Viterbo
The Via Cassia

212 km; map Touring Club Italiano Toscana

The ancient Via Cassia, well trodden before the Romans surfaced it in 154 BC, is an ideal route for travellers who want a wide-angle view of the curvaceous hills and dales of southern Tuscany and northern Lazio. As most of the Florence-Rome traffic now hurtles along the A1 motorway to the east, by car you could simply use it to make a relatively peaceful, certainly a memorable, journey between the two great cities.

Even better, you could use the Via Cassia to link several of this guide's local explorations, which are conveniently situated either side of the road. These are Local Explorations: 1, which features San Gimignano and Volterra; Local Explorations: 2, the Chianti heartland; Local Explorations: 3 including Montepulciano and the shores of Lake Trasimeno; Local Explorations: 4 including Monte Amiata; Local Explorations: 5 centering on Orvieto; Local Explorations: 6, the southern Tuscan Coast and Local Explorations: 7, Etruscan Tarquinia. It would be easy to fill a fortnight's holiday in this way.

As well as visiting the great centres of medieval and Renaissance art – Siena and Viterbo are the most outstanding – this itinerary also enables you to explore the idyllic scenery of the Val d'Orcia; to view the sturdy fortifications of villages such as Monteriggioni; wander the banks of volcanic Lake Bolsena; or drink Chianti in the shade of the vines that produce it.

THE CENTRE / *The Via Cassia*

FIRENZE

San Casciano in Val di Pesa

nelle Val di Pesa
erino Val d'Elsa

SS2

Poggibonsi

A1

Monteriggioni

Siena

SS2

Monte Oliveto Maggiore

Buonconvento

San Quirico d'Orcia
Pienza
Bagno Vignoni
Castiglione d'Orcia

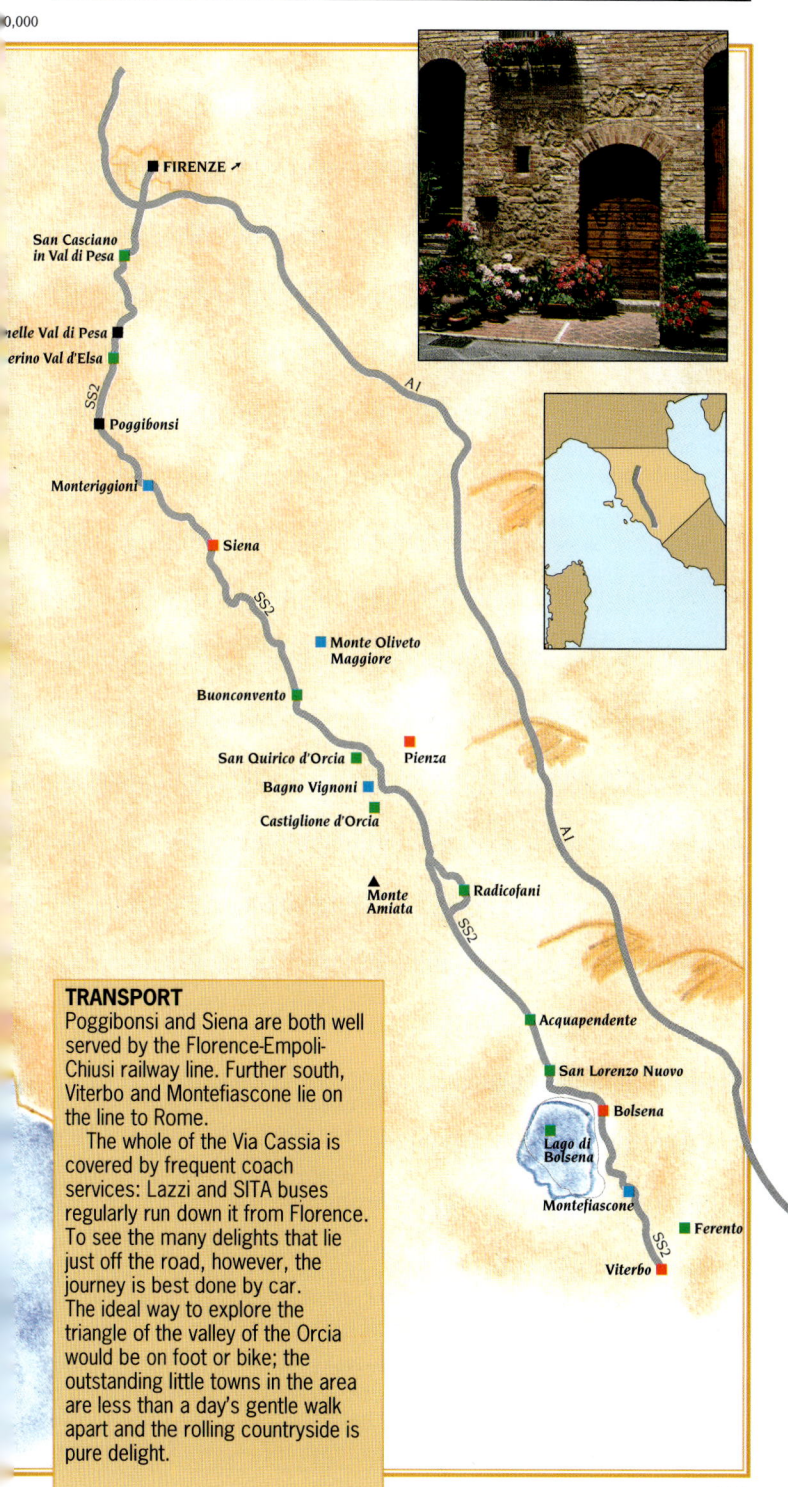

▲ Monte Amiata

Radicofani

A1

SS2

Acquapendente

San Lorenzo Nuovo

Bolsena

Lago di Bolsena

Montefiascone

Ferento

SS2

Viterbo

TRANSPORT

Poggibonsi and Siena are both well served by the Florence-Empoli-Chiusi railway line. Further south, Viterbo and Montefiascone lie on the line to Rome.

The whole of the Via Cassia is covered by frequent coach services: Lazzi and SITA buses regularly run down it from Florence. To see the many delights that lie just off the road, however, the journey is best done by car. The ideal way to explore the triangle of the valley of the Orcia would be on foot or bike; the outstanding little towns in the area are less than a day's gentle walk apart and the rolling countryside is pure delight.

SIGHTS & PLACES OF INTEREST

ACQUAPENDENTE

On the SS2, 50 km N of Viterbo. Lazio's northernmost outpost is worth a short break from the accelerator pedal. The Grand Tourists of earlier centuries, impatient to reach journey's end at Rome, however, rarely had a good word to say about the place. The **Cathedral of San Sepolcro** is the most distinguished among the handful of pretty churches. Its crepuscular 9thC **crypt** was built to the dimensions of the Holy Sepulchre and hence gave the church its name. Some fine palaces and squares enliven a short stroll through the prosperous town.

BAGNO VIGNONI ⊨ ×

Just off the SS2, 48 km SE of Siena. This gnarled hamlet holds a small but entrancing feature: instead of a square you will find at its centre a large, mossy, **stone-walled cistern** of warm sulphurous water. The properties of this hot **spring** have been vaunted since Ancient Roman times. Later visitors included Lorenzo the Magnificent who came here seeking a cure for his rheumatism. The **views** over the valley of the Orcia are punctuated to the south by the stark ruins of the castle of **Rocca d'Orcia** and its neighbouring medieval *borgo* of **Castiglione d'Orcia** which is perched on a spur of Tuscany's highest mountain, **Monte Amiata**.

Bagno Vignoni also lies on Local Explorations: 4 (page 172), an in-depth exploration of this area.

BARBERINO VAL D'ELSA ×

On the SS2, 32 km S of Florence. The Florentine Republic took particular care of the **fortifications** of Barberino in the 13thC, mainly to stop the old feudal lords of Tuscany, the early Republic's bitterest enemies, getting up to any new tricks. The imprint left by Florence is still evident and helps to make it the most attractive of the small towns on this stretch of the Via Cassia. There are no single outstanding sights but a unity of beguiling **medieval architecture** girt by sturdy walls. Sadly, over-restoration is sanitizing its charm – the craft and fancy food shops have already arrived. **Tavernelle**, 3 km N on the Via Cassia, formerly the Roman settlement of Tabernulae on the ancient route between Florence and Siena, has hidden its history behind a 20thC façade.

BOLSENA ⊨ ×

On the SS2, 31 km NW of Viterbo. Tourist information in Piazza Matteotti in lower part of old town; easiest to park down by lake. This thriving little lakeside resort noted for its mild climate doesn't make too

---

MIRACLE OF BOLSENA

Bolsena was the scene of one of the most famous of the medieval miracles that conveniently occurred when the church was having difficulty pulling the faithful into line over disputed matters of doctrine. According to tradition, a German priest on his way to Rome was celebrating mass here in 1263 when he was plagued by doubts as to whether the bread and wine really did turn into the body and blood of Christ (the doctrine of transubstantiation was a hot topic among theologians at the time). His problem was soon resolved when the host began to bleed at the moment of consecration. The Miracle of Bolsena led to the institution of the feast of Corpus Christi and the building of Orvieto Cathedral to house the blood-stained altar cloth. Poor Bolsena was only left with a bloody fragment of the altar – it is hidden in the **Miracle Chapel** of the church of **Santa Cristina**.

DETOUR – FERENTO

9 km N from Viterbo. Look out for the well-signposted turning on the right if you are heading N. After a couple of km you will come upon the melancholy **ruins** of the Roman town of Ferentium dotted about the fields. The remarkably intact **theatre**, circled by 26 tufa arches, is an impressive sight. The city was founded by the Etruscans, destroyed then rebuilt by the Romans and finally razed to the ground by the Viterbese in 1172 after the place was alleged to have become a hotbed of heresy.

THE CENTRE / *The Via Cassia*

> **EST EST EST**
> The local white wine of Montefiascone, Est Est Est, gets its name and undeserved fame from the much-told story of a bibulous 13thC German prelate. Travelling south towards Rome, he sent his valet ahead with instructions to write the word *Est* where the best wine was to be had. At Montefiascone the servant, clearly not a wine buff, enthusiastically scrawled the word three times. The priest took such a shine to it that he died from overconsumption; his pickled remains were laid to rest in the church of **San Flaviano**.

LAGO DI BOLSENA
This wide stretch of water lies in the craters of an extinct volcano and is Europe's largest lake of volcanic origin. The two islands, **Bisentina** and **Martana** (ferries from Bolsena), are the remains of small cones. Known as *il lago che si beve* (the lake you drink) for the purity of its waters, it has been fished since prehistoric times. Along with its renowned **eels** – one of Dante's victims was sent to Purgatory for over-indulging in them – the lake abbounds with perch (*pesce persico*), pike (*luccio*) and small fry (*latterini*). To see the **lakeside** at its most uncontaminated drive along the small road that hugs the western shore.

MONTE AMIATA
See *Bagno Vignoni, page* 112.

many concessions to tourism. Well worth spending a couple of hours toiling up and down the steep covered alleyways and narrow streets to work up an appetite for a memorable fish lunch in the *centro storico* or on the waterfront (see Recommended Restaurants, pages 116-17).

The best time to be here is on **July 24**, the feast day of the town's patron saint, Santa Cristina. Lurid scenes depicting the multiple tortures she suffered under the Romans are acted out by the townspeople as a procession with her image winds through the town. No one seems particularly worried that the episodes don't tally with any known historical facts.

BUONCONVENTO
On the SS2, 27 *km* SE *of Siena.* A small agricultural and industrial centre that still retains portions of its 14thC Sienese **walls**. The fact that you may never have heard of Matteo di Giovanni shouldn't put you off admiring his fine **painting of the Madonna** in the **Museo d'Arte Sacra della val d'Arbia** (*only open Mon, Tues, Sun am and Sat pm*). You'll find this low-key collection of treasures opposite the much tinkered with parish church of **Santi Pietro e Paulo.**

CASTIGLIONE D'ORCIA
See *Bagno Vignoni, page* 112.

FLORENCE
See *pages* 39-81.

> **DETOUR – MONTE OLIVETO MAGGIORE, ABBAZIA**
> *About 9 km off the* SS2. South-east of Siena lies a Tuscan desert, a barren landscape of eroded clay gulleys called the **Crete**. Here, in 1313, Bernardo Tolomei, tired of his life as a member of a rich Sienese family, founded the **Abbey of Monte Oliveto Maggiore**. Like all reformed sophisticates, he wasn't going to do things by half and also founded the new Olivetan Order, aimed at bucking up the strict Rule of St Benedict, by then grown somewhat lax. The abbey, a Renaissance jewel hidden away in the wilderness, stands witness to its success in the following two centuries as a retreat for Siena's jaded elite. Apart from the noble buildings and the cypress-ringed setting, the treasure here, embellishing the **Great Cloister,** is a grandiose cycle of 36 **frescoes** (1497-1508) on the life of St Benedict by Luca Signorelli and Giovanni Bazzi, the latter better known by the unfortunate nickname of Il Sodoma. The curious animals that creep into his pictures are reputedly portraits from his exotic menagerie. A community of monks still lives here as an enclosed order and is celebrated for restoring antique books.

Seeing the Region: 3

MONTEFIASCONE

On the SS2, 16 km N of Viterbo. A noble hill town whose foundations go back to the Etruscans. Climb up to the ruins of the **castle** (Cesare Borgia and a handful of popes slept here) for rewarding **views** over Lake Bolsena. On your way down drop into the **crypt** to see the most atmospheric part of the vast octagonal **Duomo**. At the bottom of the town, the church of **San Flaviano** is one of the strangest you'll find in this section. It is actually two churches built one on top of the other on the site of a Roman Temple to Minerva (San Flaviano's bones are kept in a recycled Roman sarcophagus).

MONTERIGGIONI ⊨ ×

Just off the SS2, 15 km NW of Siena. Well before you arrive you catch sight of this fortress village whose 13thC **walls**, still virtually intact, stand like a mighty crown on a hillock of terraced vines and olives. Built by the Sienese (1212-19) as a bastion in the struggle against the Florentines for control of the valley of the Elsa, the walls form a circle of some 600 m punctuated by 14 **square towers**. In Dante's *Inferno*, the Florentine poet likened the terrifying giants that guarded the ninth circle of Hell to the towers of Monteriggioni. Inside, apart from the simple little **church** which strides Romanesque and Gothic styles, the place seems strangely bare, with wide and windy open spaces. Top marks, though, for the romantic small **albergo** (see Recommended Hotels, page 116).

PIENZA ⊨ ×

Off the SS2, 10 km W from San Quirico d'Orcia. My favourite corner of southern Tuscany, this rural backwater of little more than 2,000 souls is one of the few examples of a Renaissance 'designer town'. Its patron was the great humanist Enea Silvio Piccolomini who, on his election as Pope Pius II, wished to glorify his native village. He even issued a Papal bull to change its name from Corsignano. Work got off to a promising start in 1495 but sadly both Pope and architect (Bernardo Rossellino) died four years later and only the central core of the grand city was ever realized. **Piazza Pio II**, built following Alberti's canons of rationality, proportion and symmetry that transformed Florentine architecture, is the focal point of the town; a 3-D version of one of those Renaissance paintings of the Ideal City. The luminous **Cathedral** takes pride of place – though for how much longer is difficult to say: the hillside behind has been slipping away ever since it was built. Inside it is soaringly Gothic – Pius had been taken by the German *Hallenkirchen* style on his travels abroad.

The massive palace to the right of the Cathedral is **Palazzo Piccolomini**, an exceedingly grand Papal *pied-à-terre* that Rossellino modelled on Palazzo Rucellai (he had been Alberti's assistant during the building of the Florentine masterpiece). Don't miss the spectacular views over the **Val d'Orcia** from the palace's triple **loggia and gardens**.

Other fine palaces surround the square including the **Palazzo Vescovile**, due at the time of writing to be the new home for the **Cathedral Museum**. The collection includes amongst its treasures a lavish **cope** embroidered for Pius II in England. The town has many other small charms worth hunting out, including the chaste little 12thC Romanesque church of old Corsignano, **Pieve di San Vito**, that stands forlorn some 15 minutes walk to the west of the centre.

Pienza is noted for its **cacio**, sheep's milk cheese claimed by locals to be the best in Italy (try telling that to a Sardinian shepherd). Foodies will go for the matured version covered in ashes. On the first Sunday of September the town is given over to a **cheese fair**.

POGGIBONSI

See *Local Explorations: 1*.

RADICOFANI

72 km SE of Siena; the SS2 now by-passes town west to west. As you leave the modern path of the Via Cassia and wind up to the stony medieval **centro storico** you will be following in the footsteps of the illustrious dead, for this was the principal staging post between Siena and Rome for all the famous travellers in past centuries. They stayed at the **Palazzo La Posta**, a Medicean villa on the edge of town.

Guests included Chateaubriand, Montaigne and Dickens. The last had a restless night; 'there is a winding, creaking, wormy, rustling, door-opening, foot-on-

THE CENTRE / *The Via Cassia*

• *Piazza San Pellegrino, Viterbo.*

staircase-falling character about this Radicofani Hotel such as I never saw, anywhere else,' he wrote. The **rocca** (castle) that crowns the hill was built in 1154 by England's only Pope, Hadrian IV. The church of **San Pietro** has some exquisite della Robbia terracotta **reliefs**: not to be missed.

SAN CASCIANO IN VAL DI PESA
On the SS2, 17 km S of central Florence. A bustling agricultural centre once heavily fortified as a bulwark to protect its mother town of Florence. Little now remains of the 14thC defences; the Second World War dealt them their final blow. The large American war **cemetery** before you arrive at the town from Florence bears witness to the fierce fighting around here in 1944. The town is on the threshold of Chianti country and from here on vines and olives keep you company as you head south.

SAN LORENZO NUOVO
On the SS2, 8 km S of Acquapendente. A neat and tidy example of enlightened 18thC town planning, San Lorenzo was built by the Papal government to rehouse the people of the old village who had been dying off down by the malaria-infested lakeside; a small star for its unusual **octagonal piazza**.

SAN QUIRICO D'ORCIA
On the SS2, 43 km SE of Siena. This modest but ancient walled *borgo* has much refined detail and a splendid setting, astride the **Orcia and Asso valleys.** The finest of its delightful churches is the Romanesque **Collegiata** church with its striking **portals**, one sporting lively 13thC lion and caryatid carvings. Visit the 16thC **Orti Leonini**, gardens where the Renaissance knocked nature into shape with miles of box hedging and little else.

From San Quirico you can branch off to explore the area further by undertaking Local Explorations: 4, pages 170-5.

SIENA
See Local Explorations: 1.

TAVERNELLE VAL DI PESA
See Barberino Val d'Elsa, page 112.

VITERBO ⇌ ✕
On the SS2, 75 km N of Rome; tourist information in Piazza dei Cadutti 16, *down Via Ascenzi from Piazza del Plebiscito; main station in Viale Trento to N of town outside walls, trains for Rome; bus station also here; parking a nightmare and mostly on* disco orario – *use any of the city gates off ring road around walls to arrive at centre.*

A provincial capital with Roman airs, celebrated for its fountains and beautiful women, Viterbo only reveals its considerable charms if you spend time on it. The large blocks of volcanic tufa give its grand buildings a forbidding aspect, but there is plenty to delight the curious and, for once, the main sights of the town are very well signposted for pedestrians.

At its heart lies a remarkable **medieval core** that has been largely

Seeing the Region: 3

left alone by later centuries. Many regard it as the best preserved of its kind in Central Italy and a saunter along the **Via San Pellegrino** is a must – the narrow street is a warren of arches, towers, balconies, open staircases and passages, best experienced on a warm summer's night. From here pass through **Piazza della Morte**, pausing to look at one of the city's oldest **fountains**, and make for nearby **Piazza San Lorenzo** to see the 13thC **Papal Palace**, celebrated both for its Gothic architecture and its illustrious history. The delicate stone lacework of the **loggia** is worth a snapshot. For some 20 years in the 13thC it was the centre of the Christian world when the papacy left a feuding Rome to set up court here. The palace also witnessed the election of Pope Gregory X after the longest conclave in history; for two years and ten months the cardinals vacillated, only reaching agreement when the people of Viterbo tore off the roof and reduced their supply of food and drink to iron rations.

From the Papal Palace walk down **Via San Lorenzo** to the historic centre of the city, **Piazza del Plebiscito**, watched over by the 14thC **Palazzo dei Priori**. Heading up from here along **Via Cavour** you can see the medieval masterpiece in the **Piazza Fontana**

RECOMMENDED HOTELS

BAGNO VIGNONI
Posta Marcucci, LL-LLL; *tel.* 0577 887112; *fax* 0577 887119; *cards accepted*.
 This modern but nevertheless tasteful hotel with 50 well-appointed rooms in a delightful village provides an ideal base for exploration of the Val d'Orcia. The swimming pool fed by the nearby hot springs is a bonus.

BOLSENA
Columbus, LL; *Viale Colesanti* 27; *tel.* 0761 799009; *fax* 0761 798172; *cards accepted*.
 The best of the town's modest hotels, this modern *albergo* has reasonably sized rooms, many with lake views, and an attractive site near the water's edge. No points for the naff decoration.

MONTERIGGIONI
Hotel Monteriggioni, LLL; *Via 1° Maggio* 4; *tel.* 0577 305009; *fax* 0577 305011; *cards accepted*.
 Restrained luxury in brilliantly restored medieval building with an enviable setting. Rooms decorated with taste; antique furniture. Breakfast in summer out in the garden backing on to the ancient town walls. A splendid small *albergo* worth the high price. Eat at Monteriggioni's highly praised restaurant next door (see Recommended Restaurants, page 117).

PIENZA
Relais Il Chiostro, LL; *Corso Rossellino*, 26; *tel.* 0578 748400; *fax* 0578 748440; *cards accepted*.
 Decent-sized rooms with a view over the Val d'Orcia: ask if one of the pair with 15thC frescoes is available. Housed in a recently restored monastery with breakfast served in the cloister. Excellent value for such a romantic spot just a few steps from Pienza's magical square.

VITERBO
Leon d'Oro, L-LL; *via della Cava* 36; *tel.* 0761 344444; *fax* 0761 344444; *cards accepted*.
 Better than average in a city not endowed with attractive hotels. Solid, if frayed comfort where commercial travellers feel at ease.

Tuscia, L-LL; *via Cairoli*, 41; *tel.* 0761 344400; *fax* 0761 345976; *cards accepted*.
 Recently modernized with Spartan rooms, but efficient, polite staff.

RECOMMENDED RESTAURANTS

BAGNO VIGNONI
Antica Osteria del Leone, LL; *Piazza del Moretto*; *tel.* 0577 887300; *cards accepted*; *closed Mon and Nov*.
 An all-Tuscan menu: start with excellent *crostini*, including *alla milza* (paté of spleen) and grilled *peperoni*; follow with a *zuppa di pane* then *scottiglia* (southern Tuscany's bung-it-all-in-and-see-what-comes-out version of stew) or *coniglio con pinoli* (rabbit with pine kernels) rounded off with the home-

Grande, the finest of the city's many fountains.

If you prefer beautiful women, stroll down from Piazza del Plebiscito along the smart **Corso Italia** in the early evening when it comes to life as the Viterbese take their *passeggiata*, mingling with the soldiers from the large army barracks outside the town. A word of warning – Viterbo is also famous for its witches. At the bottom of the Corso, just up **Via Santa Rosa**, you'll find the grotesque preserved **corpse** of the city's patron saint, Santa Rosa, inside the **church** that bears her name.

> **MACCHINA DI SANTA ROSA**
> The Viterbese have an idiosyncratic way of marking the feast day of their patron saint. On Sept 3, 100 beefy citizens stagger through the streets carrying a 100-foot high, gilded **'spire'**. But the **Macchina di Santa Rosa** has not been a great respecter of pilgrims' safety: in 1801 22 people were trampled to death by a panic-stricken crowd; in 1814 the contrivance fell on the *facchini* (porters) with dire results; in 1967 it had to be abandoned when the *facchini* ran out of breath.

made *millefoglie* pastry. Wine, of course, is strictly regional.

BARBERINO VAL D'ELSA
Il Paese dei Campanelli, LL; *Borgo Petrognano; tel. 055 8075318; cards accepted; closed Mon and Nov.*

You'll find this romantic restaurant about 2 km along the minor road from Barberino to Certaldo. Great gnocchi (potato dumplings) and a deliciously unhealthy *fritto misto* of meats and vegetables. Eating inside the prettily restored farmhouse is as pleasant as taking lunch out on the terrace.

BOLSENA
Da Picchieto, LL; *Via Porta Fiorentina 15; tel. 0761 799158; cards accepted; closed Mon and Oct.*

One of the best and most honestly-priced places offering fish from Lake Bolsena. True, you don't have lakeside views (you'll find the restaurant in the lower part of the old town) but there is a cool, vine-shaded courtyard. Try the spaghetti dressed with a *sugo di pesce* (fish sauce) followed by stewed eel or, for culinary cowards, grilled *coregone*, a fish similar to wild trout found only here and in Lake Como.

MONTERIGGIONI
Il Pozzo, LL; *Piazza Roma 2; tel. 0577 304127; cards accepted; closed Sun eve & Mon.*

Best food for miles around in the moody ruins of a medieval walled *borgo*. Strictly local cooking with superb *pici* (the local fat, hand-made pasta, pronounced peechee, or peeshee in Tuscan dialect) and a feast of wild mushrooms in the autumn.

PIENZA
La Buca delle Fate, L-LL; *Corso Rossellino 38; tel 0578 748448; cards accepted; closed Mon.*

Bustling, large *trattoria* that seems as if it ought to be in the middle of a major city rather than in this tiny Renaissance town. Short, simple menu features the best of *la cucina toscana*: a wedge of Pienza's rightly famous sheep's cheese, *cacio*, is obligatory with the end of your bottle of red *Vino Nobile* from nearby Montepulciano.

VITERBO
Trattoria Porta Romana, L-LL; *Via della Bonta'; tel. 0761 307118; cards none; closed Sun.*

Tina Palluca offers authentic Viterbese cooking in this no-frills *trattoria* off the tourist beat near the Porta Romana gateway. From the down-to-earth dishes try the *lombrichelli alla amatriciana* (literally, little earthworms, suggested by the shape of this pasta); *zucchine ripiene* (stuffed courgettes); and the *bollito di manzo* (boiled beef with onions). To finish, try the local sweet biscuits, *tozzetti*, with honeyed Aleatico wine from nearby Gradoli. Honest food at honest prices.

For fish try **La Spigola (LL**; *via della Pace,40; tel. 0761 303049; closed Wed, open evgs only*) or **Enoteca La Torre (LL**; *via della Torre, 5; tel 0761 226467; closed Sun*).

Seeing the Region: 4

The West

Between Pesaro and Spoleto
Umbria and Upland Marche - the Via Flaminia

160 km; map Touring Club Italiano Umbria Marche

This section introduces you to the oak-clad hills of Umbria and some undiscovered parts of the upland Marche by a short but pleasing journey along the Via Flaminia, one of Ancient Rome's most important highways. Besides the historic road itself, the most memorable features are the hill towns – some of Italy's proudest – with Spoleto as the climax.

Sadly, the 1997 earthquake in Umbria & the Marche has left a number of the towns on the route badly shaken. Although a number of important buildings are closed for the foreseeable future, visitors should not be put off as there is still plenty to see. We've given details of the towns worst hit in the individual entries.

La Terra dei Santi (Land of Saints), as Umbria is sometimes known, has given birth to more saints than any other Italian region. It is also the geographical heart of Italy, a charmed place which for some has a mystic quality. You can pay your respects to its greatest saint, St Francis, at the noble town of Assisi.

For most of the shorter stretch in the Marche, between Fano and Cagli, a modern *superstrada*, running parallel to our marked route, has cleared the ancient road of all but local traffic. This leaves you free to meander along its course, pondering the many remnants of its glorious past, or, if time is short, to use the dual-carriageway to get to the next attraction. Here, too, you will find the most dramatic scenery on the route, under the splendid crags of the Furlo Gorge. You can also dip your toe in the Adriatic at the historic town of Fano where the Via Flaminia meets the sea.

The Flaminian Way was built by the Consul Gaius Flaminius in 220 BC. Its importance continued into the Middle Ages when the Papal States valued it both as a strategic highway and as a pilgrim route to the shrine of St Francis.

THE WEST / Umbria and Upland Marche – the Via Flaminia

1:1,000,000

- Pesaro
- Fano
- Senigallia
- Fossombrone
- Mondavio
- Furlo
- Acqualagna
- Cagli
- Cantiano
- Sigillo
- Gualdo Tadino
- Nocera Umbra
- Assisi
- Spello
- Foligno
- Montefalco
- Trevi
- Fonti di Clitunno
- Campello sul Clitunno
- Spoleto
- Moneluco

• Trevi

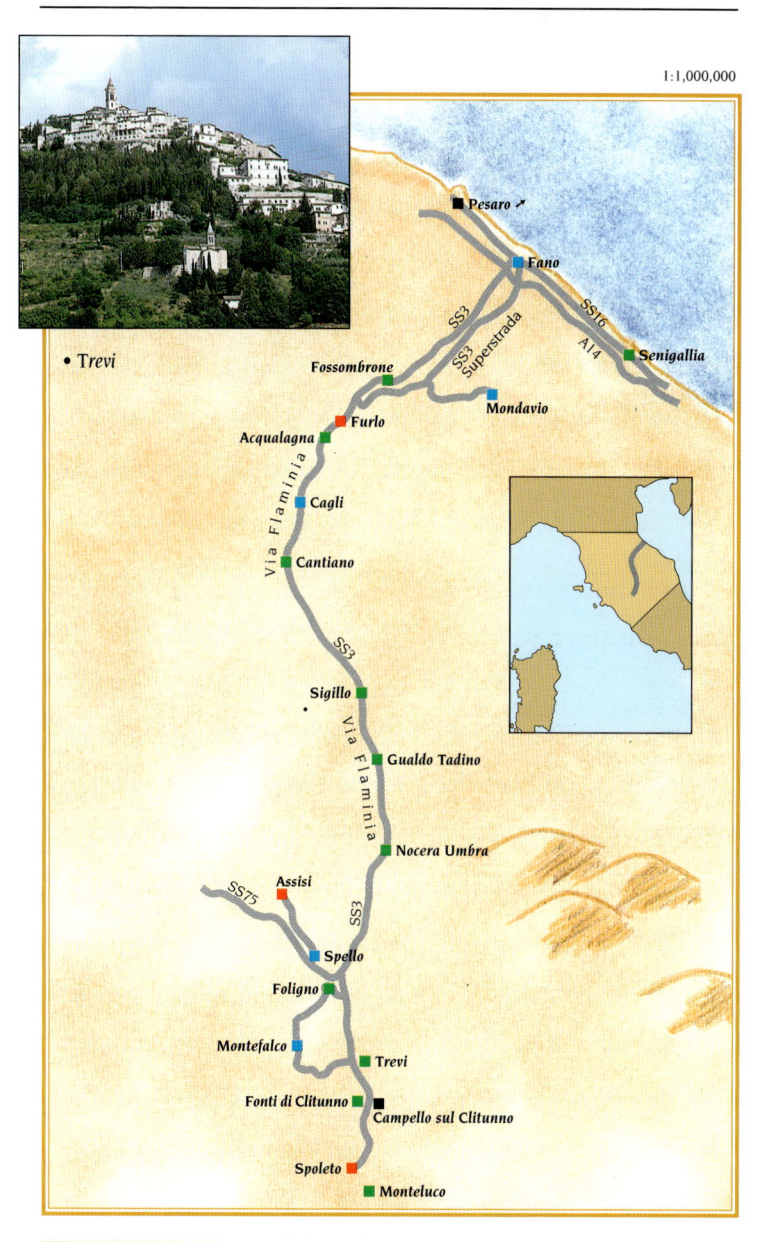

Via Flaminia

SS3 Superstrada
SS16
A14
SS3
SS75

TRANSPORT
The Umbrian stretch is well served by both trains and buses, while long-distance (Bucci) and local buses regularly ply the Via Flaminia in the Marches.

The Ancona-Rome railway line connects Spoleto and Nocera Umbra – change at Foligno for Assisi and onwards to Perugia. Fano and Senigallia lie on the main Milan-Bari east coast line.

Trips to Montefalco and Mondavio are only really feasible by car. Nearest airport to Spoleto is Rome; to Fano, Bologna. Summer-only charter flights to Adriatic coast via Rimini or Ancona (Falconara).

Seeing the Region: 4

SIGHTS & PLACES OF INTEREST

ACQUALAGNA
On the SS3, 42 km SW of Fano. The local rose-pink limestone gives a pleasing aspect to this small town, even though most of its old buildings were destroyed in the Second World War. There is little to tempt you to linger, except on the last weekend of October and the first two weekends of November, when Acqualagna welcomes visitors from all over Italy to the **truffle market** – you can smell the fungus even before you arrive.

The truffle is the Marches' greatest delicacy: if you suspect that it is overrated, try a plate of spaghetti with a truffle-flavoured sauce; or, from one of the stalls in the town's central square, a simple *crostini* (slice of toasted bread moistened with stock) topped with slivers of truffle.

THE TRUFFLE

Truffles are, weight for weight, one of the most expensive foods on Earth. Luckily, however, a little goes a long way and in Central Italy you can indulge in them without pawning your valuables.

Of some 16 species of *tartufo* found in Italy, only two are worth killing for – the *tartufo bianco* or white truffle (*Tuber magnatum Pico*) and the *tartufo nero pregiato* or black truffle (*Tuber melanosporum Vitt.*).

The white is the finest, and the costliest: *tartufi bianchi* can fetch more than £1,000 ($1,500) a kilo. The black version is cheaper. To buy them fresh you have to be here between October and the end of December for the *bianchi* and between December and March for the *neri pregiati*. In summer any fresh truffles to be found on restaurant menus will be the *tartufo d'estate* or summer truffle (*Tuber aestivum Vitt.*), a pale shadow of its superlative sisters – if these are your only experience of truffles, you will wonder what all the fuss is about.

Italian truffle hunters dig up around 100 metric tonnes of truffles a year with the help of their truffle hounds. Rarity explains the high price of these fungi: as well as growing hidden from sight underground, each species can only thrive in a very particular habitat in association with the roots of specific trees. Climate, drainage and soil alkalinity have to be just right for these sensitive growths and the most highly-prized species are the most touchy.

Experienced truffle hunters know the patches of woodland, often little more than a few metres square, where truffles grow. To avoid damaging the habitat by excessive digging, they will set their dogs to sniff out precisely where well-developed truffles lie buried. Once the hound has located a truffle, he is hauled off and given a dog biscuit; the hunter finishes off the job with a special miniature spade. Truffle patches are jealously-guarded secrets: the hunter will fill the hole afterwards and disguise it with a sprinkling of dead leaves.

In the Marches, **Acqualagna** (see Seeing the Region: 4, page 120) and **Sant'Angelo in Vado** (see Seeing the Region: 2, page 103) have truffle fairs in the late autumn, when their main squares are filled with stalls selling every imaginable truffle-based product.

San Miniato, on the southern slopes of the Arno valley to the west of Florence, is Tuscany's great centre for white truffles (the record specimen in modern times was found here in 1954 and weighed in at over 2 kg). For the finest *neri pregiati* make for **Spoleto** in southern Umbria (see pages 126-7). Although truffles are best eaten fresh within days of their discovery, there are plenty of products that try to preserve the experience. Best value are the small bottles of olive oil flavoured with truffles. Other worthwhile buys are truffle butter and tubes of truffle paste. The whole truffles preserved in glass jars are expensive and have had most of the stuffing knocked out of them in the process of conservation. To be avoided, unless you have a very perverse palate, are the liqueurs with a lump of truffle bobbing about inside the bottle.

THE WEST / Umbria and Upland Marche – the Via Flaminia

ASSISI

On the SS75, 18 km NW of Foligno. Tourist information in main Piazza del Comune 27; railway station 5 km SW of town at Santa Maria degli Angeli, hourly trains for Foligno and Perugia link with Florence-Rome line to west and Ancona-Rome line to east; buses to station and surrounding towns from bus station in Piazza Matteotti on eastern edge of town; do not attempt to drive into centre but park at one of the large car parks that surround the town - largest is underground in Piazza Matteotti; avoid Easter, Christmas and October 3-4 (Feast of St Francis) when the town is always packed with pilgrims.

This ravishingly beautiful Umbrian hill town was badly hit by the 1997 earthquake but most of its great monuments remained undamaged. The tourists have stayed away in droves since the disaster, so visit before the crowds return.

Stretched out on the lower slopes of Monte Subasio, its main thoroughfares follow the contours of the hillside and are punctuated by fine squares with balcony views over the plain below. Apart from Rome, it is Italy's greatest place of pilgrimage and you may be either deeply moved by the devotion to Italy's patron saint, the humble St Francis, or thoroughly disgusted by the tawdry cashing-in on his name.

Although the earthquake severely damaged the **Upper Basilica**, any visit to Assisi should still start with the **Basilica di San Francesco** that soars up like a mighty fortress at the western end of town. The great double-decker building, one church built on top of another, was started in 1228, two years after the death of St Francis, and consecrated in 1253. Inside, the great cycles of floor-to-ceiling **frescoes** include some of the greatest masterpieces of Italian 13th and 14thC art. For me the **Lower Basilica**, where the saint's body has lain since 1230, is the most atmospheric: the rich colours of the medieval frescoes glow in the dim light and even the most worldly among the swarm of tourists are hushed into respect. The most important works include the cycle on the **Life of St Martin** painted in 1321-6 by Simone Martini, one of the masters of the early Sienese school (first chapel on left of nave). Another great piece is Cimabue's solemn ***Madonna and Child Enthroned with Angels and***

SAINT FRANCIS

Giovanni Bernardone was born the son of a rich cloth merchant of Assisi in the winter of 1181-2, and earned the nickname of Francesco, the little Frenchman, for his love of the fairytale poetry of the French Troubadours. As a youth he was noted for his carefree ways and high spirits, but a year as a prisoner of war in Perugia, perhaps also ill health, seem to have changed his outlook as he approached his twenties. Disowned by his father for his profligate generosity to the poor, he began life wedded to 'Lady Poverty'.

In 1210 the great medieval pope, Innocent III, gave his blessing to Saint Francis and his 11 companions to become itinerant preachers and thus was born the Friars Minor, the first order of Franciscans. From their original headquarters in the tiny Porziuncola chapel on the outskirts of Assisi, the order grew with amazing speed. In 1212 he and Saint Clare, his spiritual sister, founded the first order for women, the Poor Clares, and by 1217 St Francis's message of poverty, humility and obedience had spread across Europe. He died in 1226 in the Porziuncola two years after receiving the stigmata, the marks of the five wounds of Christ. So great was his fame that his canonization followed just two years later, in 1228.

His winning combination of kindness and humility and his deep love of nature have made him one of the most popular saints of our times. But his fundamental message of absolute poverty – some even see it as an anarchic rejection of property – is strong meat for the materialistic twentieth century.

St Francis and his followers embody one of the Roman Catholic Church's perennial paradoxes: the conflict between open-hearted Christian idealism and the pragmatism required within a strictly hierarchical institution.

Seeing the Region: 4

• Assisi.

St Francis, painted in 1280: the portrait of St Francis is reckoned to be lifelike (right wall of right transept). Yet another is Pietro Lorenzetti's moving **Passion of Christ** (walls and vault of the left transept).

As was widely reported at the time, the **Upper Basilica** was damaged by the 1997 earthquake when part of the ceiling collapsed, killing a Franciscan monk. Restoration work on Giotto's celebrated cycle of 28 **frescoes** on the life of St Francis is feverishly underway but it will be many years before visitors can again see some of Italy's finest examples of early fresco work.

The town's other great church, dedicated to St Francis' spiritual sister, St Clare, lies a short distance eastwards from the central **Piazza del Comune** down Corso Mazzini. The white-and-pink striped church of **Santa Chiara** was built in 1257-65 on pure Gothic lines and decorated with lambent **frescoes**. The **body** of the saint lies in the 19thC neo-Gothic crypt. The church of **Santa Maria degli Angeli** which stands 5 km away on the plain below the city, was another major monument severely hit by the earthquake and looks set to remain closed for the foreseeable future. The small, primitive chapel, the **Porziuncola**, where St Francis's little community first gathered to worship, still stands in the centre of the domed but damaged basilica.

When St Francis was born here around 1180, Assisi could already boast a long history. To see the finest monument of Roman *Asisium* search out the **Temple of Minerva** in the central Piazza del Comune. Although now converted into a church, you are not likely to mistake it for a Christian building. It is an uncompromisingly grand Roman temple with a magnificent **portico** of lofty Corinthian columns dating from the early days of the Roman Empire (1stC BC). Goethe in his celebrated *Italian Journey* 'turned away in distaste' from the Basilica of St Francis and instead spent his time spellbound by this building. With time to spare you can explore the excavations of the **Roman forum** under the square with not a pilgrim in sight (the entrance is from

• *Santa Maria degli Angeli, near Assisi.*

THE WEST / Umbria and Upland Marche – the Via Flaminia

Museo Civico in Via Portica, just off the square).

CAGLI ×

Few foreign tourists make it to this courtly town set against a backdrop of some of the highest peaks in the northern Marches. An important staging post on the ancient Via Flaminia, it still retains its Roman grid plan, all roads leading to a proper central **square** with a florid fountain, a steely medieval town hall, and huddles of old men deep in gossip.

The hand of the great quattrocento military architect Francesco di Giorgio Martini is unmistakable in the dramatic oval **torrione** or tower to the west of the *piazza*, all that remains of the citadel that Duke Federico da Montefeltro ordered to be built above Cagli towards the end of the 15thC.

Search out the pleasing fresco of the **Madonna and Child with Saints** by Giovanni Santi – the angel to the left of the picture is said to be a portrait of Santi's son, Raphael. You will find it in the church of **San Domenico** near the hospital.

Try also to see inside the **theatre** behind the town hall, a perfect little 19thC opera house with all the trimmings (ask for a tour at the town hall).

A tortuous 10-km drive up from Cagli (follow signs from near Torrione) will take you to the windswept meadows 1,108 m up on the summit of **Monte Petrano**: grand views and a mass of wild daffodils in late spring.

CAMPELLO SUL CLITUNNO ⇔ ×

See Recommended Hotels and Restaurants, pages 127 and 129.

CANTIANO

A hoary medieval town among spectacular mountains. Worth a pause, not for any particular sight, but for its warren of old alleyways, seemingly little altered over the centuries. The finest medieval buildings stand along **Via Fiorucci** that runs off the central square. On the

•*Casare Ottaviano Augusto, Fano.*

evening of Good Friday the town stages an outstanding example of a Medieval Passion play called **La Turba**.

FANO ⇔ ×

At terminus of the SS3 on Adriatic coast. Tourist information, Viale Battisti 10, off Sassonia beach; station on SS16 in Ancona direction - main Milan-Bari line; buses leave from station for town centre, and from front of Arco di Augusto for Pesaro, Urbino, and beaches to the south; cars are not permitted within town walls - park at first available space outside walls.

The Roman colony of Fanum Fortunae took its name from a noted temple to the goddess of Fortune that once stood here. Fortune still reigns today, but in the Christian guise of the town's patron, San Fortunato. In Roman times the place was both an important port and crossroads, where the Via Flaminia from Rome met the main coastal route. Today it is an alluring small seaside resort that doubles as a busy fishing port and historic centre.

The **Arco di Augusto** provides a fitting gateway to the town. It was erected in 2 AD under orders of the Roman Emperor Augustus as part of his ambitious project to smarten up the Empire's road network and marks the arrival of the Via Flaminia at the shores of the Adriatic. On the wall of the church on the right outside the arch is a 16thC bas-relief showing the arch as it was originally built.

From here the main **Via Arco di Augusto** sets a course through the old centre (if you keep following the road it will eventually take you across the railway tracks to finish on the Sassonia beach). At the main crossroads in the centre turn right up Corso Matteotti to arrive at the central **Piazza XX Settembre**, which is decorated with a whimsical 16thC **fountain** topped by the goddess Fortune.

Among the fine buildings flanking the square stands the **Palazzo Malatesta** with a remarkable courtyard and *loggia* known as the **Corte Malatestiana**.

The palace holds the town's **Museo Civico and Pinacoteca**, a carpetbag collection including some fine Renaissance medals and paintings by Guercino, Guido Reni and Michele Giambono. The church of **Santa Maria Nuova**, just off the main square on Via de Pili, holds two treasures by Perugino, a *Madonna with Saints* and an *Annunciation* – it is probable that the young Raphael helped the Umbrian master with the first.

The town has a particularly elegant *passeggiata* in the early evening and smart, tempting shops lining the main streets. The railway cleanly splits the old town from the modern resort that has grown up along two stretches of fine beach. To the south-east runs the **Spiaggia Sassonia**, a long strand of pebbly beach with a wide promenade. To the north-west runs the shorter **Spiaggia Lido**, all sand and serried rows of beach umbrellas, the livelier of the two. Between them lies the small fishing **harbour** where you can buy the best from the freshly-landed catch – the *vongole* or baby clams are particularly good. The most economical place to eat fish here is the self-service **restaurant** near the port, run by a fishermens' co-operative (see Recommended Restaurants, page 129). Both north and south of Fano run pleasant enough beaches, which are often relatively uncrowded.

Some 20 km south is **Senigallia**, another historic centre with an outstanding long beach and worth a visit if you want to spend time on the Adriatic coast. It also has an excellent restaurant (see Recommended Restaurants, page 129).

FONTI DI CLITUNNO

On the SS3, 11 km N of Spoleto. A less-than-picturesque stretch of the Via Flaminia hides the source of the **River Clitunno**, known to the Ancient Romans as the Clitumnus. Poets from Virgil to Byron have sung the praises of this charmed spot. Among tall poplars, the waters bubble up from the rocks to form a limpid **pool** that Byron described as 'A mirror and a bath for Beauty's youngest daughters'. The white cattle reared on the banks of the river in Ancient Roman times were much sought after for sacrificial offerings to the Gods; many believed that it was the magical properties of the crystal-clear waters of the Clitumnus that rendered the animals whiter than white.

Nowadays, however, you will need a healthy imagination if the spell is not to be broken by the numerous school parties. For the poetically-minded, better perhaps to carry on north 1 km to the **Tempietto**, an exceptionally early Christian building on the river's edge, but looking for all the world like a miniature classical temple. To gain access, ring the bell at the gate.

FOLIGNO

On the SS3 29 km N of Spoleto. This is one of the few historic towns of Umbria not built on a hill top. Badly bombed during the Second World War, and further scarred by the 1997 earthquake. It nevertheless boasts a few interesting monuments. Penetrating the dreary suburbs by car is a headache, so it is only worth stopping here if you are changing bus or train to go on to Assisi.

The town's central **Piazza della Repubblica** was badly damaged by the earthquake. It brought down the town hall tower and damaged many of the surrounding buildings. However, look out for the splendid early 13thC **doorway** that graces the façade of the

---

DETOUR – MONDAVIO

Leave the Flaminia at Fossombrone for a delightful drive through the rolling Marche hills to Mondavio. Bright geraniums and spreading cedars add grace to this beautifully preserved, small red-brick medieval hill town. The imposing **fortifications** that stand out from afar were built by Francesco di Giorgio Martini, one of Italy's most celebrated Renaissance military architects, and still stand guard over the place. They now house an entertaining **'Living Museum'** (actually wax dummies) portraying life when the *Rocca* was built at the close of the 15thC for Giovanni della Rovere, son-in-law of Duke Federico da Montefeltro (see Urbino, page 000). Youngsters will savour the grisly **torture chamber**. Wander around the compact centre and stop for an ice-cream and fine views at **Al Giardino** in the little park near the square.

Duomo – a strange medley of carved animals, zodiacal symbols, an Islamic star and crescent, and one of only two portraits in Italy of the celebrated medieval emperor, Frederick II. The 18thC interior was also badly hit by the earthquake and is unlikely to reopen before 2000.

Still on the *piazza*, the face of **Palazzo Trinci**, built by Foligno's 14thC ruling lords, was also a victim of neoclassical busybodies, but its fine courtyard and main rooms have been rather better conserved and hold an unassuming civic art gallery. Wander down **Via Gramsci** from the square to see the noblest of the town's genteel if crumbling 16th and 17thC **palaces**. At the end of the road stands Foligno's least messed-about old church, **Santa Maria Infraportas**, dating from the 12thC. The Byzantine-style frescoes in the **Cappella dell'Assunta** (in the left nave) are particularly striking.

Festa fever takes over on the second weekend of September when the various quarters of the town battle out, on horseback, the **Giostra della Quintana,** a tournament (dating back to the 17thC) in which riders tilt at a swivelling target. Even if you don't stop at Foligno, you might want to know that the first edition of Dante's *Divine Comedy* was printed here in 1472 – the first book in Italian ever to be printed in Italy.

FOSSOMBRONE
On the SS3, 30 km SW of Fano. This small town on the slopes of the Metauro Valley, looks splendid from a distance. It was once the Roman Forum Sempronii. Although it has no outstanding monument, there is a delightful collection of buildings and streets that bear witness to a prosperous past. The ruins that crown the town are of a castle built by the powerful Malatesta family. The town's centre boasts a pair of **arcaded streets** lined with gracious but modest Renaissance palaces. The Mafia are here in a big way – safely locked up in one of Italy's most secure prisons on the edge of town.

FURLO ⛨ ×
Village at mouth of Furlo Gorge – see below. *See Recommended Hotels and Restaurants, pages 128 and 129.*

FURLO GORGE
The modern SS3 misses the gorge, passing instead through a 3-km tunnel. To see the gorge, turn off on to the old Flaminia, following signs for Furlo.

A gorge for lovers of gothic scenery: sheer limestone cliffs rise up on either side of the bright green waters of the Candigliano river, leaving just enough room for a narrow road to pass. At one point the ancient highway passes through a **tunnel** hewn by hand through the hard rock. The work was ordered by Emperor Vespasian in 76 AD – a remarkable feat of Roman civil engineering. The area is now a nature park and home to rare flora and fauna. You may even see a golden eagle wheeling overhead. The gorge ends abruptly as the road enters a wide valley where the Candigliano flows into the Metauro.

GUALDO TADINO
On the SS3, 33 km N of Foligno. A boom town turning out ceramics that raise *kitsch* to new heights – stop at one of the factory showrooms that engulf the ancient town and ponder how the country that spawned the Renaissance can also produce such hideous objects. Amongst the dross, however, you can discover the occasional lapse into good taste: simple painted earthenware or unglazed terracotta. The old centre was badly knocked about by the 1997 earthquake, and it will take several years until rebuilding is complete.

DETOUR – MONTEFALCO
A loop from Trevi to the west takes you up to Montefalco, the 'Balcony of Umbria' – a crow's nest town commanding some of the finest views in the region. Before strolling around the airy streets of the *Centro Storico*, walk around the walls to admire the views.

Another reason for making this detour is to see the fresco cycle, the **Life of St Francis**, in the church of **San Francesco**. Painted by the Florentine fresco painter Benozzo Gozzoli in the mid-15thC, this is one of the most spirited accounts of the saint's life.

A further attraction is **Sagrantino Passito**, the local sweet and heady red dessert wine with an alcoholic kick.

MONTELUCO
See Spoleto, page 127.

NOCERA UMBRA
On the SS3 17 km N of Foligno. This once beguiling little town with its warren of medieval streets was badly ruined by the 1997 earthquake and it will take several years until it is restored to its former beauty. It is noted for its curative waters: 5 km south-east of the town is a small spa, **Bagni di Nocera**, where you are promised a remedy for virtually any digestive disorder.

PESARO
See *Seeing the Region*: 2.

SENIGALLIA ×
See *Fano, page 124 and Recommended Restaurants, page 129*.

SIGILLO
On the SS3, some 38 km S of Cagli. Between Cagli and Sigillo the Flaminia passes through wild and empty mountain country with just a scattering of simple villages. From **Sigillo** take a twisting 9-km detour up to Val di Ranco on **Monte Cucco**, Umbria's highest peak at 1,566 m: breathtaking mountain scenery.

Some 4 km N of Sigillo on the Flaminia is **Costacciaro**, the main centre for the **Monte Cucco Regional Nature Park**. Speleologists will probably already know that one of the world's deepest potholing complexes is here, the **Grotte di Monte Cucco**. A useful map, obtainable from the information office in the centre of the village, gives details of numerous **hiking trails** in the area.

SPELLO ⚐ ×
On the SS75, 6 km NW of Foligno. Assisi's little sister, Spello also lies on the slopes of Monte Subasio and is a gem of a hill town, even if it has been over-polished for the tourists. Once the Roman town of Hispellum, its streets abound with testimony to each era of its history. Note the 1stC BC Roman **Porta Consolare**, still the main gate that pierces the town walls to the south. From here walk up Via Consolare to see inside the church of **Santa Maria Maggiore**. The first chapel on the left holds brightly restored **frescoes** by Bernardino di Betto, better known as Il Pinturicchio (literally, 'rich painting'), of the *Annunciation* and *Nativity* (1501). Looking at these beautiful works you can understand why his extravagant use of colour earned this Umbrian master his nickname. Carry on up to the central **Piazza della Repubblica** to admire the fine 13thC **Palazzo Comunale**, then make the short, sharp hike up to the **Torre Belvedere** at the top of the town for excellent views of Assisi and Spello's Roman **amphitheatre** directly below. Back in the main square there is a *cantina* selling Spello's robust red wine.

SPOLETO ⚐ ×
On the SS3, 28 km S of Foligno. Tourist information: central Piazza della Libertà 7. Station: Piazzale Polvani, N of old town; on main Rome-Ancona line; buses from station for central Piazza della Libertà; out-of-town buses from Piazza Garibaldi at N end of town. Parking: leave car outside walls as centre is compact and easy to walk. Accommodation hard to find during Festival (mid-June to mid-July).

Heading north on the SS3, your first view of this hill town, one of Umbria's finest, is dominated by the 80-m-high arches of the **Ponte delle Torri**, a 13thC aquaduct built on Roman foundations, and the bellicose 14thC **Rocca**. The modern-day Flaminia passes under the town through a tunnel but it would be a shame not to stop.

Despite a rural setting on the olive-covered slopes of southern Umbria, Spoleto is no backwater. From mid-June to mid-July it hosts the **Festival dei Due Mondi**, one of Italy's premier annual arts jamborees; and with art galleries and smart restaurants it has a decidely sophisticated air. The town is also jam-packed with eloquent monuments from its long history.

To see the major sights start in **Piazza della Libertà** in the centre of the medieval huddle of the higher, southern part of the town. To the side of the square stand the ruins of a **Roman theatre** built in the 1stC AD. Heading off along **Via Brignone** you will spot one of Spoleto's imposing Roman gateways, the **Arco di Monterone**, and yet another, the **Arco di Druso**, just round the corner in Via Arco di Druso.

Pass through the small **Piazza del Mercato** to arrive in front of the **Palaz**

THE WEST / Umbria and Upland Marche – the Via Flaminia

zo Comunale. Though rebuilt in the 18thC, it still has an impressive late 13thC **tower**. Underneath the modern wing lie the remains of a patrician **Roman house**, claimed to have been the home of Emperor Vespasian's mother (entrance in Via Visiale).

For a closer look at the great *rocca* or citadel that dominates the town, wander up Via del Municipio. It was built by the celebrated 14thC Umbrian architect Matteo Gattapone for the powerful Cardinal Albornoz. Returning down Via Saffi you will come across the dignified Romanesque church of **Sant'Eufemia**, where a right turn will bring you into the town's set-piece square **Piazza del Duomo** set-off by the 13thC **Duomo**. Flanked by a noble **bell-tower**, it has a beautiful **façade** pierced by a series of striking rose windows. Inside, see the glowing yet muted colours of Fra Filippo Lippi's **frescoes** on the life of the Virgin. These were the artist's last works and the notorious womanizer lies buried here having been reputedly poisoned in 1469 after seducing the daughter of a local noble family.

In the lower part of town to the north, hunt out **Via Cecili** to spot some of the place's oldest relics. The great poligonal blocks of stone that form the lower level of the well-preserved ancient **walls** at the side of the street date back to the city's foundation by Umbrian tribes around the 6thC BC. The square blocks above were laid shortly after the founding of the Roman colony in 241 BC. There is much more to see in the town and you could happily spend a day or two just finding your way around the labyrinth of streets.

Just south of Spoleto a small road to the east off the Via Flaminia twists up for 8 km to the ancient hill-top **sanctuary of Monteluco** where St Francis was once a hermit; the views from here are outstanding.

TREVI

Set in a sea of olive groves, this shimmering hill town tumbles down its slopes above the Flaminia. It is a delightfully unspoilt example of a medieval garrison town with plenty of crumbling stucco. On your way up, stop at the church of the **Madonna delle Lacrime** to see the luscious **fresco** of the *Adoration of the Magi*, by Umbria's native Renaissance master, Perugino.

RECOMMENDED HOTELS

ASSISI

Staying the night here allows you to savour the town after the trippers have left for the day. There is no shortage of hotels, but book early, and avoid major religious festivals, particularly around October 4, the Feast of St Francis. Some of the best:

Umbra, LL; *Via degli Archi 6; tel. 075 812240; fax 075 813653; cards accepted.*
This small hotel with a much-praised restaurant just off the main Piazza del Comune offers tranquility, a shady pergola, and fair prices.

San Francesco, LL; *Via San Francesco 48; tel. 075 812281; fax 075 816237; cards accepted.*
Middle range *albergo* with a great position right in front of the Basilica of San Francesco.

Subasio, LLL; *Via Frate Elia 2; tel. 075 812206; fax 075 816691; cards accepted.*
Assisi's grandest, with a celebrity guest list; close to the Basilica and with beautiful views from flower-decked terraces.

Dei Priori, LL; *Corso Mazzini 15; tel. 075 812237; fax 075 816804; cards accepted.*
A useful mid-price choice, this 34-room hotel is just off central Piazza del Comune.

CAMPELLO SUL CLITUNNO

Le Casaline, LL; *tel. 0743 520811; cards accepted.*
More a restaurant than a hotel, with just seven rooms in a jumble of converted farmbuildings. Idyllic setting among olive groves and rural hospitality. Turn off the Via Flaminia for village of Campello sul Clitunno and carry on another 4 km on the road for Poreta. Much in demand so book well ahead. (See also Recommended Restaurants, page 129.)

FANO

Plenty of modern hotels on the seafront but don't expect much charm. Many are closed out of season. The best three are all under same ownership and open all year:

Elisabeth Due, LL-LLL; Piazzale Amendola 2; tel. 0721 823146; fax 0721 823147; cards accepted.
Grandest in town, down on the Lido beach. The decoration is somewhat precious and the rooms not over-large, but very friendly.

Grand Hotel Elisabeth, LL; Viale Carducci 12; tel. 0721 804241; fax 0721 804242; cards accepted.
Despite name, cheaper (and quieter) sister hotel to Elisabeth Due, a few hundred metres away from Lido beach.

Corallo, L-LL; Via Leonardo da Vinci 3; tel. 0721 804200; fax 0721 803637; cards accepted.
Blockhouse hotel on Sassonia beach. Good value, friendly family hotel.

FURLO
La Ginestra, LL; tel. 0721 797033; fax 0721 700040; cards accepted.
You will find this modern restaurant with ten bedrooms in the village of Furlo at the mouth of the gorge. Airy rooms form a separate group of cottages well away from the restaurant with the cliffs of the gorge as a backdrop. Tennis courts and a swimming pool. (See also Recommended Restaurants, page 129.)

MONDAVIO
La Palomba, L; tel. 0721 97105; fax 0721 977048 cards none.
An unpretentious small albergo with modestly-priced rooms and splendid views, opposite the fortress.

SPELLO
Palazzo Bocci, LLL; Via Cavour 17; tel. 0742 301021; fax 0742 301464; cards accepted.
Swanky modern hotel in lovely converted palace just up from Santa Maria Maggiore. A pleasant alternative to staying in Assisi, if you can afford it.

Del Teatro, LL; Via Giulia 24; tel. 0742 301140; fax 0742 301612; cards accepted.
Cheaper but equally attractive alternative to the Bocci, above, housed in 18thC building in historic centre. Splendid views of Spello and Umbrian dales from tastefully furnished rooms.

SPOLETO
Gattapone, LLL; Via del Ponte 6; tel. 0743 223447; fax 0743 223448; cards accepted.
Spoleto's best: an intimate four-star hotel set in a flowery garden down by the dramatic Ponte delle Torri.

Charleston, L-LL; Piazza Collicola 10; tel. 0743 220052; fax 0743 222010; cards accepted.
Happy mix of old and new in this 18-room hotel in heart of the old town.

Nuovo Clitunno, L-LL; Piazza Sordini; tel. 0743 223340; cards accepted.
Value for money, functional and friendly, just 100 m from the Duomo.

RECOMMENDED RESTAURANTS

ASSISI
With such large numbers of foreigners there are plenty of eating places but surprisingly few outstanding ones. Three of the best:

Ristorante Hotel Umbra; LLL; Via degli Archi 6; tel. 075 812240; cards accepted; closed Tues.
Excellent regional cooking served in summer in garden. Just off main square (see Recommended Hotels, page 127).

La Fortezza, LL; Vicolo della Fortezza 2b; tel. 075 812418; cards accepted; closed Thur.
Fair prices for better-than-average Umbrian specialities – best to book ahead.

Medio Evo, LLL; Via Arco dei Priori 4b; tel. 075 813068; cards accepted; closed Wed.
The splendid medieval vaulting bumps up the price in this smart restaurant south of the main piazza.

CAGLI
Da Luchini, LL; Via Mochi 10; tel. 0721 787231; cards none; open lunch only; closed Fri.
The cagliese are noted for their love of snails, and with any luck lumache will be on the menu at this unfussy, inexpensive trattoria by the hospital.

Other specialities are home-made *tagliatelle* and *coradella d'agnello* (sauté of lamb's offal – tastier than it sounds).

CAMPELLO SUL CLITUNNO
Le Casaline, LLL; *tel. 0743 520811; cards accepted; closed Mon.*

Benedetto Zeppadoro and his family offer warm-hearted hospitality and a serious restaurant where even the bread is home-baked. Robust Umbrian country cooking. Try his range of unusual *salumi*, cured meats made from goose, deer, goat and horse, or get your teeth into wild boar stew. (See Recommended Hotels, page 127, for directions.)

FANO
La Quinta, LL; *Viale Adriatico 42; tel. 0721 808043; cards none; closed Sun.*

Overlooking the fishing harbour, this traditional fisherman's *trattoria* has simple fish dishes with no pretensions.

Self-Service del Mare, L; *Viale Adriatico; cards none; no booking; only open May-Sept.*

This self-service summer-only restaurant in a giant tent is run by a local co-operative of fishermen and must be the cheapest place to eat fish in Italy. The set meal includes wine and water. You will find it next door to the wholesale fish market at the end of the fishing harbour just before Sassonia beach.

Symposium, LLL-LLLL; *Via Cartoceto 38, Cartoceto (15 km SW of Fano); tel. 0721 898320; cards accepted; closed Mon.*

Off the beaten track, but amongst Italy's best restaurants. Take Calcinelli turning off the SS3, head for Cartoceto and follow signs to restaurant from centre of village. Seasonal menu features the best local fish and fowl. Has its feet in traditional local cooking, but its head in the stars. In summer you can eat outside. Book ahead.

FURLO
La Ginestra, LLL-LLLL; *tel. 0721 797033; cards accepted; closed Mon.*

Justly renowned. In the autumn when the truffles and wild mushrooms are at their best, Italians flock here from afar, happy to pay high prices for these delicacies. At any other time of the year you are unlikely to be disappointed by the refined regional cooking. (See also Recommended Hotels, page 128.)

If your purse does not stretch to La Ginestra, stop at the open-air **snack bar (L)** between Furlo and Acqualagna at the striking Abbey of San Vincenzo. Here you can try a *piadina* – a flat bread, filled with salami, cheese or *prosciutto crudo*, only found in the northern Marches and Romagna. While eating you can admire the ruins of the nearby Roman bridge.

SENIGALLIA
Cucinamariano, LLL; *Via Ottorino Manni; cards accepted; closed Mon.*

A new restaurant near the fort in the old part of town, that looks set for stardom. Regional cooking reinterpreted with imagination – try the excellent *antipasti*, skip the *primi* and go straight on to the superb main courses such as *faraona* (guinea fowl) stuffed with *ricotta* cheese. One of the few restaurants on the coast where you won't find fish on the menu. Excellent deserts and a huge selection of Marche wines. Best to book.

SPELLO
La Cantina, LL-LLL; *Via Cavour 2; tel. 0742 651775; cards none; closed Wed.*

Excellent restaurant in old wine cellar. The short menu depends much on the mood of the cook and what is in season. It offers the best Umbrian *cucina casalinga*, such as tagliatelle with a hearty goose sauce; rabbit cooked with wild fennel; or roast goose. Below the central *piazza*.

SPOLETO
Plenty of smart restaurants but many are pricey.

Il Tartufo, LLLL; *Piazza Garibaldi 24; tel. 0743 40236; cards accepted; closed Sun eve and Mon.*

A place for sampling the best Umbrian cooking, including dishes laced with truffles, as the name suggests. Above-average food at above-average prices.

La Barcaccia, LLL; *Piazza Fratelli Bandiera 3 (off Via Fontesecca); tel. 0743 221171; cards accepted; closed Tues.*

A humbler place than Il Tartufo, above, but popular for its home cooking.

Local Explorations: 1

Eastern Tuscany

Siena, San Gimignano and Volterra

153 km; map Touring Club Italiano Toscana

Siena, fairest city in Tuscany, demands a long visit. After the hard, masculine streets of Florence, its feminine charms are all the more alluring. Then, we suggest, you could strike west across a beautiful and constantly changing landscape to visit a string of lovely hill towns whose past was directly affected by the drawn-out power struggle between Florence and Siena and Florence's gradual stranglehold on the region. Two of them in particular, San Gimignano and Volterra, have histories of fierce independence with periods of impressive achievement. Volterra's finest hour was as the Etruscan city Velathri, and the town's Etruscan Museum is a marvellous place to investigate that enigmatic race; there are also powerful reminders of Volterra's era of Roman domination, and of its role as an independent medieval *comune*.

San Gimignano could be summed up today as a town of towers and tourists. The former are extraordinary, the latter have stripped the place of atmosphere, but it's probably the best-preserved village in Italy, with some fascinating works of art in its nooks and crannies. Beyond these three magnets, this route takes you to three more charming fortified *borgi*, a miniature Jerusalem, a *pieve* whose romantic setting inspired Puccini - and Poggibonsi: well, you might find yourself waiting for a bus or train there.

EASTERN TUSCANY / *Siena, San Gimignano and Volterra*

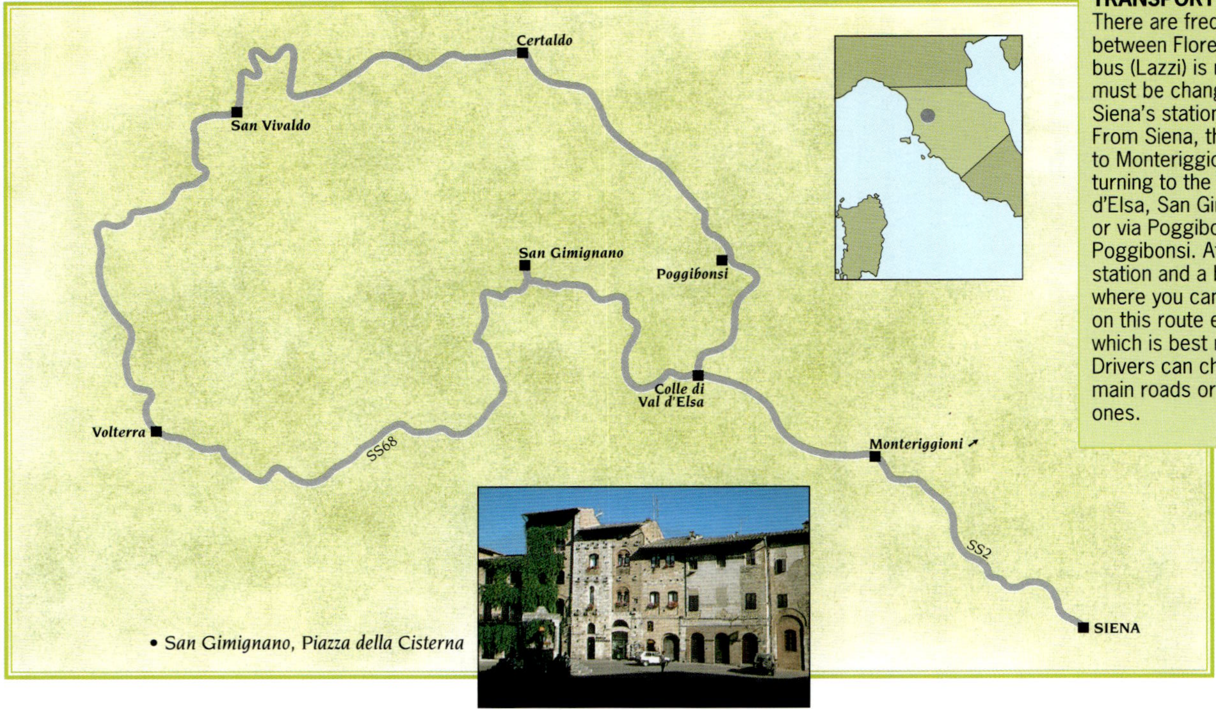

TRANSPORT

There are frequent buses and trains between Florence and Siena; the bus (Lazzi) is more direct – trains must be changed at Empoli and Siena's station is a little out of town. From Siena, there are TRA-IN buses to Monteriggioni (or rather to the turning to the village), Colle di Val d'Elsa, San Gimignano (either direct or via Poggibonsi), Volterra and Poggibonsi. At Poggibonsi there is a station and a bus terminus from where you can reach all the places on this route except San Vivaldo, which is best reached by car. Drivers can choose between fast main roads or picturesque country ones.

• *San Gimignano, Piazza della Cisterna*

1:300,000

• *Colle di Val d'Elsa.*

SIGHTS & PLACES OF INTEREST

CERTALDO
On the SS429, 42 km NW of Siena, 13 km NW of Poggibonsi. It is possible to negotiate the narrow streets up to the hill-top medieval *borgo*, but, if arriving by car, you might prefer to leave it in the large car park in the more modern town and make the stiff climb on foot.

Giovanni Boccaccio spent the closing years of his life here (he died in 1375). You will find his house in Via Boccaccio, the main street of this red-brick and rather over-restored, fortified town. His body lies in the nearby church, **Santi Michele e Iacopo**, though surely the author of the lusty *Decameron* could not have had such a stern face as that carved on his tomb. There is rather a different face in the glass sarcophagus nearby – that of the Blessed Giulia of Certaldo, now reduced to a grisly, toothy mask.

En route between Certaldo and San Gimignano, visit the **Pieve di Cellole** (see under San Gimignano, page 135). When you are 4 km away from San Gimignano, take the right turn signposted to Gambassi, then sharp right signposted to the church.

COLLE DI VAL D'ELSA ✕
On the SS68, 24 km NW of Siena. The town is split in two: 'Basso', the modern lower part, and 'Alta', the medieval *borgo* high above. If you have cause to plunge into the lower town, there is a worthwhile restaurant (see Recommended Restaurants, page 149) – and, for a snack, a pleasant café in Piazza Arnolfo di Cambio (named for the architect of Florence's Palazzo Vecchio who was born in Colle Alta in 1232). From there, car drivers must follow the signs to Colle Alta, winding their way in an uphill trail to the car park outside the walls at the top (Porta Nuova end).

Arriving on the SS68 from the direction of Volterra or San Gimignano is an easier business: you reach Colle Alta first, entering the old town by the splendid **Porta Nuova**, a 15thC fortified gateway built by Giuliano da Sangallo, with two bulging towers on either side (easier though, to park outside). From here the town stretches along a narrow ridge, a long thin line of attractive medieval and Renaissance buildings, with views on either side. In Piazza Santa Caterina you will find the ultra-serious, Michelin-starred restaurant **Arnolfo, LLL-LLLL** (*tel.* 0577 920549; *closed Tues, mid-Jan to mid-Feb and first two weeks Aug*). More suitable might be the cosy **Cantina della Fortuna, LL** (*tel.* 0577 923102), just off the piazza down Vicolo della Fontanella; at the end of this little street is a workshop making and selling engraved glass – the speciality of the town.

Beyond the piazza comes a bridge, the far end of which is straddled by **Palazzo Campagna**, built by Baccio d'Agnolo in 1539. Through the portal and into Via del Castello you will find the **Duomo**, and three small museums – **Museo Archeologico, Museo d'Arte Sacra**, and **Museo Civico** – housed in fine *palazzi*, including the *sgraffito*-decorated **Palazzo dei Priori**. You can return to the car by one of the picturesque paths that run to the side of the main road.

MONTERIGGIONI
See *Seeing the Region*: 3, *page* 114.

POGGIBONSI ✕
On the Superstrada del Palio and the SS2, 29 km NW of Siena. Not on the tourist agenda, being thoroughly industrial, with few artistic or historical lures – war damage in 1944 was much to blame. There's still the Palazzo Pretorio and Collegiata, and the pretty Romanesque Castello della Magione complex.

SAN GIMIGNANO ⇌ ✕
11 km W of Poggibonsi, 48 km NW of Siena, 57 km SW of Florence. Tourist information: 1 *Piazza del Duomo, tel.* 0577 940008.

EASTERN TUSCANY / Siena, San Gimignano and Volterra

Buses: frequent TRAIN connections with Florence and Siena, changing at Poggibonsi. You can alight outside either the south gate, Porta San Giovanni, or the north gate, Porta San Matteo. Parking: hotel guests may park inside the walls only to unload (follow signs). The town is ringed with car parks outside the walls, including a few spaces which are free of charge. You could try the large-ish free space beside the walls opposite Car Park No. 3. Steps lead up to Via Folgore da San Gimignano where turn right for the centre.

"What a terrible place to build a power station," said my companion as we approached San Gimignano, still some miles off to the north. Then, gradually, the hazy spikes which reared up from the distant hill came into focus, and were revealed to her, not as bristling industrial chimneys, but as the extraordinary, elegant medieval towers which set this town apart.

If there is one Tuscan town which has been wholeheartedly sacrificed to modern tourism, it is San Gimignano. Those towers, plus the proximity to Florence and Siena, the glorious position in a picture-book landscape, and the inhabitants' willingness to cash in on its charms have seen to that. The streets are immaculately preserved, but thronged with day trippers. Almost every shop is given over to souvenirs, and the pulse of real Italian town life is weak. High season is fair hell – a recent survey revealed that most visitors stayed an average of two hours and that their main activity was spending money on souvenirs.

If you do decide to visit, it makes sense to spend the night: even in summer the place is quiet – and cool – in the early morning and in the evening – before and after the daily invasion of coach parties.

Background
How did San Gimignano come by all its towers? Many other Tuscan towns put them up in the Middle Ages, but even then little San Gimignano was considered exceptional. In its heyday there were an amazing 76, of which a mere 13 now survive. They were built, mainly in the 12th and 13thC, as much for prestige as for protection: presumably, once the idea had caught on, no self-respecting noble family could be seen without one. The town prospered greatly in these times from its position on the Via Francigena pilgrim route to Rome. However, the plague of 1348 and later the diversion of the pilgrim route through the Val d'Elsa signalled the town's decline.

A walk around the town
Start At the northerly Porta San Matteo, **Via San Matteo** makes a fine approach to the centre, passing attractive *palazzi*, tempting food shops and *enoteche* where you can taste the local dry white wine, **La Vernaccia**, renowned for centuries, even mentioned by Dante. Before you start along Via San Matteo, you may like to turn sharp left inside the gate to visit **Sant'Agostino**, a simple, dignified 13thC church which contains, in the choir, typically lighthearted frescoes by Benozzo Gozzoli (1464) depicting the

---

DETOUR – BETWEEN SIENA AND MONTERIGGIONI
If you have time, instead of taking the main SS2, consider a backroads route between Siena and Monterigione/Colle di Val d'Elsa. The hill country of the **Montagnola**, stretching to the west and north of Siena, presents a little visited area of great beauty. As you drive on the fiddly, but almost empty roads, there are wide views of the thickly wooded landscape, with the Torre del Mangia and Duomo of Siena always present in the background. A sensible plan would be to follow the harrowing SS73 Grosseto road out of Siena, and then thankfully dive off after some 10 km towards Sociville, thereafter following your nose northwards. Places to look out for on the way are the important villas of **Castello di Celsa** and **Centinale** while the hidden monastery of **Lecceto** lies to the east. Over to the west, beyond the main SS541, are the interesting villages of **Casole d'Elsa**, **Mensano** and **Radicondoli**, also in lovely rural settings. If you are driving this route over lunchtime, bring some food and drink; you'll pass plenty of inviting picnic spots (if the weather is fine but precious few restaurants.

Local Explorations: 1

Life of St Augustine, plus his *St Sebastian* (left aisle); and a fine altarpiece depicting the *Coronation of the Virgin* by Pollaiuolo (1483).

Entering by the southerly Porta San Giovanni, you pass the prettily striped Pisan Romanesque façade of **San Francesco** (deconsecrated), and the 14thC **Palazzo Pratellesi**, now the town library. By either route you will land up in the centre, **Piazza del Duomo** and the adjoining **Piazza della Cisterna**, named for its central well of 1237. Stand in the *loggia* of the **Palazzo del Populo** to take in both *piazze* at once, the former bristling with towers, the latter surrounded by delightfully varied buildings. The **Collegiata** (ex-Duomo) is reached by a flight of steps; to its left, set back, is the baptistry *loggia*, frescoed with a youthful *Annunciation* by Ghirlandaio (1482), very affecting in its open position and attractively lit at night. Here is a little courtyard where musicians play in summer, with the entrance to the **Museo Etrusco** and **Museo d'Arte Sacra**. (Museum entrance fees are expensive for the captive tourist in San Gimignano: buy a combined ticket if you are going to visit all of them, individual ones if you are going to stick to the two 'musts', Cappella di Santa Fina and Museo Civico.)

• *San Gimignano*

The interior of the Romanesque **Collegiata** has been comprehensively painted – even the tops of the pillars are adorned with blue and white stripes, and the dark blue ceiling sparkles with a mass of gold stars. On the left of the nave are Bartolo di Fredi's *Scenes from the Old Testament* (c. 1367), full of warm detail, such as a drunken old Noah being hastily covered up to prevent him from exposing himself. On the right is the earlier fresco cycle (1333-41), attributed to Lippo Memmi, a pupil of the Sienese master Simone Martine, depicting *Scenes from the New Testament*. There are powerful images here, unusually expressive for the time: notice, for example, the figure of Judas in *The Kiss*.

On the wall inside the entrance is another *San Sebastian* by Benozzo Gozzoli, who seemed incapable of painting anything nasty. The saint, prickled all over with arrows like a hedgehog, appears entirely unaware of his problems. Higher up is Taddeo di Bartolo's *Last Judgement* (1410), which is very nasty indeed.

Along the nave on the right, the tiny **Cappella di Santa Fina** is a beautifully coloured gem – all damson ice cream and powder blue. Pay your fee, and the sacristan will whisk back the curtain to reveal the life story of Santa Fina – which was hardly a laugh a minute – by that master of contemporary (1475) detail, Ghirlandaio. The chapel was designed by architect Guiliano da Maiano, and the shrine by his brother, the fine Renaissance sculptor Benedetto.

Back in Piazza del Duomo, a passageway to the left of the tourist office leads to the courtyard of the Palazzo del Populo (town hall), with another well (there is much water under San Gimignano) and fresco fragments, mainly coats of arms, on the walls. Stairs lead up to the **Museo Civico** (*closed Mon, Nov-Feb*).

The Sala di Dante is named for the poet, who came to San Gimignano from Florence as an ambassador for the Guelf cause and addressed the town council in this room. Lippo Memmi's *Maestà* (1317) symbolizes the ideals of order and sound government, just like its model in Siena's Palazzo Pubblico by Simone Martine. Just off the Sala di Dante, there are two charming busts by Pietro Torrigiano of Santa Fina and San Gregorio.

The picture galleries contain a rich collection of Sienese paintings, plus Pinturicchio's *Madonna Assunta*, with the same background landscape that you see from San Gimignano today, and a typically pretty *Madonna* by Gozzoli. Notice, too, *San Gimignano and his Miracles* by Taddeo di Bartolo. Here, the gruesome side of Taddeo is forgotten. The wise, kind-eyed bishop sits placidly, with the town – just like it is today, a mini Manhattan – held in his lap, his miracles illustrated around him.

At the top of the stairs to the left (easily missed) is a little room frescoed in the 1320s with naive but compelling *Wedding Scenes* by Memmo di Filippucci. I want that chequered bedspread. Here too is the entrance to the Palazzo's tower, the **Torre Grossa** (separate fee), at 54 m the highest in town. There are marvellous views from the top.

Follow the sign from the Piazza to the **Rocca**, the ruined 14thC fortress in a park whose walls now enclose nothing more threatening than an olive grove with a well in the middle and a hen house to one side. If you didn't climb Torre Grossa, then take in from the watchtower here the roofs and towers of the town, and the surrounding countryside with its olive groves and stately cypresses.

A red brick path in front of the Conzorzio (headquarters of the consortium of Vernaccia producers) brings you to a little **Museo Ornitologico** – one man's collection of stuffed birds bizarrely displayed in a deconsecrated Baroque church. From here, quiet Via Quercecchio brings you back to the centre through the **Arco dei Becci**, a noble gateway in the first (12thC) of San Gimignano's three rings of walls. If you want to continue your stroll, a right turn in front of the arch down Via Innocenti will bring more fine views of the countryside. This pretty, narrow path leads to the back of 13thC **San Lorenzo** (closed). Turn left and left again down Via di Castello to reach Piazza della Cisterna. You might care to stop at the terrace of **Il Castello, L** (*tel. 0577 940878; closed Wed*) for a glass of wine or a bite to eat.

Before pressing on, try to make time for the **Pieve di Cellole**, 4 km out of San Gimignano. Leave by the Certaldo road, then left on to the road signposted Gambassi. A sharp right turn leads to the Romanesque church, romantically hidden behind four parallel rows of cypress trees; standing on a little plateau, it commands wide views. Puccini linked his beautiful *Suor Angelica* with this place.

SAN VIVALDO

On a by-road, 17 km NW of San Gimignano. With an eye to armchair pilgrims, Franciscan monks created a miniature Jerusalem in this green and pleasant land in the opening years of the 16thC. Chapels – 34 of them – dotted about the wooded slopes faithfully followed the configuration of the principal shrines of the holy city. Only 17 remain, each depicting episodes of the Passion with life-like polychrome terracotta figures set against frescoed backdrops.

Today the once-thriving community is reduced to a pair of ageing friars – ring the bell and one of them will show you around. You would be wise to see this magical place before it gets discovered.

Local Explorations: 1

THE *CONTRADE*

Once, at the height of its powers, Siena was divided into over 40 small territories or wards called *contrade*, but since the 17thC there have been just 17, each picturesquely named and each identified by its own animal insignia – snail, turtle, giraffe, elephant, goose and so on – and its own brilliantly coloured banner. Each *contrada* also has a church, dining and social club, museum and fountain. Here babies are baptized into the *contrada*, and alliegance thenceforth is unswerving. Much of a citizen's socializing is done within the confines of the *contrada*, and in times of need the *contrada* will support. This social welfare system, unique to Siena and begun in the Middle Ages, is considered a model one. Yet whilst the social benefits brought by the *contrade* are appreciated by everyone, such a tight-knit system does have its down side. Although outsiders living in Siena will readily have their children baptized into their *contrada*, they are often the first to say that the town is too provincial and lacking in buzz.

A game of slender alliance and sharp competition goes on at all times between the *contrade*. This undercurrent of rivalry is given expression twice a year, when tempers are allowed to flair – often spilling into violence – at the Palio (see The Palio, below and on page 137).

Walking around Siena, you will feel the presence of the *contrade* very strongly, easily identifying which one you are in by the wall plaques and fountains that you pass. It's worth visiting one or two of the *contrade* museums – enquire at the tourist office in Piazza del Campo for more details.

THE PALIO

Siena explodes in Palio week. The greatest of Italy's 'traditional manifestations' is integral to the lives of every citizen and there is no greater honour than that of your *contrada* winning the race. Ten of the 17 *contrade* are selected by lot to take part, each one represented by a horse – also picked by lot – and a fearless jockey, not from Siena, but from the Tuscan Maremma.

The build-up to the race itself – on July 2 and again on August 16 – is intense. Bands of costumed performers, like rival gangs of football supporters but more civilized, parade the streets with the insignia of their *contrade*.

• *Poster for Il Palio, Siena.*

• *Palio banners.*

Banners are twirled and thrown in a fantastic display. The horses are taken into the *contrade* churches to be blessed. By the time the race starts, a pagan frenzy has seized the city. In the Campo 100,000 spectators are jammed, all standing for hours in the torrid heat, to see a bare-back horse race which lasts less than two minutes. (We watched a woman nervously gnawing her handkerchief – by the end of the two minutes, she had swallowed it.)

The Palio, brutal, no-holds-barred, not for the squeamish, is best seen from a balcony if you can afford the extortionate prices (you need to buy tickets months in advance – enquire at the tourist office; tickets available from Palio Viaggi, Piazza Gramsci 7; tel. 0577 280828). If you intend to stand in the Campo, arrive early. The horses do a double circuit around you, but you see almost nothing unless you are against the barrier. Once the race is technically over, the horses and jockeys shoot off out of the Campo with a crowd of people charging after them. The atmosphere, of course, is a grand spectacle in itself.

SYMBOLS AND SAINTS
Siena is full of symbols. Take the Campo for example. The piazza itself is divided into nine sections, symbolizing the Council of Nine, or Nine Good Men, who ruled the city from the Palazzo Pubblico in medieval times. It is also seen as the Virgin Mary's cloak, spread out to safeguard her favoured city. Then look up at the façade of the Palazzo Pubblico. The windows are all decorated with the black and white

• *Symbol of San Bernardino.*

balzana, symbolic shield of the medieval communal government. Then there are the she-wolves suckling the twins, Romulus and Remus, which shoot out on either side of the central tower. Legend has it that Senius, son of Remus, founded Siena; this statue often crops up around town. The Medici balls are the symbol of repression – added after Siena was finally annexed to Florence in the 16thC. The enormous sun in the centre is the symbol of San Bernardino, who along with St Catherine (read about her in the Terzo di Camollia walk, page 144) and the Virgin Mary are the three saints closest to Siena's heart.

San Bernardino was born in 1380. During a time of great factional rivalry he preached worship of Jesus Christ rather than hatred of one another, and tried to get people to replace their divisive coats of arms with his sun symbol, which has the Greek for Christ, IHS, entwined in the middle. You can see it most prominently here on the Palazzo Pubblico and on the façade of the Duomo, but in humbler places as well. San Bernardino founded the church and monastery of **Osservanza**, which lies 2.5 km NE of the city. His heart is kept in the **Oratorio di San Bernardino** in Piazza San Francesco. So look out for the she-wolf and the sun symbol of San Bernardino, as well as coats of arms above doorways, and of course the many plaques and stickers of the *contrade*. Even the prize for winning the Palio is a symbol. The victory banner – or *palio* – is embroidered with a picture of the Virgin Mary, protectress of Siena.

Local Explorations: 1

Siena – Piazza del Campo.

SIENA
On the Superstrada del Palio, the SS2 and the SS73, 68 km S of Florence. Tourist information: Piazza del Campo 56, tel. 0577 280551. Station: 2 km NE of city centre; connecting buses to and from Piazza Antonio Gramsci; train times and tickets available from SETI, Piazza del Campo 56; the station has a left luggage office. Buses: Florence (SITA) and Siena Province (TRA-IN) buses arrive and leave from Piazza San Domenico; local buses from Piazza Gramsci. Taxis: apart from the station, there is a taxi rank in Piazza Matteoti. A bus service, using little buses to negotiate the narrow streets, operates within the city walls. Parking: the centre is closed to cars. Head for one of the signposted car parks around the edge - there are several near Piazza San Domenico and the Fortezza. The one at the station is also useful - you can easily get a taxi to your destination.

Strongly medieval, handsomely Gothic with Renaissance flourishes, suffused with all the dignity and self-respect of an old city-state, Siena should be high on every traveller's list of places to visit and revisit. The city is just right for size: its fabulous monuments and works of art are all within easy walking distance of each other. Town mansions, slotted into narrow streets, are marvels of domestic architecture.

Background
Siena was a place to be reckoned with from the early Middle Ages, becoming a republic in the 1120s. Her golden age of prosperity, good government and great artistic achievement came in the late 13th and early 14thC; her decline, accelerated by the devastating Black Death of 1348 and the overthrow of the ruling Council of Nine in 1355, was completed in the 1550s at the hands of the army of Charles V, Holy Roman Emperor, which besieged the city and decimated the population. A couple of years later, Siena was handed to Cosimo I de' Medici, its cherished independence obliterated. It became part of the Grand Duchy of Tuscany, a mere sidekick of its former arch enemy, Florence. Thereafter the Sienese turned inwards. They remained fiercely proud of their great past – their defeat in 1260 of Florence at the Battle of Monteaperti is still a source of great pride and cause for celebration – and they never forgot the importance of good community relations and social welfare (see The Contrade, page 136).

Impecunity meant that the city of Siena hardly changed over the years and today it remains much as it was in its heyday. Once tourism had brought prosperity back to the 'cracking, peeling, fading, crumbling, rotting' city, as Henry James found it, Siena was spruced up to look its best. New building is carefully regulated, and even new shop fronts must get the go-ahead. Normally a sober, provincial place, it bursts into life twice a year in July and August during The Palio (see pages 136-7); no tourist pageant this – the dearest wish of every citizen of Siena is that the horse racing for his *contrada* should win.

Orientation
Siena is built along three ridges, which meet at Piazza del Campo. In between the ridges are green valleys where no building, only garden allotments, has been allowed. Both ridges and valleys

Siena, with the Duomo in background.

are encircled by the city walls, so that both town and countryside mingle within them. Any visit to Siena should include a wander round its narrow streets, connected by aerial bridges and flights of steps, to see this unique feature.

Three principal roads meet at the Campo – Banchi di Sopra, Banchi di Sotto and Via di Città. Each of these roads curves out to one of the three ridges, and each ridge is a medieval district, or *terzo*. They are Terzo di San Martino, Terzo di Città and Terzo di Camollia, and the three walks which follow on pages 142-5 explore them, describing places of interest on the way. The principal sights in Siena, on everyone's agenda, are described below under Sights.

Sights
Piazza del Campo
One of the loveliest public spaces in the world. Mercifully, it has been preserved for pedestrians; no killer cars race round its perimeter, only the horses of the Palio (see The Palio, pages 136-7) on July 2 and August 16 each year. Summer days see hordes of tourists, but night time is magical, with voices echoing eerily off the walls of the mellow *palazzi* which surround the piazza. The Campo is shaped like a shell, dipping and curving just like a scallop, with the **Palazzo Pubblico** (see below)

at its foot, and the **Fonte Gaia** in the middle of the curve. The marble fountain is a 19thC copy of the original by Jacopo della Quercia. The nine sections into which the Campo is divided represent the Council of Nine, the model governing body of medieval Siena. The piazza is ringed by cafés and restaurants – expensive but worth it for the view and the ambience – and there is none of the tackiness that so often accompanies great sites – the Campo dei Miracoli in Pisa for example.

Palazzo Pubblico
Piazza del Campo 1. The gracious Gothic town hall, former seat of the Sienese government, was completed in 1342. Its landmark **Torre del Mangia**, which, in the words of one writer, shoots 'like a rocket into the starlit air', can be climbed for a magnificent view, both of the Campo far below and great tracts of Tuscany. The first-floor state rooms of the Palazzo Pubblico house the **Museo Civico** (*open Mar-Nov, Mon-Sat, 10 am-4 pm, Sun 9.30 am-1.30 pm; Dec-Feb 9.30 am-4.30 pm daily*). Rooms 1 to 15 could be trotted through quite quickly. To start with there are charming Sienese ceramics; then some horrid 18thC hunting scenes; then the **Sala del Risorgimento**, decorated with full-technicolour late-19thC frescoes

depicting scenes from the life of Victor Emmanuel II.

A steep flight of stairs leads up to the *loggia*, with the pathetic remains of Jacopo della Quercia's original carvings for the Fonte Gaia, which was apparently his masterpiece. He was Siena's greatest sculptor: if you have been to Lucca you will have seen his lovely tomb of Ilaria del Caretto in the Duomo there. There are views from here of the valley between Terzio di San Martino and Terzio di Città just beyond.

Next comes a series of frescoed rooms, some of the frescoes illustrating Siena's concern for good government. Those on the ceiling of Room 12 are by the Sienese Mannerist, Beccafumi. In the **chapel**, the elegant **screen** is della Quercia's; in the anti-chapel is a 15thC **bronze she-wolf** suckling the orphans, Romulus and Remus.

The museum's greatest treasures are saved up until last. In the long, rectangular **Sala del Mappamondo** is Simone Martini's **Maestà** of 1315. Maestà means the Virgin as Queen of Heaven, but here she is also head of the government of Siena. Here, too, is the unforgettable equestrian portrait of a mercenary, **Guidoriccio da Fogliano**. A huge row has raged over this picture. Is it a 16thC fake, or a genuine Simone Martini of 1330, later restored? The Museo Civico firmly believe the latter. The frescoed map by Lorenzetti after which this council chamber is named has disappeared. The **Sala della Pace**, where the Council of Nine met, is the setting for the famous and very important **Allegory of Good and Bad Government** by Ambrogio Lorenzetti, painted in 1338. The frescoes were restored in the 1980s, but the scenes of bad government are almost totally eroded: all we are left with is a dead body here, an arrest or a crumbling building there. In the scenes of good government, the king wears the colours of the *balzana* – Siena's communal shield – and rules over a city state where the people are happy, well-fed, law-abiding and industrious, their leaders wise and just. These scenes were painted in 1338, just as Siena's golden age was coming to a close; disorder and discontent were to follow, with the ravages of the Black Death in 1348, and the overthrow of the Nine in 1355.

The last room, **Sala dei Pilastri**, contains a **Maestà** by the first of Siena's great painters, Guido da Siena, dated 1221.

Duomo
Open Mar-Oct 9 am-7.30 pm; Oct-Mar 7.30 am-1.30, 2.30-5 pm. If the Campo entrances the eye, Siena's great black-and-white cathedral makes one stand open-mouthed with wonder. Built on high ground south-east of the Campo, it crowns the fair city. The Duomo was the perfect Gothic expression of Siena's golden age. It took about two centuries to construct, but by 1285 the cupola was up and the façade begun. In 1339 the Sienese overstretched themselves: they decided to turn the existing cathedral into a mere transept and build a huge new nave, making the biggest church they could conceive. But the bad times were already upon them, and the Black Death of 1348 killed off the plans once and for all. The unfinished nave still stands, its right aisle housing the Museo dell'Opera del Duomo (see page 141).

The **façade** is an astonishing sight, even by the standards of other great Tuscan cathedrals: built in pink-and-white polychrome marble, encrusted with statues, it looks good enough to eat, like a celebration Sienese cake. The lower part was designed by the great Gothic sculptor Giovanni Pisano (see under Pisa, page 92); his original statues are now in the cathedral museum – what you see are copies. The upper part was added a century later in the 1380s, except for the mosaics, which are 19thC.

The **interior** is no less exhilarating (some would say over-the-top – Ruskin's opinion was that it was 'absurd – over-striped, over-crocketed, over-gabled, a piece of costly confectionery, and faithless vanity'). You need a few moments to adjust your eyes to the dizzying black-and-white stripes before you can take anything else in. Then you can start to inspect the remarkable **marble pavement**, or rather those parts of it which are not covered for protection by drab sheets of cardboard (they should be uncovered during high season). The 56 designs, in *sgraffito* or intarsia, were produced between 1369 and 1547 by teams of Sienese artists. Beccafumi's are perhaps the most rewarding, particularly *Moses Striking Water from a Rock* and the *Sacrifice of Isaac* (between the two central crossing pillars and in front of the high altar respectively). Looking up from the floor, notice first the beautiful high altar, flanked by angels; more angels, these ones by Beccafumi, decorate the nave pillars.

Now turn to the **pulpit** in the left transept made by the father of Giovanni Pisano. This is the later, and greater, of Nicola Pisano's two magnificent, ground-breaking marble pulpits. Dating from around 1266, it was made some six years after the one in the Pisa Baptistry (see page 92).

Close by the pulpit is the Capella di San Giovanni Battista, notable for Donatello's **Baptist**, which was done two years after his similarly tortured *Maddalena*, now in the cathedral museum, Florence. Like so many great artists at the end of their lives, Donatello strove above all for expressiveness and inner truth in these works. Opposite, in the right transept, is the later (1659) **Cappella del Voto** designed in rampant Baroque style by Bernini to house a revered 13thC painting, *Madonna del Voto*. The votive offerings on the wall are mostly pretty hearts, but they also include a couple of crash helmets.

Turning to the Piccolomini Library, have a look first at the **Piccolomini Altar** to the left. The four lower statues of saints are by a young Michelangelo; the two lowest, particularly the one on the right, show something of his gifts. The **Libreria Piccolomini** *(open Mar-Oct 9 am-7.30 pm; Oct-Mar 10 am-1 pm, 2.30-5 pm; fee)* should not be overlooked. The vivid, beautifully coloured frescoes by Pinturicchio (1502-9) celebrate the life of Pope Pius II, otherwise Aeneas Sylvius Piccolomini, who was an extraordinarily profound, learned and cultured man, and head of the powerful Piccolomini family. Amongst the ten scenes, which read from the right by the window, you can pick him out visiting James II of Scotland, being made a cardinal, then pope, canonizing St Catherine, and finally arriving at Ancona, dying; black birds fly overhead to symbolize his passing. The room was built to house the Pope's library; now the cathedral choir books are on display. In the centre are the **Three Graces**, a Roman copy of a lost Greek statue by Praxiteles.

Museo dell'Opera del Duomo

Piazza del Duomo 8; open Jan-mid Mar 9 am-1.30 pm, Mar-Sept 9 am-7.30 pm, Oct 9 am-6 pm, Nov, Dec 9 am-1.30 pm. On the ground floor are Giovanni Pisano's **prophets** carved for the façade of the Duomo. Although worn, and made to be looked up at, rather than viewed at eye level, they have great presence for such early sculpture.

On the first floor, is Duccio's glorious **Maestà** (1308-11). When it graced the high altar in the cathedral, it must have been an amazing sight, painted on both sides and all in one piece, not split up, which happened in the 18thC. On the day of its inauguration, the *Maestà* was carried in stately procession to the cathedral; it launched the great age of Sienese painting.

Upstairs: more Sienese painting. Accessible from this (second) floor is an excellent viewpoint from the top of the nave wall – worth it, if you haven't staggered up the Torre del Mangia.

The **Baptistry**, located at the back of the cathedral, is described in the Terzio di Città Walk, page 143.

Pinacoteca Nazionale

Via San Pietro 29; open Tue-Sat 9 am-7 pm, Sun 8 am-1 pm, Mon 9 am-1.30 pm in summer; Tue-Sat 8.30 am-1.30 pm, 2.30-7 pm, Sun 8 am-1 pm, Mon 8.30 am-1.30 pm in winter. Sienese art flowered for two centuries, from around 1200, when Guido da Siena led the way in the prevalent Byzantine style. The true father of the Sienese School, however, was Duccio, who united Byzantine form with a Gothic grace and dignity not seen before. Thereafter, the International Gothic style was perfectly interpreted by the Sienese, particularly by Simone Martini, while the Lorenzetti brothers strove to combine Florence's interest in realism with decorative International Gothic. Yet, while the Renaissance swept Florence, Sienese artists continued in much the same vein as before. Not until the advent of the Mannerist Beccafumi, after the turn of the 16thC, was the spell was finally broken.

The Pinacoteca, housed in the lovely 14thC **Palazzo Buonsignori**, is devoted to works of the Siena School. It is the best place to follow the progress of Sienese art, as it is arranged chronologically, and contains works by all the greatest exponents.

Local Explorations: 1

Terzo di San Martino

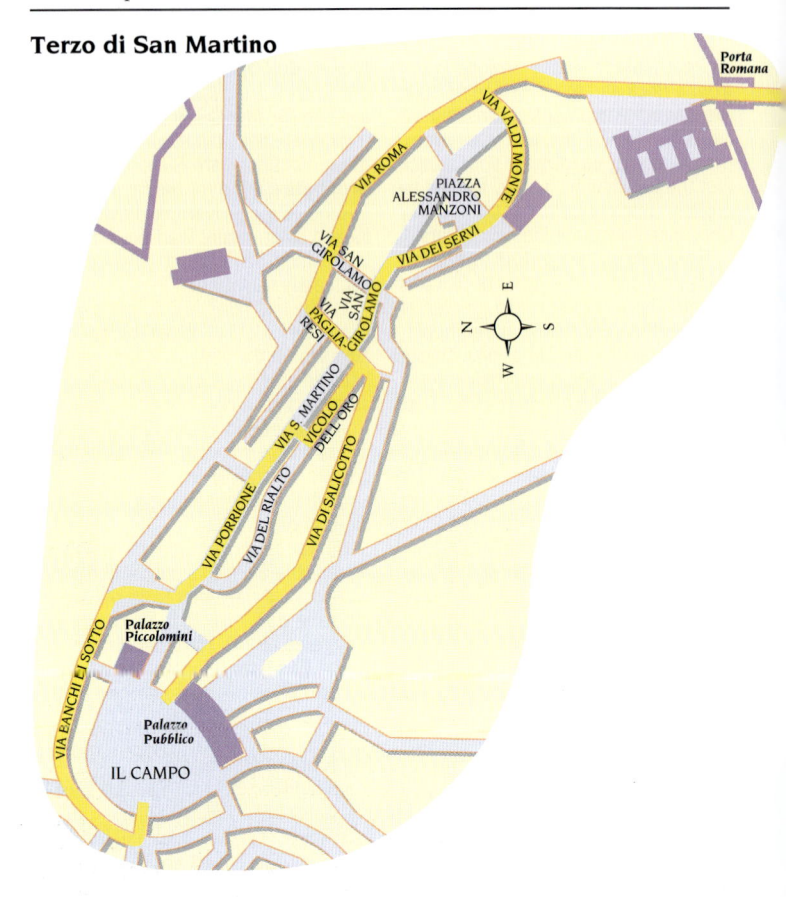

Walks
Terzo di San Martino walk - south-east of the Campo

Start The Campo. Take the Via di Salicotto down the side of the **Torre di Mangia**. This quickly leads into the heart of the **Contrada della Torre**, with its elephant and tower symbol. You will see it everywhere – on the fountain, ceramic wall plaques, even car stickers. From the fountain, there's a view of the valley between Terzo San Martino and Terzo di Città. Further along, on the street wall of No. 126, notice an old plaque of 1641 which informs you that prostitutes are forbidden in the street. Continue into Via San Girolamo (notice the copper beater at No. 15 – *contrade* emblems feature large in his work), then turn right and take Via dei Servi to **Santa Maria dei Servi**, whose bare brick, pock-marked façade is made asymmetrical by the heavy campanile squashed beside it. Inside there are some fine Sienese paintings including two *Massacre of the Innocents*, one by Pietro Lorenzetti (early 14thC), the other by Matteo di Giovanni (1492), and two altarpieces, a *Nativity* by Taddeo di Bartolo and *Madonna del Popolo* by Lippo Memmi.

Now you are in the quiet **Contrada di Valdimontone** (ram insignia), whose church hides a gloriously frescoed (Mannerist) interior. Via Valdimontone leads to Via Roma, where, through an open gate opposite, you can spy **Porta Pispini**, the fine gateway into the city from Arezzo and Perugia, dating from 1326; up Via Roma to the right is the heavily fortified **Porta Romana** of the same date.

To return to the centre, turn left along Via Roma, and then left again down Via Pagliaresi by the toy shop, passing, at No. 6, the modish *trattoria*

Terzo di Città

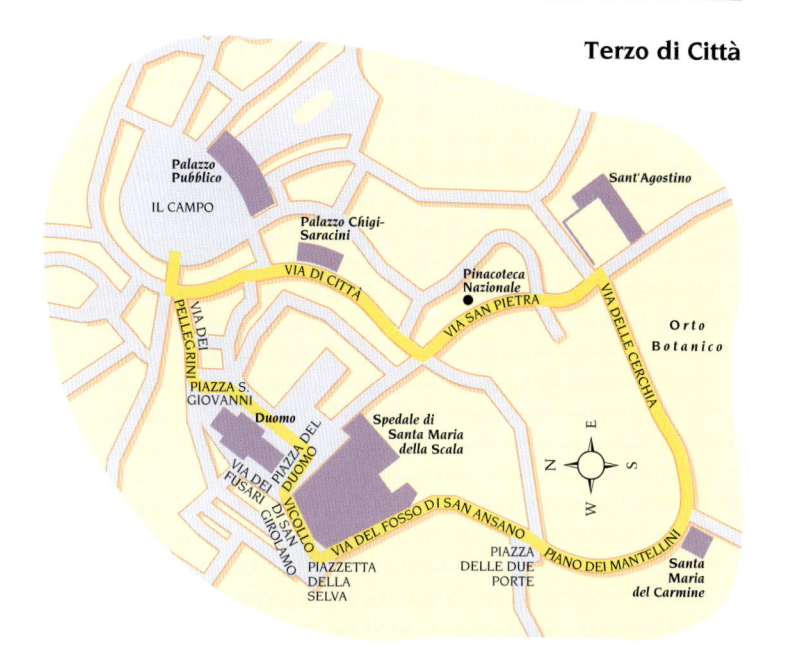

Cane e Gatto, LL-LLL (*tel. 0577 287545; closed lunch and Thurs*). At the little crossroads, take Via di Salicotto, then first right into Vicolo dell'Oro, a street of high bulging walls peppered with shutters, and of overhanging houses. Typical of Siena, flights of steps connect one quiet street to the next as they descend the ridge of the hill towards the green valley below. At the point where Vicolo dell'Oro runs into Via Rialto, take the tunnel arch to the right and turn left into Via del Porrione (note the fresco of St Martin dividing his cloak). On the left is a plaque marking the place where the Monte dei Paschi di Siena bank began in the early 17thC. Today it is one of the foremost banks in Italy and the major employer in Siena. On the right, under a vaulted brick ceiling, is the long-established **Grotta del Gallo Nero, LL-LLL** (*tel. 0577 284346; closed Mon*). Look back along pretty, curving Via del Rialto to the left. In Via del Porrione, a blackened hole in the wall serves as the workshop for **Brocchi**, selling brass and copper since 1815. Next to the church of **San Martino** is the Renaissance **Logge del Papa**, built for Pope Pius II.

From here, Via Banchi di Sotto curves around the Campo. On the left stands **Palazzo Piccolomini**, again Renaissance, by Rossellino. It now houses the **State Archives** (*open Mon-Sat 9 am-1 pm*), which include the city's illustrated account books, and Boccaccio's will. Piccolomini is a name which crops up often in Siena; it was a great Renaissance family, the most illustrious of whom, Aeneas Silvius, became Pope Pius II. His life story is illustrated in the Piccolomini Library in the Duomo (see page 141).

Terzo di Città walk -
south-west of the Campo

Start The Campo, leaving by Via dei Pellegrini. This short street leads to the back of the **Duomo** (see Sights, pages 140-1), and the entrance to its **Baptistry**, frescoed by Vecchietta and his school. The cream of Renaissance sculptors, Sienese and Florentine, collaborated on the central font, including Ghiberti and Donatello.

To see the Duomo, climb the steps and go through the archway. The building opposite the Duomo is **Ospedale di Santa Maria della Scala** (*open 10.30 am-6 pm in summer, 11 am-5 pm in winter (times vary)*). Now closed as a hospital (a modern one has been built on the outskirts), it is destined to be turned into a huge and ambitious museum, dedicated to the Sienese arts. For now, the main attractions are the 15thC frescoes in the main reception hall, the **Sala dei Pellegrini**. The history of the hospital is represented, and its function in the daily life of the city. The frescoes are be several different Sienese artists, most notably, Domenico di Bartolo. There are also various chapels (the Cappella di Santa Caterina has an altarpiece by Taddeo di Bartolo). Here too is the **Museo Archeologico** which displays local Etruscan finds. Leave Piazza del Duomo by Via dei Fusari, turning sharp left down steep Vicolo di San Girolamo, emerging in the **Contrada della Selva**, with its rhino fountain, museum and church, which has a glittering interior. Turning left down Via del Fosso di San Ansano you are suddenly in countryside, strolling past an olive grove, with the Tuscan landscape beyond, before reaching the next ridge at Piazza delle Due Porte. Ahead lies **Santa Maria del Carmine**, alternatively known as San Niccolò al Carmine, a vast expanse of soft Siena brick. Inside, over the altar: St Michael by Beccafumi. Via delle Cerchia passes through the **Contrada della Chiocciola** (snail). Next comes a rare open space amongst the buildings, much appreciated by children, and the entrance to the **Orto Botanico** (Botanical Garden; *open Mon-Fri 8 am-5 pm; Sat 8 am-noon*) maintained by the University of Siena, founded in 1784. Opposite is **Sant'Agostino**, which is closed.

From here, Via San Pietra, in the **Contrada della Tartuca** (turtle) leads to the **Pinacoteca Nazionale** (see Sights, page 141). Turn right into Via di Città, one of the three principal roads which curve away from the Campo. This is the oldest part of Siena, and it is lined with lacy *palazzi*, as well as tempting shops – such as the *pizzicheria* at No. 95, dripping with hanging hams and salamis as well as huge baskets of dried *porcini*. Finest of the houses, curving gracefully with the street and lined with a double row of three-light windows, is **Palazzo Chigi-Saracini**, whose inner courtyard with its frescoed *loggia* can be wandered into. It houses the **Accademia Musicale Chigiana**, famous for its summer master classes and its prestigious concerts (tickets available from SETI, Piazza del Campo 56). Just ahead on the right is the **Antica Drogheria Manganelli**, its former medicine cabinets now filled with gourmet foods and a fine selection of the sweet biscuits for which Siena is known, including *panforte, cavalluci* and *ricciarelli*.

Terzo di Camollia walk - north-west of the Campo

Start The Campo, at Croce del Travaglio where the three main roads – Via di Città, Banchi di Sopra and Banchi di Sotto, meet. Here is the noble **Loggia della Mercanzia** of 1417, where business transactions took place and a highly regarded tribunal met to settle commercial disputes. Take Banchi di Sopra, passing **Nannini**, famous for its cakes and biscuits. In Piazza Tolomei, where parliament used to meet before the building of the Palazzo Pubblico, is the early **Palazzo Tolomei** (1208) and opposite, the church of **San Cristoforo**. Further on is the lovely 15thC **Palazzo Salimbeni**, flanked by two other *palazzi* comprising the headquarters of the Monte di Paschi bank.

Turn left down little Costa dell'Incrociata, and beyond the **Biblioteca Comunale** take the Costa di Sant'Antonio to the **Santuario e Casa di Santa Caterina**. It was here that Catherine Bencista was born in 1347, the 25th child of a wool merchant. She died of a stroke aged 33, having become a national heroine who devoted herself to the poor as well as giving sound political advice and was canonized in 1461. Since then, the house has become embellished with a series of chapels, one where the kitchen was, another over the cell in which the saint herself lived.

If you want to return to the Campo, take Via della Galluzza from here. If you want to press on to San Domenico and the Forte di Santa Barbara, take Vicolo del Campaccio through the archway in Costa di Sant'Antonio, which ascends to both Via del Camporegio and Piazza San Domenico.

San Domenico is a great barn of a Dominican preaching church, worth entering if you want to see some more of St Catherine. Across the nave, the chapel dedicated to her is **frescoed** with vibrant scenes of the saint in religious ecstasy by Sodoma (1526). The tabernacle on the altar is by Giovanni di Stefano and contains – her head. In

EASTERN TUSCANY / *Siena, San Gimignano and Volterra*

Terzo di Camollia

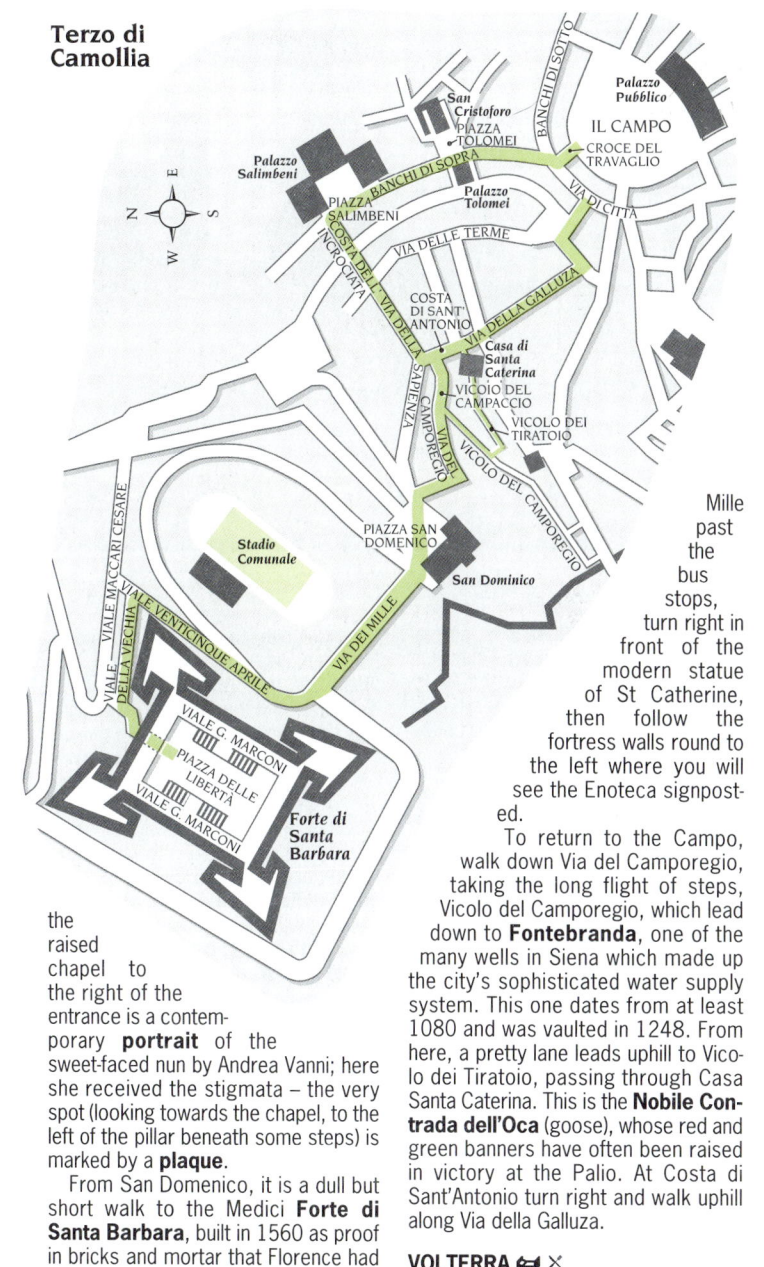

the raised chapel to the right of the entrance is a contemporary **portrait** of the sweet-faced nun by Andrea Vanni; here she received the stigmata – the very spot (looking towards the chapel, to the left of the pillar beneath some steps) is marked by a **plaque**.

From San Domenico, it is a dull but short walk to the Medici **Forte di Santa Barbara**, built in 1560 as proof in bricks and mortar that Florence had finally vanquished Siena some five years earlier. If it's between 3 pm and midnight, you might be tempted by the **Enoteca Nazionale**, a liquid library of Italian wines which you can buy or merely taste in cool, brick-vaulted surroundings (snacks also available). To find the entrance, walk along Viale dei Mille past the bus stops, turn right in front of the modern statue of St Catherine, then follow the fortress walls round to the left where you will see the Enoteca signposted.

To return to the Campo, walk down Via del Camporegio, taking the long flight of steps, Vicolo del Camporegio, which lead down to **Fontebranda**, one of the many wells in Siena which made up the city's sophisticated water supply system. This one dates from at least 1080 and was vaulted in 1248. From here, a pretty lane leads uphill to Vicolo dei Tiratoio, passing through Casa Santa Caterina. This is the **Nobile Contrada dell'Oca** (goose), whose red and green banners have often been raised in victory at the Palio. At Costa di Sant'Antonio turn right and walk uphill along Via della Galluza.

VOLTERRA

On the SS68, 50 km NW of Siena, 29 km SW of San Gimignano. Tourist information: Via Turazza 2, just off Piazza dei Priori, tel. 0588 86150. Station: Saline di Volterra, 9 km W of the town (bus connection). Bus terminal: Piazza Martiri della Libertà. Parking: possible inside the walls in Piazza Martiri della Libertà, but best left in one of the car

145

Local Explorations: 1

parks outside (which are signposted).

A sombre, lordly town perched on a windswept bluff, Volterra is one of the oldest cities in Italy. As Velathri, it was one of the leaders of the Dodecapolis, the powerful confederation of 12 Etruscan cities that held sway before Rome took over. Something of these ancient times still haunts you as you wander through the gaunt medieval streets, and the archaeological finds in the Museo Guarnacci (see page 147) vividly bring to life Volterra's Etruscan past.

The town's medieval history is a proud and turbulent one: it struggled to remain independent from the Florentines, who wanted its mines, but was brutally sacked by the Duke of Urbino on behalf of Lorenzo de' Medici in 1472; Lorenzo repented the act on his deathbed (to Savonarola). A last attempt at freedom, a rebellion of 1530, ended in failure, and Volterra remained under Florence, then the Grand Duchy of Tuscany, until the Unification of Italy in 1860. The medieval town was less than half the size of Velathri, as the ring of Etruscan walls, parts of which still stand, bear witness. The strange and beautiful landscape around Volterra echoes the mood of the city. The hills are largely bare and rolling, in hues of green, yellow, brown and black. The hill on which the town sits has long been eroding, resulting in sheer, dramatic cliffs called **Le Balze**. A place where you can park and take a

• Volterra.

wary look over the edge is signposted from the Pisa road. These clay hills offer up the town's speciality – alabaster. And though there are countless shops selling ghostly white objects of every shape, size and description, there is no sense that Volterra has sold out to the tourists, unlike San Gimignano down the road.

A walk around the town
Start In **Piazza dei Priori.** The hub of town is this evocative, severe medieval square, dominated by the **Palazzo dei Priori** (*open Mon-Sat 8.30 am-1 pm and afternoons Easter -Oct*). Dating from the early 13thC – and pre-dating the similar Palazzo Pubblico in Siena – it is the oldest civic headquarters in Tuscany, and still acts as town hall. You can visit the fine first-floor council chamber, still in use and little changed since the 13thC. Opposite is **Palazzo Pretorio**, notable for its Torre de la Porcellina, so-called for the rather stranded looking pig sticking out on a plank.

Turn right into Via Turazza to emerge in the sudden quiet of Piazza di San Giovanni, where the Baptistery (under restoration at the time of writing), the Spedale della Santa Maria Maddalena and the **Duomo**, looking much more like a pretty Pisan-style parish church than a cathedral, are gathered. Inside the Duomo, the walls are painted to

EASTERN TUSCANY / *Siena, San Gimignano and Volterra*

Volterra

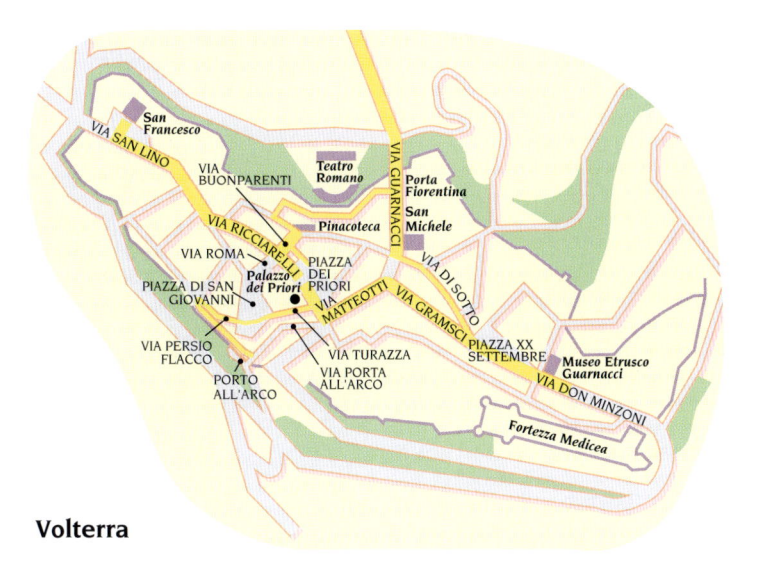

give the effect of black-and-white marble bands, hung with shields, and there's a rich coffered ceiling decorated in blue and gold. The square pulpit was created in the 16thC using 12thC Pisan reliefs. The tabernacle and marble angels around the high altar are the work of Mino da Fiesole. To the right: a remarkable polychrome wooden *Deposition* of 1228, in which four life-size figures surround Christ on his Cross.

Around the corner, in Via Roma, is a small **Museo d'Arte Sacra**, located in the Palazzo Arcivescovile. If you want to see the **Porta all'Arco**, take Via Persio Flacco behind the Baptistry, then turn left. The venerable Etruscan gateway dates from the 4thC BC, though partially rebuilt by the Romans. The three great, worn heads are around 2,700 years old. A plaque tells how the arch was saved one night during the war in 1944. Return to the centre along Via Porta all'Arco.

From the Duomo, retrace along Via Turazza, then turn right and first left down the shopping street Via Matteoti, looking up just before you turn right into Via Gramsci to see the terracotta-coloured **Palazzo Ruggieri**. In Via Gramsci are a couple of restaurants (see Recommended Restaurants, page 149), should it be lunchtime. That would set you up well for a visit to the **Museo Etrusco Guarnacci**, further along on the left past Piazza XX Settembre (V*ia Don Minzoni 15; open Mar-*

Oct 9 am-7pm daily; Oct-Mar 9 am-2 pm). The museum's collection of archaeological finds give the onlooker many clues to the mentality and beliefs of the mysterious and cultured Etruscan people. Some 600 funerary urns, which contained the ashes of the deceased, are on display having been recovered from necropoli around Volterra (some of which have disappeared with the erosion of the Balze). Many are made of alabaster (a craft which was not revived in Volterra until the 16thC), others of terracotta or tufa. They depict – some crudely, some with great skill – the preparation for death, and supposed after life of the deceased (later urns show the voyage to Hades by means of a horse-drawn wagon or *carpentum*). Upstairs, in Room XXII, is a bronze figure of a man which looks as if it had been stretched like plasticene, and could be by Giacometti. This is the mysterious 3rdC BC votive figure, strangely devoid of possessions or of clothing, dubbed **Ombra della Sera** (Shadow of the Evening). Also displayed are bronze figurines, jugs, bowls, cooking pots, fashionable ear rings, rings, dice, coins, buckles, tools, helmets. In Room XX is another highlight: the realistically carved **Urna degli Sposi** (Urn of the Married Couple), decorated with the reclining figures of an elderly couple who lived at the latter end of the Etruscan Empire, shortly before it was obliterated by the rise of the Romans.

147

Local Explorations: 1

The museum is clearly arranged, with explanations in English.

Leaving the museum, pop up Vicolo Marchi opposite for a view of the splendid **Fortezza Medicea**, which has long been a prison. Retrace to Piazza XX Settembre, and take the right-hand fork, Via di Sotto, with views of the countryside. The church of **San Michele** contains a lovely glazed terracotta *Madonna and Child* by Giovanni della Robbia. Opposite the church is an excellent local food store, specializing in cheese and meat.

Take Via Guarnacci (passing a recommendable *pizzeria*, **Ombra della Sera, L**) to Porta Fiorentina, where turn left (signposted) for an excellent view of the very impressive and well-preserved **Roman theatre**, with the **baths** beyond. In a while, the site itself, at present closed for excavations, should be open to the public.

Having seen Etruscan and Roman Volterra, plunge back into the medieval town by carrying on along the wall and, in the little piazza, turn left down the side of **Casa Torri Minucci**, one of several medieval tower houses clustered around here. A covered alley leads to the **Pinacoteca**, housed in the elegant Renaissance **Palazzo Minucci Solaini**, designed by Antonio da Sangallo the Elder.

The collection of Florentine and Sienese art (*open Mar-Nov 9 am-7 pm; Nov-Mar 9 am-1 pm*) includes a Mannerist masterpiece: Rosso Fiorentino's ***Deposition*** (1521). Taddeo di Bartolo, Luca Signorelli and Ghirlandaio are also represented.

Via Buonparenti takes you past the twin towers, joined by an aerial walkway, of the **Case Torri dei Buonparenti e Bonaguidi**, back to Piazza dei Priori.

There's one more thing you should try to see before you leave, which is just inside Porta San Francesco, along Via Ricciarelli and Via San Lino. The church of **San Francesco** has a chapel, **Cappella della Croce di Giorno**, which was frescoed in 1410 by one Cenni di Francesco with scenes, amongst others, from the *Legend of the True Cross*. There is plenty of action to detain you, as well as fascinating contemporary detail, and amusingly fanciful architecture.

RECOMMENDED HOTELS

SAN GIMIGNANO
L'Antico Pozzo, LL-LLL; *Via San Matteo 87; tel. 0577 942014; fax 0577 942117; cards accepted.*

A 15thC town house, restored with flair in 1990. Bedrooms are modishly decorated, although attention to small details is lacking.

Le Renaie, LL; *Località Pancole, 6 km N of San Gimignano off Certaldo road; tel. 0577 955044; fax 0577 955126; cards accepted; closed last three weeks Nov.*

A simple, well-run and reasonably priced country hotel with a tranquil location and a small swimming pool. Outside it looks fairly unprepossessing – a modern villa built up over the years from a simple bar and restaurant. Inside it is cool and pretty, although the decoration in the bedrooms errs on the precious.

SIENA
Certosa di Maggiano, LLL; *Via di Certosa 82, 1 km SE of Siena via Porta Romana; tel. 0577 288180; fax 0577 288189; cards accepted.*

A former Carthusian monastery, secluded in a large park, yet only minutes by taxi from the city centre, has become an exclusive hotel of great character and luxury. Business conventions are eschewed, and the sequence of beautifully decorated reception rooms has the atmosphere of a delightful country house. The service is always discreet, and the food, served in the lovely dining room, in the tranquil 14thC cloisters or under the arcades by the swimming-pool, does not disappoint.

The Via di Certosa makes a lovely road, past elegant country houses, along which to take a walk.

Palazzo Ravizza, LL; *Pian dei Mantellini 34; tel. 0577 280462; fax 0577 221597; cards accepted.*

An up-market *pensione* oozing that elusive faded charm which comes with a house that has been in the same noble family for 200 years, with quirky period furniture, comfy beds, huge bathrooms and some 'rooms with a view'. Unpretentious home cooking is served in the neat dining room, which has a ravishingly pretty ceiling, and there is a large shady terrace as well.

Santa Caterina, LL; Via Enea Silvio Piccolomini 7; tel. 0577 221105; fax 0577 271087; cards accepted; closed Jan-Mar.

Some of the rooms are too small in which to swing a suitcase; others are larger and have fresco fragments and attractive antique furniture. All are neat and well-kept with white-tiled bathrooms and there is a conservatory breakfast room with a view on to the flowery garden. Good value for money.

VOLTERRA
Villa Nencini, LL; Borgo Santo Stefano 55; tel. 0588 86386; fax 0588 80601; cards accepted.

Set just outside the town, close to the Porta San Francesco entrance, this stone house offers impressive views of the glorious sweeping countryside. Rooms are smallish but practical; some of the bathrooms need improvement – the only way to have a shower in mine was by flooding the place. There's a large swimming pool, although sadly much of the garden has been lost to an ambitious annexe, which has not yet opened.

RECOMMENDED RESTAURANTS

COLLE DI VAL D'ELSA
Antica Trattoria, LL-LLL; Piazza Arnolfo 23; tel. 0577 923747; cards accepted; closed Tues.

In the main square of the lower town, this is an old-established restaurant serving excellent Tuscan food in a comfortable setting. Attentive service; always lively.

Up in the Centro Storico is a temple of gastronomy: **Arnolfo, LLLL** (Piazza Santa Caterina 2; tel. 0577 920549; closed Tues).

SAN GIMIGNANO
La Mandragola, L-LL; Via Berignano 58; tel. 0577 940377; cards accepted; closed Thur.

A large, cool restaurant, its white walls decorated with modern pictures. Straightforward menu, delicious *bistecca Fiorentina*. Friendly service.

Along the same lines is **Osteria delle Catene, L-LL**; Via Mainardi 18; tel. 0577 941966; closed Wed which serves very tasty food under a pale rose brick vaulted ceiling. However, the huge nude painting on the wall may put you off your lunch – if it's still there.

La Terrazze, L-LL; Piazza della Cisterna 24; tel. 0577 940328; cards accepted; closed Tues, Wed lunch.

The smart restaurant of the hotel **La Cisterna, LLL-LLLL** has panoramic views over Val d'Elsa. Pasta is made on the premises – try the *fettucine all'uovo ai funghi*.

SIENA
Le Logge, L-LL; Via del Porrione 33; tel. 0577 48013; cards accepted; closed Sun.

Siena's gastronomic strength is sweets and biscuits rather than *haute cuisine*. Its restaurants tend to be somewhat disappointing. Le Logge's adventurous cooking can be erratic, but it has a great atmosphere. Attractive wood and marble dining room.

Osteria La Chiacchiera, L; costa di S. Antonio 4; tel. 0577 280631; no cards; closed Tue in winter.

A simple osteria on a narrow, steep street near Saint Catherine's house. The ambiance is rustic, wine is served behind a counter from vast containers, table tops are bare wood with rough paper mats, and the menu features excellent home-made Tuscan classics. Not overrrun by tourists (unusual in Siena). Food is wholesome and cheap.

VOLTERRA
Ombra della Sera, L-LL; Via Gramsci 70; tel. 0588 86663; cards accepted; closed Mon.

A cosy little place with wood panelling and wild boars' heads on the walls – Volterra is noted for its wild boar dishes. Here standard fare – *ribollita, risotto*, grilled radicchio – is carefully cooked and often mouthwatering.

Local Explorations: 2

<u>Central Tuscany</u>

Chianti

127 km; map Touring Club Italiano Toscana

The word Chianti is immediately evocative. It may conjure first an image of distinctive wine, perhaps a bottle adorned with the famous black cockerel, symbol of the Gallo Nero consortium of growers, or maybe a traditional straw-covered flask. Then there's Chianti the place, popularly known as 'Chiantishire' by the British, who long ago adopted the region as their own, until a more varied mix of visitors moved in – Germans particularly love it here, but there are plenty of other Europeans, and Americans too. Chianti suggests the good life in a Tuscany of beech and chestnut, vine and pasture, romantic crags and deep dark valleys thick with autumn leaves, of terraced stone-walled hillsides, lofty castles and isolated Romanesque churches, and the traditional, handsome farmhouse, called *casa colonica*. And the farms – *fattoria* – of which there are literally hundreds – devoted to the grape and to the olive.

Of course, in reality, things are nearly perfect, but not quite. Parts of Chianti are arid and suburban and certain little towns with alluring names are frankly ugly. Then there's the effects of tourism. The holiday homes and hotels (advertised by huge roadside hoardings) are filled to capacity in summer, desolate in winter, when the locals who service them must themselves travel in search of work elsewhere. The region has a manicured, commercialized veneer – even the business of wine-making is heavily automated and totally lacking in peasant *joie de vivre*, although the olive harvest is, on some *fattorie* at least, still a memorable experience (see Tuscan Olive Oil, page 156). Dig down, however, and you will find the same craftsmen, smallholders and hunters who have lived and worked in these hills for generations.

If you follow the marked route, you'll travel through the heart of Chianti, heading south from Florence on the well-worn Via Chiantigiana (SS222) to link the most interesting places on the way. A suggested detour (see under Castello di Brolio) explores one of its most beautiful corners. Leaving the steep slopes of the Monti di Chianti, the route heads towards the dry hills west of Siena, where a thin topsoil exposes the geology, and you could imagine yourself in the badlands of Dakota. Here you turn west towards the great plain of the Valdichiana and two notable small towns, Monte San Savino and Lucignano.

CENTRAL TUSCANY / *Chianti*

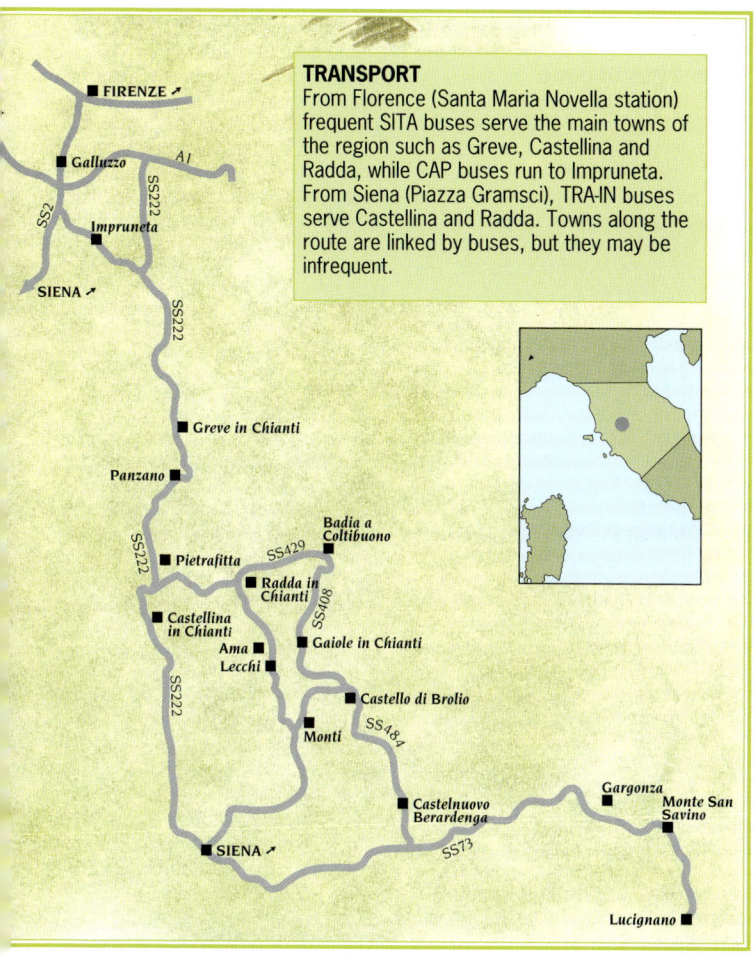

TRANSPORT
From Florence (Santa Maria Novella station) frequent SITA buses serve the main towns of the region such as Greve, Castellina and Radda, while CAP buses run to Impruneta. From Siena (Piazza Gramsci), TRA-IN buses serve Castellina and Radda. Towns along the route are linked by buses, but they may be infrequent.

SIGHTS & PLACES OF INTEREST

BADIA A COLTIBUONO
Off the SS429/408, 6 km E of Radda in Chianti. Coming from Radda, look for a sharp turning left, just before the SS429 meets the main SS22408. The road winds up through thick oak and pine woods to this former abbey tucked away in the heart of the hilly centre of the region, the Monti del Chianti. The 11thC building, with its forbidding grey stone tower, was long ago converted into a private home, and is today a well-known wine-producing estate. Its church of **San Lorenzo**, dating from 1049, can be visited, and there is a **restaurant (L-LL**; *tel.* 0577 749424; *closed* Mon, Nov-Apr) known for its spit-roasted meat.

CASTELLINA IN CHIANTI ⇔ ✕
On the SS429/SS222, 50 km S of Florence, 10 km W of Radda. The factory-like wine co-operative and hill-top *rocca* (fortress) in Castellina illustrate the town's past struggles and its present prosperity. Its commanding hill-top position made it an obvious Florentine defence post on the border of Florentine/Sienese territory, and it was fortified, fought over and besieged more than once. Today Castellina is a well-heeled little place, with an industrial suburb that has grown rich on wine.

Close to the main entrance (limited car parking), the **Via delle Volte** is a covered street, like a rather spooky tunnel, which was part of the town's defences. Skirting the edge of the hill, its windows allow inviting views of the surrounding countryside. It brings you out at the stone dolls' house church of **San Salvatore**, which contains a *Madonna and Child* by Lorenzo di Bicci. A smart shopping street, with plenty of outlets for the local wine, takes you back to the car. A path leads up to the donjon of the fortress. Rustic **La Torre, LL** (*tel.* 0577 740236; *closed* Fri), the best-known restaurant in town, is up here. Back in the street, respectable pizzas are served at jolly **Il Fondaccio, L-LL** (*tel.* 0577 741084; *closed* Mon). Opposite this restaurant is the rusticated Palazzo Squarciatupi, where you can taste local wines and olive oil of **La Castellina**.

(The **Bottega del Vino Gallo Nero**, Via della Rocca 10, is renowned for its selection of Chianti wines.)

Just outside Castellina, on the road to Radda, a sign on the left points the way to a restored Etruscan tomb, **Ipogeo Etrusco di Montecalvario**. With its entrance built into the hillside, and surrounded by pine trees, this is an evocative spot, recalling a far more mysterious people than the squabbling factions of medieval Tuscany.

CASTELLO DI BROLIO
On the SS484, at crossroads, 10 km SE of Gaiole in Chianti. The appearance of industrial buildings in the landscape announces the important wine estate of Barone Ricasole. A dark and winding avenue of cypresses leads to the hill-top **castle**, seemingly inpenetrable behind thick walls (*but open in summer 9 am-noon and 3 pm-sunset*). You will find the estate's produce on sale in the Wine House. The Ricasoli family have been associated with the castle of Brolio since the 12thC.

Not surprisingly, given its position, it was fought over, in fact destroyed, during the protracted Sienese/Florentine wrangles. In the mid-19thC it was rebuilt in Sienese Gothic style by 'Iron Baron' Ricasoli, the man who laid down the rules and formula – wrote the recipe really – for Chianti wines.

Unlikely though it seems, two interesting eating opportunities exist right here. **Osteria del C astello, L-LL** (*tel.* 0577 747194; *closed* Thurs), run by the estate, is a simple, long hut at the foot of the drive serving equally simple local dishes accompanied by Castello di Brolio wines. Just by the crossroads, in the hamlet of San Regolo, is the excellent *trattoria* **Carloni, LL** (*tel.* 0577 749549; *closed* Wed), which is packed with families on Sundays.

This local exploration takes the well-trodden central route through Chianti, stringing together the main towns and other sights of interest. All around is classic Tuscan countryside which you would only get to know if you were staying, or living, in the region. A short detour from Brolio gives a clearer impression of what it's like than staying on the main road.

At the crossroads, take the road signposted to Monti and San Marcellino. There are breath-taking views before the road passes a typical Chianti

Classico wine estate, surrounded by its own olive groves, **Castello di Cacchiano**, where you can buy direct. At the small crossroads before Monti, a signpost directs you to the *pieve* of **San Marcellino** along a lane to the right. As you enter little **Monti**, notice, on the left, the *casa colonica* with its distinctive short tower (originally the dovecot). These attractive farmhouses, mainly dating from the 18thC, are typical of Chianti, just like the *pieve* and the wine and olive oil estate. Monti has a bar/restaurant, **Tavolo Rotonda**.

If you wish to prolong the amble away from the main road, you could continue to the SS408, where turn right, then left in 2 km or so for **San Sano** (good *trattoria*).

Further on is medieval **Ama**, which produces some of the best Chianti Classico (**Castello di Ama** – tastings on offer), and then **Poggio San Polo**, with a very pleasant restaurant (see Recommended Restaurants, page 159) followed by **San Giusto in Salcio**, a pretty 11thC church in a lovely setting. By now you are practically back in Radda, which is all wrong; you could always do this little foray from there (see page 157) if it's more convenient.

CASTELNUOVO BERARDENGA ×
On the SS484, 30 km SE of Radda, 21 km E of Siena. Nothing particular to detain you in this market town, although there are two attractive villages just to the north, **Villa a Sesta** (see Recommended Restaurants, page 159) and **San Gusmé**, where there is a fairly new luxury hotel (**Villa Arceno, LLL**; *tel.* 0577 359292; *fax* 0577 359276). And 3 km or so beyond Villa a Sesta, almost back at Castello di Brolio (see page 152), a turning left leads to well-tended **San Felice**, where the wine estate of the same name produces an excellent traditional Chianti Classico Riserva, Poggio Rosso. The estate cultivates some of the grape types which were largely abandoned after Baron Ricasoli laid down the formula for Chianti.

Castelnuovo Berardenga marks the outer edge of Chianti; travelling south, the landscape of the Crete becomes bare and windswept; our route, however, turns eastwards along the margins of Chianti towards the great plain of the Valdichiana, once marshland until it was drained in the 16thC and became fertile agricultural land famous for its cattle which produce *bistecca Fiorentina*. In the opposite direction, towards Siena, is **Montaperti**, site of the battlefield where, for just one glorious and never-forgotten time, the Sienese trounced the Florentines (in 1260).

CERTOSA DI GALLUZZO
On the SS2, 6 km S of Florence. Certosa is on the outskirts of Florence, and makes a useful place for a breather if you have just discovered yourself to be still alive having negotiated the city's traffic. The monastery, founded in 1340 by the wealthy Florentine banker Niccolo Acciaiuoli, stands on a high hill outside the village of Galluzzo. In the **Palazzo degli Studi**, the works of art on display include Pontormo's Mannerist vision of the **Passion**. The Acciaiuoli family is buried in a vault beneath the imposing church of **San Lorenzo** (*open Tues-Sun 9 am-noon, 3-6 pm, 5 pm in winter*). Notice the lovely slab commemorating Cardinal Agnolo Acciaiuoli, which dates from the 16thC.

GAIOLE IN CHIANTI ⌾
On the SS408, 11 km SE of Radda in Chianti. The least instantly appealing of the Chianti wine towns, but it has no less heart than the others, and an important monthly (Monday pm) market. Wine is what will probably draw you here. The **Agricoltori Chianti Geografico** (Via Mulinaccio 10; on the SS408, on the right just before the left-hand turn to Castello di Meleto) is a winemaking co-operative started in 1961 to preserve the interests of more than a hunded small vineyard owners from Castellina, Radda and Gaiole.

Grapes from the various vineyards are mixed together as needed, with the exception of two which retain their own labels: Castello di Fagnano and La Contessa di Radda. Signposted in the village is **Montagnani** (Via Bandinelli 9) with an impressive array of Chianti Classico to taste and buy.

Propped up on various hills around Gaiole are the following places of note: **Spaltenna,** with medieval *pieve* and castle converted into a hotel (see Recommended Hotels, page 158); fortified **Barbischio**; the terrific 13thC **Castello di Vertine, Castello di Meleto,** and **Castello di Castangnoli**, set in a charming medieval village.

Local Explorations: 2

Chianti landscape.

GREVE IN CHIANTI
On the SS222, 31 km S of Florence. Probably the most important town in the region: plenty of wine shops here, notably the **Enoteca** near the church (Piazzetta di Santa Croce 8). No need to stray from the attractive, triangular **Piazza Matteotti**, which is lined by arcades and sweeps up to the rather plain church at its apex. Here is a statue of the explorer Giovanni da Verrazzano, who was born in the nearby castle of the same name. He is engulfed by market stalls every Saturday morning and during the September **wine fair** (second week). Here also is the popular restaurant **Da Verrazzano** (see Recommended Restaurants, page 159) and the hotel **Del Chianti** (see Recommended Hotels, page 158).

South of Greve is **Panzano**, noted as much for its embroidery as for its wine. As you approach, a sign on the right indicates **Montagliari**, a large *fattoria* with a well-known restaurant **Trattoria del Montagliari**, fire in cold weather, garden for summer (**L**; *tel.* 055 852184; *closed* Mon).

A little beyond Panzano, a sharp turning left leads to the soothing, creamy yellow **Pieve di San Leolino**. The Romanesque church is arranged with three naves and apses and has a lovely 13thC triptych. From the terrace there are views of the hills which encircle Panzano, bathed in sunlight and covered in thick woods and vineyards.

About 8 km south of here, off to the left, is **Pietrafitta**, a tiny, silent hamlet buried in woodland approached by a bumpy track bordered with cypresses. Perched on a rooftop, a copy of the Venus de' Medici greets your arrival. A grassy path leads to the pretty church. Back on the roadside, there's a friendly, laid-back **bar/restaurant**.

IMPRUNETA
On a by-road, 15 km S of Florence. If you inspect the massive terracotta urns which, filled with lemon or orange trees, grace the terraces of hotels or old Tuscan houses, the chances are that they will be stamped with the word 'Impruneta' and, very probably, a date reaching back into the 19thC. This is the home of raw terracotta, which you can find as pots and tiles of every shape and size. (If you decide not to stop at Impruneta, but are interested in terracotta, you could try **Zago**, about 2 km south of Strada in Chianti on the way to Greve.)

Impruneta is known for two other things besides terracotta: its long-established, hectic and happy **St Luke's Fair** held in early October, part cattle market, part general fair, with stalls bursting with local produce, sweets, nuts, wine, terracotta pots and

CENTRAL TUSCANY / Chianti

all manner of things; and its **Collegiata of Santa Maria dell'Impruneta**, overlooking the main square where the fair is held. The church, graced by a lovely 17thC portico, was bombed in 1944, but has since been restored, including its two matching chapels by Michelozzo, with lovely ceilings by Luca della Robbia, who also made the two fine tabernacles. The chapel on the right was built (c. 1450) to house a relic of the True Cross; the other to house a painting of the Madonna which was said to have been executed by St Luke and to have miraculous powers. Such was the belief in it that it was regularly loaned to Florence to help the city in times of danger. The painting you see today was done by Ignazio Hugford, the son of an Englishman who lived in Florence, after the original was found to be too faded. Nobody seemed to mind that it was now an entirely new painting; and it continued to be revered just as it had been before.

• *Chianti wine labels.*

LUCIGNANO ⚑ ×
On a by-road from Monte San Savino to Sinalunga, 8 km S of Monte San Savino.
Which medieval town planner devised the layout of Lucignano? It is refreshingly novel, consisting of four circles-within-circles, with four little piazzas at its centre, and the **Collegiata**, whose circular steps echo the shape of the streets. It is a charming place, its carefully restored 14thC houses and sunny lanes making a particularly marked contrast to the worn face of its near neighbour, Monte San Savino. 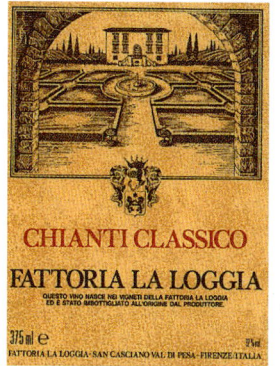
Leaving the car outside the walls, take a stroll around the town – it won't take long. Turn left inside the main gate (north side) and then first right for the Collegiata. Look back at the 14thC **Cassero** (castle) with its matching towers. Inside the **Collegiata** is a horrendous high altar by Andrea Pozzo, and a much more satisfactory pair of gilded wooden angels dating from the early 18thC.

Walk through the flowery piazza next to the church and bear left for **San Francesco**, with a softly striped Romanesque façade and pretty carved portal. Inside are frescoes of the Sienese school.

In the adjacent neat-as-a-pin piazza is **Da Toto**, where you can have a comfy bed and a good meal (see Recommended Hotels, page 158) and the **Museo Communale** (*closed Mon*). Here are paintings of the Sienese school, including the pastoral lunette by Signorelli of St Francis receiving the stigmata; the museum's showpiece, however, is the **Albero di Lucignano** (*Tree of Lucignano*), an immense gold reliquary of the 14thC, fashioned with great delicacy.

Return to the Collegiata and turn left below its steps to follow one of Lucignano's flower-filled circular streets, Vicolo del Pellegrino. Market day here is Thursday. The end of May sees **Maggiolata**, a colourful floral festival.

MONTE SAN SAVINO
On the SS73, 47 km E of Siena. A small town which sits on a balcony of hills overlooking both Chianti and Valdichiana. It has dignity and serenity, with a surprising crop of fine buildings which reflect its agricultural prosperity in times past, although today it

Local Explorations: 2

TUSCAN OLIVE OIL

"These are very precious," says Giovanni, indicating the trays of black and green olives lying on the floor of the old mill. "The harvest has now begun, and they are gathered with the greatest care. When I was a boy before the war they were picked by hand, but now a special comb is used and the olives are collected in a 'parachute' lying under the tree. It is considered a crime to shake or bash the tree as they do in the south and in Spain."

Giovanni is the owner of a fairly large *fattoria* on an estate that has been in his family for hundreds of years. His olive mill is used not only to press his own olives ("some bread, some salt, some of my olive oil and you can live forever") but those of smallholders in the neighbourhood who don't have their own mill and pay a fee to use Giovanni's.

"There are two ways of making olive oil," explains Giovanni. "There's the modern way, where you put the olives into one end of a machine and get olive oil from the other; and there's the traditional way, which of course makes for a better product. That is our method, but using modern machinery, including an electric motor instead of a donkey to turn the granite grinding stones."

The olives are first washed and stripped of their leaves by gentle vibration, then they are crushed to a pulp, stones and all, by the mill. The pulp is smeared on to nylon discs (it used to be coconut leaves) which are laid on to metal discs. Three discs are piled on top of each other and pressed. The resulting mixture of oil and water are then separated and the water drained away. The remaining solid matter is then sent down a chute into a truck, usually to be disposed of, although it may be pressed again to become *olio di sansa* for cooking.

The olive harvest begins in mid-November and continues almost until Christmas. "It is a wonderful time here," says Giovanni. "The process of making olive oil is treated with great reverence by the workers and farmers, and there is a special atmosphere in the mill, which is in operation 24 hours a day. Room temperature must be kept steady, with the door being opened or closed accordingly. A long trestle table is set up and the women bring food for their husbands. Some are eating and drinking, some resting, some working. The farmer, who has booked his slot in advance, may have many kilos of olives or just a few. He waits for a couple of hours or so while his first olives are being pressed. The moment when he collects the oil – in plastic or stainless steel vats – is a proud one. The whole process is carried out with love and commitment."

What should you look for on a bottle of olive oil? 'Extra virgin' simply means that the oleic acid content is below 1 per cent, but the best oils will have as little as 0.5 per cent. So for salads, sauces and so on your olive oil should certainly be 'extra virgin'. 'First pressing' is not terribly revealing either, since the oil resulting from a second pressing is only good for cooking. Amazingly, Italy imports a great deal of olive oil, though it is bottled here and sent out as 'Italian olive oil'. So avoid labels which say '*imbottigliato in Italia*'; it could come from anywhere – and will be of poor quality. Stick to labels which state '*prodotto in Italia*'. The production of quality olive oil is an expensive business, and L18,000 per litre is the least you can expect to pay in Italy.

presents a slightly dilapidated and gloomy air. Coming by car, you could park outside the town walls, or take a gamble and drive through **Porta Fiorentina** seeking a space in tired little Piazza Gamurrini. The narrow portal was designed by Vasari and built by Nanni di Baccio Bigio.

In the piazza are two narrow stone buildings amongst the houses: what's left of the 14thC Sienese Gothic town castle, the **Cassero**, which houses the tourist office and a **Museo di Ceramica**, and the 17thC chapel of **Santa Chiara**, whose strange interior, if you are able to see it, contains terracottas by the della Robbias and Andrea Sansovino. Sansovino, born here in 1450 (died 1529), was a sculptor and a pioneer of graceful High Renaissance architecture, not much remembered these days except perhaps for his terracotta and marble work, and for his Florentine pupil Jacopo Tatti, who took his master's surname before becoming the chief architect of his day in Venice. Monte San Savino was much fought over by Arezzo and Florence, and finally fell to the latter in 1385. Its brief moment of splendour came in 1551 when Cosimo I donated it to the brother of Julius III, the Marchese Baldovino del Monte. Although Baldovino only managed to hold on to the town for a brief 18 years, many of its fine buildings date from that period.

Walk down main **Corso Sangallo** to see the town's noblest pile, the **Palazzo Comunale**, erected by Antonio Sangallo the Elder. The airy **Loggia dei Mercanti,** opposite the Palazzo Comunale, is said to be by Sansavino and his **cloister** for the church of **Sant'Agostino** makes a beguiling stop. Inside the church, note the radiant 13thC **stained glass rose window.**

For an idyllic picnic spot, head east for 3 km to **Santa Maria delle Vertighe**, a cypress-clad hill with a rustic shrine to the Madonna overlooking the *autostrada*. The Madonna is now known as the Virgin of the Motorways, protectress of all those who travel fast by road. Her lantern was donated by the *autostrada* contractors. Beneath the surface of the shrine's Late Renaissance face-lift you can still catch glimpses of the original Romanesque church.

Some 7 km west is the preserved fortified medieval hamlet of **Gargonza**. This huddle of houses on a thickly wooded hillock sheltered Dante during his exile from Florence. In the 1970s the owner, Conte Roberto Guicciardini, turned the whole place into self-catering cottages (**LL;** *tel.* 0575 847021; *fax* 0575 847054). There are also a (somewhat basic) guest house and, outside the walls, a restaurant.

It's a beautiful, but perhaps rather dated place to stay, and because of its isolation it could benefit from a swimming pool (planning permission is currently being sought). Some of the rooms have wonderful views over the Valdichiana. In order to look around, you may have to express an interest in renting accommodation.

RADDA IN CHIANTI ⇔ ×
On the SS429, 13 km E of Castellina in Chianti, 54 km SE of Florence. A well-groomed wine-and-tourist oriented hill town set in the rocky landscape of central Chianti.

It has a miniature medieval core, its **Palazzo Comunale** encrusted with coats-of-arms; a sophisticated hotel and Michelin-starred restaurant.

In 1415 it became the capital of the Lega del Chianti, a military alliance of Florentine towns set up against Siena. The League's symbol, the *gallo nero*, or black cockerel, lives on as the trademark of the Consorzio del Marchio Storico, a consortium of some 600 wine producers who make around 80 per cent of Chianti Classico which has become famous world-wide.

The once-imposing defences of the *borgo* are now reduced to a handful of towers and meagre remains of the walls, but Radda's medieval street plan is still evident.

The Renaissance **Palazzo del Podestà** on central Piazza Ferrucci, embellished with coats-of-arms, is the most appealing building in Radda, but the main attraction here is the modest charm of the whole place – for it is surely one of Chianti's prettiest small villages.

Some 7 km north is the hamlet of **Volpaia,** an atmospheric place where nothing much seems to have changed since the Renaissance – except that the old church by the castle has now become a wine *cantina*.

RECOMMENDED HOTELS

CASTELLINA IN CHIANTI
Salivolpi, LL; Via Fiorentina; tel. and fax 0577 740484; cards accepted.

Castellina has attracted a cluster of appealing hotels. This one offers a much cheaper alternative to its two illustrious neighbours, **Tenuta de Ricavo, LLL** (tel. 0577 740221; fax 0577 741014, which occupies an entire hamlet) and **Villa Caselecchi, LLL** (tel. 0577 740240; fax 0577 741111). Salivolpi consists of two restored farm buildings (decorated with Spanish simplicity: iron fittings, exposed beams, white walls, ochre tiles) and a new bungalow set in a peaceful open position on the edge of the village. The atmosphere is calm and relaxed, and there's a spacious, well-tended garden with swimming-pool.

Another, inexpensive, family-run hotel with a pleasant atmosphere is **Il Colombaio, LL** (Via Chiantigiana on the road to Radda; tel. 0577 740444; fax 0577 740444).

GAIOLE IN CHIANTI
Castello di Spaltenna, LLL; tel. 0577 749483; fax 0577 749269; cards accepted; closed Jan, Feb.

A peacefully situated medieval castle has become a small (21-room) hotel. A popular restaurant (**LL**) is set in the great hall with minstrel's gallery. Swimming pool.

GREVE IN CHIANTI
Albergo del Chianti, L-LL; Piazza Matteotti 28; tel. 055 853763; fax 055 853763; cards accepted; closed Nov.

On Greve's triangular piazza, this is a cool, calm, neatly restored and well-run bed-and-breakfast hotel, with the surprise of an attractive swimming pool in the back garden.

Villa le Barone, LLL; Via San Leolino 19, Panzano in Chianti, 6 km S of Greve; tel. 055 852621; fax 055 852277; cards accepted; closed Nov-Mar.

Close to the charming pieve of San Leolino, this was the attractive 16thC home of the della Robbia family, and became a hotel in 1976. It still feels like a private home, and there is a peaceful woody garden and terrace around the pool with panoramic views. Well regarded restaurant.

Villa di Vignamaggio, LL; 5 km SE of Greve, on road to Lamole from SS222; tel. 055 8544800; fax 055 8544468; cards accepted; closed Nov-Mar.

The setting for Kenneth Branagh's pastoral film *Much Ado About Nothing* and a magical, deeply peaceful place to stay in self-catering (agriturismo) apartments of great taste – stone, wood, terracotta – and simplicity.

LUCIGNANO
Da Toto, L; Piazza del Tribunale 6; tel. and fax 0575 836988; cards accepted; closed Nov; restaurant closed Tue and 7 Jan-mid Feb.

Lucignano exudes charm and so does this hotel, right in the historic centre with some rooms overlooking the piazza and others the Valdichiana. Rooms are furnished in rustic style. Pergola garden (where meals are served in summer), swimming pool and car parking. Restaurant (**L**).

MONTE SAN SAVINO
Sangallo, LL; Piazza Vittorio Veneto; tel. 0575 810042; fax 0575 853648; cards accepted.

A three-star hotel just outside the town walls. Rooms are small but neat with TV, phone and shower. Attractive ground-floor bar/lounge. No restaurant, but there's one close by – see page 159. Some parking.

RADDA IN CHIANTI
Relais Fattoria Vignale, LL-LLL; Via Pianigiani 15; tel. 0577 741144; fax 0577 740263; cards accepted; closed Nov-Mar.

This is an alluring and sophisticated retreat. Situated in the village, it has lovely views across the hills from its terraces. Four interconnecting sitting rooms, decorated with murals and beautifully furnished, lead to the pool terrace where you can breakfast under a creeper-clad arbour in warm weather (there is also a brick-vaulted breakfast room). Bedrooms are cool, with waxed wooden doors, white walls, antique beds. The manageress, Silvia Kummer, runs the Vignale with consummate skill and care.

CENTRAL TUSCANY / *Chianti*

RECOMMENDED RESTAURANTS

Opening times tend to be erratic out of season; check by phone.

CASTELLINA IN CHIANTI
L'Albergaccio, LL-LLL; *Via Fiorentina 35 (towards San Donato); tel. 0577 741042; cards accepted; closed Sun.*

A relatively new restaurant with high standards of cooking and presentation and reasonable prices. A complimentary glass of *spumante* is offered with your meal.

CASTELNUOVO BERARDENGA
La Bottega del 30, L-LL; *Villa a Sesta, 6 km N of Castelnuovo Berardenga; tel. 0577 359226; cards accepted; dinner only; closed Tue, Wed.*

Well regarded, run by a Sienese chef and his French wife who take their imaginative Tuscan *cuisine* seriously. For a simple light lunch, try the nearby bar run by their daughter.

GREVE IN CHIANTI
Giovanni da Verrazzano, LL; *Piazza Matteotti 28; tel. 055 853189; cards accepted; closed Sun dinner, Mon.*

It's fun to eat on the shaded first-floor terrace/balcony overlooking the piazza around which Greve revolves. Behind, there is a large, bustling, pink-tableclothed dining room filled with local families. Straightforward food: perhaps *antipasto*, ravioli with butter and sage, *nana in sugo* (duck), and a bottle of local wine.

A handful of simple rooms are available (**L-LL**).

LUCIGNANO
See *Recommended Hotels, page 158.*

MONTE SAN SAVINO
La Terrasse, LL; *Via G. di Vittorio 2; tel. 0575 844111; cards accepted; closed Wed.*

Don't be misled by the sign 'American Bar'. Roberto Lodovichi's restaurant has a typically Tuscan interior of exposed brick and vaulted white-washed ceilings. Presentation is immaculate, service brisk. Menu strong on desserts. Some detest muzak, but we enjoyed an unobtrusive programme of classical/ moden jazz. Thirty metres

• *Local gardener with his produce.*

from the Hotel Sangallo (see Recommended Hotels, page 158).

RADDA IN CHIANTI
Il Poggio, LL; *Poggio San Polo, 6 km S of Radda, off the road to Lecchi; tel. 0577 746135; cards accepted; closed Dec-mid Feb and Mon.*

Pleasant food, nothing sensational, but the real draw is the setting, with a peaceful dining terrace overlooking the gorgeous hills. A favourite.

Il Vignale, LLL; *Via XX Settembre; tel 0577 738094; cards accepted; closed Thur.*

Associated with the hotel of the same name down the road (although under different ownership; see Recommended Hotels, page 158) and displaying the same high standards and calm sophistication. The simple dishes of Tuscany are transformed into elegant and unusual concoctions by the Italian chef/*patron* (his charming German-born wife ably presides front-of-house). Black-and-white polenta (the black achieved with squid ink) is served with a sauce of tomatoes and clams, or ricotta cheese served with a hot pear. To drink, there are excellent Fattoria Vignale wines, from the non-Chianti Classico which includes a percentage of Cabernet grapes, to both young and full-bodied Classico wines, such as the excellent full-bodied '87.

Local Explorations: 3

Tuscan-Umbrian Border

Cortona, Montepulciano and Lake Trasimeno

144 km; map Touring Club Italiano Umbria Marche

If you enjoy a lucky dip, with the emphasis on variety, this expedition is for you. Although the distances are short, it packs in dazzling hill towns, top-class pictures, great architecture, the lush broad valley of the Valdichiana and Lake Trasimeno's sheet of reed-girt silver. You'll also encounter Etruscan footprints, a Roman battle ground, a swanky spa town and a red wine to put hairs on your chest.

The metallic click of olive leaves in the breeze provides the sound track for the journey – although the din from the major roads that cross the area occasionally intrudes. Don't be afraid, however, to leave these busy highways to discover, in minutes, untouched silent villages and glorious empty countryside.

The western part of the route lies along Tuscany's Valdichiana, one of the region's main arteries, heavily farmed and dotted with light industry. On the valley's flanks stand Cortona and Montepulciano, quintessential Tuscan towns, once seen, never forgotten. Further south is Chiusi, dull at first sight but scratch the surface and you will find remarkable traces of its Etruscan forbears.

The eastern stretch of the journey centres on Italy's fourth largest lake, Lago Trasimeno. For landlocked Umbria, this is the nearest it has to a riviera and in summer its handful of resorts make a brave attempt at imitating their seaside counterparts. But, away from the campsites and holiday villas, it still has a quiet charm. Here, too, you are well advised to strike off the beaten track up into the benign hills above the lake to find your own private paradise.

TUSCAN-UMBRIAN BORDER / *Cortona, Montepulciano and Lake Trasimeno*

• *Montepuliciano*

TRANSPORT
The A1 Rome-Florence *autostrada* (Chiusi-Chianciano exit) drops you on the doorstep of this area. The main Rome-Florence railway line stops at Chiusi (bus service from the station to Montepulciano), Castiglione del Lago, Cortona and Castiglion Fiorentino, while the Ferrovia Centrale Umbra (FCU) Cortona-Perugia line takes you around the northern shore of Lake Trasimeno to Passignano and Magione.
There are regular buses from Siena and Florence to Montepulciano and Chiusi and regular services between Castiglione del Lago, Cortona, Chiusi, Chianciano and Montepulciano.

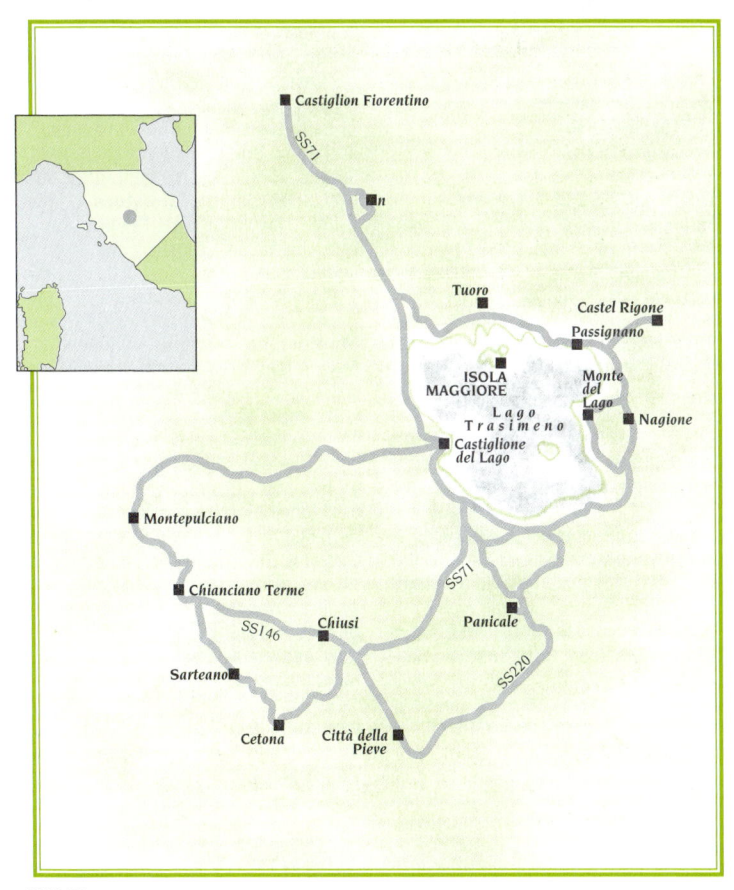

1:500,000

Local Explorations: 3

• *Lake Trasimeno.*

SIGHTS & PLACES OF INTEREST

CASTEL RIGONE
See Passignano, pages 167-8.

CASTIGLIONE DEL LAGO
On the SS71, on W shore of Lake Trasimeno. From afar, this small town presents an inviting face: its crenellated walls and turrets stand erect on a gentle hillock, once an island, now an olive-clad promontory on the western shores of Lake Trasimeno. Close-up, it is mildly disappointing, but a pretty enough place to idle away an hour or two.

The signorial 16thC **palace** of the Della Corgna family, the Renaissance lords of the lake, lies at the tip of the promontory with the town's finest prospects over the water. Attributed to the Early Baroque master, Vignola, it is decorated with some spirited **frescoes** by Il Pomarancio.

The town's most atmospheric pile is the well-preserved, four-towered 13thC **Castello**. Search out the strange defended **walkway** through the town walls leading from the castle to the Palazzo Comunale.

A minor masterpiece awaits the curious in **Santa Maria Maddalena** church on Corso Matteotti: a *Madonna and Child* with saints by Eusebio da San Giorgi (1500), a follower of Perugino.

Take an *aperitivo* at one of a handful of enticing bars and you have done this small town.

CASTIGLION FIORENTINO
On the SS71, 12 km NW of Cortona. When Arezzo ruled the town, it was known as Castillione Aretino. Then Perugia muscled in and the town was dubbed Castiglion Perugino. Finally Florence took over in 1384, changed its name for the last time, and set about giving it the typically Florentine look that remains today. This unfussy country market town, that once doubled as a sturdy garrison over the lush Valdichiana, has plenty of Tuscan grace, even if there are no three-star attractions.

At the top of the old *borgo* is the small main square, **Piazza del Municipio**, set off by a handsome 16thC **loggia**, its walls emblazoned with stone and terracotta coats of arms. Through its nine arches are quintessential Tuscan views of the olive-clad slopes of the valley. The town's **Pinacoteca** in Via del Cassero won't leave you reeling, but it does have a respectable collection of early Tuscan and Umbrian paintings and some outstanding religious goldsmiths' work. For a moment of meditation, look out the **cloisters** of the 12thC church of **San Francesco** – rank vegetation, crumbling stucco, and cool shade.

Florentine ghosts still stir in the gaunt ruins of the medieval **castle** at **Montecchio Vesponi**, 3 km south of town. High on a hill, its tall slim tower refusing to crumble away, the *castello* is the most striking in the Valdichiana. The celebrated English *condottiere*, Sir John Hawkwood, was given the castle by Florence, grateful perhaps for the fact that he no longer fought for her arch-enemy Pisa. Known to Italians as Giovanni Acuto (Sharp John), he was the last of the great foreign mercenary generals who made their fortune on the back of Italian city state rivalry. He is now best remembered by Uccello's famous equestrian fresco which decorates his tomb in Florence's cathedral (see page 49).

CETONA
See Chianciano Terme, below.

CHIANCIANO TERME
On the SS146, 12 km NW of Chiusi. Chi-

Castiglione del Lago.

anciano (pronounced key-an-*cha*-no) is one of Italy's busiest spa towns and its bottled waters grace tables across the country. Italians still flock to mineral springs as they have done since Roman times and towns such as Chianciano are big business – especially as taking the waters comes courtesy of the state health service. Chianciano's speciality is liver complaints – you won't miss the rhyming couplet at every corner *Chianciano - fegato sano* ('Chianciano – healthy liver'). Don't expect much Tuscan charm in the modern development around the four **springs** – all wide avenues, scores of swanky if faintly clinical hotels, elegant shops, smart villas and rather boring public gardens. Even if such apparently alarming treatments as *balneofangoterapia* don't whet your appetite, Chianciano is a useful place in which to find a hotel room if everywhere else is full.

For all the town's modern garb, however, it has a long history. Some believe that even the Etruscans beat a path here and it was certainly well known to the Romans. You can see the medieval face of Chianciano up in the **old town** that stands above the spa to the north, including the stern 13thC **Palazzo del Podestà,** relieved with a flourish of Renaissance coats of arms. For a beguiling, if slow, country drive, take the by-way south-east from Chianciano for Sarteano and Cetona, two hidden villages on the forested slopes of high **Monte Cetona**. Gnarled **Sarteano**, a tiny spa watched over by an imposing **castle**, boasts Etruscan roots. The medieval **borgo** has a well-preserved double ring of walls and a Renaissance **Collegiata** church in Piazza San Lorenzo, built from the ruins of Roman *Pagus Sartheanensis*.

Cetona, on the eastern slopes of Mount Cetona, is another old village worth exploring if you have time to spare. It has a pair of restaurants worth the journey (see Recommended Restaurants, page 169), and the main architectural attraction is the 12thC **Collegiata** decorated inside with precious Quattrocento **frescoes**, including an *Assumption* attributed to Pinturicchio.

The slopes of Monte Cetona are believed to have been one of the earliest sites of human habitation in Italy. The best prehistoric finds are on show in Perugia, but Cetona's **Museo Civico per la Preistoria del Monte Cetona** has an impressive collection of fragments dating from Paleolithic times up to the Bronze Age (*open daily in summer months; in winter ask for opening times at the town hall*).

CHIUSI

At the junction of the SS146 and SS326. On the main Rome-Florence railway line. Chiusi has been a thriving town for millenia: as Etruscan Camars, it was one of the most important seats of Etruscan power and was the stronghold of King Lars Porsenna, who around 507 BC swept down on Rome and briefly subjugated it. Legend holds that the Labyrinth of Porsenna, his royal tomb, laden, naturally, with treasure beyond wealth, lies buried hereabouts. Although no one has yet found it, there are plenty of other **underground Etruscan remains**. From the **Museo del Duomo** you can descend into **tunnels** dug into the soft rock thousands of years ago to collect rainwater for the city's water supply.

The fine collection of Etruscan fragments in the **Museo Archeologico Nazionale** to the left of the Duomo sketches an eloquent picture of the sophistication of Camars. In the countryside around, some 20 **tombs** from the vast necropolis that surrounded the town have been excavated – the most famous, the **Tomb of the Monkey**, is currently closed, but the 2,500-year-old painted **Tomba del Leone** (Tomb of the Lion) and the **Tomba della Pellegrina** can be visited – ask at the museum for details.

Early Christians recycled some of the Etruscan galleries for **catacombs** around the 3rdC AD – staff at the Museo della Cattedrale will arrange a visit. The **cathedral** itself is one of Tuscany's oldest, although all that remains of its most ancient incarnation are the salvaged Roman **columns** in the nave erected in the 6thC AD. It was rebuilt over the ages and finally given a thorough refit in the 19thC – the bizarre **painted mosaics** that cover every wall were done then.

CITTÀ DELLA PIEVE

On the SS71, 10 km SE of Chiusi. History is resolutely silent on the origins of this remarkably intact late medieval hill town. Pushed to one side, rarely featuring in guidebooks, even its greatest native son, the painter Pietro Vannucci, is best known to us by the name of **Il Perugino** – the man from Perugia. A number of his works decorate the local churches – best is his marvellous fresco of the **Adoration of the Magi** (1504) in the Oratory of Santa Maria dei Bianchi.

CORTONA ⚔ ✕

On the SS71, 20 km N of Castiglione del Lago. Tourist information: Via Nazionale 72, off main Piazza della Repubblica. Station to SW of town at Camucia served by stopping trains from Arezzo or Chiusi on Rome-Florence line; connecting buses to town centre. Regular coach service from Arezzo. Centre closed to traffic: try parking to the S by Porta Sant'Agostino.

Built of weathered muddy sandstone on the eastern flanks of the Valdichiana, this comes close to an ideal Tuscan hill town. The modern suburbs lie well away on the plains below, and its fine ruins, noble churches and outstanding works of art are set among proper olive groves. It can also boast an archaic pedigree. Virgil claimed that it was founded by Dardanus, the son of Zeus and Electra and the mythical ancestor of the Trojans, and it was certainly an early Umbrian stronghold which passed to the Etruscans somewhere around the 8thC BC. As with all the great Etruscan cities in Tuscany, its earliest stones have been overlayed by millenia of human life and most of what stands today is decidedly medieval. The old city on the heights now only fills part of the space once encircled by the great Etruscan **walls** which stretched for over 3 km – the **Porta Colonia** gives the best idea of the strength of these defences.

Piazza della Repubblica, a startling ensemble of steps, arches, balconies with the medieval **Palazzo Comunale** centre-stage, is the heart of the city. A short stroll to the right of the great flight of steps in front of the *palazzo* will take you to cramped **Piazza Signorelli** for an obligatory visit to the **Museo dell'Accademia Etrusca** housed in **Palazzo Pretorio**. The sharp staircase in the atmospheric courtyard of this 13thC palace takes you up to an outstanding horde of Etruscan finds including a singular **lamp** dating from the 5thC BC. Once used to light a religious sanctuary, this ornate bronze 'chandelier' has 16 oil lamps and is heavily decorated with squat figures. The eclectic museum also displays Egyptian mummies, Roman remains, late Renaissance pictures and 18thC costumes. The collection was founded in 1727 by the Etruscan Academy at Cortona, one of the first organizations to take a serious academic interest in the Etruscan civilization.

Cortona's other starred attraction is the **Museo Diocesano** in a pair of converted churches in front of the Duomo. Fra Angelico spent ten years here and the museum holds two transcendent works by him, an **Annunciation** and a **Madonna with Saints**. Cortona's own great painter, Luca Signorelli, is well represented with a particularly muscular **Deposition**.

Leaving aside plenty of time to clamber up and down Cortona's evocative alleyways, try to see the church of **San Francesco** to pay your respects at the **tomb** of Signorelli in the crypt and, just outside the walls to the south, the splendid Gothic **San Domenico.** Beside the church are public gardens with views to sigh over. The little church of **San Nicolò**, nestling amongst cypresses in a forgotten corner of town off Via San Nicolò, has some fine works by Signorelli.

Just below the *centro storico*, the Brunelleschi-inspired **dome** of the masterly Renaissance church of the **Madonna del Calcinaio** catches the eye from afar. Built at the end of the Quattrocento by the great military architect, Francesco di Giorgio Martini, its magnificent **interior** is a celebration of light and space.

The countryside around is littered with Etruscan **tombs.** Although there is often not a great deal to see, they make atmospheric spots if you are in the right frame of mind. Best of these Ozymandian remains is the **Tanella di Pitagora** (Pythagoras' Little Den), a pile of massive sandstone blocks that no one seems to be able to date with precision. (Follow the signs from the Madonna del Calcinaio.)

ISOLA MAGGIORE ⛴ ✕
See Passignano, page 167.

MONTE DEL LAGO
See Passignano, page 168.

MONTEPULCIANO ⛴ ✕
On the SS146, 9 km NW of Chianciano Terme. Tourist information: Via Ricci 9, off Piazza Grande and (summer-only) in Piazza Don Minzoni outside Porta al Prato. Best link by train is to Chiusi then bus service to town. Coaches run from Siena. Three car parks to NE of Porta al Prato following main road to E of walls.

Stretched out on a crest between the valleys of the Orcia and the Chiana, this quintessential southern Tuscan Renaissance town cuts a *bella figura* with an unfair share of stunning architecture and an excellent red wine – the aptly named Vino Nobile di Montepulciano.

Its main thoroughfare, divided into short stretches each with a different name, takes the longest possible course up the long ridge to arrive at the town's architectural and literal high point, **Piazza Grande**.

Starting at the southern, lowest, end of the old town, the town's main gate, **Porta al Prato**, was restored by Antonio da Sangallo the Elder as part of his ambitious project to improve the city's defences. Here starts the first stretch of the *corso*, **Via di Gracciano nel Corso**. The column topped by a **Marzocco**, the lion that was the symbol of Florentine dominion, catches the eye first – it was put up in 1511 to replace the figure of the Wolf of Siena. Opposite, at No. 91, is **Palazzo Avignonesi**, one of the fine palaces here by Vignola, one of the founding fathers of Baroque architecture. The Avignonesi family still lives here and is reckoned to produce the best Vino Nobile in town.

Palazzo Tarugi, across the way at No. 82, is also by Vignola. The curiosity at **Palazzo Bucelli,** No.73, is the use of recycled Etruscan funeral urns and Latin inscriptions on their bases. Renaissance meets Late Gothic in the

---

VINO NOBILE
Although this was the first Italian wine to be given the DOCG status (Denominazione di Origine Controllata e Garantita – the legal title afforded to only a handful of the country's best wines), there are those who claim that Montepulciano's grandly named wine is nothing more than a jumped-up Chianti. It is true that its principal grape, Prugnolo, is actually a clone of Chiànti's Sangiovese, but for me the result is, often – but not always – superior. This rather austere garnet-coloured wine benefits from a couple of hours airing before drinking.

The generally accepted top producer is Avignonesi, but other respectable names to look out for are Boscarelli, Gracciano, Contucci and Poliziano. Serious drinkers will go for the *riserva*, aged for a minimum of three years in oak. For ordinary gulping try the cheap but far-from-ignoble Rosso di Montepulciano.

Montepulciano.

rich façade of the church of **Sant'Agostino**, the work of Michelozzo di Bartolomeo.

Across the little square is a brick tower, the **Torre di Pulcinella**, topped by the unlikely Commedia dell'Arte figure of Pulcinella who strikes the hours, a gift to the city from a home-sick Neapolitan bishop in 1524. More fine 16thC palaces line the next stretch of the Corso, **Via di Voltaia**, the best of which is **Palazzo Cervini** at No. 21, attributed to Antonio da Sangallo the Younger, nephew of the Elder.

At the end of this stretch, step inside the church of the **Gesù** for echoes of Rome's great Jesuit Baroque churches – Andrea Pozzo who helped produce the best of them was also responsible for this church.

The last part of the town's main 16thC axis finishes in **Via dell'Opio**. A small medieval **house** at the end was the birthplace of one of the greatest Renaissance scholars, Angelo Ambrogini, better known as Il Poliziano – a penname taken from the town's Latin title, Mons Politianus. Carry on if you are happy to have a long, winding walk to Piazza Grande relieved by a visit to Duccio's **Madonna** in the church of **Santa Maria dei Servi**. Otherwise cut up **Via del Duomo**, past the noble 18thC Teatro Poliziano to arrive directly in **Piazza Grande**, the town's set-piece square strangely cut off from the rest of Montepulciano below. Originally laid out by Michelozzo in the 15thC, it is flanked by a brace of grand palaces, the Duomo and the Palazzo Comunale. The **town hall**, built over a period of 100 years and given a stony face in 1424 by Michelozzo, looks like a try-out for Florence's Palazzo Signoria with Guelf crenellations on top of its single **tower** – if you have a head for heights, climb up it for a bird's-eye view of the city and the valleys around.

The enormous Late Renaissance pile of the **Duomo** stands to the left with a blank façade that never seems to have been finished. Facing it across the square is **Palazzo Nobili-Tarugi**, perhaps Montepulciano's finest, bearing all the marks of the assured mastery of Antonio da Sangallo the Elder. Alongside the deep arcades look out for the lions and griffins that decorate the ornate **well-head**.

Palazzo Contucci on the far side of

the square from the town hall is also the work of Sangallo with Peruzzi providing the finishing touches. Its *cantine* (cellars) house the barrels of one of Montepulciano's oldest producers of Vino Nobile – they will happily show you the rambling, old-fashioned cellars and let you taste their wines. As well as Vino Nobile they make an excellent, though costly, Vin Santo.

Montepulciano's finest architectural masterpiece lies a couple of km to the south-west of town and dominates the views for miles around. The perfectly-sited, majestic Church of **San Biagio** (1518-45) is one of Italy's great Renaissance religious buildings and is the masterpiece of Antonio da Sangallo the Elder. This harmonious church of cream travertine topped by a high **dome** was built for praise, not penitence. The adjacent Canonica, or presbytery, with its elegant **loggia**, was erected years after Sangallo's death, but following his original designs.

LAGO TRASIMENO ⇌ ×

Italy's fourth largest lake, with a circumference of 45 km, barely reaches more than 6 m at its deepest; at times it seems more of a swamp than a proper lake. Its low-lying western margins are bordered by thickets of reeds and canes, while gentle hills whose slopes produce some of Umbria's best olive oil roll down to its other shores. Curiously, much of its water still drains out through an underground channel dug by the Romans. The growing number of campsites that now surround the lake lie where once the fatal malaria mosquito reigned.

The lake has been fished for thousands of years and still provides a respectable haul of pike, carp and eels – for the freshest catch make for the little fishing village on Isola Maggiore – see Passignano, page 167.

PANICALE ⇌

13 km SE of Castiglione del Lago. At the heart of this seductive little hill village to the south of Lake Trasimeno is the handsome Collegiate church of **San Michele**. Pass through the splendid Renaissance **portal** to see works by the Umbrian master **Perugino**, particularly his celebrated **fresco** of the *Martyrdom of St Sebastian* (1505). This is a fine example of that uniquely

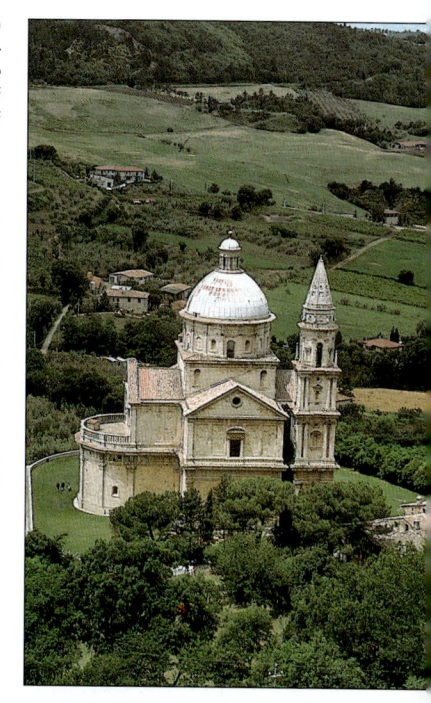

• *San Biagio, near Montepulciano.*

Italian experience of coming across great works of art still on display in the out-of-the-way places for which they were painted.

PASSIGNANO ⇌

On the SS75bis, on N shore of Lake Trasimeno. Ferries for Isola Maggiore from lakeside Lungolago Pompili. Medieval walls still enclose the old town, whose dusky stone houses clamber up the slopes of a promontory on the northern shores of Lake Trasimeno. Sad then, that an unflattering mix of lakeside villas and industry despoil the area around – out of season it can be particularly forlorn. It is, however, the best place to get a boat out to **Isola Maggiore** – not, as its name suggests, the biggest island but the prettiest with a tiny fishing village and an enchanting pair of old **churches**.

A 10-km detour north-east will take you to the atmospheric *borgo* of **Castel Rigone** with the romantic ruins of a 13thC **castle**, the magical Renaissance church of the **Madonna dei Miracoli**, and grandstand views back over **Lake Trasimeno**.

Local Explorations: 3

Clockwise round the lake is **Magione**, a major crossroad on the road to Perugia with a four-square fortified **abbey** that once belonged to the military order of the Knights of Malta. Nearby, on the lake shore, is another rather featureless Trasimeno resort, **Monte del Lago**, saved by a Quattrocento Sienese fresco in its parish church, a watchful medieval tower and fine views over the water.

SARTEANO
See *Chianciano Terme, page 163.*

TUORO
On N shore of Lake Trasimeno, 5 km W of Passignano. Summer-only tourist information at lakeside ferry-station. Tuoro, on the northern shores of Trasimeno, is an undistinguished, comfortable town with a rather messy holiday development down by the beach.

Beneath the modern veneer, however, lurks memories of Ancient Rome. For here was fought the **Battle of Trasimeno**, one of the Republic's bloodiest defeats during the Second Punic War, Rome's final conflict with its North African adversary that ended with the destruction of Carthage. It was a torrid day in June, 217 BC when the celebrated Carthaginian general, Hannibal, lured the Roman army into an ambush in which some 16,000 Roman legionaries where killed. So terrible was the slaughter that the rivers are said to have run red with blood, a fact recalled in the name of the little hamlet of **Sanguineto**. Among the dead was the Roman commander, Consul Flaminius, who a few years earlier had laid down the important Roman road, the Via Flaminia.

Recent archaeological digs in the fields to the west of Tuoro have unearthed tombs holding mass burials of bodies with limbs missing and smashed skulls. Research has dated the finds to the exact period of the battle.

The local tourist office can provide you with a map showing a pair of signposted paths through the battlefield, called the **percorso della battaglia**. The route starts about 2 km west of the centre on the track for Sanguineto – the eerie sign as you enter the area reads: '*Ricordati, viandante, che ti inoltri in un immenso sepolcreto*' – 'Remember, traveller, that you are advancing into an immense burial ground.'

RECOMMENDED HOTELS

CASTIGLIONE DEL LAGO
Miralago, LL; *Piazza Mazzini 6; tel. 075 951157; fax 075 951924; cards accepted.*

This small, recently restored *albergo* in the heart of the old town makes an ideal base from which to explore Lake Trasimeno. Welcoming staff and *al aperto* dining in summer with lovely lake views.

CORTONA
Albergo San Michele, LL; *Via Guelfa 15; tel. 0575 604348; fax 0575 630147; cards accepted.*

Sensitive restoration has retained the charm of this converted Renaissance palace a few paces from Piazza della Repubblica. Splendid public rooms and 32 spacious bedrooms, including one in the little tower with spectacular views over the roof tiles of Cortona.

Relais Il Falconiere, LLL; *Località San Martino, tel. 0575 612679, fax 0575 612927; cards accepted.*

A noble villa in its own 12-acre park three km from Cortona. Most of the original 19thC features have been lovingly retained and the nine bedrooms have been furnished with pieces of period furniture. Genuine Tuscan food in the restaurant – even the olive oil comes from the owner's own olive groves.

ISOLA MAGGIORE
Sauro, LL; *Via G Guglielmi; tel. 075 826168; fax 075 825130; cards accepted.*

A short boat trip from Passignano will take you to the only hotel on Lake Trasimeno's prettiest island – and it's traffic free. A small retreat with only 12 rooms and a restaurant (see Recommended Restaurants, page 169) – make sure you book well in advance.

MONTEPULCIANO
Il Borghetto, LL; *Borgo Buio, 7; tel. and fax 0578 757535; cards accepted.*

A little *albergo* in a 16thC palace in the heart of Montepulciano's historic centre. Bedrooms not particularly spacious, but furnished with period pieces. Avoid the second half of June when science fiction fans meet here for an annual conference.

Il Marzocco, L-LL; Piazza Savonarola, 18; tel. 0578 757262; fax 757530; cards accepted.

Montepulciano's oldest hotel, at the lower end of the Corso, stands behind the Florentine Marzocco column. Family-run, spacious and fair prices.

PANICALE
Le Grotte di Boldrino, LL; Via Virgilio Ceppari 30; tel. 075 837161; fax 075 837166; cards accepted.

Built into the walls of the castle in this splendid old village, Le Grotte has been lovingly restored and furnished with 19thC pieces. Some of the 11 bedrooms also have that rare delight in Tuscany – real baths in the bathroom. The albergo also has a noted restaurant.

PASSIGNANO
Il Gabbiano, LL; Località San Vito; tel. 075 827788; fax 075 827825; cards accepted.

Not everyone's choice, but a convenient, modern hotel on the Siena-Perugia superstrada, set among olives and woodland. The swimming pool makes up for the rather dull rooms and the high charge for breakfast.

RECOMMENDED RESTAURANTS

CETONA
La Frateria di Padre Eligio, LLLL; Convento di San Francesco; tel. 0578 238015; cards accepted; closed Tues.

The members of a community calling themselves 'Mondo X' produce the ingredients for the tables of this idyllic 13thC monastery. The cooking is anything but Spartan, each dish produced with almost mystical zeal. As one of Italy's premier restaurant reviewers put it: 'In no other place do I feel as happy as here'. This type of happiness has a price, however.

Bottega delle Piazze, LL; Strada Provinciale per S. Casciano 187; tel. 0578 244295; cards accepted; closed Mon.

In a small hamlet 9 km south of Cetona, a small country trattoria producing a refined version of regional cooking. Worth hunting out.

CORTONA
Dardano, L-LL; Via Dardano 24; tel. 0575 601944; cards accepted; closed Tues and first week of July.

This traditional breakfasting place for market traders still opens its doors at 8 am to serve hearty plates of tripe and beans. Later, the menu expands to cover other cortonese dishes, including home-made tagliatelle and ribollita.

Tonino, LLLL; Piazza Garibaldi 1; tel. 0575 630333; cards accepted; closed Tues.

Situated along the wall, overlooking the Valdichiana, it well known for its antipastissimi, an almost endless series of starters, after which you'll probably have no room – or spare change – for anything else.

La Loggetta, LL; Piazza Pescheria 3; tel. 0575 630575; cards accepted; closed Mon.

The attraction here is to eat under the loggia overlooking Cortona's lovely Piazza della Repubblica. Simple but well-cooked Tuscan fare.

ISOLA MAGGIORE
Sauro, LL-LLL; Via G. Guglielmi; tel. 075 826168; cards accepted.

Even if you are not staying at this haven on Lake Trasimeno's prettiest island (see Recommended Hotels, page 168), a meal in its restaurant is highly recommended. The speciality of the house is eel (anguilla) plus the best of the lake's other fish.

MONTEPULCIANO
Diva e Maceo, LL; Via di Gracciano nel Corso 92; tel. 0578 716951; cards none; closed Tues.

A small but rigorously Tuscan menu and particularly good homemade pasta at the lower end of the main street.

La Grotta, LL; Località San Biagio; tel. 0578 757607; cards accepted; closed Wed.

In the house where Antonio da Sangallo lived while working on the nearby church of San Biagio you will find elegant interpretations of Tuscan food in picture-book surroundings.

L'Angolo, L-LL; Via G. Galileo 20, Acquaviva; 0578 767216, cards accepted; closed Mon.

Some 9 km NE of Montepulciano on the road to Castiglione: an unpretentious family-run trattoria producing well-made food; local wine.

Local Explorations: 4

Southern Tuscany

Montalcino, Val d'Orcia and Monte Amiata

76 km; map Touring Club Italiano Toscana

The Via Cassia – known more prosaically to motorists as the SS2 – is the ancient highway between Florence and Rome, and it forms the third of our long distance routes around Central Italy – see Seeing the Region: 3. Modernized with a gravel surface by the Romans around 154 BC, it became known in medieval times as the Via Francigena, the pilgrim route from France to Rome. South of Siena it cuts through the strange, dry landscape of the Crete where erosion has whipped the clay earth into a jagged mass of cliffs and gulleys. Further on, *en route* for the wide expanse of the Lago di Bolsena, it passes through the Val d'Orcia, and it is here that you join this Local Exploration from the Via Cassia to make a south-westerly meander through an idyllic corner of Southern Tuscany.

First, a visit to Montalcino, just west of the Via Cassia, a quintessential hill town famed for its heady, long-lived Brunello wines, and, close by, the serene abbey of Sant'Antimo. Then on to San Quirico d'Orcia, and a line of charming medieval villages along the Val d'Orcia, each with its imposing *rocca*, strongholds of the Aldobrandeschi. This medieval feudal clan, of Germanic origin, put up a string of castles and had a stranglehold on a wide tract of southern Tuscany.

Leaving the Val d'Orcia, the route skirts Monte Amiata, an extinct volcano which, at 1,739 m, constitutes Tuscany's highest peak. You can walk or drive to the summit, and, in winter, ski down.

The final stretch of the route probes deep into the wild, little visited south-western corner of Tuscany to reach picturesque Roccalbegna.

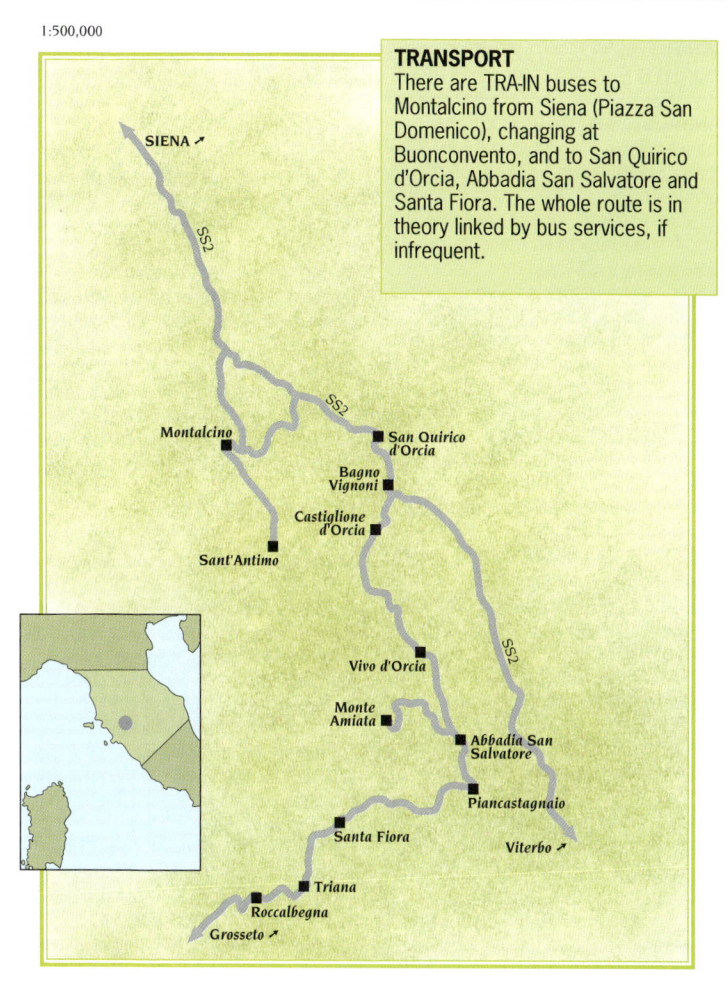

Southern Tuscany / Montalcino, Val d'Orcia and Monte Amiata

1:500,000

TRANSPORT
There are TRA-IN buses to Montalcino from Siena (Piazza San Domenico), changing at Buonconvento, and to San Quirico d'Orcia, Abbadia San Salvatore and Santa Fiora. The whole route is in theory linked by bus services, if infrequent.

• Castiglione d'Orcia

171

Local Explorations: 4

SIGHTS & PLACES OF INTEREST

ABBADIA SAN SALVATORE 🛏
6 km W of junction with SS2, 73 km SE of Siena. Set at nearly 1,000 m on the rippling slopes of Monte Amiata (see detour – Monte Amiata, below), this small, workaday town made its reputation long ago as a summer holiday and winter sports resort, a fount of medicinal springs and a base for the ascent of Tuscany's highest mountain. There are all-round views of wide tracts of Lazio, Umbria and Tuscany. The bulk of the town is modern and industrial and on the outskirts there are mercury mines: you are not far from the rough treeless uplands to the north-west they call the Colline Metallifere ('metal-bearing hills').

Abbadia San Salvatore's tiny core, however, is medieval and little changed. The rectangular **Abbadia** (abbey; to the north of town in Via del Monastero) originated in Lombard times and by the turn of the 11thC wielded great power; later it was a nest of religious painters. The Medici removed the pictures to Florence, but some notable architecture remains.

> ### DETOUR – **MONTE AMIATA**
> The main base for the ascent of Tuscany's highest mountain (1,734 m) is Abbadia San Salvatore, 14.5 km away to the east (see this page). The climb to the top is not hard: you have a choice of sleigh-lift, ski-lift or well-trodden path. The Anello della Montagna is a well signposted circle of paths which rings the mountain, and there are many other hiking trails. The lower slopes of the mountain are covered in forests of beech and chestnut, particularly beautiful in autumn. Skiers and non-walkers can drive or catch a bus nearly to the summit, where there's a car-park, a sprinkling of bars and hotels, and some rubbishy souvenir stalls. *En route* you pass the Madonna del Scout viewpoint, where the Virgin's statue is plastered with Boy Scout emblems and patches. For information on walking and skiing on the mountain call the tourist office at Abbadia San Salvatore (*Via Mentana 97; tel. 0578 778608*).

BAGNO VIGNONI 🛏 ✕
See Seeing the Region: 3, page 112.

CASTIGLIONE D'ORCIA
About 9 km S of San Quirico d'Orcia. A charming and sprightly little medieval town with narrow streets and a prettily cobbled piazza, splendidly sited below its romantic ruined **rocca**, a prominent stronghold of the Aldobrandeschi. The piazza is named after the Sienese artist Il Vecchietta (1412-80), who was born here; in the church of Santa Maria Maddalena you should find a *Madonna and Child* by him; and in Santi Stefano e Degna there are two more *Madonnas*, by Sienese heavyweights Pietro Lorenzetti and Simone Martini respectively.

MONTALCINO 🛏 ✕
On a by-road, 10 km SE of junction with SS2; 41 km SW of Siena; tourist information: Costa del Municipio 8, tel. 0577 849331; buses (from Siena) arrive at Piazza Cavour; car parking outside the walls most conveniently at Porta Cervara to the S.

If you are coming from the direction of Siena (making Montalcino the first stop on the route), leave the SS2 just south of Buonconvento. This road, signposted on the right to Montalcino, makes a lovely approach. Gently undulating vineyards and olive groves encircle the classic Tuscan hill town, securely wrapped by a girdle of walls, its steep medieval streets leading up to its highest point, the **fortezza**.

After the fall of the Sienese Republic, in 1555, a band of stalwart refugees took to Montalcino and its hilltop fortress and created the Republic of Siena at Montalcino, fending off the Florentines for four years until inevitable capitulation.

Just like Siena, Montalcino even has twice-yearly contests between rival *contrade* (town districts or wards) – but here it is archery, not horse racing. At the Palio of Siena, the bowmen of Montalcino are placed in seats of honour, in recognition of the town's service in the 1550s.

The **Palazzo Civico**, whose tower resembles the Mangia of Siena, stands on the town's main square, Piazza del Populo. Here too is a 15thC **loggia** and authentic 19thC café, **Fiaschetteria Italiana**. A short walk brings you to the *fortezza*, a ruined stronghold in a park. From its ramparts you can sometimes see Siena itself. Within the *fortezza* is an **enoteca** where you can taste the local wines, notably the deep, dark Brunello di Montalcino, one of the great wines of Italy, but sadly not cheap, even here. The local honey is also renowned, as are the biscuits called *ossi di morto* (dead men's bones).

Montalcino is an enterprising festival centre: theatre during the last half of July, music in mid-August, the archery *palio* on May 8 and again on the second Sunday in August.

PIANCASTAGNAIO

On a by-road, 5 km S of Abbadia San Salvatore. The rustic retreat of Piancastagnaio lies buried amongst groves of sweet chestnuts, the survivors of the ancient Tuscan wildwood, where there are cool scented footpaths and a few springs. Approaching from the north, the Franciscan church of **San Bartolomeo** appears on a hill to the left; it has a plain stone façade and, inside, what remains of a 14thC Sienese fresco of the *Massacre of the Innocents*.

RECOMMENDED HOTELS

ABBADIA SAN SALVATORE
La Capannina, L-LL; Vette Amiata, 14 km W of Abbadia San Salvatore; tel. 0577 789713; fax 0577 789777; cards accepted; closed Easter to July and Sept to Christmas.

Near the summit of Monte Amiata, this is a peaceful winter sports hotel which also opens in high season. The restaurant serves local dishes – probably the best bet for a meal if you are spending the day up here.

Parco Erosa, LL; Via Remedi; tel. 0577 776326; fax 0577 776326; cards accepted; closed Easter to June and Oct to Christmas.

A 42-room summer and winter sports hotel, with garden, tennis court and a view of Monte Amiata.

BAGNO VIGNONI
Posta Marcucci, LL-LLL; see Seeing the Region: 3, page 116.

MONTALCINO
Al Brunello, L-LL; Località Bellaria, 1.5 km S of Montalcino on Grossetto road; tel. 0577 849304 and fax; cards accepted.

The choice of hotels in Montalcino is surprisingly limited; this one, just out of town, is unexceptional, but set in a pleasant garden with views over the countryside. Restaurant.

In town, **Il Giglio, L-LL** (Via Saloni 5; tel. & fax 0577 848167; closed Feb) makes for a simple but very inexpensive night and also has a popular local restaurant (closed Mon).

RECOMMENDED RESTAURANTS

BAGNO VIGNONI
Antica Osteria del Leone, LL-LLL; See Seeing the Region: 3, pages 116-17.

MONTALCINO
Taverna dei Barbi, L-LL; Fattoria dei Barbi, 6 km SE of Montalcino; tel. 0577 849357; cards accepted; closed last two weeks Jan, first two weeks July, Wed and, Oct-May, Tues eve.

The Barbi estate produces Brunello wines, so kill two birds with one stone by touring the *fattoria* and eating in its rather self-consciously Tuscan-rustic tavern in the vineyards, where traditional dishes are handled with aplomb. Estate wines are naturally on offer and you can taste and buy in the adjoining *enoteca*. Makes a perfect lunch stop *en route* to the Abbey of Sant'Antimo down the road.

ROCCALBEGNA
Osteria del Vecchio Castello, LL; Via della Chiesa 2, Triana, 6 km E of Roccalbegna; tel. 0564 989192; cards accepted; closed Feb, Wed.

If you are headed for out-of-the-way Roccalbegna, you would be well advised to lunch here *en route* (booking is recommended). Apart from being the only place around, it's a congenial little restaurant serving respectable local dishes and interesting wines.

Local Explorations: 4

• *Tuscan landscape.*

Yes, and there's an Aldobrandeschi *rocca* too, rather a good one.

ROCCALBEGNA ✕
On the SS323, 43 km E of Grosseto, 16 km SW of Santa Fiora. To get to Roccalbegna you will first pass little **Triana**, fortified, with a commanding castle and a friendly *osteria* (see Recommended Restaurants, page 173).

Few people stray into this rugged corner of Tuscany. If it were more accessible it would doubtless be besieged in summer, possessing as it does those dual requisites: picturesque old houses in a dramatic setting, with fairytale castle to boot. The valley of the Albegna lies below, the slopes of Monte Labbro rise up behind. The ruined Aldobrandeschi *rocca* guards the village from its eyrie on top of Il Sasso, the 40-m high, cone-shaped crag which rears up above the village. A stiffish walk to the castle will be well rewarded by the view, over both countryside and village, with its neat grid plan streets. In the middle is the church of **Santi Pietro e Paolo** which you should look into to see its lovely triptych by Ambrogio Lorenzetti of the **Madonna and Child with Saints** (1340).

SOUTHERN TUSCANY / *Montalcino, Val d'Orcia and Monte Amiata*

SAN QUIRICO D'ORCIA
See Seeing the Region: 3, page 115.

SANTA FIORA
On a by-road, 24 km W of junction with SS2; 16 km SW of Abbadia San Salvatore.
Of the pretty villages which ring the broad base of Monte Amiata (there is also a station to the north, called Monte Amiata), Santa Fiora, on the southern slopes, is the most appealing. Here is another medieval settlement with a splendid defensive position and an Aldobrandeschi castle, although in this case all that remains is the **clock tower** which overlooks the neat piazza.

This was in fact the feudal seat of the Aldobrandeschi, whose lands and castles were eventually divided between two branches of the clan. Through marriage, Santa Fiora came into the hands of the Sforza Cesarini, whose impressive late-Renaissance *palazzo* is now the **town hall**.

Two churches and a charming public garden complete the picture. **Sante Fiora e Lucilla** (along Via Carolina) has a beautiful rose window over the entrance and fine glazed terracotta decorations on the altar and pulpit – the work of Andrea della Robbia.

A road leading downhill passes **Sant'Agostino** (often shut) which apparently contains a painted wooden *Madonna and Child* by the early 15thC Sienese sculptor Jacopo della Quercia. If it's a Saturday or Sunday, carry on to the bottom of the hill, where an 18thC water garden, **La Peschiera** will be open to view (*10 am-12.30 pm, 3.30-6.00 pm*).

VIVO D'ORCIA
A pretty hamlet surrounded by oak woods, once the site of a monastery: worth a pause on the road between Castiglione d'Orcia and Abbadia San Salvatore, perhaps for a picnic in the woods or beside its river of the same name. There's also a simple hotel with restaurant, **Amiata, L-LL** (*tel. 0577 873790 fax 0577 873764; restaurant closed Fri*).

• *Abbazia di Sant'Antimo, near Montalcino.*

DETOUR – ABBAZIA DI SANT'ANTIMO
Standing alone 10 km to the south of Montalcino in the beautiful surroundings of the Starcia valley, the Benedictine **Abbazia di Sant'Antimo** (*open daily*) is one of the most affecting of all Tuscan Romanesque churches. It's the light and the colour of the stone, the honey mixed with clotted cream of the travertine outside, the luminosity of the alabaster inside, which remains in the memory. And the music – recorded plainsong, or if you are lucky, live Gregorian chant sung by the monks at mass – which drifts round the building as you wander.

Architecturally, the early 12thC building diverges from the Tuscan Romanesque norm, having a cluster of semi-circular chapels at the east end which marks the choir, ambulatory and apse in French Romanesque style. In contrast, the campanile is square and tiered in the Northern Italian manner. There are stone carvings on the exterior and inside, the alabaster capitals on the columns are richly carved – notice in particular the second one on the right which depicts Daniel having an easy time of it in the Lion's Den.

Local Explorations: 5

<u>Western Umbria</u>

Perugia, Orvieto and Todi

80 km; map Touring Club Italiano Umbria Marche

This section is essentially about city sights. The route takes in a trio of Umbria's greatest hill towns, with only a handful of side shows on the way. But any shortcomings on the road are amply made up for by Perugia, Todi and Orvieto, which offer (amongst other things) masterpieces of the Umbrian school of Renaissance painting; one of Italy's most perfect 13thC squares; perhaps the peninsula's most splendid Gothic cathedral; and, at Orvieto, one of the most striking locations for a city in Central Italy.

Major road and rail links have made the area one of the region's wealthiest – and it shows. From Todi to Perugia (Umbria's capital), the fast dual carriageway along the wide Tiber Valley is strung with a ribbon of factories, service stations and unappetizing restaurants. However, any turning-off will take you speedily up to Umbrian hill villages that remain resolutely medieval.

Between Orvieto and Todi, the SS448 is a much calmer, more sympathetic road, taking you from the Valley of the Paglia to the Tiber. The dramatic shores of Lago di Corbara make an ideal spot for a picnic – accompanied, naturally, by a bottle of Orvieto's excellent white wine grown on volcanic soil.

Along with the attractions at the three major towns, there are two other unmissable experiences. The first is a visit to the dying village of Civita di Bagnoregio, set in its lunar landscape. The second is a taste of Lungarotti's wines at Torgiano after a visit to one of the world's best wine museums.

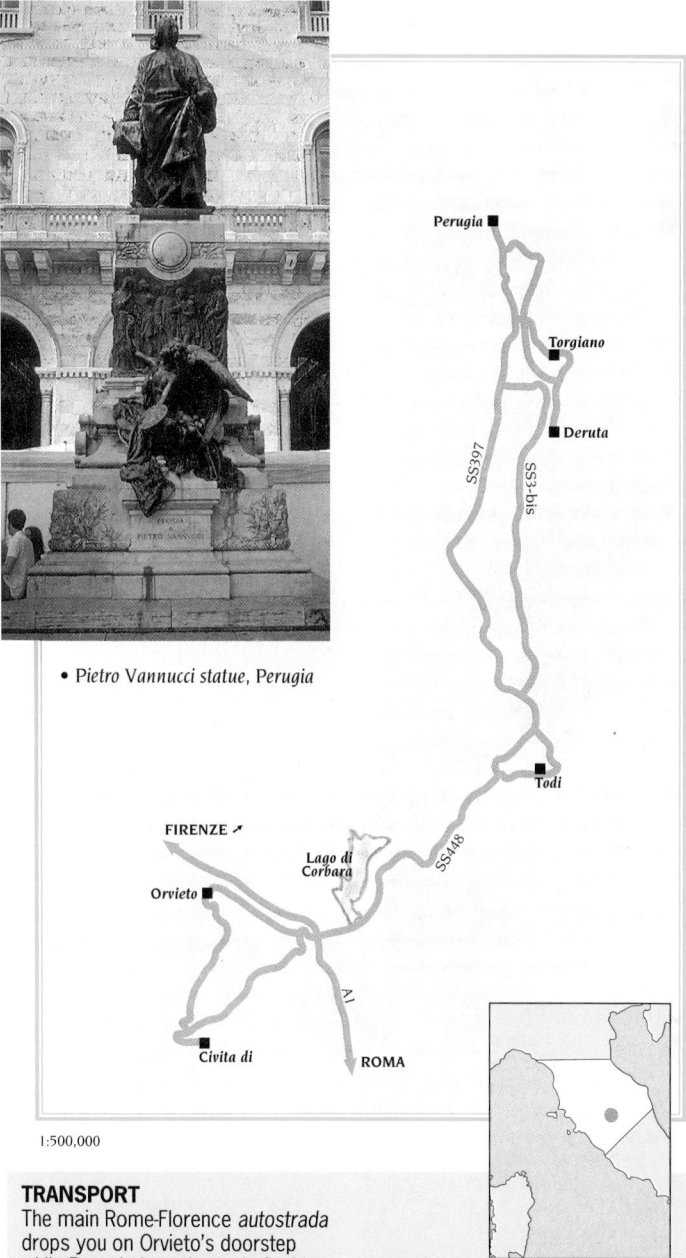

WESTERN UMBRIA / *Perugia, Orvieto and Todi*

• *Pietro Vannucci statue, Perugia*

1:500,000

TRANSPORT

The main Rome-Florence *autostrada* drops you on Orvieto's doorstep while Perugia is at the end of a fast dual-carriageway spur from the same motorway.

Local trains on the main Rome-Florence line stop at Orvieto. The Ferrovia Centrale Umbra connects Terni (on the Rome-Ancona line) with Todi and Perugia.

A convenient bus service runs between Todi and Perugia, but there are few buses onwards to Orvieto.

The closest international airport is Rome.

Local Explorations: 5

SIGHTS & PLACES OF INTEREST

CIVITA DI BAGNOREGIO
A *short detour 8 km S of Orvieto*. From the small medieval town of Bagnoregio, strike out for a couple of kilometres along the ridge to see the startling sight of **Civita di Bagnoregio**, *La città che muore* ('the dying city'). The ancient village is perched on a vertiginous pinnacle of golden volcanic tufa which is slowly, but inexorably, crumbling away. This naturally defendable site has been settled for over 2,500 years; now it only holds a few dozen people. The only way to penetrate the *borgo* is over an exhilarating roller-coaster of a footbridge. Once inside you can admire its beautifully restored houses standing in traffic-free alleys.

Come at sunset for the intoxicating play of light on the lunar **landscape** of eroded clay gulleys or *crete*.

DERUTA
On the SS3bis, 20 km S of Perugia. From the busy main road, Deruta presents a somewhat raddled face – ceramics factories, service stations, transport caffs. However, its old **centre** retains a pinch of medieval charm and a fine **collection of ancient pottery**. Deruta's ceramic industry goes back to well before the 14thC and by the Cinquecento there were more than 50 workshops here. The **Museo delle Ceramiche Locali** is housed in the Palazzo Comunale in central Piazza dei Consoli. A shame that the modern wares on sale are so uninspiring.

LAGO DI CORBARA ×
Travelling the attractive SS448 between Orvieto and Todi, you skirt the shores of **Lago di Corbara**, an artificial lake created by a 650-m dam across the Tiber. Despite being a fake, it is nonetheless a dramatic stretch of water, the steep sides of the valley lending it a touch of the fjord. On its banks is **Vissani**, one of Italy's most celebrated – and expensive – restaurants (see Recommended Restaurants, page 185).

ORVIETO ⇌ ×
On the SS71, near A1 motorway. Tourist information: Piazza Duomo in front of cathedral. Railway station at bottom of funicular railway. Park in large, well-signposted car park at Orvieto Scalo to E of town and take funicolare (funicular railway) up to centre, or in Foro Boario to SW with frequent bus service to centre.

Orvieto, one of Umbria's most dramatically sited cities, stands on a great precipitous plug of volcanic tufa – an island in the plain of the Paglia. This natural bastion, where walls have been superfluous, has been inhabited since the Iron Age.

As Etruscan Volsinii Veteres it was destroyed by the Romans in 264 BC when the townspeople rashly asked for Rome's help to suppress a slave revolt. Oddly for such a well-sited place, it seems to have been otherwise ignored by the Romans.

It regained its importance in the early Middle Ages and reached a zenith of power and building fever in the late 13thC, since when the flesh and bones of the city have remained little altered. Despite the occasional Renaissance facelift, it is still an essentially medieval city with the nastier intrusions of the 20thC kept at a distance down below at Orvieto Scalo.

The delight of Orvieto is in the detail: stay overnight to savour it early in the morning before the coaches arrive or in the evening when the cathedral façade is set alight by the setting sun. Orvieto's skyline is dominated by its magnificent **cathedral**, perhaps the finest expression of Gothic architecture in all Italy and built to celebrate the Miracle of Bolsena (see Seeing the Region: 3, page 112). Its famous **façade** in the form of a stately triptych is a *tour de force* of multi-coloured marble, sculpture and mosaics. It was begun in the opening years of the 14thC by the Sienese architect Lorenzo Maitani, who was also responsible for the delicate Biblical **carvings** that ornament the pilasters flanking the imposing portals. Inside, you must search out Luca Signorelli's celebrated cycle of frescoes on ***The End of the World*** (1477-1504). They sheath the Cappella Nuova in the right transept, a potent foretaste of Michelangelo's later *Last Judgement* in the Sistine Chapel.

The church's other great treasure rests in the chapel at the end of the left transept: a lavish **reliquary** that con-

• Opposite: Perugia

Western Umbria / *Perugia, Orvieto and Todi*

tains the blood-stained altar cloth from the Miracle of Bolsena. Wrought by the Sienese jeweller Ugolino di Vieri in 1338, it is one of the masterpieces of Italian goldsmiths' work. You can see more of his work along with handsome paintings and sculpture in the **Museo dell'Opera del Duomo** in the austere palace to the right of the cathedral.

A few paces further down the right side of the church is another museum in an ancient palace, this time the **Museo Archeologico Nazionale** filled with the contents of the Etruscan tombs that dot the countryside around. Look out for the life-size Etruscan figures in the frescoes taken from the **necropolis of Settecamini**.

Head up Via del Duomo to arrive at Orvieto's main street, **Corso Cavour,** that runs east-west along the city's heights. A left turn takes you to **Piazza della Repubblica**, the animated centre of town watched over by the curious 12-sided **bell-tower** of the 12thC church of Sant'Andrea and the medieval **town hall** tricked out with a Late Renaissance front.

Nearby is Orvieto's most splendid civil building, the four-square 13thC **Palazzo del Popolo**. After years of neglect it has recently undergone a thorough restoration during which remains of an underlying Etruscan **temple** were brought to light.

The town's most singular piece of architecture is the **Pozzo di San Patrizio**. Pope Clement VII, in the wake of the devastating Sack of Rome of 1527, had Antonio da Sangallo the Younger construct this enormous well to assure a secure water supply for Orvieto in the event of siege. The 62-m deep well has a wide double **spiral staircase** that allowed men and mules to descend and return without crossing paths. The *pozzo* is at the western end of the town by the upper station of the funicular railway and the sturdy walls of the 15thC **rocca**, or castle, that now encircle nothing more menacing than a public garden. In the park nearby are the somewhat forlorn ruins of a great Etruscan temple, the **Tempio del Belvedere**, built at the end of the 5thC BC – all that's left is part of the solid foundations.

For more substantial traces of Orvieto's Etruscan forebears, visit the **necropolis of Crocifisso del Tufo** just below the cliffs at the north-eastern edge of town – two parallel streets with cube-shaped tombs that are more than 2,500 years old.

No visit to Orvieto would be complete without trying its top-class fragrant white **wine** which comes in three versions – *secco* (dry), *amabile* (semi-sweet) and *dolce* (sweet). Labels to look out for include Barberani, Tenuta Le Velette and Castello della Sala.

PERUGIA ⊭ ×

Near the junction of the SS3-bis and the SS 75-bis superstrade. Tourist information: Piazza IV Novembre 3. Arriving by car you are well advised to follow the signs for the car park at Piazza dei Partigiani, from where a scala mobile (escalator) takes you up to Piazza Italia at the top. Arriving from the north, there is a car park on Via Sant'Antonio. The FS railway line links Perugia with Foligno (from the outlying Piazza V. Veneto), while the closer FCU line links the city with Todi and Città di Castello.

Unlike Tuscany, Umbria claims no great metropolis. Even Perugia, the regional capital and the nearest Umbria gets to bright city lights, has little more than 150,000 citizens, giving it more the atmosphere of a comfortable country town.

Today, many know it for its chocolate 'kisses', Perugina's praline *Baci*; but its history is far from sweet. For the Etruscans it was the easternmost of their key cities, and respectable remnants of the walls and gates which encircled it still survive. But its fall to Rome in 309 BC marked the beginning of a period of intermittent tussles with the Eternal City in which Perugia was invariably the loser.

After the Dark Ages, Perugia reappeared at the close of the 12thC as an independent city state. Favoured by the Papacy as a bolthole from troubled Rome, over the next century it saw five papal conclaves and the construction of its finest churches and public buildings. Trouble started in 1370 when Pope Urban V sought to appoint the tyrannical Abbot of Cluny as governor of the city. There followed 150 years of the most violent strife and tyranny, unmatched by any other city in Italy. Its great chronicler, Matarazzo, recorded the events of its most vicious years, when the bitter feud between the Oddi and the Baglioni families saw the gutters running with blood. In 1488 the Oddi family turned the main Piazza into a slaughter-house; in 1491 the Baglioni took revenge by stringing up 130 Oddi supporters from Palazzo dei Priori; by 1535 the Baglioni were practically extinct. Yet amidst the butchery, there were periodic outbursts of repentance – the cathedral was washed with wine and reconsecrated; 30 altars were erected in the main square; and when San Bernardino came to preach against the evils of the flesh, the *Perugini* made public demonstrations of contrition, building bonfires of all their worldly possessions.

As so often in the Renaissance, these violent times brought forth artistic genius – as the blood ran, Perugino and his young pupil Raphael were busily painting the city's noblest works of art. In 1540, enforced peace finally arrived in the shape of the Church, which kept the city firmly under its thumb for the next three centuries.

Nowadays, the foulest thing about the city is its suburbs – the wisest travellers slip quietly in from the Gubbio road which enters through Porta Sant'Antonio.

For a taste of essential Perugia, make for **Corso Vannucci**, the backbone of the *centro storico* which stretches from Piazza IV Novembre to Piazza Italia. Named after the city's greatest painter, Pietro Vannucci (c. 1445-1523) (better known as Il Perugino), it is the setting for Umbria's most animated and sophisticated *passeggiata*. The cosmopolitan atmosphere is partly due to Perugia's Università Italiana per Stranieri, the country's leading language and Italian culture school.
Piazza IV Novembre, has been Perugia's centre of civil and religious power since Etruscan times. Once the site of the Roman forum, the square pivots around the wedding-cake **Fontana Maggiore** (1275-78). This splendid fountain, the city's symbol, was designed by Giovanni and Nicola Pisano to stand at the head of the town's aqueduct, then newly cut from the nearby Monte Pacciano. The lower of the two marble basins is decorated with particularly fine reliefs marking out the months of the year with appropriate country labours and allegorical figures. Take your pick as to the identity of the triad dabbling their feet in the bronze cup which was added later to top out the *fontana* – some say they are nymphs, others think that they are the three Theological Virtues (Faith, Hope and Charity).

The square's scene-stealer, however, is the magnificent **Palazzo dei Priori**, one of Central Italy's Gothic gems (1293-1443). The elegant flight of steps that rises up from the square leads to one of the oldest parts of the palace, the **Sala dei Notari**, the lawyers' meeting hall. Look out for the bronze figures of the Guelf lion and Perugian griffon that guard the Gothic entrance.

However, to get to the *palazzo*'s main attraction, the **Galleria Nazionale dell'Umbria**, enter the palace by the ornate portal on the Corso and head for the third floor. Large sections of Umbria's finest art gallery have been closed in recent years for restoration, but don't be put off. This is the place to come to see the Umbrian school of painting in all its homely glory. The fine collection traces this under-sung school from its Byzantine beginnings to its golden period in the 15thC under the potent leadership of Perugino.

Siena, a seminal influence on early Umbrian painters, figures large in the earlier works: most notable is a *Madonna and Child* by Duccio. But with the 15thC, influences became more eclectic – the gallery's two greatest works are **Fra' Angelico's**, triptych of *Madonna and Child with Angels and Saints* (1437), and **Piero della Francesca's** treatment of the same subject minus angels (1475).

Of the Quattrocento Umbrian masters, **Perugino**, was the greatest. Born in nearby Città di Pieve, he raised the city from artistic obscurity to a position of considerable influence in the years of the High Renaissance. The gallery contains a dozen of his works, perhaps the most beautiful of which are the serene **Madonna and Child** and an **Adoration of the Shepherds**, a transferred fresco of 1505.

However, to see Perugino's greatest gift to the city, return to the Corso Vannucci and search out the **Collegio del Cambio** at the far end of the Plazzo dei Priori. Inside, the walls and ceiling of what once served as the city's money exchange are covered in glorious fres-

• *Perugia.*

coes reckoned to be amongst Perugino's greatest works. They are a typically Renaissance hybrid of Christian and Classical a *Nativity*, a *Transfiguration* and plenty of Greek gods added for good measure. Before the work's completion in 1507, Perugino's most famous pupil, Raphael, had joined him. It is said that the young boy was responsible for the prophets and sibyls on the right-hand wall. See if you can spot the self-portrait of the rough-hewn Perugino on the left-hand wall.

Yet another entrance to the Palazzo dei Priori on Corso Vannucci will take you to the **Sala del Collegio della Mercanzia**, once the meeting hall of the guild of merchants, entirely decorated in the early 15thC with extraordinarily fine inlaid marquetry woodwork.

The plain-faced **cathedral**, on the northern side of Piazza IV Novembre, hardly ranks as one of the top ten churches in Umbria, but it has its charms. A church has stood here for more than a thousand years, but the present building dates back to 1345. Work hadn't got very far before it was halted by the Black Death. Construction began again in 1437 and continued sporadically until 1587, but still the façade wasn't complete and that is how it remains. Happily, the most pleasing aspect is the pink-and-white marbled face visible from the square, dominated by the **statue** of Pope Julius III (1555) and the **pulpit** where San Bernardino of Siena preached against vanity.

Inside, the greatest curiosity is the town's most jealously guarded relic, nothing less than Our Lady's wedding ring. It rests in the **Cappella del Sant'Anello** and is annually given an airing with all due pomp on July 30.

Through the sacristy is the **Museo dell'Opera del Duomo**, a hoard of the cathedral's treasures, including a worthwhile *Madonna Enthroned* by Luca Signorelli (1484).

Adjoining the cathedral, note the curious Early Renaissance arched **Loggia di Braccio Fortebraccio**, sitting on top of a stretch of ancient wall. Before heading down the Corso, take a short stroll down **Via Maestà delle Volte** for a sight of some of Perugia's most characteristic High Medieval houses.

From Piazza IV Novembre, now wander along the **Corso Vannucci**, pausing for coffee or an *aperitivo* at one of the elegant bars, or to window shop outside the swanky shops. If you carry on through **Piazza della Repubblica** and **Piazza Italia** you will eventually arrive in the **Giardini Carducci**, public gardens with heart-fluttering views over the Umbrian hills. Here once stood the **Rocca Paolina**, built in 1540 by Pope Paul III on the site of the Baglioni family fortress, and from which the Papal States asserted their iron rule for three centuries over a somewhat resentful population. When the power of the Vatican was finally, if violently, shaken off in 1848, the *Perugini* celebrated by dismantling the *rocca* piece by piece over a 12-year period, until all that remained was a flat, open space.

Back up by the Palazzo dei Priori, the ancient **Via dei Priori**, takes you under the **Arco dei Priori**, beneath the *palazzo* itself, and down one of the original five *vie regali* of the old city. The first street on the right is the grim **Via della Gabbia** where prisoners were exposed to die in a metal cage during the most violent epoch of the city's history. Carry on downwards, passing through the **Porta Trasimeno** at the bottom, to reach the city's finest church, the **Oratorio di San Bernardino**, a jewel of Renaissance decoration built in 1457-61. Its rich façade is frescoed with scenes of some of the more exciting moments in the life of San Bernardino. Perugia's other outstanding church, San Pietro, lies south-east of the centre and is worth the trek along Corso Cavour (perhaps taking in on the way the Etruscan hand-me-downs in the **Museo Archeologico Nazionale dell'Umbria**) chiefly to see the richly carved choir stalls in the *presbiterio*, which are considered amongst the finest in Italy. The church also has an unfair share of excellent pictures, including four small canvasses by Perugino in the sacristy.

TODI ✉

At junction of the SS3bis and SS448, 34 km E of Orvieto. Tourist information: Piazza Umberti I, 6, off Corso Cavour. Station at Ponte Rio to N of town with connecting bus service to town centre. Centre a nightmare for cars; park near first main gate at which you arrive - ample car park at Porta Amerina.

This outstanding smallish town stands perched high above a narrow stretch of the Tiber Valley looking much like the eagle that serves as its symbol. It has an enviable inheritance of monuments from its long history and a magnificent setting in quintessential Umbrian countryside.

Ancient *Tuder*, meaning 'border', was an Umbrian city too close to Etruscan territory for comfort and around the 5thC BC the Etruscans moved in. Some of the giant blocks of stone that they used to build the town's first set of walls can still be seen. Later, the Romans patched up the walls, gave the place the status of a *municipio* and then set about expanding the hill-top site with impressive earthworks and supporting walls.

As with so many other Central Italian towns, Todi seems to have gone into hibernation during the Dark Ages only to reappear as a spirited free *comune* in the 13thC. This was its golden age, when its last set of walls and best public palaces were built. In the following centuries the town fell under the domination of the Church and, with the notable exception of its finest church, the Renaisssance passed by barely leaving a mark.

Piazza del Popolo, still the heart of Todi, stands on the heights where the Roman forum once stood and is Umbria's most architecturally pleasing square. It is framed at one end by a group of swashbuckling high medieval public buildings that confront the stately but simple Romanesque Duomo across the square.

Its southern end is taken up by the Gothic **Palazzo dei Priori,** given a sober facelift in 1514. To the left of it, Todi's two most photogenic **palaces** are linked by an outside staircase to form the Town Hall – the one with the swallow-tail crenellations is the **Palazzo del Popolo**, built between 1214 and 1228 and amongst the oldest municipal palaces in Italy. The other is the later **Palazzo del Capitano del Popolo** with a splendid set of Gothic **triple windows**. Inside there is rumoured to be an art gallery and museum of Etruscan baubles, but as they have been closed for *riordino* for as long as any one can remember, this is difficult to confirm.

The typically Umbrian **Duomo**, fronted by a flight of monumental steps, predates the civic buildings by some 100 years but was thoroughly remodelled over the subsequent centuries. Its finest feature is its **façade,** built up from a series of utterly plain rectangles set off by a large rose window. The other church to search out in the centre is **San Fortunato**, dating from the 13thC with a later, incomplete face. It stands theatrically at the top of steep steps and holds the town's nearest approximation to a great art treasure, a fine **fresco** of *The Madonna with Angels* by Masolino, Masaccio's under-appreciated collaborator in Florence's famous Brancacci Chapel.

Todi's best Roman remains are the 1stC BC **nicchioni**, a group of great semi-circular niches that once held up a Roman basilica and now close off **Piazza del Mercato Vecchio**. Nearby, just beyond the enchanting little Romanesque church of **Sant'Ilario**, is the 13thC **Scarnabecco Fountain** that served as the town's central water supply in the Middle Ages.

Todi's most revered building, however, lies outside its medieval walls on a stunning hillside site. The majestic dome of **Santa Maria della Consolazione**, to the south-west, will catch your eye from afar. Although the evidence is poor, it is generally held that this jewel of a Renaissance church is essentially the work of Bramante – with its similarity to his original plans for St Peter's in Rome, it gives an idea of how splendid the world's greatest church might have looked if Bramante had had his way and it had been built as a Greek cross, with nave and transepts of equal length. As Edward Hutton wrote: 'Rome remembered the pilgrims from the north, and how important it was to impress them, and so decided to build the long nave which obscures and obstructs the dome; and the dream of Bramante vanished. Coming into Santa Maria della Consolazione, we realize what we have lost.'

TORGIANO ⌨ ✕

Just off the SS3bis, 15 km S of Perugia.
Thanks to Giorgio Lungarotti, one of the great patriarchs of modern Italian winemaking, the **wines** of Torgiano are now some of the best in Italy. From the first bottle of Vino Rosso di Torgiano in 1964, Cantine Lungarotti now produce over three million bottles a year, the best of which is the Riserva Rubesco Monticchio.

Twenty years ago Lungarotti's wife started a small **museum** dedicated to wine. It is now, along with the Rothschilds' museum in Bordeaux, the most famous in the world. This wonderful collection is housed in the beautiful setting of the cellars of **Palazzo Baglioni** and is a must for oenophiles. Lungarotti was also the guiding hand behind the opening of the **Tre Vaselle** hotel in the medieval heart of town (see Recommended Hotels, page 185).

RECOMMENDED HOTELS

ORVIETO Villa Ciconia, LL; *Via dei Tigli 69; tel. 0763 305582; fax 0763 302077; cards accepted.*

A 16thC villa set in spreading parkland; nine bedrooms. Simple furnishing in keeping with the style of the house, with elegant iron bedsteads.

La Badia, LLL; *Orvieto Scalo; tel. 0763 301959; fax 0763 305396; cards accepted.*

The tower of this beautifully preserved former 12thC Benedictine abbey just south of the city is a notable landmark. Fine spacious rooms and an enticing swimming pool. Its restaurant serves up-market Umbrian cooking.

Virgilio, LL; *Piazza del Duomo 5/6; tel. 0763 341882; fax 0763 343797; cards none.*

Standing in the shadow of the Duomo, its chief attraction is its position. The rooms are comfortable and moderately priced, but the furnishings are modern and tasteless.

PERUGIA
Brufani, LLL; *Piazza Italia 12; tel. 075 5732541; fax 075 5720210; cards accepted.*

Stands at the southern end of Corso Vannucci. Ritzy public rooms with all the style you could want – and the prices to match. Upstairs, the bedrooms are comfortable enough, though not exceptional.

Palace Hotel Bellavista, LL; *Piazza Italia 2; tel. 075 5720741; fax 075 5729092; cards accepted.*

Little sister of the Brufani, and more economical. A complete refit has retained the atmosphere of the original building. Attractive bedrooms with period furnishing.

La Rosetta, LL; *Piazza Italia 19; tel. and fax 075 5720841; cards accepted.*

Larger of the hotels along Corso Vannucci, but by no means impersonal. Old-fashioned hospitality and punctilious service.

Locanda della Posta, LLL; *Corso Vannucci 97; tel. 075 5728925; fax 075 5732562; cards accepted.*

Western Umbria / Perugia, Orvieto and Todi

Recently refurbished with great style, it vies with the Brufani as the town's most exclusive hotel.

TODI

Bramante, LLL; Via Orvietana; 075 8948382; fax 075 8948074; cards accepted.

Stone-built hotel in a splendid position near the church of Santa Maria. Modern but restrained interior.

Residenza di Campagna, LLL; Localita' Poggio d'Asproli, via Asproli 7; tel. and fax 075 8853385; cards accepted.

This small country hotel, run by the one-time manager of a Neapolitan grand hotel, stands in woodland and was once part of a 15thC Franciscan monastery. The six ample bedrooms are decorated with theatrical style.

Hotel Villa Luisa, LL; Viale A. Cortesi 147; tel. 075 8948571; fax 8948472; cards accepted.

Standing on the slopes of the town in spacious parkland, its 40-odd bedrooms are furnished tastefully in modern style. Relaxing, hospitable atmosphere.

TORGIANO

Le Tre Vaselle, LLL; Via Garibaldi 48; 075 9880447; 075 9880214; cards accepted.

Situated just off the village's main street, more like a hamlet than a hotel, with an instant welcome and beguiling comfort (see also Recommended Restaurants, below).

RECOMMENDED RESTAURANTS

LAGO DI CORBARA

Trippini, LLL; Via Italia 8, Civitella del Lago; tel. 0744 950316; cards accepted; closed Wed.

On the slopes above the lake. Menus designed around the produce of the surrounding woodland, especially wild asparagus, mushrooms, black truffle, game and trout, according to season. Home-made bread comes flavoured with walnuts, rosemary or mint.

Vissani, LLLL; SS448, on the bank of Lago di Corbara; tel. 0744 950206; cards accepted (and just as well); closed Wed.

A recent magazine survey marked this temple to gastronomy as Italy's most expensive restaurant. Opinions vary as to whether it is amongst the best. The menu changes from day to day, roving amongst dishes fit for the better-off gods.

ORVIETO

Giglio d'Oro, LL; Piazza Duomo 8; tel. 0763 41903; cards accepted; closed Wed.

In the shadow of the Duomo, this is an elegant restaurant offering an eclectic Italian menu and surprisingly delicious puddings.

La Grotta, LL; Via Luca Signorelli 5; tel. 0763 41348; cards accepted; closed Mon.

Menu based around Umbrian cooking, with an interesting selection of *salumi* and pasta dishes – particularly good *tagliatelli agli asparagi* – followed by robust *secondi*.

PERUGIA

Aladino, LL; Via delle Prome 11; tel. 075 5720938; cards accepted; open evenings only, closed Mon and Aug.

With the emphasis on experimentation, the food here is never humdrum. Pasta is served with imaginative stuffings (pea and chervil, or parmesan and saffron), while for the main course you might find aubergines stuffed with wild boar.

Osteria del Bartolo, LLL; Via Bartolo 30; tel. 075 5731561; cards accepted; closed Sun.

One of Perugia's finer, if costlier choices, offering an inventive version of Umbrian cooking at its best.

La Bocca Mia, LL/LLL; Via Ulisse Rocchi 36; tel. 075 5723873; cards accepted; closed Sun and first three weeks Aug.

Popular with the Perugian in-crowd, it serves honest, wholesome food such as *zuppa di lenticchie* (lentil soup) and sturdy roasts.

TORGIANO

Le Melegrane, LLLL; Via Garibaldi 48; tel. 075 9880447; cards accepted.

The restaurant of Lungarotti's Tre Vaselle (see Recommended Hotels, above) has gained a national reputation for its cooking and, of course, its wine cellar. Beware the bill, however.

Local Explorations: 6

<u>South-Western Tuscany</u>

Monte Argentario, Isola del Giglio and the Lower Maremma

180 km; map Touring Club Italiano Toscana

This far south-western corner of Tuscany is for the Italophile who has grown tired of the more obvious charms further north. There are no great pictures, no sublime buildings, no grand cities, nor even any tall peaks. But this landscape of wild, windswept moorland, precarious ancient villages clinging to volcanic tufa bluffs, silent, narrow green valleys and melancholy remains of Etruscan cemeteries has a spell-binding fascination.

The journey takes in the fenny plains of the Lower Maremma, once infested by malaria. There is still a sense of abandonment. You will also see the tortured volcanic hills of the Monti Volsini to the north of Lake Bolsena. You won't want to linger by the coast, spoiled by a mess of campsites and the hectic main SS1 road. To compensate, there is the natural beauty of Monte Argentario, the striking ruins of Roman *Cosa*, the brash holiday atmosphere of Porto Santo Stefano and a great ferry trip to the wonderful Isola del Giglio. Naturalists, like the birds, will flock to the nature reserves down by Orbetello.

Canny Romans have begun to appreciate the allures of this under-sung area. Capalbio has become almost as fashionable as Rome's Via Veneto was in the 1960s, while the three small villages of Sovana, Sorano and Pitigliano seem to have more refined restaurants than the rest of Southern Tuscany put together. To Saturnia they come in droves for the hot sulphur springs, without the fuss and expense that usually goes with Italian *terme*.

The volcanic soils produce excellent mineral-flavoured wines, best of which are the red Morellino and the white Bianco di Pitigliano. Maremma cooking – peasant food at its finest – uses fish from the sea with game, including wild boar, and wild herbs. You will rarely be shocked by the bill.

SW Tuscany / Monte Argentario, Isola del Giglio and Lower Maremma

TRANSPORT

Once off the busy SS1 (Via Aurelia), the roads are relaxed and uncrowded, if slow.

Stopping trains on the main coastal Rome-La Spezia line call at Montalto, Chiarone, Ansedonia and Orbetello.

Regular boat services to Isola del Giglio and Isola di Giannutri (summer only to the latter) leave from Porto Santo Stefano. You may, with much bureaucratic fuss, take your car to Giglio, but it's not worth the effort.

Inland, coach services in these forgotten parts are few and far between, apart from short-hop local buses.

The nearest international airport is Rome.

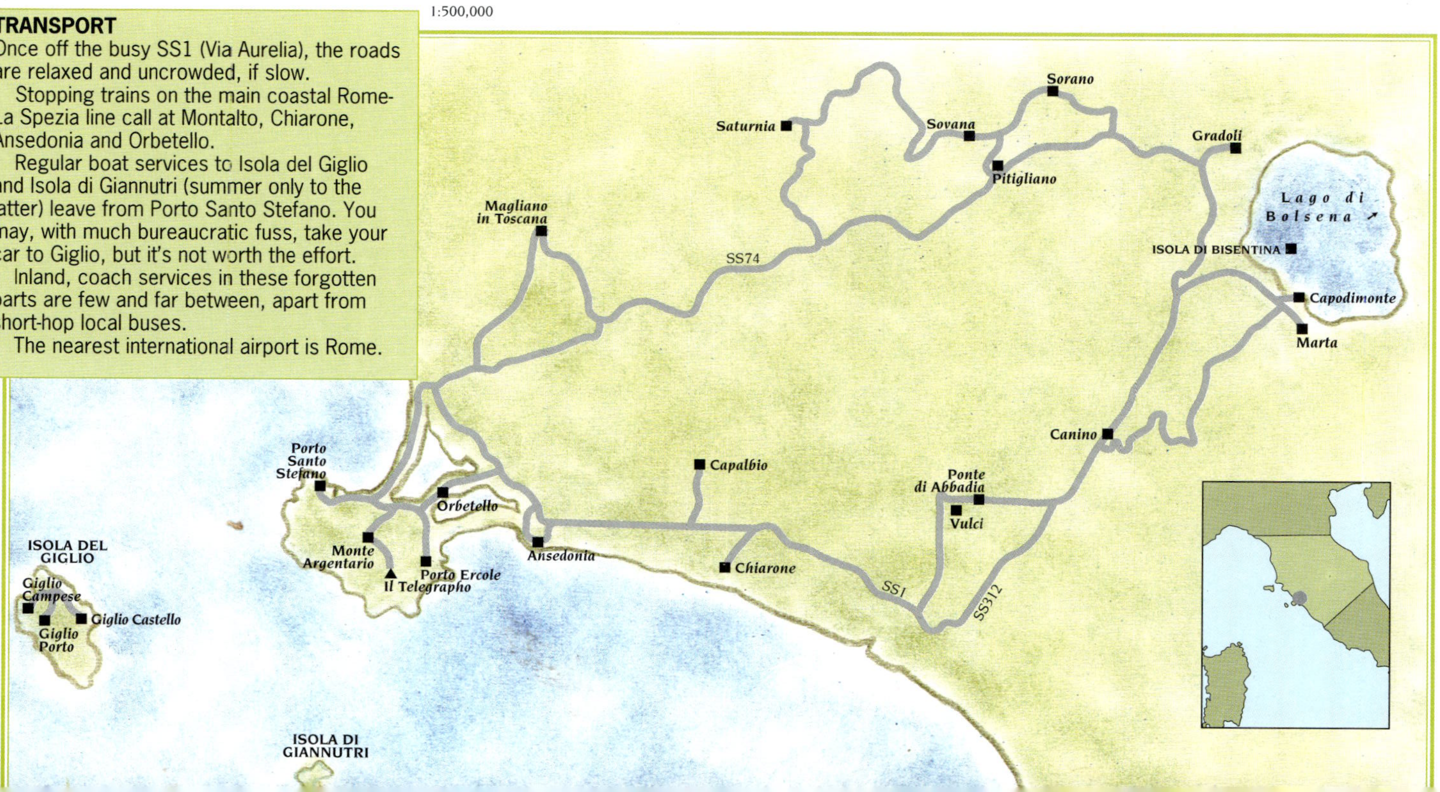

SIGHTS & PLACES OF INTEREST

ANSEDONIA 🚉
5 km S of Orbetello, just off the main SS1 Via Aurelia. Long before the ubiquitous holiday villas blighted Ansedonia's lower slopes, its promontory was the site of the important Roman colony of *Cosa*. Established in 273 BC, it thrived as a commercial centre and port despite a temporary setback when its inhabitants were said to have been driven out by a plague of mice. Things went rapidly into decline, however, with the arrival of the Visigoths in the 4thC, although the town managed to limp on until 1330 when the Sienese reduced it to rubble.

Sweeping views out over the Tyrrhenian Sea make it an atmospheric site. Its imposing **walls**, built of terrifyingly huge polygonal masses of limestone, still rise in places to a height of 8 m. Within, the ancient street plan is still visible around the **central forum**, flanked by the eloquent remains of a basilica, *curia* (council chamber), two temples and the market place. On the summit stands what is left of the city's **Acropolis**.

At the base of the promontory to the east can be traced the **Tagliata Etrusca**, Roman coastal engineering works designed to prevent the port from silting up. A little further down the coast is **Lago di Burano**, a marshy stretch of water that, since 1980, has been a World Wildlife Fund **nature reserve** – a must for waterfowl enthusiasts.

CAPALBIO ✕
20 km E of Orbetello. This medieval village on a small, green hill has become the symbol of Italy's new approach to tourism. Instead of aiming at the coach parties, it has carefully tended its modest charms in order to attract the discerning traveller. Its discovery by the fashionable left-wing political *élite* has also helped to make this quiet and manicured *borgo* the Italian socialists' weekend playground.

In 1416 it became a Sienese possession and its intact **walls** date from that period. Capalbio's most important monument is the chaste Romanesque parish church of **San Nicola**, which boasts some attractive Quattrocento frescoes. But the principal draw remains its distance from the roar of the 20thC.

CAPODIMONTE
SW *shore of Lago di Bolsena*. Capodimonte's wooded promontory and its very own Farnese fortress help make it the prettiest of Bolsena's small lakeside resorts. The **castle**, reached by a high bridge over the moat, stands apart from the rest of the village.

It was here that the beautiful Giulia Farnese was born in 1474. Married at 15, by the age of 18 she had become the mistress of Cardinal Rodrigo Borgia, later Pope Alexander VI. It was only a matter of time before her brother, Alessandro Farnese, was made Cardinal and when he himself became Pope Paul III in 1513, the fortunes of the Farnese family were secure.

This is a pleasant place for picnics, or for swimming in the unpolluted lake, although it gets busy at weekends in high summer. With time to spare, you can take the twice-daily, two-hour boat trip out to **Isola Bisentina** to see yet another of the many Farnese palaces in the area.

CANINO
15 km SW *of Lago di Bolsena*. The future Pope Paul III, Alessandro Farnese, was born here in 1468 and never lost his passion for the place:

> *If you want to live for ever*
> *Gradoli in the Summer*
> *Canino in the Winter.*

But Canino's greater fame rests on its links with the **Bonaparte family**. Pope Pius VII, hoping to sweeten Napoleon Bonaparte, allowed his brother, Lucien, to buy land here, and for good measure he dubbed him Prince of Canino. When relations between Pope and Emperor finally broke with Napoleon's high-handed arrest of Pius in 1809, Lucien fled to America. Upon the Pope's release five years later, Lucien returned to his Etruscan estates and started a lucrative new career robbing ancient graves (see Vulci, page 195).

The town's main church, the majestic **Collegiata**, contains the Neoclassical **Bonaparte Chapel**, in which Lucien is buried, along with his (and Napoleon's) father, Carlo.

CHIARONE
25 km E *of Orbetello; on the main Rome-La Spezia railway line*. Apart from miles of

sandy beach and dunes, the chief attraction here is the off-beat **Giardino dei Tarocchi**, a one-woman sculpture park 4 km out of town on the road for Pescia Fiorentina. Niki di Saint Phalle, former wife of the French sculptor Jean Tinguely (he of the mechanical creations that gyrate in the pool by Paris's Pompidou Centre), has built one of Italy's most idiosyncratic sights – a garden of vast sculptures inspired by the symbols of the Tarot. You'll either love it or hate it.

IL TELEGRAFO
See *Monte Argentario, page* 190.

ISOLA BISENTINA
See *Capodimonte, page* 188.

ISOLA DEL GIGLIO ⌘ ×
About 8 nautical miles W of the Argentario peninsula. A regular boat leaves Porto Santo Stefano for the one-hour crossing to Porto Giglio. The enchanting rocky island of Giglio, swathed in fragrant Mediterranean brushwood is, after Elba, the largest of the islands that make up the Tuscan Archipelago. Perhaps because it is small (just 5 km wide and 9 km long) it has, despite cashing in on a tourist boom in recent years, managed to keep much of its wild charm intact.

Like Capri, *Aegilium* was a modish resort in Roman times. But by the Middle Ages, the place had fallen into neglect, not helped by the depredations of pirates.

Just one road winds across the island, rising steeply from the harbour of **Giglio Porto** to reach the old walled *borgo* of **Giglio Castello** before dropping back down to the tiny beach resort of **Giglio Campese** on the western shore. A regular bus service links the three villages, although the journey can be made on foot in a couple of hours, and will give you a chance to admire the heady views and fascinating flora.

Despite the droves in July and August, the island has fewer than 20 hotels, all of modest size. Most visitors are day trippers who rarely venture from the pastel-stuccoed bars and restaurants clustered round the harbour. Outside the peak summer months, the place is paradise.

With an early morning start, and a whole day to spare, the best course is to take the bus or an uphill walk to **Giglio Castello**, some 5 km from the harbour. This medieval hamlet, built as a secure refuge from pirates, will hardly tax you with obligatory sights, but it is a lovely place in which to do nothing in particular.

You walk downhill now for a few kilometres to the small but growing resort of **Giglio Campese**, with a couple of fish restaurants to satisfy a healthy appetite before the homeward trek.

ISOLA DI GIANNUTRI
About 6 nautical miles S of Monte Argentario. Reached by summer-only boat from Porto Santo Stefano. The Greeks knew it as Artemesia, the Romans called it Dianium and built a villa, **Cala Maestra**, here in the 1stC AD; its ruins can still be seen today. After that this tiny crescent-shaped island of less than 3 sq. km seems to have been forgotten. Scarcity of fresh water has left it virtually uninhabited and even today the only buildings to be found are a few holiday cottages.

Its one beach resort, **Cala Spalmatoio**, nestles in the shelter of the crescent, while the rest of the island is edged with cavernous limestone.

GRADOLI
12 km W of Bolsena, inland from the NW shore of Lake Bolsena. Here you'll find another of the imperious Farnese **citadel-palaces** that dot the area. This one, commissioned by Cardinal Alessandro Farnese in 1513, was placed on top of a medieval fortress so that the future Pope Paul III could enjoy the cool summer zephyrs. The architect, Sangallo the Younger, built upwards from the original structure but, when the building began to shift a few years later, had to buttress it securely to prevent it toppling backwards over a ravine.

Stop off here to buy a bottle or two of **Aleatico di Gradoli**, a delicious sweet dessert wine.

LAGO DI BOLSENA
See *Seeing the Region: 3, page* 113.

MAGLIANO IN TOSCANA ×
25 km N of Orbetello. Built on the Etruscan town of Heba, it was later occupied by the Romans. Today it is little more than a village, though the sturdy **walls** which enclose it, built by the Sienese in the 15thC, and still intact,

Local Explorations: 6

make Magliano in Toscana seem grander than it is.

Inside, there is a pretty enough **Palazzo dei Priori** (1430). Magliano's most evocative landmark, the ruined 12thC Romanesque abbey of **San Bruzio,** now reduced to little more than a tower, lies a couple of km south-east, near a large Etruscan necropolis.

The village also has an extraordinary concentration of outstanding **restaurants** (see Recommended Restaurants, page 193).

MARTA
On the W shore of Lago di Bolsena. There was no lakeside promenade until early this century. Until then the rows of fishermens' houses backed on to the water with their open-ended cellars serving as fish breeding tanks. They have now been filled in, and many converted into restaurants or weekend cottages.

It is a convenient place to try the excellent **fish** from the lake: *anguilla* (eel); *luccio* (pike); *pesce persico* (perch); and *coregone*, a fish which is similar to wild trout and found only here and in Lake Como.

MONTE ARGENTARIO ⇔ ×
W of Ansedonia. The scrub-covered, limestone double peak of Monte Argentario was once an island but is now tethered to the Tuscan coast by two natural bars of silt known as *tomboli*. These unusual geological phenomena have created a shallow **lagoon**, no more than a metre deep. A walk along the southern **Tombolo di Feniglia** (closed to cars), under the shade of splendid umbrella pines and with glimpses of the lagoon, is very much worth while.

The northern **Tombolo di Giannella** is also covered in pines, but all the available space between the trees has been taken up by a string of campsites. Some years back, Argentario was a resort with a decidedly chic appeal, but its once-quaint little fishing villages have grown into tourist ghettoes with few pretentions to fashion. Nevertheless, the brash holiday atmosphere of **Porto Santo Stefano** can be infectious and around the harbour there are plenty of adequate, if pricey, places where you can eat fish. It is also the place where you catch the ferry across to **Isola del Giglio**.

Porto Ercole, on the other side of the peninsula, has airs and graces and a genuine fishing-port atmosphere. Guarding it are two incongruous Spanish 16thC **fortresses**. It was here, in 1609, that the painter **Caravaggio** died on his return to Rome from exile. He had been imprisoned in error, and was released to see his boat sailing off with all his goods. His rage brought about an attack of fever, from which he died in a nearby tavern. He was buried in the church of **Sant'Erasmo**.

You can drive to the rugged 635-m **summit** of Monte Argentario, **Il Telegrafo**, by a tortuous 11-km road for some grandstand views of the Tuscan coastline and out over the Tyrrhenian Sea as far as Elba.

ORBETELLO ×
On the SS440, off the SS1 (Via Aurelia) on the threshold of Monte Argentario. Tourist information: Piazza della Repubblica. Station, 4 km E at Orbetello Scalo with connecting buses, served by frequent trains on main Rome-La Spezia line.

This curious small town's odd position on an isthmus in the middle of a lagoon has made it an attractive and easily defended site since time immemorial. But its modern-day face owes more to Spain than to Italy. Under King Philip II, the greatest European monarch of the 16thC, the Spanish began a period of domination in Italy that was to last 150 years. So all-pervasive was their influence that a popular contemporary Italian saying had it that 'God has turned into a Spaniard'. At Orbetello they set up a major seat of power. The menacing **ramparts** and formidable **gateways**, begun by Philip II when the Spanish moved in and still bearing his arms, were built upon the Etruscan foundations of the original settlement and give the place the look of an early Spanish colonial town in Central America.

Inside the walls, the sturdy **Polveriera de Guzman**, once the Spanish arsenal, now houses an intimate **archaeological museum**. Behind the resplendent 14thC Gothic façade of the **Cathedral** the Spanish Baroque refit was less successful.

PITIGLIANO ⇔
20 km W of Lago di Bolsena. Sitting high on a vast tongue of tufa cliff and seeming to grow out of the rock, the town

SW Tuscany / Monte Argentario, Isola del Giglio and Lower Maremma

of Pitigliano is breathtaking for its position and bewitching for its unbroken medieval mould.

From its single gate, follow the arches of the enormous **aqueduct** as far as the solid unwelcoming **Fortezza**, both built in the mid-16thC by Sangallo the Younger for Count Gian Francesco Orsini, then lord of Pitigliano. The main square, thin, ilex-lined **Piazza della Repubblica**, spans the spur on which the town is built and has magnificent views out in either direction over the rugged southern Tuscan landscape.

Explore the narrow alleys behind the Baroque **Duomo** to see the best of the medieval *borgo*. Via Zuccarelli, to the southern end of the Piazza, takes you to the ruins of the town's **synagogue** and ghetto. A community was established here in 1649 by Jews fleeing from persecution in the nearby Papal States and thrived until the Nazi exterminations of the 1940s.

The locality produces a kosher white wine.

PONTE DI ABBADIA

10 km N of Montalto di Castro. Few *ponte* in Central Italy can be as magical as the narrow, single-arched **bridge** which spans the wooded cliffs way above the River Fiora. Looking dizzily downwards, you can see the tufa and travertine blocks of its 1stC BC foundations.

The single-turreted **fortified abbey** was built by the Cistercians in the

• *Porto Ercole*.

13thC as a defence against raiders from the sea; by the 16thC it was a customs house on the border between Tuscany and the Papal States.

PORTO ERCOLE AND PORTO SANTO STEFANO ⇌ ×

See Monte Argentario, page 190.

SATURNIA ⇌ ×

10 km N of Manciano. The village claims, unconvincingly, to be the oldest in Italy, having been founded by no less than Saturn himself. The Etruscans named it *Aurinia* and threw up great **walls**, sections of which can still be seen under the 15thC defences. Later it became an important Roman colony. The present village only covers a tiny part of the ancient city, fragments of which are still strewn visibly across the surrounding countryside.

Today, however, Saturnia is best known for its hot sulphur **terme** (springs) – an attraction not only for the middle-aged Romans who come to be pampered in the **spa hotel**, but also for the younger crowd who come to sport in the free **outdoor springs** further down. My first trip here was at the end of a night out with friends who thought nothing of making a three-hour detour. It has now, however, become just a bit too popular and slightly squalid – but the place does have a steamy charm.

RECOMMENDED HOTELS

ANSEDONIA
La Locanda di Ansedonia, LL; Via Aurelia Sud at the 140 km milestone; tel. 0564 881317; fax 0564 881727; cards accepted; half-board terms only in July and Aug.

A pleasant surprise on the ugly main road, this elegantly restored farmhouse offers welcoming Tuscan hospitality, local food and mosquito screens on the windows (malaria has disappeared from the Maremma, but not the mosquitoes). Breakfast in the garden. Ask for a room at the back, away from the traffic.

ISOLA DEL GIGLIO
The tourist office in Giglio Porto gives details of the many private rooms available from May to September. The island's 20 or so small hotels are booked up well in advance for July and August. Best times to visit are June and September.

Arenella, LL; Giglio Porto, by the beach; tel. 0564 809340; fax 0564 809443; cards none; closed end Sept-end May.

Sensible choice for families, with a handful of larger 'apartments', this peaceful *albergo* has a glorious terrace with sea views and homely cooking.

Pardini's Hermitage, LL-LLL; only reached by hotel's own boat from Giglio Porto; tel. 0564 809034; fax 0564 809177; cards accepted; closed Oct-Mar.

Giglio's most enchanting, on a tiny private cove with just 12 rooms and beautiful grounds. Impeccable service, family management that treats guests as old friends, delicious fresh fish from outdoor barbecue and swimming from rocks – *simplicamente paradiso*.

Castello Monticello, LL; 2 km before Giglio Castello on island's only road; tel. 0564 809252; fax 0564 809473; cards accepted; closed mid-Nov to mid-Mar.

Splendid location in unspoilt countryside with sweeping views out to sea, this villa-cum-castle is ideal if you want to be away from the bustle of Giglio Porto or Campese.

PITIGLIANO Guastini, L; Piazza Petruccioli 4; tel. 0564 616065; fax 0564 616652; cards none.

Somewhat anonymous and austere, this typical small-town hotel has nonetheless splendid views, honest prices and a passable restaurant.

PORTO ERCOLE
Il Pellicano, LLL+; Cala dei Santi; tel. 0564 833801; fax 0564 833418; cards accepted; closed Nov-Mar.

Strictly for wealthy honeymooners or football pools winners, this seaside retreat has a fabulous setting in a villa-style complex and frankly outrageous prices. Both the quality and the bills in the restaurant are legendary.

SATURNIA
Villa Clodia, LL; Via Italia 43; tel. and fax 0564 601212; cards accepted.

An alternative choice to the pretentious and over-priced Hotel delle Terme, it has ten peaceful bedrooms and a swimming pool in the centre of this fashionable village. Breakfast is, somewhat oddly, *all'inglese*.

SOVANA
Sovana's two delightful little *alberghi* face each other across its enchanting main square and both double as excellent restaurants (see Recommended Restaurants, page 193):

Scilla, L-LL; Via di Sotto 3; tel. 0564 616531; fax 0564 614329; cards accepted.

Eight comfortable rooms in a medieval *palazzetto*, marginally cheaper than the Taverna Etrusca.

Taverna Etrusca, LL; Piazza del Pretorio 16; tel. 0564 616183; fax 0564 614193; cards accepted.

Sprucer, newer version of the Scilla opposite, but same size.

RECOMMENDED RESTAURANTS

CAPALBIO
Da Maria, LL; Via Comunale 3; tel. 0564 896014; cards accepted; closed Tues.

This popular and justly praised restaurant on the threshold of the old *borgo* is hung with hunting trophies and offers the best authentic *cucina Maremmana*: sturdy soups of *ceci* (chickpeas) and *fagioli* (beans), grilled suckling pig and game are available in the autumn.

ISOLA DEL GIGLIO

The little harbour boasts a number of first-rate fish restaurants with little to choose betweeen them – but **Vecchia Pergola** (LL; Via T. de Revel 31; tel. 0564 809080; cards none; closed Tues) with a lovely summer terrace is perhaps the most pleasant.

The best two restaurants on the island are up in Giglio Castello: **Trione** (LL; tel. 0564 806266; cards accepted) in the small square in front of the castle; and **Da Maria** (LL; tel. 0564 806062; cards accepted; closed Wed) on Via Casamatta. Both offer fish and fowl, cooked with dedication and imagination.

MAGLIANO IN TOSCANA

A haven for gastronomes, with no less than three outstanding restaurants, all charging fair prices:

Antica Trattoria Aurora, LL; Chiasso Lavagnini 12; tel. 0564 592030; cards accepted; closed Wed.

No surprise that booking is essential at this superb restaurant that successfully marries traditional cucina toscana with modern fantasy. Try the acquacotta (the Maremma peasant soup, literally 'cooked water'), here elevated to sublime heights. In summer you can eat in the charming courtyard.

Da Guido, LL; Via Roma 18; tel. 0564 592447; cards accepted; closed Tues.

Rigorously faithful rendering of Maremma home cooking – substantial primi and meaty main dishes.

Da Sandra, LL; Via Garibaldi 20; tel. 0564 592196; cards accepted; closed Mon.

Small trattoria on the town's main street with a Toscanissimo menu – try coniglio all'uva (rabbit with grapes) if it's offered; drink red Morellino wine.

ORBETELLO

Il Nocchino, LL; Via dei Mille 64; tel. 0564 860329; cards none; open evenings only, closed Wed.

An osteria which hasn't lost its old identity. Traditional seafood cucina, but with originality: delicate fishy antipasti with vegetables or squid ink risotto, followed perhaps by mixed grilled fish.

PORTO SANTO STEFANO

Orlando, LL-LLL; Via Breschi 3; tel.0564 812788; cards accepted; closed Thur in winter.

Above-average cooking at a fairish price, with particularly appetizing antipasti di mare (seafood starters) and the speciality zuppa di pesce, which has to be ordered in advance.

Il Veliero, LLL; Via Panoramica 149/151; tel. 0564 812226; cards accepted; closed Mon eve.

Above the town, with terrace, overlooking the sea. Eclectic all-fish menu, varies according to availability; round it off with a mouthwatering dessert.

Dal Greco, LLL; Via del Molo 12; tel. 0564 814885; cards accepted; closed Tues.

A relatively sophisticated place, with a limited menu (almost entirely fish-based), immaculate service, with the emphasis on presentation.

SATURNIA

Bacco e Cerere, LL; Via Mazzini 4; tel. 0564 601235; cards accepted; closed Tues.

Small restaurant above a wine shop and delicatessen, serving rustic food imaginatively adapted to modern tastes and served with Tuscan wines.

Da Caino, LL-LLL; Via Canonica 3, Montemerano; tel. 0564 602817; cards accepted; closed Wed and Thurs lunch.

In the medieval borgo of Montemerano, half way between Saturnia and Manciano. Despite its sophistication, this much-praised restaurant retains the character of a traditional osteria, cooking seasonal local food.

SOVANA

Scilla, LL; Via di Sotto 3; tel. 0564 616531; cards accepted; closed Tues.

Menu based almost entirely on Maremma dishes, with especially good vegetable soups followed by manzo (beef) in red wine or cinghiale (wild boar), (see Recommended Hotels, page 192).

Taverna Etrusca, LL; Piazza del Pretorio 16a; tel. 0564 616183; cards accepted; closed Mon.

Locally inspired dishes with a touch of creativity. Flowery terrace in the summer, (see also Recommended Hotels, page 192).

Local Explorations: 6

• *Bathing in the hot springs at Saturnia.*

SORANO

10 km N *of Pitigliano*. Visiting Sorano is always dramatic. The majestic tufa cliffs on which the village teeters cannot bear the weight and whole chunks of the town are slipping away. Little by little, street after street is declared uninhabitable and allowed to crumble away unchecked. A law of 1929 helped villagers to set up home elsewhere and since then the tide of decay has been hindered only through the efforts of a growing community of artists and potters who have turned it into a notable craft centre.

The strange juxtaposition of medieval splendour and desolation gives the place a slightly melancholy atmosphere. Presiding over it are two castles, the impregnable 16thC **Fortezza Orsini**, by the town entrance and, higher up, the square battlements of the older **Sasso Leopoldini**.

SOVANA ↔ ×

8 km NE *of Pitigliano*. This ancient capital of the Aldobrandeschi family reached the height of its importance in the middle of the 12thC before slipping quietly into oblivion. Its fortunes were linked with those of Hildebrand, who, as Pope Gregory VII (1073-85), was one of the greatest popes of the Middle Ages. Thereafter it fell into decline, ravaged by malaria (as late as the 19thC, guidebooks advised travellers to visit only in the winter months) and attacks from the Sienese armies.

Barely a village, this solitary place with an abandoned feel sits on a spur which stretches from the ruins of its Aldobrandeschi *rocca* at one end to the lonesome cathedral at the other. Stroll down **Via di Mezzo**, the main street paved in a herring-bone pattern with ancient terracotta bricks, to reach **Piazza del Pretorio** with its fine group of buildings. The 13thC **Santa Maria**, with a triple nave, built on the shape of a square and supported by octagonal pillars, is an outstanding medieval church. Inside, its pride and joy is a splendid, remarkably early *ciborio*, a tabernacle and canopy over the main altar dating back to the 8th or 9thC.

Opposite stands the **Palazzo Pretorio**, which now contains a small museum of Etruscan finds, flanked by the **Loggia del Capitano**. To the side of **Palazzo Bourbon del Monte** (in the same square) are the ruins of the town's oldest church, **San Mamiliano**, built on the foundations of an Etrusco-Roman building.

At the far end of Via di Mezzo, past the legendary **birthplace** of Hildebrand, the exceptional **Cathedral** was already an antique when it was given a pleasing Romanesque aspect in the 12thC. Its dome dates back to the 10thC while the barbaric sculptures around the entrance are even earlier. Only high walls and a tower are left of the **castle**, but it is still a striking sight.

• *Sorano.*

The surrounding countryside is littered with **Etruscan tombs,** particularly to the west. The finest of these is the temple-like **Tomba Ildebranda**, which is cut straight out of the face of the tufa rock.

VULCI

11 km N of Montalto di Castro. A fertile imagination is useful to appreciate this moody archaeological site, so little has been left by 19thC grave robbers. Vulci was one of the 12 great cities of the Etruscan dodecapolis. Now, all that remains is windswept, flat moorland, littered with plundered tombs. The destruction began in 1828, when a plough broke through into an Etruscan tomb near the village of Canino. The owner, Prince Lucien Bonaparte (see Canino, page 188), soon began to exploit the new discovery by excavating tomb after tomb and selling off their contents with great rapidity; as each grave was plundered, it was filled with debris. On his death, the Roman Torlonia family bought up his estates and continued the destruction.

Now the wealth of Vulci is scattered among the museums of the West, with perhaps an even greater quantity of Etruscan treasures remaining uncatalogued in private hands. As early as 1840, it was reported that a staggering 30,000 tombs had been 'discovered', but it wasn't until 1857 that any proper archaeological investigation of the area began. When D.H.Lawrence visited in 1927, he commented upon the irony that the Etruscans should have left their fortunes to the Bonapartes. Nowadays, there is little left to find, but modern *tombaroli,* or grave robbers, still practise their trade.

Local Explorations: 7

Northern Lazio

Southern Etruria – the Etruscan Trail

180 km; map Touring Club Italiano Toscana or Lazio

Many of the greatest Etruscan cities lay to the south of Tuscany in modern-day northern Lazio. This tour in an area little visited by the foreign traveller takes in the best of these ancient sites, which offer a fascinating insight into the civilization that preceded Rome in Central Italy. As a contrast, you'll also see some outlandish and exquisite sights from later centuries in the shape of Mannerist monsters, villas and gardens.

Long before the Etruscans, this area was torn by volcanic activity which has cast the landscape into fantastic shapes – from the beautiful crater lake of Lago di Vico to the great plugs of volcanic rock that support precarious medieval villages high above the road. Its monuments, too, were forged by fire: the volcanic tufa provided the ideal rock in which the Etruscans could dig their warren-like funeral chambers and this easily cut stone provided the distinctive building blocks for medieval Viterbo and the Late Renaissance pile of Caprarola. It also provided the just medium for some of Italy's strangest stone carvings, the giant monsters at Bomarzo.

In Tuscany, the Etruscan cities continued to grow and prosper in later ages, blotting out most traces of their distant founders. Here, often due to malaria, their great settlements withered away leaving only small villages huddled besides the ruins. It is here, therefore, that the most complete relics of this fascinating if shadowy civilization remain and few will fail to be profoundly affected by the tomb paintings at Tarquinia.

To round the journey off, the tour includes Villa Lante in Bagnaia. Thoughts of volcanoes, monsters and ancient Etruscans can be put behind you as you take in the prospect of this peerless example of a Late Renaissance pleasure ground, surely amongst the great gardens of Italy.

NORTHERN LAZIO / *Southern Etruria – the Etruscan Trail*

TRANSPORT

A trio of ancient Roman roads traverse this area. The coastal Via Aurelia passes under the walls of Tarquinia; the Via Cassia, from Rome to Florence, passes Sutri and Vetralla; and the Via Flaminia, to the east, goes through Civita Castellana on its way northwards to the Adriatic coast.

Travelling by rail, the Rome-La Spezia line serves Tarquinia, while the stopping Rome-Florence train halts a few kilometres outside Civita Castellana, and the private Roma-Nord line stops at Capranica. Bus services follow the three main ancient highways, but few cross east-west. The nearest international airport is Rome.

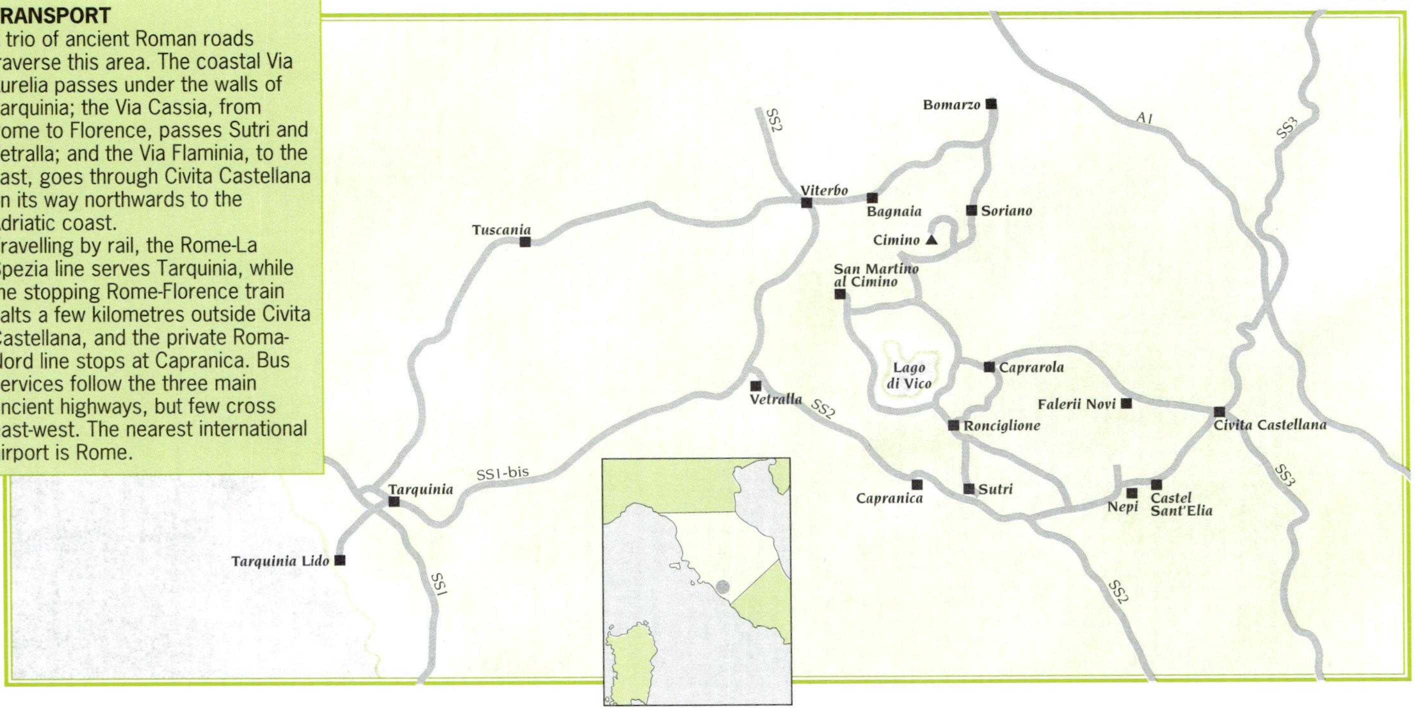

The gardens at Villa Lante.

SIGHTS & PLACES OF INTEREST

BAGNAIA ×
3 km E of Viterbo. The gardens of **Villa Lante**, which stand above this small town, are amongst the most handsome in all Central Italy. This text-book Late Renaissance pleasure ground was laid out by the Mannerist master Vignola in 1566 as a summer retreat for Cardinal Gambara, Bishop of Viterbo – look out for his emblem, a prawn, carved in the most unlikely corners of the garden.

Here, nature has been thoroughly knocked into shape: five open **terraces** on a steep slope are linked by flights of steps and elegant **fountains**, all framed by manicured hedges of box and yew. In keeping with the fashion of the time, water is ever present, from the gentle double cascades which trickle down from the garden's highest point, through the long stone **dining table** where the central channel of running water was designed to act as a wine-cooler, to the lower parterre, with its **giochi d'acqua**, the hidden fountains of water which the saucy cleric could turn on his unsuspecting guests.

The villa itself, or more accurately pair of villas, is really just a couple of pavilions designed to embellish the gardens. One of them has delightful frescoes showing the gardens as they looked when first constructed.

If you have time, wander around the medieval part of Bagnaia which stands behind the main piazza – plenty of earthy charm in stark contrast to the perfection of the gardens.

BOMARZO
20 km NE of Viterbo. Follow the signs that take you below the ramparts of the village to arrive at **Il Parco dei Mostri** (The Park of Monsters), one of the strangest sights in northern Lazio.

Sometime around the middle of the 16thC, Vicino Orsini, a bastard son of the rich Roman Orsini family, created a Late Renaissance 'theme park', embellishing the slopes of a large natural amphitheatre with a host of enormous stone sculptures. The natural outcrops of tufa rock in what he called his *sacro bosco* (sacred wood) were hewn into strange monsters and fantastical beasts – three-headed dogs, an elephant crushing a soldier, a giant mangling a woman. Time and lichen have helped to mould them into the wild, wooded landscape, but their contorted features are as powerful as ever. Not surprisingly, Dali raved about them, and so do the coachloads of schoolchildren who come here every year in the early summer months.

CAPRANICA
On the SS2 Via Cassia, 25 km S of Viterbo. The town's most striking feature is the way it suddenly towers up above you, a dramatic exclamation mark on your journey along the old Via Cassia. A stop is not obligatory, but if you do, cut

through the modern town to explore the **16thC quarter** with its fine Late Renaissance palaces and, over a narrow bridge and through a towered gateway, the fortified **medieval village**, the oldest part of the town.

CAPRAROLA

18 km SE *of Viterbo*. The village of Caprarola lies in the shadow of **Villa Farnese**, surely one of the most striking villas in Central Italy. Arriving in the centre of the town, the fortified palace stands majestically at the summit of the main street.

When Alessandro Farnese became Pope Paul III in 1534, the fortunes of the Farnese family were made. It was his nephew, another Cardinal Alessandro Farnese, who commissioned Vignola to build the pentagonal Villa Farnese, on the foundations of an earlier fortress.

By 1559, work had begun. The palace was to rise up above a series of theatrical ramps and terraces and was to be reached along a suitably grand approach road which stretched the whole length of the town. No expense was spared on this example of the Renaissance ideal well past its sell-by date.

From the great circular central courtyard, the **Scala Regia,** a spiral stairway that puts others in the shade, leads up to the *piano nobile*. Most of the rooms here are decorated with Federico and Taddeo Zuccaris's sumptuous frescoes to the glory of the Farnese family. The **Sala del Mappamondo**, decorated with maps of the then known world, comes as a relief – for once the Farnese's exploits take second place.

To the rear, Vignola laid out parterre gardens linked to the *piano nobile* by bridges spanning the deep moat of the original fortress. Once the approach road had been cleaved through the town below, the place was given a facelift to suit its new status and small *palazzi* were added here and there to accommodate members of the Farnese retinue. The remainder of the population were discretely moved on to two new quarters – Borgo Corsica (on the left of the central street) and Borgo Sardegna (to the right).

CASTEL SANT'ELIA

See *Nepi, page 200*.

CIMINO, MONTE

4 *km* SW *of Soriano del Cimino*. A dead-end turning off the road from Soriano takes you up through woods of chestnut and hazelnut to *La Faggeta*, the stand of beech which clothes the 1,000-m peak of Monte Cimino. Though crowded at weekends in the high summer, for the rest of the time this fine beauty spot is a perfect place for a lunch-time break. There are plenty of picnic sites and a *pizzeria* with picture-postcard views.

CIVITA CASTELLANA ✕

On the SS3 *Via Flaminia*. Built on the heights at the confluence of two rivers, this is the site of the ancient town of *Falerii Veteres*, home of the war-like Faliscan tribe later absorbed by the Etruscans. In the 4thC BC it was a thriving city and a noted producer of pottery produced for export on an almost industrial scale.

In 241 BC the Romans, seeing its power and impregnable position, destroyed the town and forced the Faliscan people to move to **Falerii Novi** on the much more vulnerable nearby plain.

There they stayed until the troubled 8thC when they crept back to the safety of the ancient site, renaming it Civita Castellana, and by the 12thC it had been rebuilt as a papal stronghold.

The present town is rather frayed around the edges but has a modest elegance and a striking medieval core. Its finest building is its intimate **Duomo**. The façade sports a fine columned portico (1210), while its simple interior is flanked by Classical columns and its floor is decorated with rich marble *cosmati* mosaic work. The **crypt** down below may well date back to the 8thC and its columns may date from an even earlier period.

The town's other winning building is the **castle** built by Cardinal Rodrigo Borgia, later Pope Alessandro VI. In the 19thC it was turned into a prison to hold some of the Vatican court's most notable convicts; now it is a museum.

The site of the former city, **Falerii Novi**, stands about 6 km west of the town on the road towards Fabrica di Roma and merits a visit. The eerie vision of over 2 km of almost intact high walls looms up a little way from the road, in the middle of farm land. The beautiful arches that pierce the massive blocks of moss-covered tufa stone are now guarded only by trees, while inside all that remains is the ruined church and monastery reduced to farm buildings.

FALERII NOVI
See Civita Castellana, page 199 and above.

NEPI
20 km SW of Civita Castellana. Surrounded by its high **walls** of Etruscan origin, Nepi was one of the gateways to Ancient Etruria. The **castle** on top didn't arrive until the end of the 15thC when Rodrigo Borgia, the future Pope Alessandro VI, had it built for his infamous daughter Lucrezia. It was the son of another Pope, the Farnese Paul III, who got Antonio da Sangallo the Younger to remodel it. Modern Nepi is in a sad state of neglect, with many churches and *palazzi* abandoned and decaying, though there are signs that the tide may be turning.

Some 3 km east of the town, on the road towards Civita Castellana, under the cliffs of a gorge below **Castel Sant'Elia**, stands an old **basilica** built on the site of a Roman temple to Diana. The present church dates back to the early 11thC, but parts of its 8thC predecessor were incorporated into it. Inside, the colonnades have recycled Roman capitals.

RONCIGLIONE ⇔ ×
4 km SE of Lago Vico. Dickens described this town as a pigsty, though it has to be said he rarely had anything favourable to say about his travels in Italy. The medieval part of present-day Ronciglione is certainly rather worn around the edges. Its small main square, oddly hemmed in by a ruined church (it used to be the cathedral until part of it toppled over into the ravine behind) and a castle, seem to have been forgotten by the rest of the town. But its main **avenue**, probably designed by Antonio di Sangallo, has a certain grandeur and the town's vast **cathedral**, completed in 1695 to designs by the Baroque masters Pietro da Cortona and Carlo Rainaldi, is striking.

SAN MARTINO AL CIMINO
5 km S of Viterbo. Once through the **gateway** at the foot of the village (its design attributed to Borromini) you enter a world whose neatness and order has a northern atmosphere explained by the fact that the land was given to the French Cistercian order in the 13thC.

At the higher end, the Gothic **Abbey of San Martino** keeps an eye over the parallel streets of terraced houses, models of enlightened 17thC town planning. To the side of it stands a modest *palazzo* built by Donna Olimpia Pamphili, nicknamed the *papessa*. In 1644, she single-handedly propelled her aged brother-in-law, Innocent X, to the throne of St Peter in return for which he gave her the lands of San Martino. During Innocent's 11-year reign, she rebuilt much of the village, filling many of the houses, it is said, with reformed whores and ex-convicts. Her spare time was spent running the Vatican, taking decisions on domestic government and foreign policy and selling appointments and offices to the highest bidder. She died here of the plague in 1657.

SORIANO ⇔ ×
17 km E of Viterbo. Sitting on the slopes of Monte Cimino, its dominating feature is the huge 13thC **Orsini fortress**, whose muscular walls seem to place the rest of the town at its mercy. Nevertheless, life in the lively piazza beneath it seems happy enough.

The potential star attraction lies unloved at the foot of the town, on the road towards Viterbo. The **Palazzo Chigi-Albani** has been shut up for years, although a notice states that it is 'under restoration'. Begun in 1562, probably to a design by Vignola, its glory is said to be an outstanding Baroque fountain called the **Fontana Papacqua**. There is rumoured to be a custodian who will let you see it – perhaps you'll have better luck finding him than I did.

SUTRI
On the SS2 Via Cassia, 30 km S of Viterbo. Like so many Etruscan towns, the date of its foundation is unknown, though some put it as early as 1000 BC.

The city sits theatrically on a crag of tufa rock, encircled by its medieval walls (parts of their Cyclopean Etruscan foundations can still be seen in places). Inside there are several noteworthy *palazzi*, but the major attractions lie outside to the south.

The rather overgrown 1stC BC Roman **amphitheatre** is cut out of solid rock and could hold 6,000 people; even a *vomitorium* was thoughtfully provided for when the excitement of the *spettacolo* became too much.

Nearby, the origins of **Santa Maria del Parto** are decidedly pre-Christian. It was hewn out of the rock in the 6th or 7thC BC as an Etruscan burial chamber. It was converted into a church in the Middle Ages and decorated with the frescoes which remain today.

The hills and woods surrounding it are honeycombed with chambers and catacombs, many converted into chapels, later abandoned.

RECOMMENDED HOTELS

Northern Lazio suffers from a lack of attractive hotels and you may do better at Bolsena (see Seeing the Region: 3) or Orvieto (see Local Explorations: 6). Here are the best of the few:

RONCIGLIONE
Sans Soucis, LL; *Punta del Lago on Lago di Vico, NW of Ronciglione; tel. 0761 612052; fax 0761 612053; cards accepted.*

Small *albergo* on lakeside with beach, pretty garden, and fine views.

SORIANO
La Bastia, LL; *Via Giovanni XXIII; tel. 0761 745383; fax 0761 745383; cards accepted.*

This smallish hotel in modern Italian style stands just outside town up a well-signposted track. Slightly precious, but sound value. Come here if you want a room with a spectacular view of the Tiber plain and the Appennine foothills.

TARQUINIA
Tarconte, LL; *Via Tuscia 19; tel. 0766 856141; fax 0766 856585; cards accepted.*

This 1970s-style hotel is the best in the area. Inside all is bright and clean with modern paintings keeping company with 'Etruscan' decorations.

RECOMMENDED RESTAURANTS

BAGNAIA
Biscetti, LL; *Via Gandin 11; tel. 0761 288252; cards accepted; closed Thur and July.*

Sophisticated versions of Lazio specialities in large helpings. Rather dowdy decorations let down the fine cooking.

CIVITA CASTELLANA
L'Altra Bottiglia, LLL; *Via delle Palme 14; tel. 0761 517403; cards accepted; dinner only except Sun lunch; closed Wed and Aug.*

Decidedly elegant establishment with a menu strictly tied to season and local produce – unusual *primi* – and outstanding sweets.

RONCIGLIONE
Lido dei Pioppi, LL-LLL; *Punta del Lago; tel. 0761 612029; cards accepted; closed Mon.*

Just outside town as you reach the lake, take the well-marked track to this favourite haunt of epicurean Romans. Sitting on the lake-side terrace, try the lake fish, including perch and eel.

SORIANO
Ai Tre Scalini, L-LL; *Via Vittorio Emanuele III, 1; tel. 0761 745970; cards none; closed Wed and second half June.*

Friendly, family-run restaurant with wild mushrooms from Monte Cimino a feature on the menu. Its simple but excellent cooking has earned it a reputation far beyond the local beat.

TARQUINIA
Il Bersagliere, LL-LLL; *Via Benedetto Croce 2; tel. 0766 856047; cards accepted; closed Sun eve and Mon.*

The best in town with *laziale* cooking and the chance to eat outdoors in summer.

TUSCANIA
Al Gallo, LL; *Via del Gallo, 22; tel. 0761 443388; cards accepted; closed Mon.*

A gastronomic haven in an antique *palazzo*. In the beautifully designed dining room that blends the rustic and the refined, you'll sample some of the best food in northern Lazio.

Façade of San Pietro, Tuscania.

TARQUINIA

Off the coastal SS1 Via Aurelia, 50 km SE of Orbetello. If you only have time or inclination to visit one Etruscan site, this is the one to make for. Of all the Etruscan cities, Tarxuna, home of the legendary Tarquins, was perhaps the greatest. Said to have been founded in the 11thC BC by Tarchon, brother of Tyrrhenus, by the 9thC BC it had become one of the principal settlements in Italy. When the Tarquins ruled Rome it is reckoned that its population numbered around 100,000. They lived on a site just to the east of the modern town guarded by an 8-km wall. It is now a sweeping open moorland, littered with a vast warren of tombs. Of the 6,000 underground burial chambers excavated so far, 62 are decorated with remarkably well-preserved **wall paintings** – the most eloquent remains that these mysterious people have left us.

Most of the important tombs (the best among them are the **Tomba dell'Orco** and the **Tomba dei Leopardi**) lie on either side of the road to the south-east of the city (they are opened in rotation). The underground rooms are now empty, their furnishings having been removed to the city's museum or sold off further afield by the *tombaroli* who have made a tidy income over the centuries from their plunder. The glorious paintings depict scenes of everyday life: the hunt, a man at dinner with his wife, or being bitten by a dog, or making love.

Why the city moved from here in around the 7thC to its present site is not clear. It was then known as Corgnitum, later Corneto and it was only this century, during the 1920s when Fascist Italy strove to recapture its Imperial glory, that it was renamed Tarquinia.

Present-day Tarquinia, ringed by medieval walls, has been much knocked about over the centuries but contains one of Etruria's best museums and several fine buildings. **Palazzo Vitelleschi** was built by the ruling family in the early years of the 15thC, a Renaissance building whose detail harks back to the earlier Gothic period. The *palazzo* now houses the **Museo Nazionale Tarquiniese**, a superb collection of some of the best Etruscan finds of the area – most notably two half-sized winged horses dating back to the 4th-3rdC BC and some of the bawdiest painted pottery imaginable.

Of the town's handful of interesting churches, the finest stands within the walls of the ruined **castle**. The beautiful Romanesque church of **Santa Maria di Castello** has an harmonious interior, lit by two rose windows, and shelters under a fine rib-vaulted ceiling and simple central dome.

Sun, sea and sand await you down at **Tarquinia Lido**, a few kilometres away on the coast. Heavily developed, it is standing room only during the summer months, and the proximity of the industrial port of Civitavecchia places something of a question mark over the purity of the water.

TUSCANIA ×

25 km W of Viterbo. The undertow of history has shifted modern Tuscania westwards from the site of its original foundation. Its **medieval wall** encircles only a small part of the area covered by its Etruscan predecessor. The rudimentary ruins of the ancient city stand forlornly exposed on a nearby moor.

Before the Romans conquered Tuscania in the 3rdC BC, it was a large, thriving Etruscan city. Under Rome it continued to prosper, particularly as it lay on the important Roman **Via Clodia**, tracts of which can still be seen today.

Its decline began with the arrival of the Longobards from the north in AD 569 and in 774 Charlemagne handed the city over to the papacy. Two remarkable churches, built on the site of ancient temples, were left behind on the **Colle San Pietro** as the town shrank. When they were partially rebuilt in the 12thC, the hill was still encircled with towers, though over the next century these were quarried for the building of the new medieval town on the adjoining hill, **Colle del Rivellino**.

San Pietro stands in the shadow of two hulking towers. On its magnificent 12thC **façade**, the rose window above the marble portal is flanked by fantastical carvings that look deeply pagan to the modern eye. The stern triple-naved interior is paved with kaleidoscopic **cosmati mosaics**, while below it the marble-pillared **crypt** has an atmosphere which is almost Islamic.

Further down the hill, on the other side of the Via Clodia, **Santa Maria Maggiore** was the cathedral until the 9thC. Its fine white marbled portal is flanked by rather battered statues of St Peter and St Paul but yet again strange mythical beings cast an unholy shadow over the stonework of its façade. After San Pietro's severity, this interior is altogether lighter and more harmonious.

Before returning to the main road, you come across the ruins of the **Bagno della Regina**, thermal baths whose *caldarium*, or warm room, and a few mosaics can still be seen.

The medieval town, which stands a little way off, has had more than its fair share of trials and tribulations over the centuries, the last of which was a disasterous earthquake in 1971, from which it is still recovering. Most of its churches date back to the 12thC, but what hasn't been achieved by foreign sackings has been seen to by earthquakes.

Outside the city walls, the fine adjoining Renaissance church of **Santa Maria del Riposo** is notable for its richly decorated altarpiece (1534) that dominates its otherwise restrained interior. Next door, the former monastery houses the **Museo Nazionale Tuscanense**. The major attraction here is a collection of some 30 Etruscan sarcophaghi, discovered only 20 years ago, belonging to successive generations of the same family and dating back to the 3rd-1stC BC.

As in so much of Etruria, the city's *necropoli* were almost entirely destroyed during the 19thC. The main culprits here were the Campanari family who gave first refusal for the best of the loot to the Vatican, busy setting up the Gregorian Museum at the time.

VETRALLA

13 km S of Viterbo along the SS2 Via Cassia. The town was badly damaged by Allied bombing in 1944 and, while its castle was destroyed, its vast **cathedral** escaped unharmed. Parts of the lower church date back to the 12thC (the crypt is paved with *cosmati* mosaics) but the remainder of the building is stolidly 18thC.

VICO, LAGO DI

10 km SE of Viterbo. According to mythology, Hercules made Lago di Vico when he drove his club into the ground; pulling it out, water trickled in. The *lago*, the smallest of northern Lazio's three volcanic lakes, is 18 km in circumference. Its woods and meadowland make it perhaps the most beautiful of the lakes, visible from the surrounding road but hard to reach, unless you leave the car behind. The lakeside and surrounding area is now a nature reserve.

VITERBO

See Seeing the Region: 3, pages 115-16.

Local Explorations: 8

Western Tuscany

The Upper Maremma and Metal Hills

180 km; map Touring Club Italiano Toscana

An exploration in a minor key, this section is for the open-minded traveller who wants more than the standard starred attractions. The melancholy plains of the coastal Maremma or the featureless Colline Metallifere, or Metal Hills, may not be text-book Tuscany, but they provide the setting for a string of curiosities that are worth searching out.

The marked route takes in the atmospheric ruins of a trio of great Etruscan cities, essential stops for those drawn to this ancient civilization, even if what remains is meagre. Ruins, too, but of a much later period, are the draw at the romantic Gothic Abbey of San Galgano.

The geothermal hardware around Larderello may not provide an obvious tourist spectacle, but the miles of bright steel piping give a nonetheless intriguing dimension to the rolling Metal Hills. Here, too, you can get up close to some of nature's strangest geological displays – bubbling mud pools and hissing plumes of sulphurous steam.

Massa Marittima, the area's only pukka historic town, boasts one of Tuscany's top ten cathedrals and a warren of medieval byways in which to get lost. Many may be tempted to give Grosseto, the other major town on the route, a wide berth. But even here there is compensation: excellent local cooking.

Other reasons to come to this part of Tuscany might include a taste of Sassicaia, one of Italy's most outstanding fine wines, or a ferry trip out to the island of Elba – despite its inevitable popularity as a mass tourist destination, it is still big enough to harbour unspoilt hideaways.

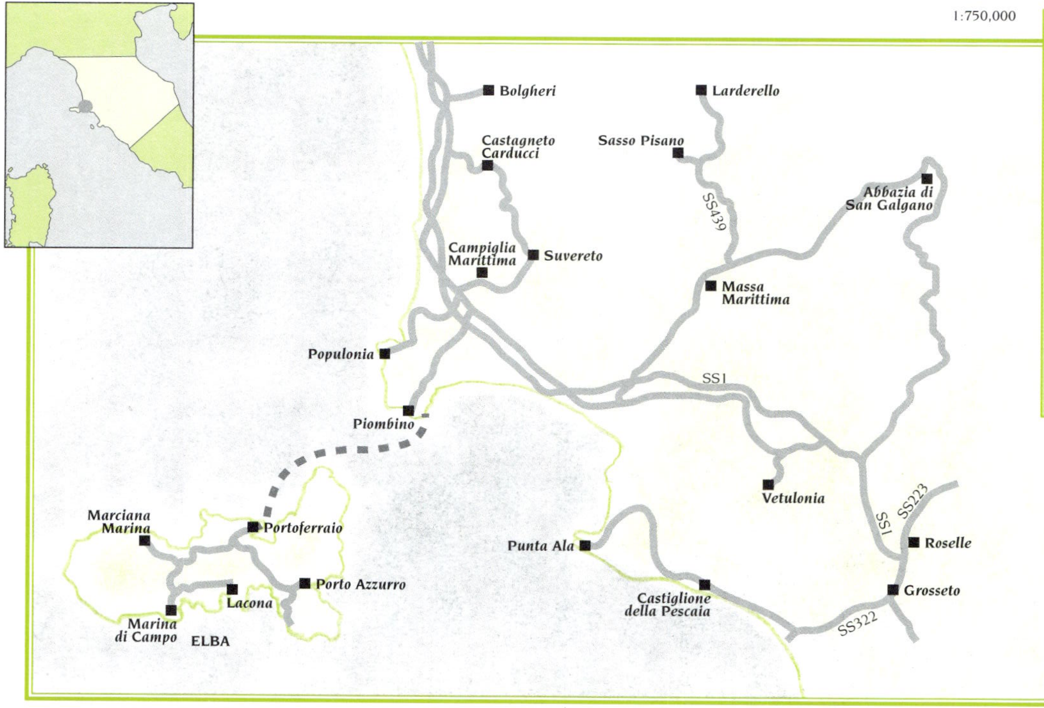

WESTERN TUSCANY / *The Upper Maremma and Metal Hills*

TRANSPORT

Much of this route lies on either side of the SS1, the old Roman Via Aurelia that runs north along the Tyrrhenian coast: not the loveliest of highways, but convenient. Parallel to it is the main Rome-Pisa railway line which serves Grosseto and Piombino (for ferries to Elba). The main hub for local and long-distance buses is Grosseto. There is a regular bus service to Larderello from Massa Marittima.

SIGHTS & PLACES OF INTEREST

BOLGHERI
Some 5 km off the SS1. A scene-stealing approach road and one of Italy's most lauded wines provide two good reasons to leave the Via Aurelia to visit this *borgo* grouped around a 17thC castle. From the old Roman road to the centre of town runs a dead-straight, 5-km **avenue of bottle-green cypress trees**, many now sadly infected with a parasitic fungus – see the avenue before they die off.

Sassicaia, a wine that owes more to claret than Chianti, is made entirely from cabernet sauvignon grapes and was developed by the Marchese Mario Incisa della Rocchetta with a star-studded team of consultants on his Tenuta San Guido that lies at the start of the cypress avenue. The estate now produces 90,000 bottles a year of this legendary wine which are snapped up by international wine buffs at around L65,000 a bottle.

CAMPIGLIA MARITTIMA ×
See Castagneto Carducci, below.

CASTAGNETO CARDUCCI ⇌ ×
Follow the up-and-down backroad off the SS1 (Via Aurelia) to discover a string of sleepy villages set in vineyards and olive groves, backed by green hills and facing out to sea. Inside the medieval walls of **Castagneto Carducci** is the house where the Nobel prize-winning Italian poet, Giosuè Carducci (1835-1907), spent part of his youth. Further on, **Suvereto** has a handsome Romanesque church, San Giusto – look out for the Byzantine touches evident on the porchway – and a sturdy medieval town hall.

Campiglia Marittima, is a small town that still retains much of its medieval character: alleyways of stern stone houses and the ruins of the castle on the hill above. In the cemetery, the little Romanesque church of San Giovanni has some curious inlay work on the side entrance featuring the Greek myth of Meleager and his celebrated hunt for the Calydonian boar.

CASTIGLIONE DELLA PESCAIA ⇌
× On the SS322, 22 km NW of Grosseto. The pleasure boats now outnumber the fishing smacks in the old port, but this seaside resort remains one of the most attractive on the Maremma coast. The fine beach runs into shady woods of umbrella pines, and above the modern town the old medieval *borgo*, **Castiglione Castello**, stands within turretted, thick Pisan walls. To the northwest, deep in Mediterranean scrub, is the exclusive little resort of **Punta Ala** – the only thing to ruffle a stay in one of its handful of smart but synthetic hotels is the bill.

ELBA ⇌ ×
Regular ferry service with car transport from Piombino, operated by Toremar and Navarma; crossing time about one hour. Tourist information: Portoferraio at Calata Italia 26. Buses for whole island from bus station at Viale Elba 20.

Lush Mediterranean *macchia*, a gentle climate and limpid seas have made Italy's third largest island a favourite Euro-tourist destination, best avoided in July and August. Its high mountains are crowned with evergreen oak and chestnut while lower down wild stretches of broom, eucalyptus, agave and cork oak give way to steep slopes of vines and olive trees. Its long coastline alternates between inviting coves and plunging cliffs and on its beaches iron pyrites glisten in the sand.

For long before the tourist boom, Elba built its wealth on its iron ore. To the Ancient Greeks it was *Aethalia*, or 'sooty' for the smoke from its foundries; much of the prosperity of the Etruscans was based on Elban iron.

Portoferraio, the gateway to Elba and its main town, was rebuilt by Cosimo de' Medici in the 16thC and its old centre is worth lingering in. The main beach resorts are **Marciana Marina**, **Marina di Campo**, **Lacona**, and **Porto Azzurro**, but all roads on Elba are attractive, if tortuous, and will lead you to hidden corners well off the tourist beat.

The island's most celebrated guest was Napoleon, who spent nine months in exile here in 1814-15 – visit both **Villa dei Mulini**, his Portoferraio residence, and his summer home at **San Martino**, 10 km into the hills.

GROSSETO ×
On the SS1 & SS322, 12 km inland from sea. The urban sprawl of the Marem-

ma's commercial centre holds few tangible sights for the visitor. Badly mauled in the Second World War, what remains of its historic centre, enclosed within a six-sided Medicean fortress, is lost in a grid of modern streets. Italian towns, however dire, usually have a saving grace; in this case it is the food. *La cucina grossetana*, simple and filling, is some of the best in the Maremma and includes an excellent version of *acquacotta*; artichoke (*carciofi*) risotto; wild boar in a sweet and sour stew (*agrodolce*); and – if you dare – *granelli alla maremmana*, a mixed-fry of ram, calf and horse testicles.

LARDERELLO

On the SS439, 29 km N of Massa Marittima. If you begin to tire of Tuscany's Renaissance treasures, here is the perfect antidote – 60 km of shimmering stainless steel tubes shooting across the landscape, harnessing super-heated underground steam to generate around 500 megawatts of pollution-free power. This corner of the **Colline Metallifere**, the Metal Hills, has a surreal beauty despite the cooling towers and generating plants that dominate the valleys. Larderello takes its name from Francesco de Larderel, a Frenchman who first tapped the local *soffioni* – awesome pools of mud, billowing sulphurous vapours – in 1818, to produce borax. A free **museum**, which is housed in his original works, is filled with sepia photographs of frowsty old aristocrats posing in front of improbable machines and wooden models in glass cases. Nearby, you can peer at a bubbling **soffione**.

If your curiosity is whetted by these volcanic phenomena, head south past the chestnut-clad slopes of **Aia dei Diavoli**, the Devils' Yard, to **Sasso Pisano**, following the yellow signs for the *fumarole e putizze*. Just before the little village, by a car park to the left, you will come across the *fumarole*. At first they resemble nothing more than a smouldering slag heap; at closer quarters you can see that it is a mass of steaming vents in an encrustation of salts. Further along the road, following the signs for Pomerance, plumes of steam (the *putizze* of the signs) begin to appear in the strangest places – from the middle of vegetable plots, vineyards and front gardens.

• *Portoferraio, Elba.*

Neighbours chat over the fence, oblivious to the hiss of steam and the smell of sulphur that hangs in the air.

MASSA MARITTIMA

On the SS439, 20 km inland from sea. Tourist information: Via Parenti 22, by Piazza Garibaldi. Nearest train station 19 km away at Massa-Follonica on main Rome-Pisa line; buses meet trains.

The most attractive town in the Maremma and once one of the most important in the Sienese Republic, Massa Marittima has preserved its medieval glory thanks to the anopheles mosquito. From the close of the 14thC until the surrounding marshes were drained in the 19thC, malaria managed to reduce this once-thriving mining centre to a ghost town. In the Middle Ages, copper and silver mines assured its prosperity and paid for the building of the oldest quarter, the **Città Vecchia**. Its **Duomo**, a masterpiece of the Pisan Romanesque-Gothic style, has to be one of the finest in Tuscany and stands in state on a platform at a dramatic angle to **Piazza Garibaldi**. Amongst the fine carving inside, look out for the monolithic **font** with relief sculpture by Giroldo da Como (1267) and the 14thC Arch of San Cerbone at the side of the main altar.

From the piazza head up steep **Via Moncini** to explore the **Città Nuova**, the higher quarter laid out in 1228, shortly after the city declared itself a free *comune*. Here the finest monument is the **Fortezza dei Senesi**, built as a grandiose symbol of power in the wake of Siena's conquest of the town in 1335. There are plenty of other beguiling sights around town including a **Pinacoteca** in the **Palazzo Pretorio** on Piazza Garibaldi with a *Maestà* by Ambrogio Lorenzetti, and a modern museum dedicated to mining, arranged in a warren of tunnels under the Città Vecchia, which was used as air-raid shelters in the Second World War. The entrance to the **Miniera Museo** is found in Via Corridoni.

POPULONIA
Off the SS1, N of Piombino. Where now stands a medieval *rocca* surrounded by a huddle of houses, once stood Etruscan Pupluna, or Populonia, one of the 12 cities of the Dodecapolis. It built its prosperity in the 3rdC BC by smelting iron ore from Elba, and much of the sprawling **necropolis** that encircles the little Gulf of Baratti lies buried under slag heaps from the ancient furnaces. Although there is not much to see, it is a potent spot for those bitten by curiosity about the Etruscans.

PUNTA ALA
See Castiglione della Pescaia.

SASSO PISANO
See Larderello, page 207.

SUVERETO
See Castagneto Carducci, page 206.

VETULONIA
It was not until the end of the 19thC that the little medieval village of Colonna di Buriano, *just off the SS1 (Via Aurelia) NW of Grosseto*, was discovered to have been the site of **Vetulonia**, another of the 12 cities of the Etruscan Dodecapolis. Since then, excavations have brought to light a great necropolis and the remains of colossal walls. The best finds are now in Florence and much of the rest is in the small local museum that is firmly closed for 'rearrangement'. Still, you can find the great 5thC BC polygonal blocks of stone of the city's oldest **walls** up on the highest part of town, and visit the **necropolis** that lies amidst olive groves 3 km north-east.

> ### SAN GALGANO, ABBAZIA DI
> *Off the SS441, near junction with SS73.* This great French Cistercian abbey built in honour of a local hermit, San Galgano, was once one of the most powerful in Tuscany. Today it is a glorious Gothic ruin, its vast **nave** open to the sun and echoing to the sound of dipping swallows. To the left of the church is a small hill, **Monte Siepi**, crowned with the circular Romanesque church of **San Galgano**. Make the sharp climb in order to see a ravishing **fresco** of the *Madonna Enthroned* by Ambrogio Lorenzetti in the small side chapel, and the curious boulder in the centre of the church. San Galgano, as a sign of his renunciation of the world, is said to have plunged his sword into this rock from whenceforth it served him as an improvized cross.

> ### DETOUR – ROSELLE
> *Off the SS223, 10 km NE of Grosseto.* Perhaps one of the most important cities in northern Etruria and another member of the Dodecapolis, Etruscan Roselle fell to Rome at the end of the 3rdC BC but limped on to the late Middle Ages when it was finally abandoned. You can still see an awesome tract of its original **walls** that reach a height of 5 m and date back to as early as the 6thC BC. Archeological excavations are still underway and have now brought to light substantial remains of the Roman city. Again a fascinating corner if you are following an Etruscan trail.

RECOMMENDED HOTELS

CASTAGNETO CARDUCCI
Zi Martino, LL; *loc. San Giusto* 264; *tel.* 0565 766000; *fax* 0565 763444; *cards accepted.*
A small, comfortable three-star hotel, recently opened by the welcoming owners of the adjoining *trattoria*.

CASTIGLIONE DELLA PESCAIA
Hotel Corallo, LL; *Via N. Sauro* 1; *tel.* 0564 933668; *fax* 0564 936268; *cards accepted.*
Fourteen bedrooms, each with a balcony, air-conditioning and every convenience, attached to a family-run fish restaurant.

ELBA – PORTOFERRAIO
Villa Ombrosa, LL; *Via De Gasperi* 3; *tel.* 0565 914363; *fax* 0565 915672; *cards accepted.*
A quiet hotel, looking out over the Spiaggia delle Ghiaie, not far from Napoleon's Palazzina dei Mulini.

Hotel Bahia, LLL; *loc. Cavoli*; *tel.* 0565 987055; *fax* 0565 987020; *cards accepted.*
A comfortable new 60-bedroom hotel, set in gardens of olive and prickly pear, with friendly service.

MASSA MARITTIMA
Il Sole, LL; *Corso della Libertà* 43; *tel.* 0566 901971; *fax* 0566 901959; *cards accepted.*
Massa's best central hotel.

PUNTA ALA
Piccolo Hotel Alleluja, LLL; *Punta Ala*; *tel.* 0564 922050; *fax* 0564 920734; *cards accepted.*
Despite its name, the most inviting of the resort's four hotels, decorated with stylish rusticity, encircled with Mediterranean *macchia* and complete with pool and tennis court.

RECOMMENDED RESTAURANTS

CAMPIGLIA MARITTIMA
Pizzica, LL; *Piazza della Vittoria* 2; *tel.* 0565 838383; *cards accepted; closed Mon.*
As well as a restaurant, with an eclectic selection of Tuscan dishes, it is also an *enoteca* with an extensive stock of Tuscan wines.

CASTAGNETO CARDUCCI
Zi Martino, L; *loc. San Giusto* 262; *tel.* 0565 763666; *cards accepted; closed Mon.*
A chance to taste honest Tuscan food at more than honest prices.

CASTIGLIONE DELLA PESCAIA
Hotel Corallo, LL-LLL; *Via N. Sauro* 1; *tel.* 0564 933668; *cards accepted; closed Tues.*
The inventive menu is based around fish, varying according to the daily catch, accompanied by an extensive choice of Tuscan wines.

ELBA – CAPOLIVERI
Il Chiasso, LL; *Via N. Sauro, Capoliveri*; *tel.* 0565 968709; *cards accepted; closed Tues.*
Reckoned by many to be the island's best for both its cooking and atmosphere; excellent value, too.

Luciano, LL; *loc. Scaglieri della Biodola, Portoferraio*; *tel.* 0565 969952; *cards accepted; closed Wed.*
An interesting menu, particularly the fishy *antipasti*. Overlooks the Golfo della Biodola.

Rendez-Vous da Marcello, LL; *Piazza della Vittoria* 1, *Marciana Marina*; *tel..* 0565 99251; *cards accepted; closed Wed in winter.*
Well known for a triad of *antipasti* called La Brasiliana, Il Tronchetto and La Patata di Marcello, followed by excellent fish *secondi*.

GROSSETO
Osteria del Ponte Rotto, LL; *Via Scansanese* 36; *tel.* 0564 409373; *cards accepted; closed Wed.*
The best *cucina grossetana*, on the banks of the River Ombrone.

MASSA MARITTIMA
Robust *massetano* dishes and a few imports from **Enoteca Grassini**, (**L**; *Via della Libertà* 1; *tel.* 0566 940149; *cards accepted; closed Sun*); another sound choice for genuine local cooking is **Taverna del Vecchio Borgo** (**LL**; *Via Parenti* 12; *tel.* 0566 903950; *cards accepted; closed Sun eve and Mon.*)

Local Explorations: 9

<u>Umbria-Marche Appennines</u>

Gubbio and its Mountains

160 km; map Touring Club Italiano Umbria & Marche

A chance to get away from the plains and up into the mountains that divide Central Italy: to exchange your city shoes for a pair of hiking boots and explore some of the natural beauty of this relatively remote part of Central Italy; or, if you wish, to swap the claustrophobia of the art gallery for that of Italy's most famous caves. This is an area to explore if you want to get a feel for what life was like in the region a century ago.

The route takes in a pair of outstanding Umbrian towns, Gubbio and Città di Castello, but for most of the way forsakes high culture in search of the simple pleasures of a string of lesser-known towns and villages in majestic settings amongst the Appennine peaks of the region.

As you thread your way under looming crags, past densely wooded hills, across farmland divided into pinched strips of field, squeezing through threatening limestone gorges, and just once crossing a mountain pass (at a modest 700 m), the Appennines remain the central ever-changing feature of the tour. Rising to a maximum of 1,700 m, these are no giants in comparison to the Alps or the Gran Sasso, further south. Instead, the majesty is altogether gentler – and the roads are relatively easy and rarely crowded.

Once away from the Tiber Valley, the pastures are poorly suited to intensive modern farming. Farms are small and ill-constructed, reflecting the poverty which blighted the area until the 1970s. The strips of barley or maize, divided up by single rows of vines, recall the centuries-old system of *mezzadria*, still a bitter memory for many of the older farmers, by which the peasant had to give half of his meagre produce to his *padrone* in return for the use of the land.

On the remoter stretches of the route, the main livelihood is the cutting of the forest covering the mountain slopes for firewood. In a few villages, the ancient trade of charcoal burning still continues.

UMBRIA-MARCHE APPENNINES / *Gubbio and its Mountains*

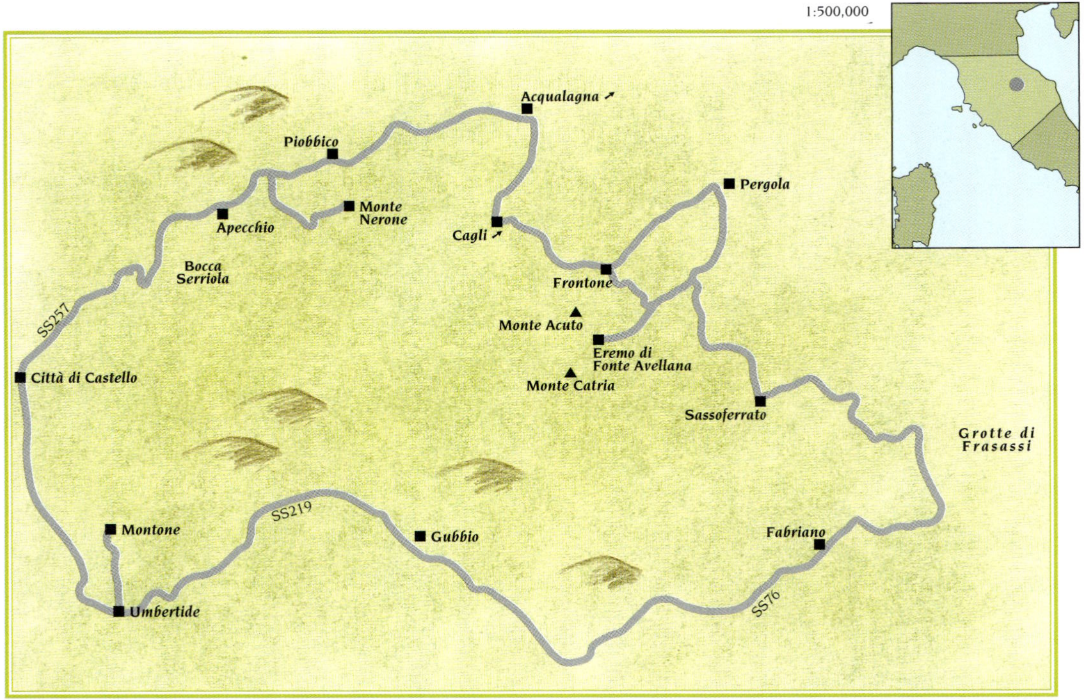

TRANSPORT

A car is the ideal way to make the most of this mountainous area, but you could get by on public transport. The Upper Tiber Valley, in which lie Città di Castello and Umbertide, is an important transport artery served by regular bus and train services from Perugia. Buses from Perugia will also get you to Gubbio, as will trains to Fossato di Vico (regular connecting buses for Gubbio) on the main Rome-Ancona line.
Across the mountains, Fabriano also lies on the Rome-Ancona line, from which an infrequent branch-line service takes you to Sassoferrato and Pergola.
For the remainder of the circuit, local bus services link town to town, often coinciding with school starting and finishing hours.
The nearest airports are Perugia and Ancona, neither of them on international routes, though there are some charter flights serving Ancona in summer.

1:500,000

Local Explorations: 9

SIGHTS & PLACES OF INTEREST

ACQUALAGNA
See *Seeing the Region*: 4, *page* 120.

APECCHIO
On SS257, 28 km NE of Città di Castello. This dour mountain village with a strong medieval stamp nestles deep in the Appennines. No great monuments, but plenty of local colour. In the mountains around, charcoal burners still build their fires and the wrinkled elderly widows who linger in the streets look as if they are from a movie set. Best sights are the hump-back **medieval bridge** and the extensive cellars of **Palazzo Ubaldini** which house a fossil museum.

Around 4 km north-east of Apecchio on the SS257 follow the sign off to **Monte Nerone**: the road snakes up to the peak of this craggy limestone mountain. On the way, pause to see the **Mappamondo**, the world's largest globe. Even if you don't turn off, you can catch sight of it from the road, high up on a crag.

The man who built it is currently arguing with the local authority over a little matter of planning permission: his latest ploy is to build the world's largest string of rosary beads.

South-east of Apecchio the SS257 winds its way to Città di Castello over the **Bocca Serriola**, a wild but not excessively high pass (730 m) over the Appennines.

BOCCA SERRIOLA
See *Apecchio, above*.

CAGLI
See *Seeing the Region*: 4, *page* 123.

CITTÀ DI CASTELLO ⊷ ✕
On SS3bis, 17 km S of Sansepolcro. Tourist information: Viale De Cesare 2/b. Station; Piazza Repubblica, SE of town, served by the local Ferrovia Centrale Umbra which runs from Sansepolcro down to Perugia. Regular bus service from Arezzo S along the SS3bis from Piazza Garibaldi (which is just outside walls to the E). Parking: best to leave car at one of the gates through the city walls - Piazza Garibaldi to E is convenient.

Umbria's northernmost town lies on the plains of the Upper Tiber Valley, hemmed in by well-preserved early 16thC walls. Once the important Roman town of *Tifernum Tiberinum* (its inhabitants are still known as *tifernati*), it was razed to the ground in 542 by the Gothic King Totila. Not until the mid-15thC was the city resurrected, with the rise to power of the Vitelli family. Their enlightened rule drew artists such as Raphael and Luca Signorelli. The Vitelli's reign, however, was short-lived: in 1502 Vitellozzo Vitelli was invited by Cesare Borgia to a banquet where he was inhospitably strangled between courses. From then on it remained in the hands of the Papal States until the Unification of Italy.

Città di Castello's best offering is the **Pinacoteca Comunale**, both for its collection and the building itself. You'll find it on the southern edge of town (Via della Cannoniera 22) in one of the three Vitelli palaces here. Look out for the florid **sgraffito** decorations on the garden front designed by Vasari, and the exuberant **frescoes** by Cristofano Gherardi that embellish the **monumental staircase**. The best works that Raphael painted for the town were plundered by Napoleon and only a much damaged processional **standard** by him remains. The real glory of the gallery, however, is the **Martyrdom of St Sebastian** (about 1498) by Luca Signorelli, whose skill at drawing the human figure prefigured Michelangelo. There are a number of other outstanding pictures and grandly frescoed rooms to distract your attention.

Hunt out the **Museo Capitolare** next door to the Baroque-fronted **Duomo** on the main **Corso Cavour** to admire the *Tesoro di Canoscio*, a remarkably early set of liturgical silver dating from the 7thC, and a glittering silver-gilt 12thC altarfront. The town's most handsome palace stands beside the Duomo - the severe Late Gothic **Palazzo dei Priori** (1322-38). Its striking similarity to Gubbio's magnificent Palazzo dei Consuli is easily explained – the same architect, Angelo da Orvieto, designed them both. Alberto Burri (1915-95), one of Italy's most important 20thC artists, was born here and some 200 of his works are on show in **Palazzo Albizzini** on Via Albizzini. His abstract expressionist canvasses built up from such things as torn sacking and tar have a haunting, melancholy impact. In 1990 the artist donated larger, more recent works that are dramatically displayed in the converted **Seccatoi Tabacchi**, or tobacco drying sheds, in Via Francesco Pierucci.

At Villa Garavelle, 2 km from the town centre on the road for Perugia, is the **Museo delle Tradizioni Populari**, one of Central Italy's better museums dedicated to rural life in bygone ages. There is also an unlikely **model railway collection**, a legacy from the villa's previous owner.

FABRIANO ⇔ ×
On the SS76, 34 km E of Gubbio. Even back in the 14thC, Fabriano's **paper mills** were producing a million sheets of paper a year and it was here that watermarked paper was invented. Its paper is still used the world over for banknotes and quality art paper. So proud is the town of its traditional industry that it has dedicated an interesting modern museum to it – you'll find the **Museo della Carta** in the former monastery of San Domenico to the south of the town on Largo Fratelli Spacca. The best place to buy Fabriano paper is **Antica Cartoleria Lotti** under the portico of the Palazzo Comunale. While the industrial sprawl of the suburbs promises little, it is worth penetrating to the heart of the town to see the opera-set main **Piazza del Comune** flanked by the Gothic **Palazzo del Podestà** with swallow-tail battlements. Centre-stage is a smaller version of Perugia's famous **fountain** built at the close of the 13thC.

The town was the birthplace of Gentile da Fabriano, Italy's greatest master of the late 14thC International Gothic style of painting. You will have to make do, however, with works by his followers, best of whom was Allegretto di Nuzio – you can find his work in the **Pinacoteca Comunale** in tiny **Piazza Umberto I** behind the main square, and in the **Duomo** next door. Also in the Duomo are some handsome **frescoes** by Orazio Gentileschi, a 17thC follower of Caravaggio who ended his days as court painter to King Charles I of England.

FONTE AVELLANA, MONASTERY OF
Best road (17 km) from Pergola via Serra San Abbondio; shorter from Frontone but a rougher ride. On the flanks of **Monte Catria**, the **Monastery of Fonte Avellana** was founded in 980, visited by Dante in 1310, and once presided over by St Peter Damian. Its setting in the high mountains is breathtaking. One of the handful of the remaining aged Camaldolesi monks will show you the fine vaulted *scriptorium,* where monks copied out manuscripts, and the Dante Alighieri **Library** with rows of rare *Seicento* books.

GROTTE DI FRASASSI (FRASASSI CAVES)
10 km E of Sassoferrato, well signposted. Make for the plunging Frasassi Gorge for a 'journey to the centre of the Earth' through the **Grotte di Frasassi**, Italy's largest and most famous complex of caves. Some 13 km of limestone caverns have so far been explored and it is reckoned that they may run for up to 35 km. Only one and a half km of this crystalline wonderland is open to the public. Equipped with walkways and theatrical lighting, it includes the awesome **Grotta Grande del Vento**, so vast that Milan Cathedral would fit comfortably inside, and some of the most extravagantly fanciful **stalagmites and stalactites** you are ever likely to see. The guided tour lasts for around an hour; dress warmly as the temperature inside is a constantly low 14°C.

Even if you don't have time to see the caves, stop to admire the splendid backdrop of the **Frasassi Gorge** and the Romanesque **church** in the little spa of **San Vittore delle Chiuse** (right by the cave ticket office and car park). This tiny, perfectly square *chiesetta* was built in the 12thC on chastely simple lines and is one of the prettiest of its kind in the Marche. (To see inside ask for the keys at the tobacconist's opposite.) Some guidebooks still talk enthusiastically of another fine dramatic limestone gorge nearby called the **Gola della Rossa**: it is now an enormous quarry. In a region sorely blighted by quarries, it must be the worst example of this type of 20thC vandalism.

FRONTONE ×
Off the SS424, half-way between Cagli and Pergola. Above the shapeless modern village stands a steep hill with just enough room on top for an imposing **castle** and medieval **borghetto**. As the last of a string of natural defences running from the sea to the impassable Appennines, it has been fortified since

the pre-Roman times, when the Eugubines (from Gubbio) dominated the region. The well-restored **rocca** once helped to defend the southern border of the Duke of Montefeltro's lands and some consider the triangular tower at the western end to be the work of Duke Federico's favourite architect, Francesco di Giorgio Martini.

This windswept look-out (note the size of the rocks on the roofs to stop the tiles blowing off) gives a splendid prospect of the surrounding mountains, dominated by **Monte Catria** (1,700 m) and **Monte Acuto** (1,527 m). Having dubbed itself the *Little Switzerland of the Marches* the town built a chairlift to the top of **Monte Acuto** in the late 1970s, since when it has rusted away, unused. You can drive up to the top of these twin peaks from Frontone; the journey is especially rewarding in May and June when the Alpine flora on the upland meadowlands is in full flower.

GUBBIO ⚔ ✕

On the SS219. Tourist information: Piazza Oderisi 6 (on Corso Garibaldi). Nearest station 20 km away at Fossato di Vico; connecting bus service to Gubbio. Regular bus service to/from Perugia. Large free car park by Roman Amphitheatre.

Bare-boned Gubbio is amongst Italy's finest embodiments of a late medieval city. Stacked up on the terraces of steep Monte Ingino, its ashen palaces and churches stand warily aloof from the fertile plains below, little changed from the early 14thC, when most of its fine buildings were erected. But the noted bronze Eugubine Tablets (see Palazzo dei Consoli museum, pages 215-18) bear witness to the city's ancient roots as one of the oldest Umbrian centres.

Roman *Iguvium*, destroyed by the Goths in the 6thC, extended further into the plain where the ruins of the Augustan **amphitheatre** now stand. During the 12th and 13thC it managed to keep its head high as a free city state, despite the arrival in 1155 of Frederick Barbarossa: his threat to destroy the city was only averted by the intervention of its bishop, San Ubaldo, now Gubbio's patron saint. In 1376, to escape the clutches of a local tyrant, the city gave itself to the Montefeltro Lords of Urbino who ruled until the Duchy of Urbino was handed over to the Papal States in 1631.

As you arrive you will probably find yourself at the foot of the town in **Piazza Quaranta Martiri**, whose name commemorates 40 citizens killed in Nazi reprisals. From here follow narrow **Via Cavour** hemmed in by towering palaces built of Gubbio's steely-grey limestone. You will find yourself at the bottom of the town's finest street, **Via dei Consoli**. As you climb past rather too many souvenir and fancy food shops, note the small arched door next to the main entrance of many of the palaces. Known as a **porta del morto** (door of the dead), this was once thought to have been a ceremonial doorway only used when residents made their last exit, as corpses, from the house. Nowadays the doors are reckoned to have had a defensive purpose, as an easily defendable entrance

---

FRANCIS AND THE WOLF

The name of St Francis of Assisi is inextricably linked with Gubbio thanks to the legend of the Wolf of Gubbio. The celebrated early account of the saint's life, the *Little Flowers of St Francis*, recounts how a singularly large and fierce wolf was terrorizing the town and indiscriminately including both animals and townsfolk in its diet. St Francis, who happened to be staying here at the time, decided to take the matter in hand and sallied forth to the animal's lair to negotiate a truce. Cowed by the saint's stern words, the wolf agreed to mend his anti-social ways in exchange for assurances that he would be regularly fed by the people of Gubbio until he died. The pact was sealed with a paw shake. The animal then lived for two years in Gubbio, tamely going from door to door, until it died of old age. Tradition has it that a little Franciscan church in Via Savelli della Porta stands on the site of the grotto where the wolf lived after its conversion and was buried with full honours. It is alleged that the skeleton of a giant wolf was unearthed there early in the 20thC, but no one quite remembers what happened to the bones.

Near Gubbio.

when the main door was barricaded up. In a little *largo* or small square half way up Via dei Consoli is the delightful **Palazzo del Bargello**, perhaps Gubbio's most elegant small 14thC palace and home to the city's medieval police chief. In front is a tinkling Renaissance fountain, known as the **Fountain of the Mad** – popular tradition holds that if you run around it enough times you are guaranteed to go crazy.

Carry on up and you arrive at Gubbio's glory, the **Piazza della Signoria**. Built as a great balcony out over the town, it is shored up by enormous **arches** (take the road that runs below the square to see the true might of the structure). Standing to one side is the gaunt **Palazzo dei Consoli**, one of the finest medieval civic buildings in all Italy. Built of bone-white, clean-cut blocks of local stone, approached by a majestic flight of fan-shaped **steps**, and crowned with an elegant **bell tower**, it was erected between 1332 and 1349 to designs by the architect Angelo da Orvieto. The great sombre interior guards the town's **museum and art gallery**. Here you can examine the celebrated **Eugubine Tablets**, seven

RECOMMENDED HOTELS

CITTÀ DI CASTELLO
Tiferno, LL; Piazza Raffaello Sanzio 13; tel. 075 8550331; fax 075 8521196; cards accepted; closed second half of July.
The best in town, a smart, old-fashioned four-star hotel in a dignified old palace in the heart of the *centro storico*. Always popular, so make sure you book well ahead.

Le Mura, LL; Via Borgo Farinario; tel. 075 8521070; fax 075 8521350; cards accepted.
A new hotel in an old shell next to the *Pinacoteca*. Honest prices, courteous staff, and a three-minute walk from the centre make it highly recommendable. Double glazing in the 35 rooms assures quiet.

FABRIANO
Aristos, LL; Via Cavour 103; tel. 0732 22308; fax 0732 21459; cards none; closed part of Sept.
Intimate three-star hotel with just eight rooms, to east of old town and convenient for centre.

Old Ranch, L-LL; loc. Piaggia d'Olmo (2 km from centre - take road W for Sassoferrato then right on small road for Cantia); tel. and fax 0732 627610; cards accepted; closed July.
A country house restaurant in the hills with acclaimed cooking (see Recommended Restaurants, page 217). Its nine bedrooms are in various outbuildings around the park – it is much more relaxing than staying in the centre of town.

Janus, LL-LLL; Piazza Matteotti 45; tel. 0732 4191; fax 0732 5714; cards accepted; closed most of Aug.
Big, four-star hotel by large car park at eastern gate through city walls. Professional, but just a touch anonymous – more for businessmen than tourists.

GUBBIO
Gubbio boasts a surprising number of excellent hotels and plenty of visitors, so it is necessary to telephone or fax ahead.

Park Hotel ai Cappuccini, LLL; Via Tifernate; tel. 075 9234; fax 075 9220323; cards accepted.
Gubbio's smartest hotel, but out on a limb to the west of town. Top-class service and the choicest *modernissimo* decorative style in an enchanting converted monastery make up for its inconvenient location (see Recommended Restaurants, page 217).

Bosone, LL; Via XX Settembre 22; tel. 075 9220688; fax 075 9220552; cards accepted.
Solid comfort, unchanged for decades, in this central but peaceful small traditional *albergo*. A place where you'd happily return.

Villa Montegranelli, LL; loc. Monteluiano (4 km SW of town down Via Buozzi); tel. 075 9220185; fax 075 9273372; cards accepted.
A superb hotel in an elegant 18thC villa with handsome grounds. Not cheap, but excellent value for what you pay. Its restaurant is one of the best in the area (see Recommended Restaurants, page 217).

RECOMMENDED RESTAURANTS

Most restaurants in this area pride themselves on sticking to local traditional cooking. The grander establishments offer old favourites 'reinterpreted'. Truffles abound, as do game, excellent salamis and hams, imaginative stuffed pasta, and the occasional cut of wild boar and wild mushrooms in the autumn. Even in Gubbio, prices have still not hit the heights of those charged in Tuscany.

CITTÀ DI CASTELLO
Amici Miei, LL; Via del Monte 2; tel. 075 8559904; cards accepted; closed Wed.
Family-run restaurant with a refined atmosphere in the cellars of a 16thC palace. Uninhibited reinterpretation of regional cooking with such dishes as pasta stuffed with radicchio and pork

fillet with capers.

Il Bersaglio, LL; Via V.E. Orlando 14; tel. 075 855534; cards accepted; closed Wed.

Strictly Umbrian menu at this slightly cheaper-than-average place south of centre on road to Umbertide.

FABRIANO
Old Ranch, LL; loc. Piaggia d'Olmo, (2 km from centre - take road west for Sassoferrato then right on small road for Cantia); tel. 0732 627610; cards accepted; closed Tues and July.

Country house restaurant with rooms (see Recommended Hotels, page 216) in the hills above Fabriano. Great home-made pasta and an acclaimed *fritto misto* (mixed fried meats and vegetables). Tables in garden in summer.

Villa del Grillo, LL-LLL; loc. Rocchetta (5 km NE of centre); tel. 0732 625690; cards accepted; closed Sun eve and Mon.

Rustic elegance in a lovingly restored 18thC villa. Outstanding menu that wavers between the best traditional cooking and refined international dishes. High standards, but value for money.

FRONTONE
Taverna della Rocca, L; Via Leopardi 20 (up in Frontone Castello); tel. 0721 786109; cards none; closed Wed.

The better of the pair of restaurants below the castle, in what was once the stables. Utterly basic peasant food, but well prepared and cheap – home-made pasta and a super-abundance of charcoal-grilled meat.

Il Daino, L-LL; Via Roma 19; tel. 0721 786101; cards accepted ; closed Mon.

Simple setting in the modern village below the castle but exceptionally good local cooking with the best ingredients – in season wild boar and game. Their *coratella d'agnello* (a sauté of lamb offal) sounds off-putting but is truly delicious..

GUBBIO
Ample choice of good if pricey restaurants, with the grandest trying to outdo each other in dishes laced with the area's plentiful black truffles.

Taverna del Lupo, LLL; Via Ansidei 21; tel. 075 9274368; cards accepted; closed Mon.

My favourite choice in Gubbio for a special occasion. Ultra-refined versions of Eugubine dishes with a blowout menu *degustazione*. Restrained elegance, medieval vaulting.

Park Hotel ai Cappuccini, LLL; Via Tifernate; tel. 075 9234; cards accepted; closed Mon.

Although out of town, the modern classy restaurant at this excellent hotel (see Recommended Hotels, page 216) is well worth the trip. The finest local ingredients turned into imaginative dishes.

Bargello, L-LL; Via dei Consoli 37; tel. 075 9273724; cards accepted; closed Mon.

Opposite Palazzo del Bargello, this popular restaurant and *pizzeria* in an ancient cellar is the place if you are on a tight budget. Excellent *primi* and pizzas from a wood-fired oven.

Villa Montegranelli, LLL; loc. Monteluiano (4 km SW of town down Via Buozzi); tel. 075 9220185; cards accepted.

Acclaimed cooking in an elegant 18thC villa with handsome grounds. Accent on imaginative treatment of Umbrian classics with moments of inspired fantasy such as pasta with chicken livers, marrow flowers and apple. Also has rooms (see Recommended Hotels, page 216).

bronze plates, dug up in 1444 near the Roman amphitheatre, with some of the only inscriptions ever found in the ancient Umbrian language. As this tribal tongue never appears to have had written characters, it is here rendered phonetically using the Etruscan alphabet (on the four 2ndC BC plates); the inscriptions appear in Latin on the later 1stC BC plates. The text describes arcane religious rituals and has provided some of the few insights to Italy's pre-Roman history and languages. Pictures to look out for are examples of Gubbio's very own early school of painting led by **Ottaviano Nelli**. There are two curiosities: the score of 14thC **latrines** dotted about the palace, and the 18thC anonymous **portrait** of a man in the act of making the supremely rude Italian gesture with the left hand in the crook of the right arm.

Follow the signs for the Duomo, climbing the steep steps of **Via Ducale**, pausing to glance down through an iron grating at the enormous 16thC wooden barrel in the cellar half way up. At the top of the alley are the **Palazzo Ducale** and the **Duomo**. If you have visited Urbino (Seeing the Region: 2, pages 104-5), no prizes for guessing who were responsible for the Ducal Palace. Its noble courtyard could have only been built by Francesco di Giorgio Martini for Duke Federico da Montefeltro. After years of neglect, the interior of this urbane Renaissance palace is undergoing thorough restorations which look set to run for years.

For such a special town, the time-worn Duomo is disappointing and need not detain you. Better to search out the church of **Santa Maria Nuova** at the end of Via Savelli della Porta to see the early 15thC fresco of the **Madonna del Belvedere**, the acknowledged masterpiece of Ottaviano Nelli.

Close by (you won't miss the signs) is the **Funivia**, a shaky-looking chairlift that will whisk you to the top of **Monte Ingino** and the **Basilica** dedicated to the town's patron, San Ubaldo. The celebrated race of the *Tre Ceri* on the saint's feast day (May 15), when three teams of burly citizens race up here from the town bearing the three enormous wooden *ceri* (literally candles), ranks with Siena's *Palio* as an outstanding example of Italian festive collective madness. When not in use, the *ceri* are kept in the Basilica.

If you can't face a return journey on the *funivia*, a winding downhill path through the woods will take you back to the centre.

In Renaissance times the city was famed for its fine **painted ceramics**, a tradition still carried on today: you will find plenty of excellent examples of this brightly-coloured *maiolica* ware in the shops on Via dei Consoli.

MONTE ACUTO, MONTE CATRIA, MONTE NERONE
See Frontone, pages 213-14, Fonte Avellana, page 213 and Apecchio, page 212.

MONTONE
Between Città di Castello and Umbertide, a 6-km detour off the SS3bis dual-carriageway. Here is an archetypal medieval Umbrian hill village celebrated as the home base of the Fortebraccio family who produced a pair of Italy's most celebrated *condottiere* (mercenary generals). There is no single outstanding sight, but lashings of Umbrian charm. In summer, visitors fill the pinched cobbled streets and the place has recently been gripped by a fever of restoration work. In 1473 Carlo Fortebraccio, then General to the Venetian Army, bequeathed to the town its most treasured possession, a **spine** from Christ's Crown of Thorns which is still paraded through the streets with much ceremony on Easter Monday.

PERGOLA
On the SS424, 20 km E of Cagli. This shapely small town set in the vineyard-dotted valley of the Cesano has a refined and distinctly 18thC air. It also had – and might again have the celebrated **Bronzi Dorati**. These extraordinary Roman gilded bronze equestrian statues, found near Pergola in 1946 and dating from the 1stC AD, are at the centre of a long-running row between the town council, which wants to keep them here, and the regional authorities, which have prepared a special room for them at the archaeological museum in Ancona. For a number of years, the Pergolesi actually bricked them up out of everyone's reach in an old convent. At the time of writing they have been taken off to Florence for 'restoration', and no one knows where or when they will return. In the meantime, console your-

UMBRIA-MARCHE APPENNINES / *Gubbio and its Mountains*

Traditional ceramics, Gubbio.

self with an ice cream at the *Gelateria Antica* in the main **Corso**, or try a bottle or two of *Vernaccia*, a heavily perfumed purple wine peculiar to the town. The Saturday **market** is a particularly lively example of the Marche country market.

PIOBBICO

On the SS257, 10 km E of Apecchio. Ignore the small modern nucleus along the main road and make for the higher end of town where you'll find a splendid **castle** and the **borghetto**, a cluster of crumbling medieval houses clinging like limpets to the surrounding hillside. Originally built in the 13thC by the ruling Brancaleoni family, the castle was given an elegant Renaissance facelift in the 1570s. After years of sad neglect, it is now being restored – a large portion is complete and open to the public between June and September at weekends. Even when closed, it's worth walking up to peer into the courtyard.

The town is celebrated in Italy for being home to the *Club dei Brutti*, an association for the world's downtrodden uglies – their motto reads 'Ugliness is a virtue; beauty is slavery'.

SASSOFERRATO

18 km S of Pergola. A prosperous little town watched over by a solid **citadel** and a medieval *borgo* high on a ridge above the modern sprawl. Follow the museum signs to wind up to the top, park and stroll through the hushed cobbled streets, past a fine Gothic Franciscan church to arrive at intimate **Piazza Matteotti** with its elegant arcades. The palace with the double ramp staircase, **Palazzo dei Priori**, houses the best finds from the Roman city of *Sentinum* which lay just to the south of the present town (ask at the nearby *biblioteca comunale* to see the **Museo Archeologico**; *closed Sun*).

The **scavi archeologici** (ruins of Sentinum) just south of town are strictly for the expert and difficult to find – blink as you drive past and you'll miss them. The Museo delle Tradizioni Popolari (a collection of old farm implements) and the modern art gallery are being reorganized – this may take many years.

Some 4 km out of town on the road for Genga and the Frasassi Caves (see page 213), look out for the huge building in the form of an ocean liner beached on the hillside – an architectural folly in dubious taste, which has become a restaurant.

UMBERTIDE

On the SS3bis dual-carriageway, 20 km S of Città di Castello. The ugly sprawl of factories along the approaches to this old town don't make for favourable first impressions. It's worth pausing, though, to see the historic centre, if only to admire a fine painting in the church of **Santa Croce** – a moving **Deposition** by Luca Signorelli. The sturdy 14thC **rocca**, or castle, can be visited, but for no very good reason.

Local Explorations: 10

The Marches

Inland from Ancona – Hill Towns of the Central Marche

176 km; map Touring Club Italiano Umbria Marche

The corrugated valleys that score the heartland of the Marche have been cut by rushing torrents that run down from the Appennines to the Adriatic Sea. If you follow this route, you'll see some of the most outstanding stately small towns that lie on the heights above these rivers, stoutly walled places that once guarded the fertile valleys below. You will have to grapple briefly with the worst of a modern city if you decide to stop at frantic Ancona, the regional capital and a spicy sea port. But the finest coastline on the Northern Adriatic awaits you on the nearby Conero Riviera.

Exploring this area is a tantalizing experience. From the crest of every hill you will see medieval fortified villages stretching off to the horizon. Yet once away from the straight roads which follow the valley bottoms, the lanes leading to even the major towns meander along the natural contours until you begin to wonder whether they have any real intention of getting you there at all.

Take it slowly and savour the mellow charm of this land, ordered by man for centuries, gridded with vineyards which produce Verdicchio wines; stop off, perhaps, at some of the smaller villages, too numerous to have their praises sung individually.

Each town has its own particular mark, sometimes a religious shrine or a festival, sometimes a clutch of masterpieces by the great Venetian painter Lorenzo Lotto, who spent much of his life working in the area. All have their own jealously-guarded, distinctive character. To this day, the Italian concept of *campanilismo* – the absolute belief in the supremacy of your native town and scorn for those that stand across the valley – is hardly more manifest than in these *marchigiani* foothills. Perhaps the reason for the poor communications here is not simply geographical.

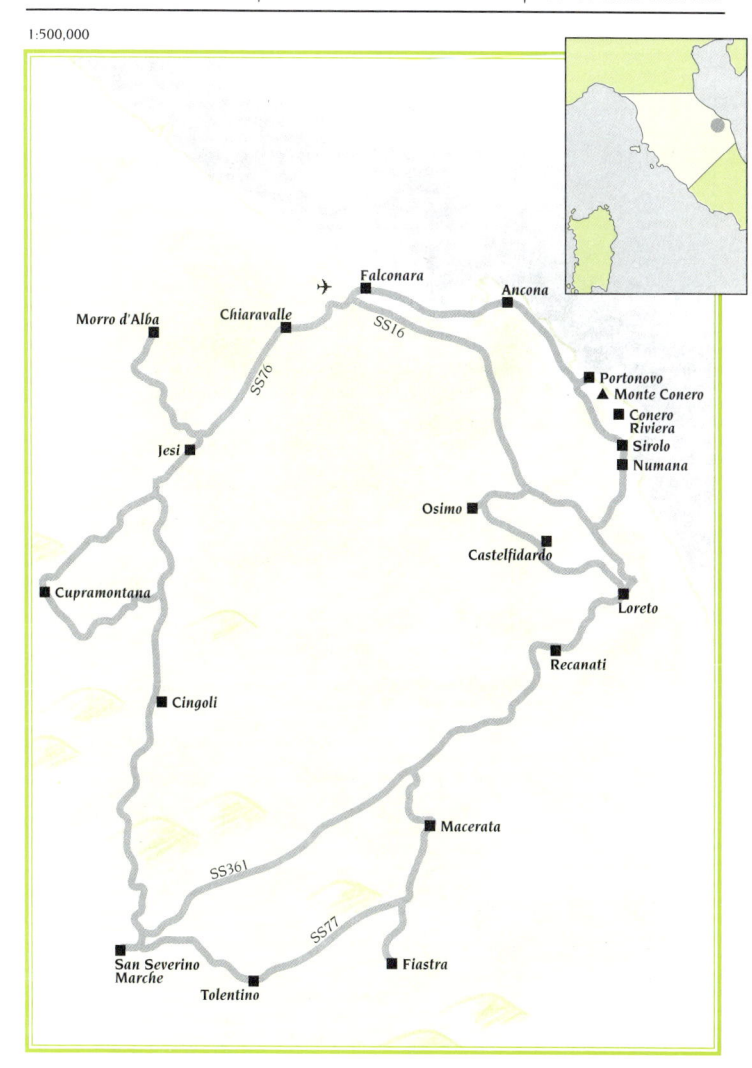

THE MARCHES / *Inland from Ancona – Hill Towns of the Central Marche*

1:500,000

TRANSPORT

Ancona is the main crossroads for public transport: its railway station stands at the junction of two important lines. The coastal mainline links the southern ports of Brindisi and Bari with Bologna, Milan and several international destinations, while a second line heads inland, stopping at Falconara, Jesi and Fabriano before crossing the Appennines and on to Rome.

Bus services from Ancona's Piazza Stamira link most of the towns on the route.

Down at Ancona's port, six ferry lines will take you and your car to the Greek mainland and islands, and to Turkey. In peacetime, this is the most important ferry port for former Yugoslavia.

The narrow coastal road along the Conero Riviera is best avoided in July and August. Away from the sea and Ancona, the roads are excellent and generally quiet.

Ancona's airport, 10 km to the north-west at Falconara, handles cut-price international charter flights from May to September.

• *San Ciriaco.*

SIGHTS & PLACES OF INTEREST

ANCONA ⇌ ✕

Exit Ancona Nord or Sud from A14 motorway. Tourist information: Stazione Centrale west of port and at ferry terminal in summer. Frequent trains run on both main Milan-Bari and Rome-Ancona lines. Ferries to Venice, Bari, Greece, Turkey and, in better times, to former Yugoslavia: information and bookings at Stazione Marittima on port. Bus terminal serving most places on this itinerary and a number of Italy's main cities in central Piazza Stamira. Air terminal for Raffaello Sanzio Airport (Ancona) at Piazza Roma 21. Parking difficult – a nightmare in the morning – expensive but central underground car park at Piazza Stamira usually has space (well signposted until you get near).

Many visitors are only too happy to bid *addio* to Ancona, the capital of the Marche and the largest city in the region. Badly bombed in the Second World War and brought to its knees by a major earthquake in 1972, it has few remaining monuments from its long history and many of its cracked buildings still await a face-lift. Give it time, though, and you may, like me, acquire a taste for the salt and spice of this restless sea port.

Built on two hills that form an amphitheatre around the harbour, it was settled in the 4thC BC by Greek colonists from Syracuse. Later, the Romans exploited its sheltered anchorage and in 115 AD, under Emperor Trajan, the present harbour walls were raised: the stately ceremonial marble **arch** standing forlornly at the end of the docks marks his achievement.

In the Middle Ages, the forces of the German Emperors, the Church and the Venetian Republic each made sure that Ancona was never able to establish itself as a powerful maritime republic. In 1532 it slid compliantly into the hands of the Papal States where it remained until the Unification of Italy.

The oldest part of town straddles **Colle Guasco**, the hill above the port. On its peak, high above the agitation of the modern city, stands Ancona's finest church and its most obvious landmark, the medieval **Cathedral of San Ciriaco**, a pleasing mix of Romanesque and Gothic styles. The austere interior is picked out with exotic Byzantine touches, a painted wooden **roof** in the form of an upturned boat, and a soaring 12-sided **cupola** – a place in which to linger when the summer heat becomes unbearable. In the crypt you can glimpse the remains of an ancient pagan **temple** that provided the foundation for the church.

To see the rest of the best, avoid the squalid area around the railway station and start your walk from the bottom of **Corso Stamira** down by the ferry docks. After noting the Venetian-Gothic façade of the ruined church of **San Agostino**, cut across to nearby **Piazza della Repubblica** where **Corso Garibaldi** and **Corso Mazzini** begin – these two *corsi* complete the city's trinity of parallel main streets. The grimy 19thC **Teatro delle Muse** that boxes in the square has been *in restauro* for so long that no one can remember what it's like inside.

From here take a brief detour up Corso Mazzini to see the 16thC **Fontana del Calamo**, a regimented row of 13 masked spouts. Next to the fountain is my favourite port of call, a **kiosk** that sells oysters and other fresh shellfish to be eaten standing up with a class of dry white wine or sparkling *prosecco*, a great restorative.

Back down in Piazza della Repubblica, amble along **Via della Loggia** to see the statue-decked **Loggia dei Mercanti**, an outstanding example of florid Late Venetian-Gothic (the influence of Venice is never very far away here). Further on is the singular 13thC front of **Santa Maria della Piazza**:

• *Opposite: Church of Santa Maria, Conero Riviera.*

THE MARCHES / *Inland from Ancona – Hill Towns of the Central Marche*

Local Explorations: 10

rows of blind arches and plenty of fidgety carving. Inside, a glass panel has been set into the pavement allowing you to see the **remains** of the even older church below.

From Via della Loggia walk up to **Piazza del Plebiscito**, ruled over by a resplendent if cracked **statue** of Pope Clement XII. Over his shoulder is the Neoclassical church of **San Domenico** with a stirring **Titian** *Crucifixion* above the high altar. As you climb up from the square on Via Pizzecolli you are in the heart of the oldest part of the city. **Palazzo Bosdari**, at No. 17, guards Ancona's **Pinacoteca**: paintings to look for here are Crivelli's chilly *Madonna and Child*, Titian's *Virgin with Child and Saints*, and Lorenzo Lotto's *Sacra Conversazione*.

Further up Via Pizzecolli you can rest your legs as you admire the bird's-eye views of the port from **Piazza Stracca**. A few paces on is **Palazzo Ferretti**, home of the **Museo Archeologico delle Marche**, an outstanding collection of antique nick-nacks – black and red Attic **vases**, Etruscan **bronzes**, Iron Age **jewellery**. Most guide books tell you that the **Bronzi Dorati**, a group of celebrated Roman equestrian statues, are *in restauro*, but see Pergola (Local Explorations: 9, pages 218-19) for the real story.

As you wind onwards and upwards through deserted Piazza del Senato and up Via Giovanni XXIII you will catch glimpses of the ruins of the **Roman amphitheatre** behind – dilatory digging has been going on for years and one day it may be worth stopping to look. A last effort and you are on the summit of **Colle Guasco**, with breathtaking views out to sea and the white, wind-blown face of the cathedral behind you. Now take a sprightly walk back down to the town for a fish lunch or oysters by the fountain.

CASTELFIDARDO
Off road for Loreto, 6 km SE of Osimo.
This statuesque hill town was the scene of a celebrated battle in the fight for the Unification of Italy, when the Piemontese army routed the 'crusaders' of the Papal forces in 1860. It now styles itself the world capital of the accordion. In its **Museo Internazionale della Fisarmonica** you can see more than 150 examples of the instrument. The town still turns them out by the gross and claims that the piano accordion was developed here in 1863 from the more primitive Austrian squeeze box.

CHIARAVALLE
Off the SS76, 12 km NE of Jesi. The **Abbazia di Chiaravalle**, a daughter foundation of the great Cistercian Abbey of Clairvaux in France, is one of Italy's oldest Cistercian-Gothic constructions. It was founded in 1126, just ten years after St Bernard opened Clairvaux. Anywhere else it would be an important historic site, but here it is little loved, and lost in the mess of modern Chiaravalle.

CINGOLI
On the SS502, 24 km S of Jesi. A windy walled town built on a hill that receives the last rays of the sun when all around is in shadow. *'Non e' ancor notte a Cingoli'* ('It's not yet night at Cingoli'), goes a popular Marche saying, meaning, 'Don't count your chickens before they are hatched'. The place has also earned the title 'The Balcony of the Marche' for its sweeping panoramas – the best views are from behind the church of **San Francesco**. Climb up Corso Garibaldi to **Piazza Vittorio Emanuele**, once the **forum** of Roman *Cingulum* and still the heart of this stone-built town. To one side stands a fine 16thC Renaissance **town hall** with a much earlier **clock tower**. Inside is the smart, newly arranged **Museo Archeologico** with interesting Bronze Age lumber (to see the collection call at the library (*Biblioteca Comunale*) in Via Mazzini I). The library also houses the town's **Pinacoteca**, or art gallery, with another of the Marche's serendipity paintings by Lorenzo Lotto, this time a sumptuous *Madonna of the Rosary*. Cingoli's brief moment of glory came with the one-year papacy of its son, Pius VIII, in 1829. It was he who ordered a new façade for the Late Baroque **Duomo** on the main piazza, never finished due to his early death. Behind the town hall is hushed **Via del Podestà**, Cingoli's most atmospheric street.

CONERO RIVIERA ⇋ ×
Take the Ancona Sud exit from A14 motorway to join the coast road. Well signposted for Conero Riviera if leaving from the centre of Ancona.

Just south of Ancona rises the solitary limestone peak of **Monte Conero**, whose steep slopes slide down to the sea and the prettiest **beaches** on the whole of the Northern Adriatic shore. The beauty of the place means that its three small resorts offer standing room only in July and August. Come in May, June or September.

From Ancona, the first port of call is **Portonovo**, the smallest retreat on the Riviera. Gasp at the picture-postcard views out to sea as you wind down the dead-end road to this collection of hotels, restaurants, campsites and make-shift beach huts on a narrow strip of beach. The strand is split in two by the **Fortino Napoleonico**, a squat, window-less fort built in 1808 by Napoleon's Italian viceroy to fight off British ships. It has now been converted into a most singular **hotel** (see Recommended Hotels, page 228).

At the end of the road, where the evergreen oaks that smother the mountain come down to the sea, stands the early Romanesque church of **Santa Maria**. Built between 1034 and 1048, its curious form is unique in Italy and looks as if it might be more at home in Normandy – at the time of writing it is closed for serious restoration work but the sign promises imminent re-opening. Back on the main road, the Conero trail skirts the base of the mountain with sweeping views inland. Around 8 km south from the junction for Portonovo, follow signs for Monte Conero to drive up to **Badia di San Pietro**, built in the 12thC as a Benedictine Hermitage and now a fine hotel (see Recommended Hotels, page 228). This is the highest point on the mountain reachable by car and worth the journey for the views. The whole area was declared a regional **nature park** in 1987 and a web of signposted footpaths covers the peak – maps and information from the Consorzio del Parco del Conero at Sirolo. On the summit (572 m) traces of a **paleolithic settlement** dating back 100,000 years have been discovered – the earliest signs of human presence in the region.

The southern spur of Conero shelters the Riviera's two chief resorts. **Sirolo** is the most attractive, with a spruce **medieval centre** and a tree-lined, balcony **piazza** that teeters high above the sea. The mass of campsites and hotels below the old town runs seamlessly into more of the same at **Numana**. Here the authorities, anxious to get the most from the short season, have killed the golden goose and allowed the virtually uncontrolled construction of hotels and campsites. Still, it has a fine long **beach** to the south and an **archaeological museum** (*Via La Fenice 4*) documenting the history of the Piceni tribes who lived here until Rome muscled in).

To escape from the crowds, make for one of the many small isolated **coves** only accessible by boat – regular services in season from Numana, Sirolo and Portonovo.

CUPRAMONTANA

10-km detour off main SS76. This small *borgo* is one of the most important centres for the Marche's famous white wine, **Verdicchio**. The vine-clad hills hereabouts recall the background of a Renaissance fresco. Forget the old prejudice that Verdicchio is a cheap and nasty wine in a waisted 'Gina Lollobrigida' bottle: it has come a long way since its launch in the 1960s and many producers now make outstanding wine. Its peculiar, slightly bitter finish is unmistakable and makes it a perfect partner for Adriatic shellfish. The town's **Cantina Sociale**, or co-operative winery, is one of the best larger producers and also makes an excellent champagne-method sparkler. Visitors are welcome, purchasers even more so.

FIASTRA

On the SS78. A noble old **abbey**, a **nature park** and some of the Marche's best **Roman remains** lie just south of Macerata at Fiastra. The serene **Abbazia di Fiastra** (*open May-June weekends only; July-Sept daily*) is another of the great Cistercian abbeys founded under the patronage of Clairvaux in France (see also Chiaravalle, page 224). Apart from its splendid setting, it has delightful **frescoes** by the Salimbeni brothers and a fine Renaissance **cloister**. Part of the building now houses an **archaeological museum** with finds from nearby Urbs Salvia, and a collection of antique rural artefacts. The whole area is a **Riserva Naturale**, an idyllic spot for country rambles and protected by the World Wildlife Fund.

A few kilometres further south stand

Local Explorations: 10

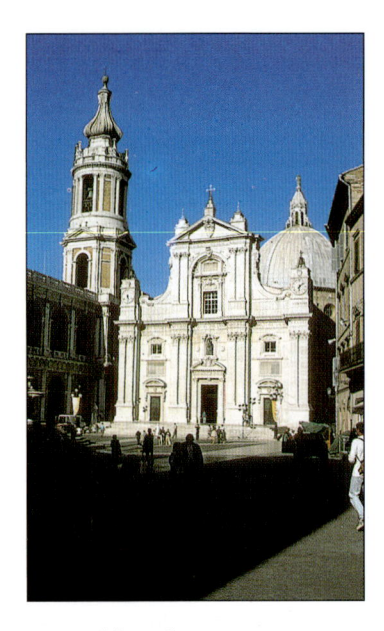

• *Piazza della Madonna, Loreto.*

the remains of **Urbs Salvia**, a city founded in the 1stC BC and, like so many of the Marche's Roman towns, wiped out by Alaric in 408 AD. For once this is an archaeological site with things you can actually see – the **amphitheatre**, which was built in the 2ndC AD, is one of the region's most conspicuous Roman ruins.

JESI ×
On the SS76 dual carriageway, 25 km W of Ancona's centre. Tourist information: central Piazza Repubblica 9. Station in Viale Trieste, SE of centre; frequent trains on Rome-Ancona line. Short-term pay parking below walls (spaces marked with blue lines) using special tickets which are sold in newsagents and bars.

Don't be put off by the ugly encircling main roads and heavy industry: once in the *Centro Storico*, you can breathe the sophisticated atmosphere and feel the lively pulse that distinguish one of the most beguiling towns hereabouts. Its most striking feature greets you as you arrive – a belt of massive **14thC walls**, built on Roman foundations, strengthened with buttresses and impregnable **towers**, and topped by houses.

The main streets of the walled historic centre run along a narrow ridge and there is much to tempt you to explore. Start in **Piazza Federico II** which lies at the north-eastern end of the town where the Roman forum of *Aesis* once lay. Its name recalls the birth here of the fabled medieval Hohenstaufen Emperor Frederick II in a tent on December 26 1194. Frederick, known as *Stupor Mundi* for his stirring deeds, endeared himself even more to Jesi when he later called it his special city, its very name seeming to recall that of Jesus.

The 18thC face of the **Duomo**, the robust **caryatids** on the palace to the left of the church and the **obelisk** in the centre give the square a decidedly Late Baroque tone.

A few steps down **Via Pergolesi** and you will be in Piazza Colocci, in front of Jesi's most handsome building, **Palazzo della Signoria**. This text-book Renaissance palace was built in the late 15thC by Francesco di Giorgio Martini, the Sienese genius best known for his military architecture. The large rampant **lion** above the entrance is the symbol of the power the city once held. Inside note the three-tiered **courtyard** with brick piers on the first level, marble on the second and wooden on the third.

Carry on along Via Pergolesi to **Piazza della Repubblica**. Jesi's largest square is dominated by the town's 18thC theatre, **Teatro Pergolesi**, home to a prestigious autumn **opera** season and named after the composer **Pergolesi** who was born here in 1710. From here the long principal thoroughfare, **Corso Matteotti**, runs straight as an arrow to end at an **arch** built in honour of Pope Clement XII in 1734. Stroll down the street in the early evening, seemingly with half the town's population, for a most civilized *passeggiata*. On parallel **Via XV Settembre** stands Jesi's most flamboyant building, **Palazzo Pianetti**. Apart from its hundred windows, the bland façade little prepares you for the over-the-top Rococo flourishes inside. The most extravagant part is the sugar-candy stucco work in the long **galleria**. The over-blown decoration alone would merit a visit; the added bonus of the civic **art gallery** (Pinacoteca Comunale) makes it obligatory for here is kept a small group of some of Lorenzo Lotto's finest works – *The Judgement of Santa Lucia*, a *Visitation*, an *Annunciation* and a restless *Deposition*.

Some 12 km north of Jesi is the pleasing rocky village of **Morro d'Alba**, worth a journey if only to try its celebrated red country wine, *Lacrime di Morro d'Alba* – no one knows how it got its name, which translates as Tears of Morro d'Alba.

LORETO ⚓ ✕

Exit Loreto/Porto Recanati from the A14 motorway, on the SS77. Railway station E out of town at bottom of hill serves main Milan-Bari line with connecting bus service to centre. Pay parking relatively easy except on religious feast days.

You don't have to believe in the cult of the Virgin Mary to appreciate Loreto – but it helps. This is one of the most important **shrines** to the Madonna in Europe, or indeed anywhere, and the town exists only to service the thousands of pilgrims who travel here from around the world. The great dome of the **Sanctuario della Santa Casa** dominates the countryside for miles around; below it stands the focus of worship, the rustic **cottage** from Nazareth that is said to have witnessed the Annunciation and the childhood of Jesus (see Legend of the Holy House, this page). Although the *Santa Casa* arrived, according to tradition, in 1294, it was not until 1507 that the Vatican finally approved of Loreto as a place of pilgrimage, though work on the church had begun in 1468. It was Pope Julius II who decided to pull out all the stops and give the primitive cottage a fit setting. The result is a showcase of work by many of the most celebrated names of Late Renaissance Italy and gives believers and unbelievers alike good reason to come here.

The church was begun on Gothic lines, but later architects, including Bramante and Sansovino, gave it a thorough Late-Renaissance treatment. Inside, under the dome, is the great **marble facing** that protects the Holy House, carried out in the 16thC to Bramante's designs by Andrea Sansovino, Antonio da Sangallo the Younger and by Gian Cristoforo Romano, the renowned medal designer. Notice how around its base, centuries of kneeling pilgrims have worn deep furrows in the marble.

The curious **statue** of the Black Madonna of Loreto within the walls of the *Santa Casa* is a modern copy of the original destroyed in a fire in 1921. Some claim that the tradition of the Black Madonnas to be found in many famous shrines is a reference to the prophetic line referring to Mary in the *Song of Solomon, I am black, but comely*; others, more prosaically inclined, point out that the statues were often carved in dark hardwoods, later further blackened by the smoke of votive candles. At the bottom of the right nave are the church's greatest artistic treasures – gem-stone coloured **frescoes** in the Sacristy of St Mark by Melozzo da Forli, and Luca Signorelli's noble **frescoes** in the nearby Sacristy of St John.

Piazza della Madonna, the elegant set-piece square with a delicate Baroque **fountain** that fronts the Sanctuary is flanked on two sides by the arcades of the 16thC **Palazzo Apostolico**. The **Museo-Pinacoteca** inside preserves a fine group of late works by Lorenzo Lotto (the Venetian master retired and died in the monastery here

---

THE LEGEND OF THE HOLY HOUSE

The simple cottage at Nazareth where the Annunciation took place and where the Holy Family lived, so the legend goes, was borne away by angels in 1291 as the Saracens descended on the Holy Land. It first touched ground on a hill in Dalmatia. Here it stayed until December 10, 1294 when, following its poor reception by the locals, it again took off, this time to land across the Adriatic Sea in a laurel grove (*lauretum*, hence Loreto) infested by bandits. Adjustments were hurriedly made and the house moved off again, this time to end up a few miles away in the middle of a public highway on the top of the hill of Loreto.

Experts in our more sceptical age now suggest that the bricks of Mary's house were brought from Palestine in the ships of the retreating Crusaders. To this day the *marchigiani* light enormous bonfires on the eve of December 10, the Feast of the Translation of the Holy House, to help the *Santa Casa* on its way.

Local Explorations: 10

RECOMMENDED HOTELS

ANCONA
Unless you are waiting for a ferry, little reason to stay in chaotic Ancona. You would be better off lodging at nearby Portonovo, July and August excepted (see under Conero Riviera, below). The best two are:

Grand Hotel Palace, LLL; *Lungomare Vanvitelli 24; tel. 071 201813; fax 071 2074832; cards accepted.*

Restrained opulence with traditional high standards – and high prices – in this grand but not excessively large hotel down by the port at the foot of Monte Guasco.

Grand Hotel Roma & Pace, LL; *Via Leopardi 1; tel. 071 202007; fax 071 2074736; cards accepted.*

A classic 19thC hotel in the heart of town on a cross-street between Corso Garibaldi and Corso Stamira. Masses of moth-eaten charm. Stalin tried to get a job here as a night porter in 1907, but was turned down.

CONERO RIVIERA
Hotel prices shoot up in the high season (July and August); bargains for the rest of the year. The Riviera's most attractive hotels are at Portonovo:

Emilia, LL-LLL; *Via Collina di Portonovo 149; tel. 071 801145; fax 071 801330; cards accepted.*

Well away from the beach, this modern hotel stands high on the slopes of Monte Conero. Distinctive character given by enormous collection of contemporary art, smart bedrooms and awesome views. Superb food in the restaurant, but prices are sky high (see Recommended Restaurants, page 229).

Fortino Napoleonico, LLL; *Portonovo; tel. 071 801450; fax 071 801454; cards accepted.*

Surely one of the region's oddest hotels: a converted one-storey Napoleonic fort right on the beach. Prices drop considerably out of season. Rooms are spacious but gloomy (only narrow slits for windows). Public rooms in Imperial style, densely wooded grounds and swimming pool within the ramparts.

Excelsior La Fonte, LL; *Via Poggio, Portonovo; tel. 071 801470; fax 071 801474; cards accepted.*

A short walk up from the beach, this cheerful Spanish Colonial-style hotel has plenty of sunny terraces and a fine restaurant; value for money.

If you don't want to be near the beach try:

Monteconero, LL; *Monte Conero, Sirolo; tel. 071 9330592; fax 071 9330365; cards accepted; closed Nov-Easter.*

Take the road up Monte Conero to this converted monastery, 500 m above sea level with glorious views out to sea. The modern rooms give few signs of their historic origins.

LORETO
No shortage of beds in this major pilgrim centre, with many establishments run by religious orders. Best profane choice is:

Villa Tetlameya, LLL; *Via Villa Costantina 187 (1.5 km E along Via Maccari); tel. 071 978863; fax 976639; cards accepted.*

Loreto's out-of-town four-star hotel with just eight fine rooms set in a tranquil park.

Orlando, L-LL; *Via Villa Costantina 89; tel. 071 978501; fax 071 978501; cards accepted.*

Excellent economic choice on same road as Villa Tetlameya, above.

MACERATA
Nothing sparkling here – and what there is gets packed out in July for the opera festival.

Della Piaggia, LL; *Via Santa Maria della Porta 18; tel. 0733 230387; fax 0733 233660; cards accepted.*

The best in the historic centre, near Piazza San Giovanni car park. Sober, family-run hotel, modern but tasteful.

THE MARCHES / Inland from Ancona – Hill Towns of the Central Marche

Villa Quiete, LL; Valle Cascia, Montecassiano; tel. 0733 599559; fax 0733 599559; cards accepted.

Some 5 km N of Macerata towards Osimo, this large villa has delightful gardens but variable rooms – lives up to its name, though. Also a chance to glimpse the medieval town hall in the village of Montecassiano.

RECOMMENDED RESTAURANTS

ANCONA

The city is famous for *brodetto*, its saffron-tinged fish stew, and there is no shortage of other seafood on menus.

Teatro Strabacco, L-LL; Via G. Oberdan 2; tel. 071 54213; cards accepted; closed Mon.

Open late with a good choice of *anconetana* specialities, you can also just take a snack here while listening to one of the many live music concerts that the owner organises.

Passetto, LLL; Piazza IV Novembre; tel. 071 33214; cards accepted; closed Wed.

Ancona's classiest restaurant with a terrace for the summer. Refined fish dishes and a vast wine cellar. At end of town furthest from Colle Guasco.

La Moretta, LLL; Piazza del Plebiscito 52; tel. 071 202317; cards accepted; closed Sun.

Somewhat prissy, but imaginative fish cookery. Tables in summer on Ancona's most attractive square. Perfect pasta dressed with seafood.

Osteria del Pozzo, L-LL; Via Bonda, off Piazza del Plebiscito; tel. 071 2073996; cards none.

This cheap and cheerful *trattoria* in a narrow street in the old town is the lunchtime choice for locals: delicious, simple fish dishes – fried squid, for example – with no frills.

CONERO RIVIERA

The two best restaurants are in hotels at Portonovo (see also Recommended Hotels, page 228):

Emilia, LLL; Via Collina di Portonovo 149; tel. 071 801145; cards accepted; closed Mon, except summer.

Above the resort on the slopes of Monte Conero, you pay a premium for the splendid sea views. Acclaimed seafood.

Fortino Napoleonico, LLL; Portonovo; tel. 071 801450; cards accepted; closed Mon (except summer).

Imperial style in the grand dining room of this Napoleonic fort right on the beach (see also Recommended Hotels, page 228). French touches to the imaginative fish dishes. Menu also has a cheese tart *con custard inglese*.

JESI

Galeazzi, LL; Via Mura Occidentali 5; tel. 0731 57944; cards none; closed Mon.

Horrible setting in modern block, but heavenly *gnocchi ripieni* (small stuffed dumplings) and other earthy local dishes. The pick of local Verdicchio and red *Rosso Conero*.

Hostaria Santa Lucia, LLLL; Via Marche 2/b; tel. 0731 64409; cards accepted; closed Sun and Mon.

You can taste the sea in the outstanding fish dishes in this smart restaurant; try the good value *menu degustazione* for the best.

LORETO

Orlando Barabani, LL; Via Villa Costantina 93; tel. 071 977696; cards accepted; closed Wed.

Tables *al aperto* in summer with outstanding regional fare and plenty of meaty options if you have grown tired of fish.

Andreina, LL; Via Buffolareccia 14 (2 km out on SS77 towards sea); tel. 071 970124; cards accepted; closed Tues.

Family-run restaurant with superior *marchigiano* menu – excellent hams and salami, also plenty of game.

MACERATA

Da Secondo, LLL; Via Pescheria Vecchia 26; tel. 0733 260912; cards accepted; closed Mon.

Everyone's favourite choice in Macerata, with classic regional dishes and few surprises. Outdoor tables in summer. Behind main Piazza della Libertà off Via Don Minzoni.

in 1556) and an unusual collection of Renaissance ceramic **pharmacist's jars**. Hidden away in a corner are also some 70 carved blocks of box wood used until the 1940s to stamp designs on pilgrims' bodies which were then indelibly tattooed as permanent souvenirs of their pilgrimage to Loreto. Today the keepsakes on sale are less durable but equally grotesque.

MACERATA ⚐ ✕

On the SS485, 25 km from the Macerata exit on the A14 motorway. Tourist information: Piazza della Libertà 12. Station S of town on Piazza XXV Aprile; on Civitanova Marche-Fabriano branchline connecting with main lines. Easiest to park to SE of town near Sferisterio.

A provincial capital of measured dignity and solid, if unostentatious wealth, its centre was almost entirely built between the 16th and 19thC. Some may find it dull. Its open-air **opera festival** in July has found an international following and takes place in the 7,000-seater **Sferisterio** – a monster of a Neoclassical arena erected by private subscription in the 1820s. As you are transported by a Verdi aria, you might care to know that the arena was originally built as a stadium for *pallone*, or Italian football.

For such a distinguished town, there are relatively few eye-catching monuments or treasures. The Renaissance two-tiered **arcades** of the **Loggia dei Mercanti** on central **Piazza della Libertà** is the most striking piece of architecture in Macerata.

The best of the city's palaces line **Corso Matteotti**, the road that leaves the square at the side of the Loggia, while **Corso della Repubblica** will take you to Piazza Vittorio Veneto and the civic **gallery and museum**.

Here is a mixed bag of works by Umbro-Marchigiani painters – most important is **Carlo Crivelli's** *Madonna and Child*. If you do have time to kill, you might examine the dusty old carriages in the **Museo delle Carrozze** or brush up your modern Italian history in one of the country's best museums dedicated to the Unification of Italy and wartime resistance – you will find them in the same *palazzo* as the pictures.

MORRO D'ALBA

See Jesi, pages 226-7.

OSIMO

4 km off the SS16, 19 km S of Ancona. The town's compact warm brick **Centro Storico** rides the crest of a hill above the mess of the modern expansion below. Most of Osimo's best buildings date from the 17th and 18thC, but signs of its ancient past sometimes show through.

Drop into the atrium of the **Palazzo Comunale** in main Piazza del Comune to see a dozen **statues** from Roman Auximum and hunt out the mighty blocks of the Roman **walls** above Via Fonte Magna. The **mosaic pavement** of the **Duomo** is a fine relic of medieval times. The old Romanesque church of San Francesco has been smothered inside and out in High Baroque to celebrate its later reincarnation as the **Sanctuary** dedicated to **San Giuseppe da Copertino** (1603-63), the patron saint of those taking exams. Thanks to his celebrated capacity for levitation, he is also invoked by American pilots for their protection.

PORTONOVO

And other places marked on the Conero Riviera, see Conero Riviera, pages 224-5.

RECANATI

On the SS77, 7 km SW of Loreto. This dignified small town strung out along the crest of a hill was renowned in the 16th and 17thC for its commercial fair, one of the most important in the Papal States. Its wide streets and comfortable buildings still have a mercantile character. Nowadays, however, it is close to the heart of many Italians as the birthplace of one the country's greatest poets, Giacomo Leopardi (1798-1837). He spent a hothouse childhood, self-imprisoned in his father's classics-filled library and for the rest of his life tried to recapture in his pessimistic verse the illusion of happiness, glimpsed fleetingly as a youth in Recanati.

Palazzo Leopardi, at the southern edge of town, where he was born and brought up, has memorabilia, manuscripts and a library. Around almost every corner, plaques mark spots referred to in his poems. Recanati was also the home town of the great tenor Beniamino Gigli and part of the **Museo Civico** in Palazzo Comunale on central **Piazza Leopardi** holds a collection of

THE MARCHES / *Inland from Ancona – Hill Towns of the Central Marche*

his costumes from some 30 operas, a mock-up of his dressing-room and some of the many presents that he received, including a walking stick from Verdi.

In the same palace is Recanati's treasure, a **room with three of Lorenzo Lotto's finest pictures**, including a most strange *Annunciation* packed with almost breathless narrative detail.

SAN SEVERINO MARCHE
On the SS361, 26 km W of Macerata. Founded around 550 AD after the Goths had destroyed the Roman *Septembeda* further down the hill, this beguiling town has a happy mix of medieval and Renaissance buildings. Its outstanding feature is its unusual elliptical main square, **Piazza del Popolo**, circled by shady arcades. Before taking your *aperitivo* here, search out the **Pinacoteca**, at Via Salimbeni 39, in order to see Pinturicchio's sumptuous **Madonna della Pace** and earthy pictures by the local Salimbeni brothers.

You can see more of their endearing work in the nearby Romanesque church of **San Lorenzo in Doliolo**.

TOLENTINO
On the SS77, 18 km SW of Macerata. Pil-

• *Recanati.*

grims come from across Central Italy to this good-looking medieval town to visit the shrine of St Nicholas of Tolentino (1245-1305). A multitude of miracles have been attributed to the Augustinian friar, who passed the last thirty years of his life here. Even if you don't have any favours to ask of St Nicholas, visit his handsome **Basilica** to marvel at the grandiose 14thC Giottoesque **frescoes** in the Gothic **Cappellone di San Nicolà**.

History was made in 1797 at **Palazzo Parisani-Bezzi** (Via della Pace) when Napoleon, in the wake of his successful invasion of the Papal States, forced Pope Pius VI to sign the Peace of Tolentino.

If you enjoy riddles, make for the central **Piazza della Libertà** to try and figure out the three clock faces on one of the Marche's oddest medieval **clock towers**. As if the mix of Napoleon, flying saints and chronological puzzles was not enough, Tolentino also boasts **The International Museum of Caricature and Humour in Art** – which reopened in early 1995 in its new home, Palazzo Sangallo.

Local Explorations: 11

North-Western Tuscany

The Garfagnana, Lunigiana and Versilia Coast

220 km; map Touring Club Italiano Toscana

Following the marked route makes an unpredictable journey that switchbacks its way between a couple of Italy's smartest seaside resorts and some of Tuscany's remotest uplands. It is a journey for the Italophile with a yen for variety, much of it through decidedly un-Tuscan countryside where hiking boots – or even skis are more useful than a volume on Renaissance art, and where a good phrase book is the most useful of all.

The deep valley of the River Serchio, cleft between the marble peaks of the Apuan Alps and the Appennines, forms the Garfagnana. Here the attractions are the velvet green-landscape and the decrepit villages, atmospheric places of no importance from which the young and fit have departed. But to taste the real Garfagnana you must leave the main road that runs along the valley bottom and head uphill to the remote, silent hamlets of this unsung region.

Wilder scenery tinged with a melancholy air awaits you in the Lunigiana, Tuscany's northernmost corner that covers the basin of the River Magra. The beauty of this isolated area has been tarnished by the arrival of the A15 motorway, but again, off the main road, 'undiscovered' delights lie hidden in the Appennines.

The narrow coastal strip at the feet of the Apuan Alps is known as the Versilia and provides a stark contrast to the desolation of the rest of the route. Here you can unpack your bathing costume and evening wear to visit two of Italy's most elegant resorts, or don your sunglasses to see the dazzling marble quarries of Carrara, surely amongst the most striking sights in all Italy.

> **VERSILIA**
> The narrow stretch of coast between Forte dei Marmi and Viareggio is known as the Versilia. In the Middle Ages it was caught up in a continual tug-of-war between the surrounding powers – Lucca, Pisa, Genoa and Florence – who sought control over the Via Francigena, an important medieval highway that ran through here, hemmed in by the sea and the Apuan Alps. The marble quarries and silver mines were an added attraction. However, it was not until the malarial swamps down by the sea were drained in the 19thC that the area found its modern vocation as a celebrated holiday riviera. Now tourism and stone quarrying live uncomfortably together.

NW Tuscany / The Garfagnana, Lunigiana and Versilia Coast

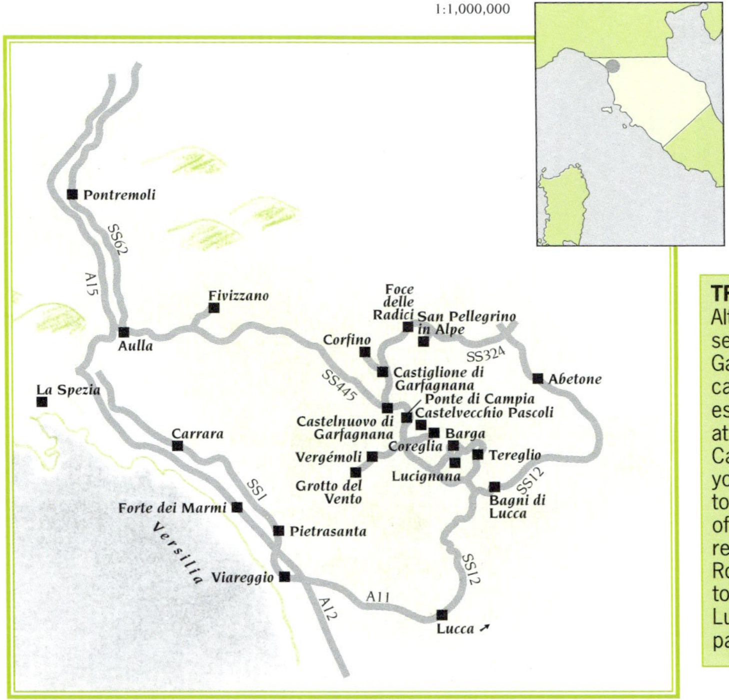

TRANSPORT

Although the main centres are well served by train, to explore both the Garfagnana and Lunigiana in depth a car or sturdy walking boots are essential. The Lucca-Aulla rail line stops at Bagni di Lucca, Barga, and Castelnuovo di Garfagnano. From Aulla you can traverse the Lunigiana by rail to Pontremoli and onwards to the plain of the Po. All the Versilia coastal resorts lie along the main La Spezia-Rome line. The main centre for buses to nearly all the places on this tour is Lucca (see Seeing the Region: 1, pages 85-88).

DETOUR – GROTTA DEL VENTO

Tuscany's grandest **caves** lie at the end of this short detour, a diversion worth taking for the dramatic scenery alone. Head south-west from Barga up the valley of the Turrite di Gallicano, a white torrent that rushes down from the marble mountains of the Apuan Alps. Along the way stop to marvel at **Vergemoli**, a hamlet perched improbably high above the road. The crystalline wonderland of the **Grotta del Vento**, or Cave of the Wind, at Fornovolasco, penetrates the mountain for some 4 km. From April to September you can choose between five guided tours of graded difficulty; in winter the caves are only open on Sundays.

Local Explorations: 11

SIGHTS & PLACES OF INTEREST

ABETONE
On the SS12, W of Garfagnana. Tuscany's joker in the pack, a larch-cloaked ski resort at its liveliest in mid-winter. In summer, you might want to stop here to explore the spreading forests that cover these high Appennine slopes – ski lifts will take you up to cool mountain air when Florence shimmers in the heat.

AULLA
See Lunigiana, below.

BAGNI DI LUCCA
On the SS12, 26 km NE of Lucca. This little spa town on the threshold of the Garfagnana had its heyday in the early 19thC under the patronage of the self-styled Queen of Etruria, Napoleon's imperious sister, Elisa Bacciocchi. Princes and poets from across Europe – Byron, Heine and Shelley amongst them – gathered here to take the salty, sulphurous waters. And in 1838 when the **Casino** was opened, they could try their luck at the world's first roulette tables. English expatriots took to the place with such gusto that they made themselves at home with an incongruous neo-Gothic Anglican **church and cemetery**.

Even if Bagni di Lucca's splendour is somewhat tarnished, it remains a likeable backwater with an endearing air of faded northern gentility. Its **bath-houses** still function and, amongst a host of cures, offer the possibility of sweating away your ills in a natural rock **cave** fed by steam from the hot springs.

BARGA
Off the SS445, 30 km N of Lucca. The nearest you will find to a proper town in the Garfagnana, Barga repays a visit. Passing the ugly industrial suburb of Fornaci di Barga, leave the plain to make for the narrow streets of the old quarter. In the Middle Ages this was a powerful fortress town and it is still uncompromisingly medieval. At the top, set off by a grassy terrace called the **Arringo**, stands the **Duomo**. The origins of this outstanding Lombard Gothic church date back to the 9thC. Inside, get close up to the relief carvings on the 12thC **pulpit** – masterpieces of Romanesque sculpture. Back outside, the views of the Garfagnana from the Arringo are splendid.

Some 4 km north-west of Barga is the hamlet of Castelvecchio, now called **Castelvecchio Pascoli**, in honour of the great Italian poet, Giovanni Pascoli (1855-1912) who spent the final years of his life here. Both his house, left as it

---

LUNIGIANA
The A15 motorway effortlessly grinds through Tuscany's northernmost outpost, the wilderness of the **Lunigiana**, a vaguely defined area that covers the basin of the River Magra. Off the main highway, the chief attractions are the landscapes – wild rocks convulsed in primeval cataclysms and thickly-woven mats of holm oak, beech and hornbeam. The gnarled villages, watched over by tumble-down Malaspina castles, cling on with the tenacity of tree roots. Once this was the homeland of the *Luni*, an ancient tribe whose origins lie in prehistory.

At **Pontremoli**, the largest town in the area, you can see a collection of fascinating stylized statues called *stele*, some dating back to the Bronze Age, that the Luni left behind. You will find the **Museo delle Statue-Stele della Lunigiana** in the Castello del Piagnaro that crowns the town. Around the castle are the narrow streets and slate-roofed, stacked-up houses of Pontremoli's inviting medieval heart. You will also see how the town is divided into two old quarters. In the 14thC the ruling warlord, Castruccio Castracani, split the town with sturdy walls to keep the warring Guelf and Ghibelline factions apart.

At the southern end of the Lunigiana, **Fivizzano** is a small commercial centre still enclosed in its Florentine walls. **Piazza Medicea**, ringed with Renaissance *palazzi*, is a stern reminder of the suzerainty of Florence. **Aulla**, the region's only other important town, has little to offer other than the **Fortezza della Brunella**, a dramatically-sited 16thC castle with an exceptionally well-organized local natural history museum.

was on the day he died, and his tomb can be visited.

A few kilometres further along the SS445 is **Ponte di Campia**, the official gateway to the Garfagnana. The snack-bar by the bridge is reckoned by locals to be one of the best places to eat the celebrated vegetable *torte*, or rustic pies, of the region.

CARRARA ×
Off the SS1, 6 km inland from coast. Carrara's marble quarries have been worked over the millenia and many of the greatest masterpieces of Western art have been carved from its prized stone. From afar, the Apuan Alps that rear up behind the town glisten as if with snow; drive up to see the dazzling whiteness of the quarry faces and scree slopes of marble waste. A visit to the lunar landscape of the oldest *cave*, or quarries, at **Colonnata** and **Fantiscritti** is an unforgettable experience – take your sunglasses. The town itself now sprawls down to the sea, and apart from the great blocks of marble that litter the place, has few obvious charms. Its Pisan-style 11thC **Duomo**, in white and grey marble naturally, is worth a glance, and the **Museo Civico del Marmo** in Viale XX Settembre, just out of town, tells you everything you could wish to know about Carrara marble (*closed Sun*). If you head up to Colonnata to see the quarries, you should also try the unlikely local speciality, *lardo di Colonnata* – the fattiest belly pork, flavoured with spices and packed into marble jars to be seasoned for at least six months in damp caves; its faintly rancid edge is an acquired taste.

CASTELNUOVO DI GARFAGNANA ×
On the SS445, 15 km NW of Barga. The centre of the historic capital of the Garfagnana was totally devastated during the Second World War, but both its medieval ***rocca***, on the main square, and the nearby 16thC **Duomo** in grey sandstone, have been sensitively rebuilt. This market town for the isolated villages of the area makes a good place to observe the self-reliant, almost anarchic people of the Garfagnana.

For a roller-coaster ride up into the Appennines that divide Tuscany from Emilia-Romagna, leave the SS445 at Castelnuovo and drive north on the SS324. After around 7 km, **Castiglione di Garfagnana** looms up, a sturdy windswept *borgo* fortified by Lucca in the 14thC. Here you can either turn off for utter tranquility up at the mountain resort of **Corfino** and the meadows and woodlands of the Pania di Corfino **nature reserve**, or stay on the main road to climb ever upwards towards **Foce delle Radici** (1,529 m), the highest point on the route and the watershed of the Appennines. A brief detour south from here will take you to **San Pellegrino in Alpe**, for breathtaking views and the **Santuario di San Pellegrino**, a hermitage founded in the 7thC.

CASTELVECCHIO PASCOLI
See Barga, page 234.

CASTIGLIONE DI GARFAGNANA ⌂ ×
See Castelnuovo di Garfagnana, this page.

COREGLIA AND TEREGLIO
See Lucignana, page 236.

CORFINO
See Castelnuovo di Garfagnana, this page.

FIVIZZANO
See Lunigiana, page 234.

FORTE DEI MARMI ⌂ ×
Off the A12 and SS1, 15 km NW of Viareggio. Forte dei Marmi once ranked as one of Italy's most fashionable seaside resorts. Though it has grown rapidly since its heyday before the Second World War, it still clings on to a certain style. Its wonderfully wide and long strand of fine sand is backed by elegant villas set in shady gardens and luxury hotels with prices to make your head spin. If you want to see the Italian upper middle classes at play, this is one place to come.

LUCCA
See Seeing the Region: 1, pages 85-8.

LUCIGNANA
On by-road off the SS445. Named, so its inhabitants claim, for the quality of its light, this typical Garfagnana village is one of a string of tiny places that dot the Appennine slopes between Bagni di Lucca and Barga. Few people, let alone tourists, pass through these enchanting hamlets. Typically, they contain a few battered grey-stone houses, a bar and

Local Explorations: 11

vegetable shop, and grass growing between the cobbles of the main street. One of the hamlets, **Coreglia Antelminelli**, takes its name from its heart-shape and boasts a museum of *figurine di gesso*, or plaster statues, for which the area is well known.

Tereglio is built on a narrow ridge with just enough room for a single road and two rows of dwellings. An area to explore if you are a pioneering traveller.

PIETRASANTA
On the SS1, 3 km inland from sea. The most interesting corner on the Versilia coastal strip, this marble town was founded by Lucca in 1255 as a bulwark against Pisa. At first glance, its historic centre seems like the standard-issue higgledy-piggledy heap of old houses; look carefully, however, and you will see its underlying rectangular, checker-board layout. Most of its finest monuments are grouped around the imposing **Piazza del Duomo**, with the marble-faced **Duomo** taking pride of place.

PONTE DI CAMPIA
See Barga, page 235.

PONTREMOLI ✕
See Lunigiana, page 234.

SAN PELLEGRINO IN ALPE
See Castelnuovo di Garfagnana, page 235.

VERGEMOLI
See Detour - Grotta del Vento, page 233.

VIAREGGIO ✕
Off the A12 and SS1, 20 km N of Pisa. Tourist information: Viale Carducci 10. Station on main La Spezia-Rome line in Piazza Dante. The largest seaside resort on the Tyrrhenian Sea and one of Italy's smartest. Its long, gently-sloping beach is backed by the **Lungomare**, a 3-km promenade flanked by oleander, tamarisk and palms. The endless parade of luxury hotels is lightened by the occasional flourish of turn-of-the-century Liberty architecture and shady gardens. It still boasts a real fishing port – one of the most important in Tuscany – and a pair of delightful **pinete**, or pine woods, the last vestiges of the Mediterranean *macchia* that once covered the area. Thanks to its mild climate and celebrated Lenten **Carnival**, it manages to be a lively place all year round.

RECOMMENDED HOTELS

BAGNI DI LUCCA
Bridge Hotel, L-LL; *Piazza di Ponte a Serraglio 5; tel. 0583 805324; fax 0583 805324; cards accepted.*

The English name is the only reference to Bagni di Lucca's former popularity with the British that you'll find at this small, modern, family-run hotel by the river; three-star rooms at less than the usual three-star prices.

Locanda Maiola, L-LL; *Via Controneria, loc. Villa; tel. and fax 0583 86296; fax none; cards none.*

Just seven bedrooms in a converted farmhouse up in the hills to the east of town. But the real reason to stay here is to sample the outstanding home cooking served in the restaurant (residents only) – try the chicken fried with artichokes and courgettes.

CASTIGLIONE DI GARFAGNANA
Il Casone di Profecchia, L-LL; *on the SS324 at Casone di Profecchia; tel. 0583 649030; cards accepted.*

A restaurant-with-rooms (see Recommended Restaurants, page 237) in the 18thC barracks that once housed the troops who guarded the frontier between Tuscany and Modena. On the main road 17 km northeast of town.

FORTE DEI MARMI
There are some 100 hotels to choose from, ranging from the five-star **Augustus, LLL** in Viale Morin, a Liberty-style palace set in a jewel of a garden, to humble but still pricey one-star *pensioni*. Two middle-range places stand out:

Tirreno, LL; *Viale Morin 7; tel. 0584 787444; fax 0584 787137; cards accepted; closed Oct to Easter.*

Peaceful garden and 50 m from the sea – try and get a room in the 19thC villa rather than the modern wing.

Franceschi, LL-LLL; *Via XX Settembre 19; tel. 0584 787114; fax 0584*

787471; *cards accepted*.
Discreet comfort with great style.

VIAREGGIO
No shortage of hotels – the problem is choosing one that won't break the bank. Here are three choices:

Palace Hotel, LLL; *Via F. Gioia 2; tel. 0584 46134; fax 0584 47351; cards accepted*.
One of the town's best in a grand turn-of-the-century mansion that dominates the sea-front. Near beach and pine woods, with five-star prices.

Garden, LL; *Via Foscolo 70; tel. 0584 44025; fax 0584 45445; cards accepted*.
One of Viareggio's oldest, with considerable style. Convenient, but noisy.

RECOMMENDED RESTAURANTS

CARRARA
Soldaini, LL; *Via Mazzini 11; tel. 0585 71459; cards accepted; closed Mon*.
Noted restaurant much frequented by locals, with both fish and meat – pasta with *pesto* and superb fish soup.

CASTELNUOVO DI GARFAGNANA
Osteria Vecchio Mulino, L-LL; *Via V. Emanuele 12; tel. 0583 62192; cards accepted; closed Sun*.
Opened as an *osteria* in 1890, it offers a wide range of *spuntini*, or snacks – savoury-filled pastries made from chestnut, maize or buckwheat flours, accompanied by cheeses and cured pork meats.

CASTIGLIONE DI GARFAGNANA
Il Casone di Profecchia, L; *on the SS324 at Casone di Profecchia; tel. 0583 649030; cards accepted*.
In the stables of the old barracks (see Recommended Hotels, page 236) with simple Garfagnana food – from toasted polenta with mushrooms through to *necci*, chestnut flour fritters with fresh ricotta cheese. On the main road 17 km north-east of town.

COLONNATA DI CARRARA
Da Venanzio, LL; *Piazza Palestro, 3; tel. 0585 73617; cards accepted; closed Sun eve and Thurs*.
A good place to brave *lardo di Colonnata*; otherwise, plenty of other hearty alternatives to put hairs on a quarryman's chest.

FORTE DEI MARMI
Lorenzo, LLL-LLLL; *Via Carducci 61; tel. 0584 84030; cards accepted; closed Mon in winter*.
Book in advance for the town's best restaurant – both fish and meat on the inventive menu and fair prices for such high quality.

La Barca, LLL; *Viale Italico, 3; tel. 0584 89323; cards accepted; closed Tues*.
Fish restaurant with slightly less shocking bills than Lo Squalo Charlie.

PONTREMOLI
Locanda Bacciottini, L; *Via Ricci Armani, 4; tel. 0187 830120; cards none; closed Sun evg and Mon*.
Plenty of authentic old-world appeal and a mouth-watering range of *antipasti*. The local pasta, *testaroli*, dressed with pesto, is a must.

VIAREGGIO
Romano, LLLL; *Via Mazzini, 102; tel. 0584 31382; cards accepted; closed Mon*.
Among the finest of Viareggio's exclusive fish restaurants. Its lavish menu has earned it national fame.

Giorgio, LL; *Via Zanardelli; tel. 0584 44493; cards accepted; closed Wed*.
A popular *trattoria* where it's as well to book your table in advance. After the appetizing *antipasti*, choose your *secondi* from the display of fresh fish.

INDEX

Abbadia San Salvatore 172
  hotels 173
abbeys
  Abbadia San Salvatore 172
  Abbazia di Chiaravalle 224
  Abbazia di Fiastra 225
  Abbazia di San Galgano 208
  Abbazia di Sant'Antimo 175
  Magione 168
  Monte Oliveto Maggiore 113
  Ponte de Abbadio 191
  San Bruzio, Magliano in Toscana 190
  San Martino al Cimino 200
Abetone 234
Acqualagna 120
Acquapendente 112
Aia del Diavolo 207
Ama 153
Ancona 222-4
  hotels 228
  restaurants 229
Anghiari 100
  hotels 108
  restaurants 108-9
Ansedonia 188
  hotels 192
Apecchio 212
Archiano 95
architects, A-Z 29-34
Arezzo 100-1
  hotels 108
  restaurants 109
artists, A-Z 29-34
Assisi 121-3
  hotels 127
  restaurants 128
Aulla 234

Badia a Coltibuono 152
Bagnaia 198
  restaurants 201
Bagni di Lucca 234
  hotels 236
  restaurants 237
Bagni di Nocera 126
Bagno Vignoni 112
  hotels 116
  restaurants 116-17
Barberino Val d'Elsa 112
  restaurants 117
Barbischio 153
Barga 234-5
beaches
  Conero Riviera 225
  Fano 124

Forte dei Marmi 235
  restaurants 235
Viareggio 236
Bisentina 113
Bocca Serriola 212
Bocca Trabaria Pass 101
Bolgheri 206
Bolsena 112-13
  hotels 116
  restaurants 117
Bomarzo 198
Borgo Pace 101
  hotels 108
  restaurants 109
Buonconvento 113

Cagli 123
  restaurants 128-9
Cala Maestra 189
Cala Spalmatoio 189
Campello sul Clitunno
  hotels 127
  restaurants 129
Campiglia Marittima 206
  restaurants 209
Canino 188
Cantiano 123
Capalbio 188
  restaurants 192-3
Capodimonte 188
Capoliveri, restaurants 209
Capraia 84
Capranica 198-9
Caprarola 199
Carrara 235
  restaurants 237
Casole d'Elsa 133
Castagneto Carducci 206
  hotels 209
  restaurants 209
Castelfidardo 224
Castellina in Chianti 152
  hotels 158
  restaurants 159
Castello di Brolio 152-3
Castello di Cacchiano 153
Castelnuovo Berardenga 153
  restaurants 159
Castelnuovo di Garfagnana 235
  restaurants 237
Castelvecchio Pascoli 234-5
Castiglion Fiorentino 162
Castiglione del Lago 162
  hotels 168
Castiglione della Pescaia 206

hotels 209
  restaurants 209
Castiglione di Garfagnana 235
  hotels 236
  restaurants 237
Castiglione d'Orcia 172
castles
  Bolgheri 206
  Capodimonte 188
  Castel Rigone 167
  Castel Sant'Elia 200
  Castello dell'Imperatore, Prato 94
  Castello di Brolio 152
  Castello di Castangnoli 153
  Castello di Meleto 153
  Castello di Vertine 153
  Castiglione 206
  Castiglione del Lago 162
  Castiglione di Garfagnana 235
  Castiglione d'Orcia 112, 172
  Fortezza della Brunella, Aulla 234
  Frontone 213
  Gradara 102
  Montalcino 172-3
  Monte San Savino 157
  Montecchio Vesponi 162
  Nepi 200
  Piobicco 219
  Rocca d'Orcia 112
  Sarteano 163
  Sorano 194
cathedrals
  Duomo, Fabriano 213
  Duomo, Florence 48-50
  Duomo, Jesi 226
  Duomo, Massa Marittima 207-8
  Duomo, Pistoia 92
  Duomo, Siena 140-1
  Duomo, Volterra 146-7
  Orbetello 190
  Orvieto 178, 180
  Perugia 182
  Pisa, Campo dei Miracoli 91-2
  Ronciglione 200
  San Ciriaco, Ancona 222
  Sovana 194

Vetralla 203
Certaldo 132
Certosa di Galluzzo 153
Cetona 163
Chianciano Terme 162-3
Chiaravalle 224
Chiarone 188-9
Chiusi 163-4
churches
  Basilica di San Francesco, Assisi 121-2
  Collegiata, Canino 188
  Collegiata, Cetona 163
  Collegiata, Lucignano 155
  Collegiata, San Gimignano 134-5
  Collegiata of Santa Maria dell'Impruneta 155
  Collegiata, Sarteano 163
  Duomo, Barga 234
  Florence 56-61, 73
  Montepulciano 166, 167
  Perugia 183
  Pisa 90
  Sanctuario della Santa Casa, Loreto 227
  Santa Maria della Consolazione, Todi 184
  Siena 144-5
  Tuscania 203
Cingoli 224
Citt del Castello 212-13
  hotels 216
  restaurants 216-17
Citt della Pieve 164
Civita Castellana 199-200
  restaurants 201
Civita di Bagnoregio 178
Colle di Val d'Elsa 132
  restaurants 132, 149
Colline Metallifere 207
Colonnata di Carrara 235
  restaurants 237
Conero Riviera 224-5
  hotels 228
  restaurants 229
Coreglia

238

INDEX

Antelminelli 236
Corfino 235
Cortona 164-5
  hotels 168
  restaurants 169
Costacciaro 126
Cupramontana 225

Deruta 178

Elba 206
  hotels 209
  restaurants 209
Etruscan remains
  Chiusi 164
  Cortona 164,165
  Ipogeo Etrusco
    di Montecalvario
    152
  Orvieto 180
  Perugia 180, 183
  Populonia 208
  Roselle 208
  Saturnia 191
  Sovana 194
  Sutri 200
  Tarquinia 202
  Todi 183
  Tuscania 203
  Vetulonia 208
  Villa Artimino 95
  Volterra 147-8
  Vulci 194

Fabriano 213
  hotels 216
  restaurants 217
Falerii Novi 199-200
Fano 123-4
  hotels 127-8
  restaurants 129
Fantiscritti 235
Ferento 112
Fiastra 225-6
Fiesole 77
Figline Valdarno 107
Fivizzano 234
Florence 39-41
  countryside
    around 77
  Duomo 48-50
  east of the
    Duomo 70-3
  festivals 43
  hotels 78-9
  north of the
    Duomo 68-70
  Oltrarno 73-6
  Palazzo Pitti 53-4
  restaurants 79-81
  sights and places
    of interest 42-8,
    50-3,54-61
  south of the Duomo
    64-8
  Uffizi 61-3
Foligno 124-5
Fonte di Clitunno 124

food 35-6
Forte dei Marmi 235
  hotels 236
  restaurants 237
Fossombrone 125
Frasassi caves 213
Frontone 213-14
  restaurants 217
Furlo
  hotels 128
  restaurants 129
Furlo Gorge 125

Gaiole in Chianti 153
  hotels 158
Gargonza 157
Giglio Campese 189
Giglio Castello 189
Giglio Porto 189
Gradara 102
Gradoli 189
Greve in Chianti 154
  hotels 158
  restaurants 159
Grosseto 206-7
  restaurants 209
Grotte di Frasassi
  213
Gualdo Tadino 125
Gubbio 214-15,218
  festivals 218
  hotels 216
  restaurants 217

Impruneta 154-5
Isola Bisentina 188
Isola del Giglio 189
  hotels 192
  restaurants 193
Isola d'Elba *see*
  Elba Isola di
  Giannutri 189
Isola Maggiore 167
  hotels 168
  restaurants 169
Italy, Central,
  history 21-5

Jesi 226-7
  restaurants 229

Lacona 206
Lago di Bolsena 113
Lago di Corbara 178
  restaurants 185
Lago di Vico 203
Lago Trasimeno 167
Larderello 207
Lazio, North,
  wines 38
Le Marche *see*
  Marche
Livorno 84-5
  restaurants 96-7
Loreto 227,230
  hotels 228
  restaurants 229
Lucca 85-6

hotels 96
  restaurants 97
  sights and places
    of interest 86-9
Lucignana 235-6
Lucignano 155
  hotels 158
Lunigiana 234

Macerata 230
  hotels 228-9
  restaurants 229
Magione 168
Magliano in
  Toscana 189-90
  restaurants 193
Marche food 36
  wines 38
Marciana Marina 206
Marina di Campo 206
Marina di Pisa 87
  restaurants 87
Marta 190
Martana 113
Massa Marittima
  207-8
  hotels 209
  restaurants 209
Mensano 133
Mercatello sul
  Metauro 101
monasteries
  Certosa di
    Galluzzo 153
  Fonte Avellana 213
  Lecceto 133
Mondavio 124
  hotels 128
Monsummano 90
Montagliari 154
Montagnola 133
Montalcino 172-3
  hotels 173
  restaurants 173
Montaperti 153
Monte Acuta 213,
  214
Monte Amiata 112,
  172
Monte Argentario
  190
Monte Catria 213,
  214
Monte Cetona 163
Monte Cimino 199
Monte Conero 225
  hotels 228
Monte Cucco 126
Monte del Lago 168
Monte Ingino 218
Monte Nerone 212
Monte Petrano 123
Monte San Savino
  155,157
  hotels 158
  restaurants 159
Montecassiano,
  hotels 229

Montecatini Alto 90
Montecatini Terme
  89-90
  hotels 96
Montecchio
  Vesponi 162
Montefalco 125
Montefiascone 114
Montepulciano 165-7
  hotels 168-9
  restaurants 169
Monterchi 101
Monteriggioni 114
  restaurants 117
Montevarchi 107
Monti 153
Montone 218
Morro d'Alba 227
Mugello 77

Nepi 200
Nocera Umbra 126
Numana 225

Orbetello 190
  restaurants 193
Orvieto 178,180
  hotels 184
  restaurants 185
Osimo 230

Padule de
  Fucecchio 88
Paduletta di
  Ramona 88
palaces
  Castiglione
    del Lago 162
  Fivizzano 234
  Florence 52-5, 66-
    8,73
  Gradoli 189
  Macerata 230
  Montepulciano
    165, 166-7
Palazzo Albizzini,
  Citt del Castello
  212
Palazzo Apostolico,
  Loreto 227, 230
Palazzo Chigi-
  Albani, Soriano
  200
Palazzo Datini,
  Prato 94
Palazzo dei
  Consoli, Gubbio
  215
Palazzo dei Priori,
  Citti del Castello
  212
Palazzo del
  Bargello 215
Palazzo della
  Signoria,Jesi 226
Palazzo Ducale,
  Gubbio 218
Palazzo Ducale,

239

Index

Pesaro 102
Palazzo Ducale, Urbania 104
Palazzo Ducale, Urbino 105-6
Palazzo Leopardi, Recanati 230-1
Palazzo Parisani-Bezzi, Tolentino 231
Palazzo Pianetti, Jesi 226
Palazzo Taglieschi, Anghiari 100
Palazzo Trinci, Foligno 125
Palazzo Ubaldini, Apecchio 212
Palazzo Vitelleschi, Tarquinia 202
Papal Palace, Viterbo 116
Pienza 114
San Gimignano 134
San Martino al Cimino 200
Siena 141,144
Todi 183
Volterra 146,148
Panicale 167
hotels 169
Panzano 154
Parco dei Mostri 198
Parco Demidoff, Pratolino 77
Passignano 167-8
hotels 169
Pergola 218-19
Perugia 180-3
hotels 184-5
restaurants 185
Pesaro 101-2
hotels 108
restaurants 109
Piancastagnaio 173-4
Pienza 114
hotels 116
restaurants 117
Pietrafitta 154
Pietrasanta 236
Piobicco 219
Pisa 90-2
Campo dei Miracoli 91-2
hotels 96
restaurants 97
Pistoia 92-3
hotels 96
restaurants 97
Pitigliano 190-1
hotels 192
Poggibonsi 132
restaurants 149
Poggio a Caiano 95
Poggio San Polo 153
Ponte de Abbadio 191
Pontremoli 234

restaurants 237
Populonia 208
Porto Azzuro 206
Porto Ercole 190
hotels 192
Porto Novo, hotels 228
Porto Santo Stephano 190
restaurants 193
Portoferraio 206
hotels 209
restaurants 209
Portonovo 225
restaurants 229
Prato 94-5
hotels 96
restaurants 97
Pratolino, Parco Demidoff 77
prehistoric remains Cetona 163
Monte Conero 225
Pontremoli 234
Punta Ala 206
hotels 209

Radda in Chianti 157
hotels 158
restaurants 159
Radicofani 114-15
Radicondoli 133
Recanati 230-1
Renaissance 27-8
Roccalbegna 174
restaurants 173
Roman remains
Ancona 222,224
Ansedonia 188
Arezzo 100
Assisi 122
Bronzi Dorati, Pergola 218
Cala Maestra 189
Cingoli 224
Falerii Novi 199-200
Fano 123
Ferento 112
Gubbio 214
Osimo 230
Sassoferrato 219
Saturnia 191
Spello 126
Spoleto 126-7
Sutri 201
Tuscania 203
Urbs Salvia, Fiastra 225-6
Volterra 148
Ronciglione 200
hotels 201
restaurants 201
Roselle 208

San Casciano in Val di Pesa 115
San Felice 153

San Gimignano 133-5
hotels 148
restaurants 149
San Giovanni Valdarno 107
San Giusto in Salcio 153
San Gusm 153
San Lorenzo Nuovo 115
San Martino 206
San Martino al Cimino 200
San Miniato 120
San Pellegrino in Alpe 235
San Quirico d'Orcia 115
San Sano 153
San Severino Marche 231
San Vittore della Chiuse 213
San Vivaldo 135
Sanguineto 168
Sansepolcro 103-4
restaurants 109
Santa Fiora 175
Santa Maria del Parto 201
Santa Maria delle Vertighe 157
Sant'Angelo in Vado 103
Sarteano 163
Sasso Pisano 207
Sassoferrato 219
Saturnia 191
hotels 192
restaurants 193
Senigallia, restaurants 129
Settignano 77
shrines
Loreto 227
St Nicholas of Tolentino 231
Siena 138-9
Contrado 136
hotels 148-9
Palio 136-7
restaurants 149
sights 139-41
walks 142-5
Sigillo 126
Sirolo 225
Sorano 194-5
Soriano 200
hotels 201
restaurants 201
Sovana hotels 192
restaurants 193
Spaltenna 153
Spello 126
hotels 128
restaurants 129
Spoleto 126-7
hotels 128

restaurants 129
Sutri 200-1
Suvereto 206

Tarquinia 202-3
hotels 201
restaurants 201
Tarquinia Lido 202-3
Tereglio 236
Tirrenia 87
Todi 183-4
hotels 185
Tolentino 231
Torgiano 184
hotels 185
restaurants 185
Trevi 127
Triana 174
restaurants 173
Tuoro 168
Tuscania 203
restaurants 201
Tuscany food 35-6
wines 37-8

Umbertide 219
Umbria food 36
wines 38
Umbrian remains, Eugubine Tablets, Gubbio 215,218
Urbania 104
restaurants 109
Urbino 104-7
hotels 108
restaurants 109

Valdarno, The 107
Versilia 232
Vetralla 203
Vetulonia 208
Viareggio 236
hotels 237
restaurants 237
Villa a Sesta 153
villas
Lucchese 88
Medici 77,95,114
Montagnola 133
Villa dei Mulini, Elba 206
Villa Farnese, Caprarola 199
Villa Lante, Bagnaia 198
Vinci 95
Viterbo 115-17
hotels 116
restaurants 117
Vivo d'Orcia 175
Volpaia 157
Volterra 145-8
hotels 149
restaurants 149
Vulci 194
wines 37-8

Zago 154